Truman Capote

George Plimpton is the editor of *Paris Review*. He has written several books, many of them about sport, and, with Jean Stein, was the author of the original 'oral biography', *Edie*. He lives in New York City.

by GEORGE PLIMPTON

The Rabbit's Umbrella (juvenile)

Out of My League

Writers at Work, Volumes I–IX (ed.)

Paper Lion

The Bogey Man

American Literary Anthologies, Volumes I–III (ed.)

American Journey: The Life and Times of Robert F. Kennedy (with Jean Stein)

Pierre's Book (ed.)

Mad Ducks and Bears

One for the Record

One More July

Shadow Box

Sports (with Neil Leifer)

A Sports Bestiary (with Arnold Roth)

Edie: An American Biography (with Jean Stein)

D.V. (with Christopher Hemphill)

Fireworks: A History and Celebration

Open Net

The Curious Case of Sidd Finch

The Best of Plimpton

Chronicles of Courage (with Jean Kennedy Smith)

The Writer's Chapbook

The Paris Review Anthology (ed.)

The Morton Book of Sports (ed.)

The X-Factor

In Which Various Friends, Enemies,
Acquaintances, *and* Detractors *Recall*

His Turbulent Career

George Plimpton

PICADOR

For Sarah D. and Sarah P.

Note to the Reader

A word about the present volume: this "oral biography" is the third such work with which I have been involved, the previous two being *An American Journey: The Life and Times of Robert F. Kennedy* and *Edie*. The form is particularly appealing for a number of reasons, not the least of which is that the reader is treated to information delivered firsthand, as if one had happened in on a large gathering, perhaps a cocktail party, in this cave of Truman Capote's acquaintances. With a glass in hand (probably a vodka) our reader moves from group to group and listens in on personal reminiscences, opinions, vitriol, and anecdote. In this case, by some amazing stroke of good fortune the reader proceeds in the chronological order of Truman's life, so that the first group is from Monroeville, Alabama, on through his turbulent career, until the final conversations overheard are those murmured by the mourners at Crooked Pond.

First-time readers may be put off by the idiosyncrasies of the form—the staccato rhythms of the text, the contradictions in the evidence about a particular episode, and especially the fact that the editors of oral biography do not have the luxury of being guides and interpreters of the subject's life: they are more or less at the mercy of others' verbiage. Traditionalists, or those who may wish a more complete portrait of Truman, would be urged to read Gerald Clarke's official biography, *Capote*—a work that was of immeasurable help in the research for gathering the witnesses for what follows.

I have made every effort to reach those who agreed to be interviewed to be sure they had not (to use that unfortunate politician's usage) "misspoke," and in a few cases I have been unsuccessful. In the event of any questions arising as to the use or contents of the material, the necessary corrections will obviously be included in future editions.

I am indebted to a number of people—Gloria Jones, who recommended the project during her employ at Doubleday; those who conducted interviews (Roderick Coupe, Anne Fulenwider, Fayette Hickox, Gia Kourlas, Susan Morgan, David Robbins); and Sarah Dudley, who helped shape the book in its early stages. I am especially grateful to Susan Morgan and Anne Fulenwider, whose help and guidance in all departments of the preparation of this work have been invaluable . . . to such a degree that both deserve coauthorship.

Contents

Contents

Contents

Truman Capote

Truman Capote stands beside a garden gate in Monroeville. Almost certainly Harper Lee in her novel *To Kill a Mockingbird* modeled the character Dill after Truman, who was her next-door neighbor: "He wore blue linen shorts that buttoned to his shirt, his hair was snow white and stuck to his head like dandruff; he was a year my senior but I towered over him. As he told us [an] old tale his blue eyes would lighten and darken; his laugh was sudden and happy; he habitually pulled at a cowlick in the center of his forehead . . . We came to know [him] as a pocket Merlin, whose head teemed with eccentric plans, strange longings, and quaint fancies." *(Courtesy of Karen Lerner)*

Monroeville ❖ 1924–1931

CHAPTER ONE   *In Which the Reader
Is Introduced to Monroeville (pop. 1,800),
Harper Lee, and Goes to TC's First
Big Party*

MATTHEW RHODES *(resident)* If you come into
Monroeville from the south side, after those miles of
cotton fields on either side of the road, first you pass
the Vanity Fair lot, the biggest employer in town.
They do mostly woman's lingerie. That was how they
got their start, but now they manufacture Lee jeans
and they do polo shirts. Then you'll pass the
community college. It used to be the Patrick Henry
Community College and now it's Alabama
Southern—I have no idea what they have against
Patrick Henry. Then a little restaurant row—
McDonald's, Hardees, and a little diner called
Radley's, after Boo Radley of Harper Lee's *To Kill a
Mockingbird*.

Then you pull up on the square. A lot of the
shopfronts have changed over the years. Jennie
Faulk, Truman's aunt, had her millinery shop on the
square, but you wouldn't recognize where it was. A
lot of small businesses are on the square: a few
attorneys, a travel agency, a movie rental, a Christian
bookshop, a furniture shop, and then Dickie

Williams's drugstore. If you want to know any gossip, you go to Dickie and talk to him. He markets himself as a self-styled local historian, though his stories about Truman are somewhat limited. One of them is that this short little man walked in and in this real high-pitched voice declared, "I want a small black comb about this long—that's all I want, nothing else." That's one story. Then he tells the story of when he asked Truman, "How do you know that what you write will be successful?" And Truman had said, "It's like baseball. It's hard getting that first hit, but once you do, the rest is easy." That's about all, though Dickie does as much as he can to please the tourists who come to town . . . he's very respectful of the Faulk family, who raised Truman, and Harper Lee's family.

Then, in the center of the square, you've got the old courthouse built at the turn of the century and the new courthouse next door built in the 1960s. Harper Lee—everyone calls her Nelle—depicts the old courthouse as "sagging" in *To Kill a Mockingbird*, but they've invested a lot of money over the last few years to lift the sag so the courthouse doesn't fall in on itself. When you walk upstairs into the main courtroom, the first thing you see is a plaque above the door that says: "This room was used as a model for the courtroom scene in *To Kill a Mockingbird*." In the center of the room are the different exhibits that switch from time to time—an exhibit on the Indians in the area, on the War of 1812 or the Creek Indian War. In the back corner is the Truman Capote–Harper Lee exhibit. Not much there. We've got six signed photos from Gregory Peck, who played Atticus in *To Kill a Mockingbird*. We've got four signed copies of different books by Truman and one table of xeroxes of different letters from the New York Public Library when he either writes from Monroeville or mentions Monroeville. We have the *Life* magazine that has Truman and the two actors who played the killers in *In Cold Blood* on the cover. We've got an original script to the movie. . . . We haven't gotten a thing from Harper Lee herself though she lives in town. We've had to go through private individuals to get what we have.

The lot on the square where the Faulk house stood, where Truman grew up, is now vacant. The first one burned in 1940, and then Jennie Faulk moved the family to a small house outside of town while they rebuilt. The second house was torn down in 1988. Remnants of the stone wall that ran around the yard are still there. In the back corner there's a little Sno-Kone stand that's open a few hours after school for the kids to come over. Of course, they don't have the slightest idea of who lived on that lot.

Harper Lee lived next door. Astonishing to think that two famous writers came out of such a small Alabama town. They tried to put up a billboard mentioning that it was the hometown of Harper Lee and Truman Capote. For the longest time Nelle fought it. There is very little recognition of her at all—she's turned down any attempt to have a Harper Lee Day.

She lives in a small, one-story brick ranch. It has a chain-link fence running around it and a little carport off to one side. With all the talk about how reclusive she is and how she dislikes public attention, you sort of build up this grandiose image of a fortress, a J. D. Salinger type of thing with the tunnel, the guard dogs, and the guard tower. Then you see it, and you're disappointed because you've built it up so much in your mind. In a town like Monroeville, I know darn well Harper Lee knows exactly who I am and exactly what I've been doing. When I first moved to Monroeville three years ago, I was going to write a book about what her novel and what Capote's work had done to change people's perceptions of the Deep South, race relations, and life in a small Alabama town. I sent her a letter to tell her that I was doing it. She wrote back. Basically, she wrote thanking me for the kind letter, but that I could never have her permission to go ahead with the project. The people in town who tried to capitalize by giving interviews really didn't know her at all. I shouldn't put much stock in what they had to say, because the people who knew her best were the ones who don't talk about her. At the end of the letter, she had a curious suggestion. She suggested that I write about William Barrett Travis, who had a law practice near Monroeville, or perhaps Rube Burrough, who was a turn-of-the-century bank robber who lived in south Alabama.

EUGENE WALTER (*writer*) They're all hopping mad because they don't feel that you have to go that intimately into people's lives. It's a very Southern tradition to go very deeply into other people's lives, but it's kept within the parlor. Behind the fan! Draw the shutters and pour the jambamy, let's go to work! But not publicly.

MATTHEW RHODES One of my first days in town, I was in conversation with one of the lifelong inhabitants of Monroeville. After several minutes, I noticed that he was looking at me with an odd expression on his face. Finally he said, "You're not from around here, are you?"

"No, I'm originally from Virginia."

"Well, hell, you're a Yankee!" he said.

When I pointed out that Virginia is south of the Mason-Dixon line, he said, deadly serious, "Son, you'll learn something real quick around here. Anybody north of Birmingham is a Yankee!"

However long you've lived here, it is impossible, no matter how hard you try, to escape the shadow of Harper Lee and Truman Capote. There has hardly been a day that has gone by that one or both of their names isn't mentioned.

Truman remains an enigma in Monroeville. Several members of his family still live in the area, and each of them tries, in varying degrees, to maintain a shroud of secrecy about him. Other than some preliminary work which the museum in the courthouse has done, as well as a small mention on a billboard outside of town, it is hard to find any sort of remembrance of his life here. A historical marker has recently been placed on the lot where the Faulk family home once stood, and of course there are a few old-timers around who remember Truman and the town back then and don't mind reminiscing.

JENNINGS FAULK CARTER (*cousin*) It was quite different back then. All the roads, of course, were dirt except around the square in Monroeville, and there were great big oak trees bordering it—horse-wagon racks that you could tie wagons to. Farmers came to town on Saturday afternoon and shopped. Now Monroeville is deserted on Saturday afternoon.

DR. CLAIRE BAYLES (*professor*) In the hot dry weather we had such clouds of dust that you had to leave all the windows open. We just dusted and dusted, but you could still write your name on every mirror in the house by lunchtime. I remember the cattle drive on Camden Highway. When I was about three or four my daddy carried me out to the porch to see a herd of oxen being driven toward market, not by cowboys, but guys in bib overalls with long sticks, driving them downtown. He said, "Honey, I bet this is the last one there'll ever be down this road." He was about right. There wasn't but one more I can remember after that.

MARIE RUDISILL (*aunt*) Truman comes from a family, the Faulks, that goes way back and had to struggle through the Civil War and afterward. A tough line of people. You're not going to find people having afternoon teas. Ida [Electra Henderson] Faulk held her family together after the Civil War. She went down and worked in the cotton fields. We were brought up that way; we were tough. When I came back from college, I worked in that store downtown. I swept the sidewalk in the morning, I swept the store. I wasn't allowed to play all summer. I was taught to work.

ANDREAS BROWN (*literary archivist*) Capote's mother, Lillie Mae Faulk, was said to be a great Southern beauty. Not in the sense that we consider great beauties today, but at that time she was considered a very attractive and charming woman. By all accounts the prettiest girl thereabouts, just an inch or so above five feet, dark blond hair, barely seventeen, but today what we might refer to as a bubblehead. She certainly was irresponsible, childlike, a case of arrested development in the sense that she pursued adolescent values well into her thirties. She married the first fellow that came along who had any money, Arch Persons, and abandoned her son Truman to her relatives when he was about two, just a baby, really, and went off hoping to live the high life with her husband. She won a beauty contest sponsored by Lux, one of many, many regional winners. Capote expanded this, of course, into her winning the contest for Miss Alabama in the Miss America contest. A typical Capote exaggeration. Eventually, she divorced her husband, left her child in Monroeville, Alabama, with the Faulks, and went off to New York to seek fame and fortune. In Monroeville she would visit her son very briefly, sometimes for a day, but she didn't stay very long. Monroeville, Alabama, wasn't her idea of glamour.

JENNINGS FAULK CARTER Lillie Mae left Truman at Jennie and Callie and Sook's when she went up to New York. They were used to children. So they took Truman, like just automatic, you know. They didn't even think about it. It was a great old big rambling house with a hall down the center and everybody had a bedroom. Truman always slept by himself. Normally you'd put two boys in one bed in a room, but Sook and Jennie knew he didn't want to sleep with anybody, so they would fix me a pallet on the floor. They just sort of bent to his whims, even though he was a child.

Jennie was a hard-nosed business woman, but she liked Truman, and she liked to hear him talk. She would sort of prompt him to expound a little bit. Of course if he got too wild, she'd tell him right quickly, "You're just lying, Truman, just get off that."

TRUMAN CAPOTE *As a child I lived for long periods of time on the Carters' farm, small then but today a considerable property. The house was lighted by oil lamps in those days; water was pumped from a well and carried, and the only warmth was provided by fireplaces and stoves, and the only entertainment was what we ourselves manufactured. In the evenings, after supper, likely as not my uncle Jennings, a handsome, very virile man, would play the piano accompanied by his pretty wife, my mother's younger sister.*

MARIANNE MOATES (*resident*) Mary Ida Faulk, who married Jennings Carter, reminded me of a little bantam rooster. She was a tiny woman, and if something didn't go right, she would just lambast you up one side and down the other. But she was totally generous too. She opened her home to friends and relatives. She was active in the community, she gardened, she did things with her friends. In their retirement age she and Jennings got a motorcycle and went up into the Carolinas. On a motorcycle! Sometimes she was very hard to please and stubborn about some things. Jennings had two mules, one named Mary and the other named Ida, so that should give a little bit of insight into how he felt about her.

MARIE RUDISILL Truman never had a center in his life. He never had the devotion of his mother or his father. The only stability Truman ever had in his life when his mother left him and went to work was at Monroeville with that bunch of old maids, Mary Ida, Callie, Jennie, and Sook. There was the sense of being loved, but it was not the right kind of love. Sook encouraged Truman, you know, to dress up in ladies' clothes. She wouldn't let him ride a bicycle and she wouldn't let him do this for fear he would be hurt. Just pampered, pampered. She was doing the wrong thing for him.

JENNINGS FAULK CARTER We all called her Sook, that was all she was ever known by. When she was a young girl, she had some type of fever, probably typhoid fever, and while it had not really affected her mentally, she was a little bit childlike in her attitude about things. She was a lot more companionable to children than she was to adults. She managed the household, and that was her job in the Faulk family . . . to see that food was on the table and the clothes were ironed and beds were made.

Every night Jennie Faulk would bring home from her millinery shop on the square what she called the money sack—a little canvas bag with the change and quite a few bills out of the cash register. She would deposit it on a table in the house. Sook would slip her hand in that money sack and get a handful of change. Jennie probably suspicioned what Sook was doing, it was just another way of letting Sook have money. She'd only get a handful of change— whether it was just her own honesty or they had an understanding, I don't know—and she would do this once a week, and usually on a Saturday. Then she would divide this money among Truman and me, and she would keep some for herself.

Sook wasn't a particularly shy person—she would talk to guests in the house and, of course, Sunday dinner she always passed everything and she would enter in the conversation. But she wouldn't go to town to shop; she did all her shopping on the telephone. She didn't go to church, and the only movie I think she ever saw was *Gone With the Wind*. She didn't think much of that; she said it wasn't really like her daddy said it was. She had a vice, if that's a vice: she chewed tobacco. Her favorite brand was Brown

Mule. She would send Truman or me or the girlfriend Harper Lee up to town to buy her a plug of Brown Mule. We didn't think a thing about it; we thought that was just part of life . . . just like Miss Jennie, Truman's aunt, would come in from the store at night and go to a closet back there and pour herself out about that much of her medicine. She would down that medicine in one gulp and then she'd come back in to have supper. That was accepted too. Jennie was taking her medicine. Course, when we got older we discovered that her medicine was Ezra Brooks bourbon, something like that, you know.

MARIE RUDISILL Sook had been completely shoved in the background all her life. She wasn't a mental elephant or anything like that, but she had her own little dream world. And she gave that to Truman. There was no reality in her life. She was a free soul, a free bird. They'd go off in the woods and they'd fly kites. They'd cut these gorgeous pictures out of every magazine in the world and paste them on the kites. Lie on the grass and fly the kites.

TRUMAN CAPOTE *Once more, the creek. The taste of raw turnip on my tongue, the flow of summer water embracing my nakedness. And there, just there, swiveling, tangoing on the sun-dappled surface, the exquisitely limber and lethal cottonmouth moccasin. But I'm not afraid; am I?*

NANCIE B. ROBINSON *(resident)* He was dressed in white from head to toe—white linen shirt, white linen pants, white socks, and white shoes, even a white tie. We walked to the tennis court, which was a couple of blocks down the street from my house. We played on a red clay court. Truman got too hot after a while, and went and sat on a bench. He sat with one leg going in one direction, one leg going in the other, his arms stretched out on the back of the bench. His hair was falling down in his face. He would blow upward to clear it away, and it would flop back down. Truman was such a beautiful child; absolutely gorgeous. He had the prettiest complexion.

DR. CLAIRE BAYLES My only real memory of Capote is seeing him at the swimming hole when he was between seven and eleven. The other kids who normally swam there just stood around with their mouths open and looked at him for a minute or two because he had on a dressmaker's swimsuit with a shirt and little tailored shorts—a real wild print, probably Hawaiian. All the rest of us had on these little drab, stringy, cotton swimsuits. He must have stood out like a bird of paradise in a flock of scrawny turkeys. We were just awfully impressed with his swimsuit. I heard a couple of other kids talking and one of them said he was staying with the Faulks and that his mother had brought him that fine swimsuit from New Orleans. From what I heard, the Faulks always dressed him up like Little Lord Fauntleroy. You know, I think it must have been real rough on him. He probably would have rather been wearing bib overalls and little khaki shorts like all the other boys.

JENNINGS FAULK CARTER We didn't think anything about maybe taking a shirt off and hanging it on a bush or something, but Truman was not like that. You didn't touch his clothes. He would wear clean clothes almost every day, which is unheard of in children, especially country children, because the wash is done by hand. But that was something that Sook and Jennie just put up with: they tolerated his being clean and neat all the time. We deliberately tried to dirty him sometimes, but that's just children, the way children act. You can't believe how athletic he was when he was young. He was real muscular. He could chin himself. He could out-chin me and out-chin his girlfriend, Nelle. He could climb rope bare-handed, and he could do things that none of us could do that were amazing to a country kid . . . like get on that rock fence around the Faulk house, four feet off the ground, and do a cartwheel, which would flabbergast all of us. None of us could do that sort of thing. But, by the same token, he would not fight anybody. In those days, kids seemed to think that you had to be tough, you had to be able to wrestle and fight and hit back and all that and not take anything off anybody. There wasn't a great deal of conversation. First off there'd be a lick, somebody would hit somebody, and then later there might

be a discussion, but usually it was hit first and talk later. But
Truman wouldn't do that, he would never hit anybody.

I have to keep accenting how clever he was and how fast he
could think. When he first started school in Monroeville, he could
already read and write; he thought the teacher and the other
classmates would be real proud of him. But they weren't; they
ostracized him. The teacher didn't realize that he was a prodigy, and
she tried to treat him just like the regular students. So his life was
miserable in school. Miss Jennie lived close enough to the school so
that every day at dinner he could walk home and have a hot meal.
Sometimes one of the classroom bullies would confront him after
he'd left the schoolyard. Truman would say, "You know, my father
had me take lessons from Jack Dempsey; I could knock you out. But
I won't, I'll just show you something else." The bully would just be
standing, looking at him, and all of a sudden Truman would turn
one of his cartwheels. He could do marvelous cartwheels, roll on his
hands and land on his feet, and then stop and rotate back and end
up standing with his feet right where he had been talking to this
bully. And this would just flabbergast the kid, and he would forget
all about picking on Truman. The first thing, he'd be out there trying
to do cartwheels too, and couldn't, you know. By the same token, he
was kind of lazy. He would connive to get Nelle and me to do the
physical part of any game and he would be the brains. Like one of
his favorite games was to play school in the backyard where they
had a huge pile of cut stove wood. He would get Nelle and me to
arrange the sticks of stove wood like a desk and a chair, directing all
of this and telling us to move this piece of wood here and move that
piece of wood there. And then he would teach school and we would
sit there on those uncomfortable piles of stove wood, you know. I
guess you'd say Truman was more mature as a younger person. In
these games of teaching school, he always seemed to have superior
knowledge to us, and would always discuss something that we didn't
know anything about.

He and Mr. Lee, Harper's father, would get to discussing the
words and the crossword puzzle, first thing you know they'd be
playing some game between themselves . . . make up a sentence

using the words that started with the same letter like the "sun that's shining is sinking in the sky."

He'd invented a circus and charged admission. Of course, Nelle and I never saw any of the money. Jennie had read in the paper (that and the Bible was about all that she ever did read) that some two-headed chicken had been born that fascinated all of us when she read it out loud to us. So for his next circus, Truman was going to exhibit a two-headed chicken. He wasn't very creative with his hands but he could always get Nelle and me to do it. So we ended up building the chicken for him. It looked pretty much like a two-headed chicken when we got through.

TRUMAN CAPOTE . . . *I started writing when I was about eight. Writing was always an obsession with me, quite simply something I had to do, and I don't understand exactly why this should have been true. It was as if I were an oyster and somebody forced a grain of sand into my shell—a grain of sand that I didn't know was there and didn't particularly welcome. Then a pearl started forming around the grain, and it irritated me, made me angry, tortured me sometimes. But the oyster can't help becoming obsessed with the pearl.*

MARIE RUDISILL I knew Truman'd be a writer. The old Negro woman who lived in our house always said, "That boy's gonna be a writer, because he's always writing lewd things on the sidewalks all over town." Truman was a very unique child. He could tell absolutely unreal things, just out of the clear. I thought he might be an actor. He danced and all that. His father worked on riverboats, on the Streckfus Steamboat Line which ran up and down the Mississippi River. Truman would go on the boat with his father for the weekend or something and he'd tap-dance. What the hell. Not a big deal. Truman was a real good dancer though he never took a dancing lesson . . . he was just . . . innovative.

JENNINGS FAULK CARTER He was one of the few I ever knew who knew what he wanted to do with his life. He wanted to write, and there's no question about it. He had a little pocket notebook that he would write little scenes in. Sometimes we'd be walking in the woods, and he would see a particularly striking scene of a tree limb bending over a creek, and he would stop and actually write this down. He filed these things away. He had an old trunk he used to keep up under Sook's bed that he would put his papers in, and he had a little key, and he would lock this trunk up and they were in there. You weren't to touch his writings.

NANCIE B. ROBINSON One time, I went with Truman next door to see Harper Lee. We played in the yard for a long time, climbing the chinaberry trees, and we got really hot and tired. We went into the house to a back bedroom where Nelle's father had an office. There was an old typewriter on the desk in the room, and Nelle grabbed some paper and put it in the typewriter. Truman started telling a story, and while he talked Nelle typed it. Well, they would not let me help with the story, so I just grabbed my paper dolls and went home!

JENNINGS FAULK CARTER Nelle, by the same token, never showed an interest in writing. She read a lot. There's no question that *To Kill a Mockingbird* is Nelle's book. Truman probably helped her. He helped her find a publisher, probably proofread some of it, but it's her story. The only time I've ever heard him say anything about Nelle's book was that he remarked, "She got a Pulitzer, and I've never, never done that." I forget how he put it, but you could tell he was hurt badly. That as much writing as he had done, he had never won it, but Nelle had.

He wrote because he wanted to be a writer. Just like I flew because I wanted to be an aviator. I think he wrote because of the idea of manipulating the words to where it could entertain me and you. I think that's what he was after.

TRUMAN CAPOTE *Harper Lee . . . wanted to be a lawyer, like her father and her sister, and cared only about hanging around the courthouse and playing golf. She was extremely articulate on every kind of constitutional law known to man and in fact did go to law school, came within one week of graduating, and then decided she wanted to write instead.*

. . . When we were children, I had a typewriter and worked every day in a little room I used as an office. I convinced her she ought to write, too, so we would work there each day for two or three hours. She didn't really want to, but I held her to it. We kept up that routine for quite a long time.

JENNINGS FAULK CARTER He loved to read and stay up at night. We all got up at daylight. It would be eight o'clock. I would have already been in the fields, and he'd be lying up there in bed! That's a different lifestyle. He was lying up there in bed and in pajamas. Jennie and Sook, they'd put up with it and bring him coffee in bed. He was sittin' up there enjoying himself . . . so outgoing and jolly and friendly that, hell, you just loved to see him. Then, about three or four in the afternoon, he'd kind of wind down. He'd be in the living room, curled up in the corner somewhere where he could get light on the book, sitting on the floor with his knees up under his chin. He wouldn't speak to you, wouldn't look up, wouldn't even know you were in the house. He had something different inside of his personality.

I know the most fun we had with Truman, and with Nelle, would be when we'd be playing some kind of imaginative game, and Truman would be leading it. That was always great fun for me, because he would always make it so alive, just like you were there. He'd take you off to a castle in Arabia or something and it was so different from anything we could imagine . . . from what we were familiar with or even read about.

EUGENE WALTER I knew him as "Bulldog" Persons. He used to come to Mobile from Monroeville to a dentist here because his lower jaw was being corrected. He belonged, as I did, to something called the Sunshine Club. The *Mobile Press-Register* had a children's page called the Sunshine Page. It was for children who wanted to write, or thought they wanted to write, and there were little poems and little stories and there were always prizes. At the end of the year, someone won a pony or a dog. They never offered cats, so I never sent in any text. Every Saturday, if you belonged to the Sunshine Club, you had free tickets for the Saturday matinees at the Lyric

Theater, which was a glorious theater—now torn down. That's where I met Truman—little butterball thing, not really very fat, but oddly bull terrier-like. I really thought he was like a troll. In the lobby of the Lyric, a charming old lobby with black-and-white tiled marble floors, I said to myself, "There's a troll . . . a *troll*." I was fascinated. Also in the Sunshine Club was a boy, J. L. B.—very tall, and he was a bully. He was mean to Truman, real nasty to him, saying, "You runt!"—things like that. At this one matinee, Truman backed off to the other end of the lobby, charged full speed ahead, and put his little head right into J.L.'s most delicate masculine parts. J.L. bent over doubled, coughing, and never bothered Truman again. From that moment on, I always called him Bulldog. J.L. was killed in the war. I think maybe Truman put a hex on him.

When he was a member of the Sunshine Club, Truman won a competition for a piece he wrote called "Old Mr. Busybody." It was to be published on the Sunshine Page in two sections—one Saturday and the next Sunday. But his aunt realized that he had written about their next-door neighbor and called off publication. Truman had used an eccentric recluse for Mr. Busybody. The person described served as inspiration for the character in *Other Voices, Other Rooms* as well as in the recluse in Nelle Harper Lee's novel *To Kill a Mockingbird*. Truman pretended all of his life that "Old Mr. Busybody" had been published . . . that his first publication was on the Sunshine Page. He liked the joke of "Old Mr. Busybody," Part One, Sunshine Page. But it was never published. Nobody knows what happened to "Old Mr. Busybody," because his aunt grabbed it in a hurry and ran it back to Monroeville. Because Truman said in some interviews here and there that his first published piece was the Sunshine Club's "Old Mr. Busybody," there are people working on their doctorates, or whatever, searching the files of the *Mobile Press-Register* to this day.

VIRGINIA TAYLOR *(resident)* Truman, when he got tired of staying with his cousins in their store, would spin around on the stools in the drugstore next door. Truman's father, Archie, came to town one day to do some visiting. He arrived in a blue convertible with two ladies in the back seat; because they didn't know anyone in town they never got out of the car. Archie asked Truman if he would like to take them for a ride. Truman didn't have a driver's license. Anyway Truman took the keys and asked me if I wanted to go along. I wasn't really taken with Truman. I got in the car anyway, maybe I liked the car or something! I still remember that it was real scary for me and also for the ladies in the back seat. He couldn't even see over the steering wheel, but he drove so fast that it seemed at some points the car was up on two wheels. It was obvious to the ladies in the back that Truman didn't know anything about driving, but they couldn't do anything about it. We rode out on the Peterman Highway and back. Once in town Truman handed over the keys like nothing had happened. Archie was lucky to get his car back! I'll bet he got a talking-to by those ladies in the back seat!

JENNINGS FAULK CARTER He [Arch Persons] was a personable man, and real quiet. You would think that every word rolling out of his mouth was the gospel, but most of it was just some scheme to get money out of you somewhere. He even conned me into flying him over the South one time in an airplane. He never paid the gas bill, the hotel bill, or anything. I picked up the tab. Yet I flew him from city to city to city to city before I finally delivered him back to Mobile. We were gone three or four days and there's no telling what it cost.

He installed this boxer in Jennie's house, putting him in training. The boxer would get up every morning at daylight and run around the square in his running shorts. Well, that just horrified all the women in Monroeville that a man would do such things. Arch did other things too, he buried a man alive on the school ground. That used to be a stunt in the thirties, to see how long a man could survive without air. They kept him in the ground for a day or two, and charged admission to come and see. And then dug him up, and he was about half dead, but he was still alive.

ARCH PERSONS *(father)* [in a letter to Marie Rudisill] As you know, Truman spent two-thirds of his boyhood in Monroeville because my job caused me to have to live both in New Orleans and in St. Louis, mostly in high-class hotels, but other than this we did not suffer any hardships, as I had a good job and an interesting one. It has been said that I squandered $35,000 of Lillie Mae's money during the eight years we were married when the fact is I never knew Lillie Mae to have over $150 during that period and then only on one or two occasions. I made a good salary and was steadily employed and had annual railroad passes for both her and myself during all of that time and she was certainly not deprived of a good living.

As you know, Lillie Mae took Truman to New York, though having agreed at the time of the divorce that he should remain with Sook in Monroeville, accessible to both of us. However, this turned out well for him and I am glad for that reason though it deprived me of almost his entire childhood.

JENNINGS FAULK CARTER When Truman was in the second grade, he learned that he'd have to leave Monroeville and go back up North with his mother. He said he wanted to throw a party so grand that everybody would remember him. He decided to have a Halloween costume party. With Nelle and me, he planned it for weeks ahead of time—a party on a Friday night he wanted it to be . . . unheard of because children didn't have nighttime parties; it meant that parents from out in the country would have to bring their children into town at dark and then either stay the night or return home over dark and dusty roads. But Truman got his way. He went full speed ahead. He thought up dozens of games for the children to play. One game consisted of a series of cardboard boxes with a hole in the top of each one through which the children were to reach their hand down to try to guess what was inside. One box had in it a huge terrapin that we'd found. Truman turned it over on its back; in the box it scratched and wiggled. Truman hinted that it was a wildcat, a skunk or a snake in there and some of the children were terrified. Nobody ever guessed a terrapin. In another box Truman had mashed up oranges and bananas in a glob. People thought it was mashed grapes or chitlins. The third box had a turkey wing duster. Everybody guessed that one. Out in the yard another game involved Truman's Tri Motor Ford pedal airplane. An incline was built from the back porch down the steps, and we'd take turns climbing aboard, zipping down the incline and gliding to a stop near the pecan tree. Another game was bobbing for apples. Beneath the pecan tree, we set up the washstand with four big tubs full of water. Jennie had ordered these apples for Sook from the Northwest, so big that it was hard for a child to get a bite. Everybody tried, but not many of Sook's apples got ruined . . . just teeth marks.

Now a soot-black man named John White was to tend to the apple bobbing. John used to work for Truman's grandfather in the fields. He didn't like Jennie and he wouldn't work for her, but on this night he agreed to tend the apples. Truman wanted him dressed in a white suit, shirt, and shoes. Jennie made him a white hat.

John White was so proud of what he was going to do at Truman's party that he talked to everybody about it. It got around town. The day before the party, Sheriff Farish came to see Jennie in his patrol car. This meant he was there on official business. He was dressed in a khaki uniform with a dark tie and a military campaign hat, big boots, and he wore a gun belt with a big revolver in it. He was formidable-looking . . . supposedly killed several people with his revolver: an Indian, a white man, and several Negroes. The patrol car had a front windshield that could be rolled out. There was a purple light on top of the car. The siren was mounted on the window post, so to crank it the sheriff had to reach outside the car. The handle was wired down, with good reason, because when he parked the car, the first thing kids went for was the handle. Jennie came out to the front gate to see him. He stood almost at attention by his car like he was dreading what he had to say. He called Truman "Mr. Truman," so we knew it was important. He said he'd heard that "Mr. Truman" had invited Negroes to his party. "Now I don't believe it's true," he said, "but a lot of people do. The talk is that he wants to show the people in Monroeville a thing or two before he goes back up North. And he's got some darkies in these costumes that nobody can identify and won't know they're colored until after the party. Then the damage will be done. The Klan is all worked up over this, and they're going to hold a meeting on the schoolhouse grounds the night of the party to look into it."

The sheriff said the Klan would hold their meeting and then march down Alabama Avenue in front of Jennie's house on their way to the town square. The sheriff said he had warned the Klan not to throw anything, or yell anything, or do anything to interrupt her party. But he said, "You know how the Klan is—they haven't had any excitement in a long time. Unless they can stir something up, people won't pay their dues and the Chief Dragon gets upset."

Miss Jennie didn't have too much education, but she had a dignity that would make people stand back in awe. She said, "Sheriff, no such funny business will take place under my roof. And I do not need to remind you of your duties, I'm sure. Good day to you, sir."

Maybe it was because of that but Jennie got into the spirit of the party. She invited some neighbors and some of her best customers at her millinery store who happened to be landowners, shop owners, and politicians. She had Aunt Lizzie, the cook, make divinity candy, pulled-molasses candy, cookies, cakes. She set up card tables for the adults to play Rook. Sook was all atwitter, fixing punch in the cut-glass punch bowl. Jennie said they'd buy the newfangled paper cups for kids no matter what they cost and adults could use the cut-glass cups.

When we were thinking of whom to invite, Nelle had the idea of inviting the Boular children—Sonny and Sally. Sonny, really a young man, was a recluse, the inspiration for Boo Radley in Nelle's *To Kill a Mockingbird*. The Boular house was in the corner next to the schoolyard with a great fence of fruit trees, scuppernong arbors, and a wire fence around it. Kids had developed a legend about Sonny— that he was dangerous, and if you got over the fence, he would stab you with a butcher knife. There wasn't anything wrong with his mind. It's just that he was kept at home and was enormously shy. We had never seen him out of his yard, so we wondered what kind of costume he would come dressed in, figuring it would be something extraordinary because he was such an unusual person.

We thought the night of the party would never come. When it finally did, Nelle and I painted our faces. Truman had a Chinese face of Fu Manchu. The comic books and newspapers were featuring the Chinese tong wars in California, and I think Sook and Truman figured that the Chinese would fit in real good as a Devil. So Truman's costume looked Chinese, with a buttoned-up collar coat and a loose shirt that hung over his trousers. His face was painted yellow and his eyebrows arched up. He had on a skullcap, and someone had plaited him a horsehair pigtail that hung down the back of his shirt. When the party started he took a pen and pencil to judge the different costumes. Kids lined up to ride the airplane down the ramp. There was a drove of folks bobbing for apples. John White looked like an apparition in white . . . and with his black skin he blended into the background behind the washtubs.

Today you wouldn't put any importance on it, but back then Jennie had a phonograph that played flat, round records. You had to wind it up and then it would play one record at a time . . . an amazing piece of entertainment, because very few people at that time even had radios. Jennie had gotten a young colored boy to change the records on the phonograph so we could have music all the time. Adults came back to the hall door to listen to the music and check on their children.

The party was in full swing. Sally and Sonny hadn't shown, but Nelle and I were so interested in the little airplane that we hadn't noticed. Every time we could, we jumped in and rode it down the ramp. About this time we heard a commotion in the front part of the house. We could hear Sally screaming, "They've got Sonny over at Mr. Lee's! They're going to hang him!"

Everybody rushed around and somebody hollered, "Call the sheriff!" Truman said, "Quick, let's go through the hedge." So we ran around the back while people streamed out the front of the house. We cut through our passage in the fence and hurried next door to the Lees' porch. Nelle's father with his undershirt on was wading out through these sheet-covered Klansmen on the street. He was a big, dignified man, and he was slinging people out of the way. The Klansmen didn't give him any resistance. They moved out of the way. He was a member of the state legislature, editor of the *Monroe Journal,* and an upstanding citizen. Nobody wanted to cross him . . . only the one with the green fringe on his hood, the Chief Dragon, who was standing by this strange figure in an odd costume. Whoever it was had on a series of cardboard boxes, painted silver, taped together, starting with a square box on the head with eyeholes cut—a mechanical man, a robot . . . it was almost impossible for him to walk.

Mr. Lee got the tape unwrapped from around the box on the robot's head. When he pulled the box off, it was Sonny Boular—his face as white as a sheet, his hair long and shaggy, stringing over his ears, tears and sweat streaming down his face. He looked wild and frightened. Mr. Lee turned and addressed the crowd almost as if he was in a courtroom. He said, "Look at what your foolishness has done. You've scared this boy nearly to death because you wanted to believe something that wasn't true. You bunch of grown men should be ashamed."

The adults from Jennie's kept coming over from next door, so that soon it was a solid line of the most influential people in Monroeville. The men looked mad and formidable. The Klan members began to slowly melt away. Some ground their torches in the dirt. They never continued their march to the square. They drifted back to the schoolyard and got back into their cars and left.

We learned from Sally that she had helped dress Sonny in this robot costume. When the two left their house together to come to the party, they ran into the Klansmen starting up the street. The lead Klansmen had spotted Sonny in his costume, and assuming that the robot was a Negro in disguise, he yelled, "There's one of them there!" Sonny had tried to run, but after taking a few steps in his cardboard boxes, he fell down in Mr. Lee's yard.

The next morning we took some of the leftover party refreshments to our tree house. Truman was bubbling over with talk. He had his notebook. He said, "How does it feel to see history in front of your eyes? We saw the Ku Klux Klan commit suicide. Didn't you see the people's faces? The Klan will never have any more support in this county. Nobody will back them. They died last night." Truman said, "Did you see Sonny's tears? Did you see the stubble on his face? He *shaves!*"

GEORGE PLIMPTON Parties had been going on when I visited Monroeville a few years ago. Halloween two or three days before. Cardboard skeletons were still hanging in the windows. We drove by a house with trees in the front yard draped with long strips of toilet paper . . . the custom being in these parts to decorate someone's place this way if you don't like them. "Let's roll so-and-so's yard," is how they say it. Our guide, a Monroeville resident, said the home was a local schoolteacher's. I remember wondering how the teacher had reacted in front of the class the next day.

I'd hoped to "visit" Harper Lee and chat with her about Truman. Childhood friends, of course. Astonishing to think that two writers of such world renown had come out of a small town two hours of hard driving from any place one had ever heard of. Alas, we were told that she had left town to play in a golf tournament in Maine. Golf is one of her passions. Another is crime, and she apparently spends her days in the courthouse following the various criminal cases which come under that jurisdiction.

We parked the car and moseyed around the site of the Faulk house, where Truman had grown up. Weeds. The stones of the foundation. Do I remember a tree, which could have been the inspiration for *The Grass Harp?*

We had lunch at the Vanity Fair Golf and Tennis Club, where Harper Lee tees it up. Fancy clubhouse. Strange to think of a golf club in Monroeville—much less with such a name. We heard an odd bit of news—that Harper Lee was not playing golf in Maine at all. She was still in town, waiting for us to pull out, perhaps watching us through the slats of the venetian blinds as we passed by.

We paid a visit to the town cemetery, passing through a small plot once reserved for the blacks of the community. One of the stones was engraved "Sweet Tooth" and a number of the others "Gone But Not Forgotten." In the main part of the cemetery we paused by Truman's mother's headstone—her maiden name, Lillie Mae Faulk, and her birth and death dates engraved at the top, and then listed below are her two "consorts," Julien Archulus Persons and Joseph G. Capote. The stone is handsome. Our guide said, "We just love our dead folks around here."

Truman's name appears at the bottom of the list along with his dates. The date of his death is wrong, one day off. I am reminded that William Faulkner's headstone at Oxford, Mississippi, has an engraver's error, a misplaced apostrophe. An endemic problem with Southern writers?

In fact, Truman's remains don't lie there. Neither do his mother's.

JENNINGS FAULK CARTER Truman was in Europe or somewhere when Lillie Mae died. He cabled, and had her cremated. So he got back at her tenfold, because I'm sure wherever she is she regrets being cremated. Worse than that, they lost the ashes. Joe [Capote] put the ashes in one of these mausoleum things, but you have to pay rent, and then he quit paying rent on it. So she doesn't exist anymore.

If Lillie Mae was here sitting over there, she would be so sweet: she would tell you these touching tales about Truman when he was a boy, and you would almost cry and you would think of how loving she is . . . that there's never been a mother like her.

New York, Greenwich ❖ 1933–1944

CHAPTER TWO   *In Which TC Arrives in New York, Goes to a Succession of Schools, Fails Math, and Meets Some New Friends*

Truman (third from left in front row) in a group photograph of his class at Manhattan's Franklin School. It was the fourth and final school of his teenage years—the others being Trinity, St. John's Military Academy (a miserable choice; he lasted only a year before being returned to Trinity), and Greenwich High School. *(Truman Capote Papers, The New York Public Library)*

ANDREAS BROWN When Lillie Mae, or Nina, as everyone in New York knew her, divorced Arch Persons and came to New York to start a new glamorous life, she found herself Joe Capote, who was a successful Cuban businessman. He adored her

---

and immediately provided her with the lifestyle for which she was impatiently waiting—a beautiful apartment, nice clothes, everything else. That's the impression you get from everything that is available. She was very ambitious about being accepted into society. Very ambitious. She wanted to be a member of café society, as it was called in those days, and she pursued it with determination. She entertained, spent money, lived well . . .

JOHN KNOWLES *(writer)* Truman often talked about himself. Oh, my God, yes. Endlessly. Sometimes you wondered whether he was doing it with some ulterior motive to get you, to set up something inside you, or whether he was really telling the truth. The first time I became involved with his famous technique, which he worked to a turn on me, was just after I first met him: Truman began telling me his life story. This terrible, tragic story. The central tragedy (as he saw it) in his life is a scene: Truman is two years old. He wakes up in an utterly strange room, empty. He yells, but he's locked in there. He's petrified, doesn't know where he is—which is in some dumpy hotel in the Deep South—and his parents have gone out to get drunk and dance; they have locked this tiny little boy in this room. That was his image of terror, and I think it was his way of symbolizing the insecurity of his youth—this image of that kind of abandonment. He started with that harrowing story. Then he'd go on to tell about his going to military school. They were going to make a man out of Truman, so he went to a series of military schools. Can you picture that?—seeing Truman in a military uniform? Obviously it wasn't going to work out.

CLARENCE BRUNER-SMITH *(schoolmaster)* As soon as young Truman arrived, his mother enrolled him in Trinity. When I came to Trinity in 1927 the tuition in the high school was $300. This year it's $16,500 for the upper school, $15,000 for the kindergarten. In Truman's day there were around 350 to 400 students through grade twelve. A day started with chapel. Every morning. Truman would have taken algebra, and also Latin, because we start Latin in the sixth grade. He did dreadfully. His grades in math were incredible. But he was never in danger of being sent to another school. We had some very brilliant kids, and some pretty dull ones, but we coped with it. Truman remained a child, I think, all his life. Certainly he was a very explosive kid. I think it was in the fourth grade that he got down on the floor on his back in the headmaster's outer office and pounded his feet up in the air the way a young child might.

CRAWFORD HART (*classmate*) Since classes at Trinity were small, his presence was felt, probably because of his ability to relate tales of his youth in the South, many of which were the basis for future work. Truman excelled in floor exercises in the gymnasium, and had gymnastics been as popular then as it is today, he truly could have been a candidate for possible Olympic consideration. I can remember him doing cartwheels; it reminded me of a pinwheel going at full speed. He had little use for team sports, preferring instead to perfect his tumbling, skating, dancing, and writing. I add writing here because I think he took delight in getting his articles (compositions, to be more exact) printed in the Trinity School paper while the rest of us struggled to catch up with him.

Truman and I both transferred to Greenwich High School, Greenwich, Connecticut, after our freshman year at Trinity. Truman's family had purchased a home in the Millbrook section of town.

PHOEBE PIERCE VREELAND (*writer*) I met him when I was about twelve and he was a year or so older . . . at a party given by some people called Jaeger who lived in Millbrook, which is a section in Greenwich, an attractive place, wonderful houses, and you drive in through pillars and the driveways wind around and it's heavily wooded. That's where Truman's parents had moved. Everybody knew everybody there. The Jaegers were a marvelous family, very atypical. The mother was a German village belle and the father a fabulous guy named Hans Otto Jaeger, a brilliant chemical engineer—the only human being I've ever seen who really had dueling scars on his face. They were giving a Christmas party and that's when I met Truman. He picked me out and started to tell me a story, a riddle, like the lady and the tiger, but more abstruse, and I knew the answer. From that moment on we spent years in each other's pockets. We called each other on the telephone until our parents said, "We'll rip it out if you don't stop it!" We went everywhere together. One of the pleasures about Truman was swimming. We used to spend our whole summer in this swimming lake, the color of strong tea. On the upper and lower lake we'd go skating in the winter. Truman was a marvelous ice skater. Really marvelous! A wonderful dancer.

CRAWFORD HART He jitterbugged to some of the fastest music we could find. We'd stand and watch. Whether it was in the gymnasium, on the ice, or on the dance floor, Truman's physical characteristics and blond hair set him apart.

PHOEBE PIERCE VREELAND Truman asked me to marry him maybe when we were both about fifteen or sixteen. We figured—one of the real practical plans of youth—that since we got along, why shouldn't we get married. We'll be buddies forever. It seemed right at the time. I thought it was a perfectly swell idea. But I got involved—I went to the dance with somebody else—and that's when he got very cross and stamped on my picture. But he got over it. We went to the movies. We were thrown out of the Pickwick Theater. It was one of those grandiose old theaters, the only theater in town, Moorish, a huge place, the clouds would drift across the sky above the screen. If you wanted to go to a movie of recent vintage, you went to Stamford, which, you know, was a *real* place. You never knew what was going to drift into the Pickwick. Truman and I would go on weekends and they hated us. *They hated us.* Occasionally we would fortify ourselves with some apricot brandy, oh God, but usually not. As we sat there, we would rewrite the movies at the top of our voices, screaming with laughter: "She should have said . . ." "He should have said . . ." "Well, he's hopeless anyway, but if he had only said . . ." It was awful, I mean, from the point of view of the Pickwick. "Out!" We were thrown out of the Pickwick more often than the dust. Dear, dear! Golden afternoons in the Pickwick Theater. One of the people who came to call on the Capotes in Greenwich was a wonderful man who was French, the Count of something, and he had one of the great automobiles of the world with the pipes coming out of the hood, black with red leather. He gave Truman and me a ride in it. "Drive it by the Pickwick," we said. "Right by the Pickwick!" And we'd wave at them as we went by.

In those Greenwich years we talked all the time. We read *The New Yorker*—in those days, a great icon. We listened to jazz. We loved jazz. We went to used-record stores and jazz bars. We went into New York together a lot—to the Stork Club and El Morocco. We saved up our money and went there. I don't know why they let us in but they did. We were such a curious couple. Truman and I used to take those old trains back. The midnight train—the milk train! I have slept on that milk train!

Finding Truman was something marvelous for me because, like most adolescents who care terribly about writing and do not care very much about the kind of world that's around them, you begin to think that you're insane! Am I sane? Does anyone know what I'm talking about?

I cannot emphasize enough that from the moment I met Truman there was only one thing he knew he was going to be and that was a writer. That's what he cared about. That's all he cared about at Greenwich High. What did algebra have to do with anything? That's when Ms. Catherine Wood came around. She was a wonderful woman. The quintessential teacher. If you put her in a room with a hundred women and you said, "Who's the teacher?" people would pick her—tall and radiant, benign but not a fool by any means. She took him in hand and schooled him thoroughly in grammar and the fundamentals, the structure of poetry, and she taught him, and also interceded with the other teachers so he could walk around things like algebra.

Always from the time I knew him when he was twelve or thirteen, he was fascinated by society. When he was in Greenwich he knew people who were terribly boring, but he was interested in their houses and the way they lived. He was always fascinated by the intricacies of that society. People who loved him and knew him said, "For God's sake, how can you stand those people?" We'd make fun of him in a nice way: "How can you hang out with those idiots?" But that was his thing.

So I spent a lot of time at his house. I knew his parents, Nina

and Joe, quite well. I knew her until she died. She and Truman were
a strange pair. In the first place, which no one has ever said, they
looked so much alike. You may say, "But they're mother and child,
why shouldn't they?" But I mean, *uncannily*—the same coloring, the
same high forehead, the same color eyes set in the face, the same
mouth, the same body structure. Rather slim upper body, heavy hips
and heavy legs.

Nina was the first Southern woman I had ever met. Now you talk
Southern. She was a real Southern child. Amazed at everything.
Amazed at Schrafft's. *Amazed*. That's saying something. She was a
darling, charming, original person, but we just gazed at one another
across this gulf. She scared me. Because she was not like a mother.
Now, Greenwich was by no means a boring place as suburbs go—
there were a lot of interesting, eccentric, amusing people—but she
was quite outside of my experience. She was also (this shows you
how times change) the only divorced mother that I knew. So this
made her sort of exotic. Nina was a belle. She was. She was
extremely attractive, very attractive sexually. She could be charming
but you never felt she meant it. I hope I have not given you the
impression that Nina was some hotsy-totsy person flinging herself
around the furniture. She was beautifully dressed, she had a great
feeling for style—her hair and everything. I always remember her
jewelry. She loved amethysts and always wore them and Joe gave
them to her for her birthday. A very beautifully mannered woman.

I was only about eleven when I met her. She was the only mother
I met who was not a mother kind of mother at all. She was lovely to
Truman at one point and terrible the next, so he was constantly
ricocheting. She'd insult him in front of people. "You gonna wind up
in the guttah," and all this stuff. You never knew what she was going
to do next and that is not any fun to live with. Joe was absolutely
adorable, much nicer to Truman.

Now as for Joe, at that time Joe was a darling guy, wonderful fun.
If she was the first divorcée mother I met, he was the first Cuban.
He had a wonderful accent, a Cuban accent, which is nothing like
Puerto Rican or Spanish. He was funny, humorous, he taught me
how to rhumba. But Nina was his life and he didn't know really how
to handle the whole thing. Of course, he couldn't handle his

financial life. He wound up in Sing Sing for embezzlement—
something like that. I'll never forget that, I mean—Sing Sing!! That's
where Jimmy Cagney goes to jail. Not the nice guy who taught you
how to do the rhumba.

ELEANOR FRIEDE *(editor)* Joe was a little round man, just a little
bigger than Nina. I didn't think he was a very attractive man,
although he liked women. Nina was very jealous. He couldn't look
sideways at a woman but she'd say, "I'll get the carving knife!" He was
Latin, as you know, Cuban, and I gather that he did play around. I
loved Nina, I liked Joe. The first time that I brought Donald Friede,
whom I met in the fall of 1950, to a party at 1060 Park Avenue, their
apartment in New York, she took him aside, this little martinet,
beautifully dressed and so coiffed, and she took him to the kitchen,
where she got a carving knife, and she said, "I want to know your
intentions about that girl. She is my favorite girl, and I want you to
know if you hurt her, believe me, you see *this* . . ." Brandishing the
knife. She wasn't drunk, but that's just the way she was.

She was tiny, Truman's height. She had brown eyes and blond
hair. I met her at the racetrack, Belmont, with a lady friend of mine,
a gal from Texas, Lyn White. I'm not a race fan, but Lyn dragged me
there and afterward we always went with Joe and Nina who were
betting, horsey friends. Joe Capote was a gambler (that was his
downfall) and Nina loved it too.

Lyn White, who was so funny with her Texas accent, would tell
the joke about "What does Joe Capote do for a living?" and he would
say he was in *shits*. He had a Cuban accent, and he was with
Wamsutta sheets, but he couldn't say "sheets," he'd say, "I'm in
shits." Scatological humor. Joe was always in "shits."

The relationship with Truman was a bit of a mystery to me. Nina
adored Truman. She once told me at lunch—we were such good
buddies she'd tell me what she did in bed—"Oh, I just wish Truman
would find a nice girl and settle down. I want some grandchildren."
Now, I mean, how could . . . well, I couldn't be the one to say,
"Come on, Nina, I mean he might be petsy with Lee Radziwill, but
he ain't gonna get married." I couldn't say that to her because she
really had talked herself into thinking that it was going to happen.

She adored him. At one point I remember she was telling me, "I swear on the most precious thing in the whole world to me, Truman being killed by a car in the street . . ." She was very proud of him. She didn't call up and say, "Have you seen Truman's story in *Esquire*?"—that would be too bourgeois. She treasured him and valued him. Of course, she knew about his male friends. I had a favorite picture of Truman—Donald Windham, Joe, Nina, and Truman in Venice, you know, the usual Venice picture. For some reason or another those photographers in the Piazza San Marco always get you looking at your best. I don't know whether they put a filter on the camera lens or what, but everybody was beautiful: Don and Truman in Venice. That was before Jack Dunphy, and I'm sure Nina knew about that. Or she didn't let it sink in, or maybe, you know, she rewove it for herself.

Nina was a tough little martinet with him. I remember late one afternoon, sitting on the couch, a couple of us, and Truman came through in some kind of outfit, very chic, all dressed up in kind of a strange tie and things, and Nina said, "Where are you going?" He said, "Well, I'm only going over to Bennett Cerf's for dinner." She said, "Well, what about that gray suit we just bought at Brooks Brothers, you go back in there and put on the gray suit." "But it's only Bennett and Phyllis . . ."

Anyway, he did traipse back to his room. He came back out in the gray flannel suit, looking wonderful, but he had on the patent-leather pumps. She said, "Oh, go ahead." Afterward, Truman said, "Oh, my crazy mother." He could be kind of disparaging about her, but that was long after she was dead.

PHOEBE PIERCE VREELAND Things went from bad to worse with Joe and Nina. It was especially difficult for Nina. For women in the suburbs in those days, unless you were truly suburban—that is to say, you liked squash, golf, gardening, good causes, antique collecting, something of that sort—it was a horror show. There was nothing to do. No men around all day . . . people reaching for the bottle or pills, or for their tennis instructor. Truman was very proud and he never complained. But he saw that it was just getting worse and worse. He was the one who really got them to move back to

New York. He packed up the stuff. I remember him helping. He was going to New York and that's when they moved to 1060 Park.

CLARENCE BRUNER-SMITH In New York, Truman came back to Trinity for a while before transferring to Franklin. I never taught Truman, but the man who did teach him in the ninth grade brought me quite a lengthy story one day. He said, "Bruner, I want you to read this." Well, I read it, and I said to his teacher, "Who claims to have written it?" He said, "Truman Capote." Well, he had, undoubtedly. One of Capote's most distinguishing qualities as a writer was that he could interpret the inside of the brain of a child.

The head of the Lower School, John Langford, who was a remarkable teacher, was prescient in a way, because he kept some poems that Truman wrote . . . and which were sold at auction not too many years ago, for what I thought were ridiculous sums of money, since they weren't particularly distinguished, in my estimation.

CAROL MARCUS MATTHAU (*friend*) I was about thirteen. We lived at the Park Lane. The apartment had huge rooms with transoms over the bedroom doors. My sister had two boys who came to visit her after school every day. I knew the name of one of them, Truman Capote, which I couldn't forget. I had never met him, because every day I came home from school and closed my door. I did the same thing every day. I was very academic. I didn't know I was a girl yet. I would come home and do my homework. I'd have fantasies about the speech I'd make when I got the Nobel Prize and so on. After my homework I would take a bath and then I'd come back into my room to pick out what I would wear to dinner. I did that every day. The same thing.

One evening I came out of the tub and was standing stark naked in my bedroom. I looked up and there was this face in the transom—a very bright-colored face with yellow-gold hair, china blues, pink and white. He looked like an old valentine with this beautiful smile on his face. I gasped. I didn't know whether to jump for the bed and pull the covers over me or try to get to the loo and grab my robe.

He said, "Oh no, no! Don't *move,* please! You are directly from the moon. You were made on the moon. I *know* you are made of moonbeams; I am looking at them right now."

I was sort of lulled and transfixed because I'd never heard anyone speak like that before. Finally, I ran and got my robe and put it on. I opened the door and saw this high ladder propped up against the wall. Truman was sitting on the top of it. He got down and came toward me saying, "Oh, there is not a single question about it. Look at you! Your eyes, your nose, your face—you didn't come from this world. You don't belong here . . ." and so on. He was maybe fifteen or sixteen.

PHOEBE PIERCE VREELAND The Marcuses lived at the Park Lane Hotel when it was on Park Avenue. There are people who always live in hotels. Strange people. Mr. Marcus, who was a tycoon in aviation to begin with, was a very intense, dark man. A presence who just *sat* there in this hotel apartment with the beige carpets and glass lusters on the lamps. Carol and her younger sister, Elinor, and everybody else had a great time except Mr. Marcus. During the great Saroyan uproar, when Carol was being romanced by William Saroyan, Mr. Marcus did not care for the idea of his darling daughter marrying this lunatic, and said so. Mr. Marcus just hated this dirty bohemian, and Saroyan, of course, returned the hatred with interest. I remember once when he was calling on Carol, he left with a very elaborate ashtray, just put it in his pocket and walked out. Carol said, "Oh, he always does that." A gesture of contempt, you know. Carol didn't seem to mind. Of course she eventually married him. You would have thought Mr. Marcus would have been horrified by Truman. But he wasn't. That was something I never failed to enjoy. Truman would say, "Rah! Rah! Rah! We're going to see the so-and-sos," and I would say, "Oh my God, talk about putting your head in the oven." But it would always turn out for the best. I've seen this happen over and over again. Mr. Marcus would on principle disapprove of everything about Truman. And without Truman trying . . . after a half hour or an hour, they would be buddies. They really would. It wasn't because Mr. Marcus knew that Truman had no designs on his daughter. He liked him.

ANDREAS BROWN On many occasions he told people he never graduated from high school. He did. From Franklin School here in New York City, a private school on the Upper West Side. He did very poorly, flunked a number of his courses, often cutting class. He didn't do as much important or sophisticated writing in his early years as he claimed. He was not the polished, finished writer at the age of fifteen and sixteen and seventeen he claimed to be. It certainly was vastly superior to what the average high school kid achieves, but it was not of *New Yorker* quality. He purposefully created the special persona of a child prodigy. Much of that stemmed from the fact that Capote, small in stature, appeared extraordinarily young for his age. When he was twenty, he looked fourteen. When he was sixteen, he looked ten. When he was thirty, he looked eighteen. Capote capitalized on that. He got a kick out of people thinking he was fifteen when he was twenty-two, and when he was twenty-two he was doing some excellent writing. So people would read something and look at Capote and say, "My God, you're a child prodigy!" He loved that and he perpetuated it; then he began to embroider and tell people, "Well, when I was in junior high school, I entered *Scholastic* magazine's national competition for junior high school, high school writing, and I won national awards." The truth is, he was never published in *Scholastic* magazine and won no national awards so far as we could determine after a thorough search.

HAROLD PRINCE (*theater director*) My memory of him at Franklin is this odd fish out of water in an all-Jewish boys' school on Eighty-ninth Street and Central Park West. A year or two before he graduated, (class of '43; I was class of '44), I passed this blond waif, very bizarre, moving up the staircase to a classroom. My only connection to him was that we both wrote for the school literary magazine—the *Red & Blue*. I had literary aspirations; I wanted to be a playwright. I read his poetry in the literary magazine. He wrote exclusively poetry at Franklin. I don't remember reading a word of narrative. And of course as a narrative writer his strong suit was his beautiful poetic imagery. He was one of the editors—even then a towering literary presence in the school. He won the school's prize for original writing the year he graduated. I won the literary prize the next year. I was kind of sparked by him more than anything else, sparked by how successful he was being so young. I decided that I would give myself until twenty-one to be equally successful.

When the Truman Capote memorial exhibit was arranged at the New York Public Library, I happened to walk through it. I was in the library for their annual Christmas party, which is one of the great parties in the world—hundreds of kids and their parents just wandering about. I was looking at the various exhibits and I saw "Truman Capote." I went upstairs. I was alone. I made my way along the glass cases backward, chronologically, because I'd entered the room the wrong way. I got to the end and I thought, "I wonder if there'll be anything about Franklin," because people keep saying that Truman denied he went there, and there was the literary magazine and my name . . . on the same page! I wanted to turn around and cry out, "Hey! Hey!" I was very moved by that, I came home, told my kids, told my wife. I told the story for a few days to everyone I met.

1944–1945

CHAPTER THREE   *In Which TC Joins*
The New Yorker, Upsets Robert Frost,
Writes His First Stories, and Joins the New
York Artistic World

Truman on the set of Jean Cocteau's *Parent Terrible*. *(Karl Bissinger)*

TRUMAN CAPOTE *The last thing in the world I would do was waste my time going to college, because I knew what I wanted to do. I had, by that time, read a tremendous amount and was really a very accomplished writer. I had no reason to go to college. The only reason to go to college is if you want to be a doctor, a lawyer, or something in a highly specialized field. I could subtract at one time after I did a lot of things with a tutor, but then, afterward, it faded away and now I can't subtract. I can add, but I can't subtract. But if you want to be a writer, and you are a writer already, and you can spell, there's no reason to go to college.*

NATALIA MURRAY *(editor)* He was hired as a messenger and an office boy for the art department at *The New Yorker* magazine. One of his duties was to sharpen pencils. He was bringing his pencils back to the studio when Harold Ross, the editor, encountered him. He turned around, looked at Truman, and asked, "What's that?" Truman, walking down the corridor with his pencils, looked like a little ballerina.

They're not even copy boys, they're messengers. They run around delivering book copies, manuscripts. With thirty-odd editors reading everything we write, there's always an enormous amount of paperwork, shuffling of galleys around the office, eight, ten, twelve sets of galleys for one small piece constantly in circulation. I remember Truman in the corridor with his cape. I don't know what Truman was being paid in those days. Fifteen dollars a week or something. I remember one fellow, getting thirteen dollars a week, asked for fourteen dollars a week and they fired him. They knew the answer to *that* kind of impertinence.

BRENDAN GILL *(writer)* He was a very young office boy, and though he denied it to me years afterward when I wrote about him in my book about *The New Yorker,* with his golden hair and the opera cape he wore, he was an absolutely gorgeous apparition, fluttering, flitting up and down the corridors of the magazine. He was indeed tiny. He did have golden hair at that time, though he eventually became bald, which radically altered his appearance, along with the rotundity of his face. He and Miss Terry, our office manager, were an extraordinary couple. They were both the same size and they got on wonderfully well. He had always adored elderly women and he adored Miss Terry, who was quite vicious, and was a bigot about almost everything, which also suited Truman. But he *was* an office boy. Afterward he boasted of how before our art meetings (he was in charge of putting drawings on an easel) he had opened the envelopes in the mailroom, and often pushed some of the contents under the table, thereby performing an editorial function all by himself. After he left, when they moved the table out from the wall and reorganized the room, scores of drawings were discovered that Truman had professed his contempt for by discarding. The buck had stopped there with him all those years ago. But, as far as we knew, Truman was just a singular vision in the corridor. When it turned out to our astonishment that he was a real writer and better than most of the people on the magazine, he made many of the staff uneasy.

BARBARA LAWRENCE *(editor)* Truman used to come and stand behind my desk a great deal. I remember once he told me that he wrote short stories. I remember thinking, "Oh my God. Don't tell me I'm going to have to read some of those!" Much later, when I had begun to look at his stories, he said to me, "Now, honey, I remember when I told you that I wrote short stories and I knew what you thought. You thought, 'Oh my God!' "

BRENDAN GILL Truman liked to tell the story about how, as a kind of nursemaid, he used to take Thurber to a girlfriend's house and hang around until after the assignation, when he'd help Thurber, who was blind, get dressed. Truman resented having to do that, according to his story, so he avenged himself by putting on Thurber's socks inside out, knowing that Helen Thurber, who had dressed him that morning, would notice upon undressing him that evening that something had happened. Thurber would have been hard pressed to explain. It's a nice sort of Maupassant story. Which has everything wrong with it except Truman's skill in telling it. If Mrs. Thurber was able and willing to dress the aging reprobate in the morning, why wouldn't his girlfriend, having presumably helped to undress him, be equally willing to dress him? Why would little Truman be pressed into service? Kind friends were quick to pass the story on to Helen, who, not denying the existence of the girlfriend, denied that Truman had played any such role in Thurber's sufficiently awkward amatory life.

CAROL MARCUS MATTHAU *The New Yorker* sent him to write a piece for "Talk of the Town" about a seminar that Robert Frost was having up in New England. He wrote exactly what he thought of Robert Frost and was fired instantly. That's what he told me. He thought Frost was a big pompous ass and that it was pathetic to see everyone hanging on every word.

GEORGE PLIMPTON Truman's story was that, sitting in the front row at the reading, he had reached down to scratch his ankle. He had a stiff neck, from the flu or something, and when he went to straighten up, he found he couldn't . . . and that Frost would look down and assume he'd fallen asleep. So in this weird bent-over crouch Truman left his seat and crept down the aisle to get out. He had let it be known that he worked for *The New Yorker,* though probably not as a lowly copy boy. Frost saw him, of course. He somehow assumed this was *The New Yorker*'s reaction to his reading. He said as much. He closed the book from which he was reading, threw it out into the room, and refused to go on. Truman said that Frost had a good arm—well, he didn't put it that way—and had actually hit him in the back of the neck. All this got back to *The New Yorker* and Truman was fired—I suspect more for passing himself off as a *New Yorker* critic than anything else.

ELEANOR FRIEDE Truman was living at 1060 Park at the time. There were two great bedrooms; one was Truman's, and the other was Nina and Joe's, and off the hallway between them was a large bathroom, which I guess was shared. It was one of those old-fashioned apartments, with servants' quarters in the back, and a big living room where she gave the parties which overflowed the whole apartment. Nina gave a lot of parties, great parties, people all over the place, sitting on the bed. I remember going into her bedroom, and there sitting in the middle of the bed would be Bea Lillie telling funnies. I mean that was the kind of party she gave. I don't know how she knew Bea Lillie, but she was there. Maybe she met her at the racetrack, I don't really know. I didn't ask Nina, "How come you know Bea *Lillie?*"

DORIS LILLY *(writer)* Very sweet. Nina, his mother, really crazy, wonderful Southern woman. You know the kind. She had that apartment on Eighty-seventh Street and Park . . . really too far uptown. Kind of the boondocks. But that house sparkled. That floor was waxed twice a week. I mean *clean,* you have no idea how clean that apartment was. Nina washed her hair every single day. She had no hair at all, it was so very, very fine. Truman had very fine hair, you know. Nina's hair was all wispy, it almost wasn't even hair because she washed it so much. She was small, diminutive, and had a Southern voice—she use to "tawk like tha-ut," and cooked! We used to have wonderful dinners up there. I remember Carson McCullers. The reason I remember Carson McCullers is that I would say, "Who is the lady drinking that dark brown drink?" She drank. Oy-yoy-yoy. Bourbon, I guess. Black, it was so dark. A great glass of straight bourbon. People who are heavy drinkers drink very slowly. She took a little sip and another little sip. You think they're never going to drink it and then, by the time you turn around again, they've finished it. There were a lot of other writers. Jim Agee. I remember meeting him. Anyway, Nina would make the most luscious, incredibly delicious, unbelievable buffet suppers that I've ever had in my whole living life. Southern food that she would cook herself. The Capotes never seemed to be without money. They didn't have any, as I found out later. But they didn't look like they didn't. Joe worked hard. And Truman would sit in the kitchen at night and type. He had a little tiny typewriter. She complained, Nina, about the noise. He typed with big margins because then he would have more pages, you see. He liked big type and he made big margins. That way he'd get more pages faster.

BARBARA LAWRENCE I used to think he looked almost fetal. His funny, mincing little walk, the baby voice, the infantile gestures. We all used to go out for lunch at the Forty-fifth Street Automat. You couldn't walk down the street with him when people weren't gaping at him. At the time he was living in a Park Avenue apartment with his parents—his mother and his stepfather, Joe Capote.

We used to like to go up to his apartment when his parents weren't there. He gave us liquor and good things to eat. He once gave me a beautiful little Limoges cup and saucer for my birthday. I realized much later that it must have come out of his mother's tea set. We were up there quite a lot and one night he said he had written a story that he wanted to read for us. After he'd finished it I was quite astonished and thought, "My God, he has a lot of talent." It seemed to me that the story should end earlier than it did. He agreed. That was the first story he sold—to Whit and Hallie Burnett, *Story* magazine. "My Side of the Matter." On the basis of that very small criticism of the ending, which he agreed with, he asked me if he could bring me his stories. I said, "Sure." The first one he brought me was "Miriam." I think that was the second story he sold. He used to bring them down one at a time and we'd go over them. He was just nineteen at the time but absolutely professional. No amateur sensibilities, absolutely professional. If I made a suggestion and he thought it was helpful, he went home immediately and rewrote. Sometimes he'd come back the next day with everything taken care of. He very quickly made up for that innocence, that abysmal ignorance of his of the matter-of-fact daily world. Actually I think he was always very sophisticated. Usually, someone that age with their first stories feels vulnerable, defensive. Not Truman.

VIRGINIA CARR (*professor*) The story is that Carson McCullers's sister, Rita Smith, really discovered Truman—that wonderful short story "Miriam," which she had recommended being published. Carson thought that she was going to move over to Random House to be with Bob Linscott, who had moved from Houghton Mifflin and was trying to take as many of his authors with him as he could, but Carson said, "I can't just leave Houghton Mifflin; they've been

good to me. But I want to recommend to you someone in my stead."
And that was Truman.

PHYLLIS CERF WAGNER (*friend*) I first met Truman at a dinner party
Bennett [Cerf] and I were having. In those days you had to even
everything up. God forbid you had a woman sitting next to another
woman or a man sitting next to a man. There were certain people
who were ladies without husbands . . . like Peggy Pulitzer and Edna
Ferber. Edna was very . . . touchy . . . if you didn't even things out.
So the day before the dinner party I panicked because though I had
it properly evened out, women began to call and tell me that they
could come but that their husbands were heading for Washington or
wherever. I was just undone. Edna Ferber was so gallant, so
wonderful to me on the phone when I called her to explain I wasn't
even. She said, "You have to remember, my dear, that it's for dining,
not mating."

Well, be that as it may, I was panicked. I called Bennett and I
asked, "Don't you have any male authors we can invite?"

Well, there were two that he could think of. One was Lloyd
Morris, who's a professor at Columbia, and the other was a brand-
new author Bob Linscott had just signed on at Random House
named Truman Capote. He said, "Why don't you call them and
invite them?"

Well, I did, and they both said they could come. Well, the first
guest to arrive was Edna Ferber. Christopher Cerf, our son, then
about six years old, came down, as was the custom, in his pajamas
and neat little robe we had bought at Brooks Brothers to say hello to
the guests and then good night; off he went upstairs. The doorbell
rang and our butler came in and said, "Are you expecting a child?"
Bennett said, "Yes! That's Truman Capote!" Well, in he came, and
the thing that I remember most is Edna Ferber saying, "To even out
the dinner table the Cerfs have gotten their child dressed up in a
dinner jacket!"

MARGUERITE YOUNG (*writer*) I thought he was very beautiful when
he was young. I was very fond of him—as close to him as you can
imagine. There was never a day for seven years he didn't call me.

Never a day. He was hilarious over the telephone. I hardly went anywhere. He kept me informed about what was going on in literary circles. I would say, "Well, all this scandal and all this gossip, Truman, I'm so glad they don't have anything about me to gossip about."

"Ohhhh, but they do! You're the most sensational one of all."

I said, "How so? I'm not a drug addict, I'm not an alcoholic, I'm not a lesbian, I'm just quietly . . ."

He said, "But that's the scandal. They don't have anything on you!"

BARBARA LAWRENCE I was getting more and more fascinated by his talent, but I had also just taken a nerve-racking new job. By this time he was bringing me early chapters of *Other Voices*. But it was obvious that he no longer needed my help. When I told him this, all he said was "Honey, I don't want to make a fool of myself."

LEO LERMAN (*editor*) Truman came into my life. It was the end of Hitler's war. I couldn't make out . . . was he a small boy? . . . a real small boy? . . . which I doubted . . . was he some kind of elf? Anyway, I liked him right away. We spent the evening. It was very *gemütlich,* and then we were going away, coming down the stairs, he jumped on my back and remained that way. That's how it began.

I carried him in the direction of Third Avenue. We were going west. I finally put him down. Wasn't very heavy, but he was incredibly sturdy. It was more cohesive, New York, then. You would see people.

GRAY FOY (*editor*) Leo's house was at Ninety-fourth and Lexington. Number 1453. That was the date of the fall of Constantinople. Leo always used to say that after that date all Culture went to the West. The house was always brimming over   the literary world. The dance world, the dancers were almost the nicest people. They weren't the Russian school with egos that were like stilettos. Everybody came. Marcel Duchamp, Marlene Dietrich, Maria Callas, William Faulkner, Evelyn Waugh, everybody that you can think of, a kind of clearinghouse in a way. It was usually somewhat impromptu. The guests got very little at first, rather cheap red wine, and cheese.

LEO LERMAN Four-story house and a basement. It was full of love and things and darkness, because those houses always were. People didn't come for drinking, they didn't come for eating. We couldn't afford liquor. We had four gallons of nasty red wine that I don't think anybody ever drank. We had five pounds of cheddar and port and some old biscuits. People came for one another, to see one another and talk. There were all the chums who came: Tennessee, Truman, Gore, Mr. Faulkner, who would have at one another occasionally, Henry Green whose real name was Henry York.

GRAY FOY Ladies would often bring things like chickens or whatever, feeling sorry for Leo because he stayed in bed most of the time. He received in bed. It was rather like a levee. He decided early on that rather than go to college, he was going to go to bed, which I think is rather sensible in a way. George Weidenfeld used to come with his mother, as recessive as wallpaper, you know; he would just sit there, and you would never think that he was going to turn into the sort of sex god that he became later, and the darling of the European set and all those rich women . . .

MARGUERITE YOUNG Truman and I used to play with these ancient paper dolls. Leo was in bed wearing his Turkish fez and robe. Leo has a thing—he can't light matches. You can't strike one near him because he would faint dead away—a childhood trauma. So Truman would come over to light his stove and make coffee for him. Or Marlene Dietrich would come to turn on the stove . . . Truman and I would play with these ancient paper dolls and talk with Leo all night long. We were all such good friends.

LEO LERMAN They sat on the floor, they sat on chairs, they sat on the landings. One of those miracle evenings I went up four flights of stairs to my bedroom and there was Cathleen Nesbitt asleep on the bed. Sitting at the side of the bed was Nora Kaye. I remember passing Tilly Losch on the landing, kissing Martha Graham's hand, which struck me, I must say. In the bedroom, Rudy Nureyev was sitting on the floor and people were telling him how he should do *Pétrouchka*.

The only stuffed animal we've ever had was a great white owl. He guarded the house. There was a whole wall in the front parlor of late-eighteenth-century gouaches of Vesuvius's eruption. They terrified Ken Tynan—he would not go into that room. I never quite understood why, but I was deeply interested and pleased. We had a very early collection of Tiffany lamps. Mr. Cecil Beaton came in and said, "Isn't that lovely?" We knew instantly we should get more because he was going to go out and buy them. In those days, you'd get them for twelve dollars, fifteen dollars in those marvelous junk shops on Third Avenue.

PHOEBE PIERCE VREELAND One of the things that was so marvelous about Leo's parties was that they were on Sunday night, which is still a psychological dead night. It was the mixture that was such fun—the ballet boys and the eccentrics and then you'd have the top kind of people and wonderful: John LaTouche and Julie Harris and Todd Bolender and John Garfield and Marguerite Young, all sorts mixed up together. Nobody went with anybody, they just showed up—"I'll see you at Leo's," "See you at Leo's," and everybody'd drift over on Sunday night. Group and regroup and go out later and have dinner. New York at that time was really a thrilling place. You felt the world opening up—all sorts of people who were dancers and painters . . . John LaTouche. Oh, I adore John LaTouche. The first time I was ever allowed to go to the theater by myself, I took Truman of course and we went to see *Cabin in the Sky*, for which LaTouche wrote the lyrics. LaTouche was just marvelous. Once I met him at the Blue Angel. For some mysterious reason he had a fried egg on his hand. I said to him, "How did you get into this situation, LaTouche?" He said, "Honey, I have no idea." So I said to the waiter, "Waiter, could we have a plate, a napkin, and a fresh drink for the gentleman?" So the waiter came. He slipped the fried egg off LaTouche's hand and put it on the plate, handed him the napkin, and LaTouche said, "My, I ad-*mire* that." He was just a darling man. These were the kinds of people who were around. Truman fit in and got a wonderful reception because people were fascinated by the arts, but particularly by literature. People didn't talk about money all the time, or movie rights. Truman was right in the middle of it.

ARTHUR GOLD (*pianist*) We met him at Leo Lerman's. *Le tout* New York was there every Sunday. We went trudging up the stairs and at the top of the stairs was a young man sitting on the floor in front of the door. I thought he was perhaps fourteen or fifteen. So I said, "Little boy, is there anything I can do for you? Are you all right?"
   "I'm just tired."

ROBERT FIZDALE (*pianist*) Truman came in and Leo said, "Hello, Truman, do you want to lie down?" in a very concerned tone of voice. The boy looked so pale and weak that you thought perhaps climbing up the stairs was too much for him. That was our first impression.

GORE VIDAL (*writer*) I met Truman at Anaïs Nin's. Truman was brought by Mary Louise Aswell, who was a great power for all of us because we were all trying to get our handicraft into *Harper's Bazaar,* where she was the fiction editor. It had to do with the sheer brilliance of George Davis, who was number one there, the best editor in the business, with Leo Lerman as number two and Mary Louise Aswell as number three. Davis was the one editor associated with the stratosphere of literature. After all, he lived with Auden and Benjamin Britten, the Bowleses and Carson McCullers. That was, for us, as high as you could go. If he'd worked for the *Reader's Digest,* we would have all aimed for there too. So Mary took me to Anaïs's on Tenth Street. My novel *Williwaw* was about to come out. Truman said, "How does it feel to be an *enfant terrr-ible?*"

DIANA VREELAND (*fashion editor*) I was one of his first fans. I remember meeting him. I remember *exactly.* I went to George Davis's for a little cocktail party for Truman's friends. I went into a very crowded room. I was the only girl. Everybody else were chaps. Lying across the sofa full length was Truman. We became friends immediately and we were always friends. Always, always. His particular charm was an endless, nonexplanation of anything.

Everything was said and nothing was explained. I don't know how to say it otherwise.

PHOEBE PIERCE VREELAND Mary Louise Aswell, who was a great influence on Truman, a wonderful editor, very rigorous, she always used to say, "Be careful, Truman, of that foolish world." And Pearl Kazin too, and all those who cared for him. It wasn't just social climbing. I mean that's ridiculous for someone of the subtlety of Truman's personality and mind. There was something that he wanted in that group, that world, and exactly what it was frightened me so much.

PEARL KAZIN BELL (editor) I met him when I first went to work for Harper's Bazaar right after the war. Mary Louise Aswell was the fiction editor. They published very good fiction and poetry in those days, because it was before Harold Ross died and The New Yorker was able to use subtle, experimental fiction. But in those days they were not doing that, so writers like Jean Stafford and Eudora Welty were all published in Harper's Bazaar. One day I was sitting there and this extraordinary little creature danced in. I don't know how old he was—he must have been about twenty-five or twenty-six then— and he absolutely charmed me to pieces.

Mary Louise Aswell was terrifically important to him and Truman never lost touch with her. It was she who used to keep me informed of what was going on in his life. She was my Gentile mother—and every Jewish girl should have one! She was absolutely marvelous. A Philadelphia Quaker, she was married for a time to Edward Aswell, who had become Thomas Wolfe's editor after Maxwell Perkins had died. She was a woman of incredible charm, very nervous, very high-strung, but when she turned on the charm you couldn't deny her anything at all. She eventually began to live with this wonderful woman named Agnes Sims, a painter, also from Philadelphia, who had lived in Santa Fe for a long time. It was a great place for lesbians in the 1920s and 1930s, rather highborn lesbians who went out there and were not persecuted in any way. Mary Louise wasn't beautiful, but she had a wonderfully animated face. Truman was always trying to get her to dress differently. He regarded himself as a great authority on women's fashion. Once he took her to Bergdorf and made her buy a suit that was very attractive, but it wasn't for her and she felt very uncomfortable in it. She kept saying, "Oh dear, I can't sit down in this." Truman said, "You have to suffer to be beautiful."

George Davis was the one who gave Truman his first start. The very first story, "Miriam," was published in *Mademoiselle*. A great editor. Carson McCullers's sister, Rita Smith, was his assistant. She was not at all like Carson. She was a dumpy little woman, very much devoted to her sister. I think that deep down she was rather jealous of her, but she seemed very devoted.

GRAY FOY Rita Smith, Carson McCullers's sister, was as nice as Carson was not nice—a kind, languorous Southern woman. She lasted quite a long time. George Davis was very much in the Brooklyn Heights set, with Oliver Smith and all of those people, over there, haunting the wharves. The Brooklyn Navy Yard, lots of sailors, the world of Hart Crane . . .

PHOEBE PIERCE VREELAND *Mademoiselle*'s office, where Rita Smith worked, was in the Chanin Building, and as fortune would have it there was a giant version of the Brass Rail on the ground floor. Rita was known at the Brass Rail. She bought a story of mine; she said, "Well, there's something wrong, honey, with just that little section there." I said, "Show me, Rita, what you mean." She said, "Oh, we'll just go down to the Brass Rail and talk it over." She used to drink "double bourbs," as she called them: "I'll have a double bourb, honey." I had a couple of drinks to go with her, oh, just hanging off the barstool at that point, but nothing fazed her. The next morning, after I came to, I looked back over the story and she was right. It took me about three days to pull myself together.

Truman and her sister, Carson, got along quite well. Of course, you have to remember that the South was really where nobody went, I mean *nobody* went to the South, though there were a lot of people from the South who came here. That's one of the reasons that Truman and the Smiths got along so well: they were all Southern. I think perhaps that Truman was kind of homesick. He liked that household that they had out there in Nyack. God knows it was too much. "Mother" was the character of the family. Mrs. Smith, oh, she was a personality.

"Mrs. Smith, don't you think you should stop drinking Guinness stout for breakfast?"

"Honey, it's so nourishing."

All her children were geniuses. "Brotherman," whose given name was Lamar, played the piano. I've heard amateur pianists, but he was the worst I have ever heard in my life. You know the gag about playing with mittens on? "Oh, you're so marvelous, Brotherman," said Mother. They were a pair. It was some household, though perhaps not weird by Truman's standards. They were fine as far as he was concerned. Boy!

I spent the most humiliating moment of my life there. It was when they were remodeling the house in Nyack. Carson was upstairs with her usual unspecified illness. Bilious was my diagnosis. Finally I could stand it no longer, and I said, "Mrs. Smith, I'd like to use the ladies' room." With the remodeling in progress, there was a bathroom on the main floor, but it was a skeleton, all the fixtures, but there were no walls. Mrs. Smith said, "Go right ahead, honey," pointing to the bathroom! I was very young then, I didn't know what to do. Nowadays I'd say, "For heaven's sake, don't do that to me. I'll go upstairs." But I did what she told me, and she said, "All right, everybody, close your eyes!" That's what happened. You know your worst nightmare is you're walking naked down the street. This is worse!

I remember Rita used to say, "Bye, Mom, bye, Mom!" And she'd take her coffee cup and hang it on the bough of the tree outside the house. Rita took the bus every day from Nyack. Carson, you either liked her a lot or you didn't like her a lot. There was always something a little stagy about Carson's Southernness, like the change from Lulu Smith to Carson McCullers.

1946

CHAPTER FOUR   *In Which TC Is*
Accepted into a Writers' Colony in
Upstate New York and into a New Circle
of Friends and Meets Newton Arvin

The stone mansion, the center of the writers' and artists' colony at Yaddo near Saratoga
Springs in upstate New York. Truman's friend (at the time) Carson McCullers was
instrumental in getting him admitted. Also in residence that summer were Leo Lerman,
Marguerite Young, John Malcolm Brinnin, Katherine Anne Porter, and the two
academics Howard Doughty and Newton Arvin, both of whom had relationships with
Truman, Newton's by far the more significant. *(Courtesy of Yaddo)*

TRUMAN CAPOTE
[letter to Robert Linscott, editor at Random House]

dear bob

have come, am here, am slowly freezing to death; my fingers are pencils of ice. but really, all told, i told, i think this is quite a place, at least so far. the company is fairly good. here at the moment are: agnes smedley, carson, howard doughty (he is very pleasant), leo lerman (who is keeping himself in control), ralph bates, marguerite young, and arriving today St. Katherine Anne P.

I have a bedroom in the mansion (there are bats circulating in some of the rooms, and leo keeps his light on all night, for the wind blows eerily, doors creak, and the faint cheep cheep of the bats cry in the towers above: no kidding. my studio is quite a distance from the house, and is enormous. it s a remodeled barn, and sitting in the loft is an old-fashioned barouche: i keep thinking of Rudyard's phantom rickshaw, which is all very disconcerting. that is where I am now, in the studio, and you cannot imagine how cold it is, though there is a fine pot-bellied stove. however, I can't seem to keep the damn thing going. it is only ten o'clock in the morning but i think i will have to warm my gizzard with a shot of whiskey. from the studio i can see the mountains, and there are buttercups blooming outside the door.

barbara phoned before i left, and told me what a delightful luncheon she'd had with you. i am finishing up my story today and tomorrow, then i'm going to let it cool for maybe two weeks, and work on Other Voices, *before typing it off to send. Will mail you a carbon, of course.*

sorry to write such a damn dull letter, but haven't acclimated myself enough yet to give much of a report. will try to do better next time . . .

best,   t

HORTENSE CALISHER *(writer)* The trees at Yaddo are out of German opera. Some are so huge as to seem almost imaginary. At any moment Wotan will roar. The building known as the Mansion comes into view; if you have approached by car from the highway you may already have glimpsed its turret . . . A tycoon's taste now confronts you. Railroad baron second-class, fin de siècle American, grim-walled from without, lit with pink Tiffany lamps from within. And inside the faint absurdity persists.

In the legendary drawing room, whose filigree ironwork doors open on a sky that on occasion can supply double rainbows, but more ordinarily, bats . . . a phoenix-on-flames fireside, two Dutch ice sleighs, a cardinal's chair nearly twice human height, and a window of stained-glass Indians, above a fountain whose tinkle, I strive to remind myself, has nothing to do with the squatting position of its marble female nude. While, from the adjacent music room, wooden angels with trumpets blow the 1880s straight into one's ear.

JOE CALDWELL *(writer)* At Yaddo, we're called not fellows, not residents, but "guests," the whole idea being that we are the guests of Katrina and Spencer Trask. One of the reasons it may have occurred to them about leaving this mammoth fifty-five-room mansion to creative people was that there was no point in giving it to any of their friends, or any of their relatives, because they all had one just like it! Spencer Trask was a financier and a successful businessman—the New York Central Railroad, and helped back Adolph Ochs so he could buy the *New York Times*. They had four children, two who died not long after they were born. Christina lived to about nine and Spencer Jr. to about five. Both died at the same time, of diphtheria. The story is this—that the two of them were walking through Yaddo one day and since they had no children agreed that it should be a place for writers, painters, and composers where in peaceful surroundings they could work untroubled by the disruptions that plague even the most dedicated creative people.

Elizabeth Ames was the first mistress of Yaddo. It was her idea that this was a great house and that you were guests. Her most enduring contribution was something called "quiet hours." The only time you can ever make any noise is between four in the afternoon until ten at night. At eight o'clock in the morning a lunch box (carrot sticks, sandwich, fresh fruit, a cookie) and a thermos of tea or coffee with your name on it is set out on a shelf in the back of the mansion to take to your studio so there'll be no interruption during the day itself . . . so you can really work like a coal miner. The men wore jackets to dinner and then afterward there would be at least an hour of amiable conversation among the different guests, Elizabeth Ames presiding.

In the old days they had chicken on Sunday, spaghetti on Monday, stew on Tuesday, turkey on Wednesday, eggplant on Thursday, fish on Friday, and ham on Saturday. One time somebody said to the director, "Can't we change the menu?" "No, we find it easier to change the guests."

In the winter the mansion is closed. The guests eat in the library over the garage. One winter one of the other guests asked me, "What's the mansion like? What's it like?" And I said, "Well, it's big." And she said, "What do you mean it's big?" I said, "It's big." I didn't know what else to say. She said, "Come on, you're a writer." I said, "It's big."

It's not cozy . . . it's grand. There's an enormous fireplace and above it there's a mosaic of the phoenix, and underneath it says in Latin, "Conquered by the flames, Yaddo rises again to peace." There's a great staircase going up to the second floor and just above the landing there's an enormous Tiffany window of a woman with her hands raised called "Hope."

ELIZABETH BISHOP (poet) I didn't like it in summer because of the incessant coming and going, but the winter was rather different. There were six of us and just by luck we all liked each other and had a very good time. I wrote one poem, I think, in that whole stretch. The first time I liked the horses, I'm afraid. In the summer—I think this still goes on—you can walk through the Whitney estate to the track. A friend and I used to walk there early in the morning and sit at the track and have coffee and blueberry muffins while they exercised the horses. I loved that. We went to a sale of yearlings in August and that was beautiful. The sale was in a big tent. The grooms had dustpans and brooms with brass handles and they'd go around after the little colts and sweep up the manure. That's what I remember best about Yaddo.

JOE CALDWELL They didn't have admissions committees then. I think Elizabeth Ames appealed to people like Malcolm Cowley and Dwight Macdonald and asked, "Who are the good writers?" They would tell her and she would invite them. She had no idea what to expect. One time John Cheever was going from some room or another back to his own room stark naked. And, as heaven would have it, somebody was bringing some visitors through the hallway. What John did was to back up against the wall, hold his arms out, and say to the people as they passed by, "I'm a ghost." They just kept right on going.

LEO LERMAN When we were at Yaddo, the main house was closed because of the war. We lived in the wings and in various studios. There were eight of us. Katherine Anne Porter came for a weekend. She was a grand visiting lady, with jewels, and a very Southern accent. To the day she died . . . I always told her, "Dear, I always see you stark naked on your belly on a fur rug, kicking your heels in the air." She rather liked that.

MARGUERITE YOUNG Truman was hilarious at Yaddo. I went with him, Newton Arvin, Carson McCullers, and Jerre Mangione to one of the great hotels in Saratoga Springs (either the Grand Union or the USA) because we wanted to see the first television. We went in and looked. Truman said, "This thing has no future whatever." And we all agreed, no future whatever.

LEO LERMAN Carson McCullers drank a great deal of wine. She was always impecunious. Once she told us she had to go "into town," meaning New York. About seven o'clock in the morning we got up to escort her to the train—she seemed helpless at all times in a most determined way. We got to the train. She had to be sort of hoisted onto it. Once hoisted, she turned and said she'd got no money. But there was a kind of strange crackling noise from her bosom. She's quite flat-chested to the best of my knowledge, but her bosom seemed fuller than usual, which wasn't much. Lo and behold, she had been accumulating royalty checks and so forth, and these were all pinned underneath her shirt. Checks. I don't think there was any money, just checks. Her bosom grew.

JOHNNY NICHOLSON (*restaurateur*) Carson had a very good Southern sense of humor. But on a very dramatic side. George Davis used to say, "You know, when you're not looking, she throws her cane away and does a jig on one foot."

VIRGINIA CARR Both Carson and Truman had the ability to transform the truth and to keep fine-tuning it. Carson started telling a story to Edward Newhouse, who used to write for *The New Yorker,* about how her father set himself on fire smoking on the sofa. He was so absentminded that the fire had really blazed up before he noticed. Just then the Yaddo dinner bell rang. The story was interrupted. Edward could hardly wait to get back with Carson to find out what happened. When they got back together Carson said, "Oh, Edward, you believe that story? I must be improving. The last time I told it no one believed me." There was no stopping her. She liked to tell the story about the time she leaped on a horse when a mounted policeman had left it to graze and galloped off. She told it so much that people could not verify that it was untrue. Truman was like that.

ALFRED KAZIN (*critic*) Of course, not everyone at Yaddo was as charmed with Carson as I was. I remember playing poker with Carson and Katherine Anne Porter; an amateurish shuffling of cards by Carson mysteriously drove Katherine Anne mad with fury and ended with Katherine and me walking down Union Avenue on a lovely Sunday afternoon. The young girls promenading the avenue in their springtime best irritated Katherine Anne as much as Carson had. She had nothing good to say about any of them. I thought this remarkable, considering that Katherine Anne (once a bathing beauty in Mack Sennett's Hollywood comedies) was not only talented but in face and figure quite a dazzler. But I learned (especially at Yaddo) to look at writers with appreciation even when I could not see beginning or end to the commotion that mysteriously possessed them.

TRUMAN CAPOTE

[letter to Marie Louise Aswell, editor at *Harper's Bazaar*]

marylou, my angel,

well, I knew it was too good to last: i'm in trouble, and it's all leo's fault. according to Mrs. Ames, howard doughty and I are "insistently persecuting" him. see, leo has a real aberration about snakes: he makes me escort him every day from the mansion to his studio; but he has dramatized the whole thing to such a ridiculous extent that everybody here thought he was half-way joking. so yesterday howard came to my studio for lunch. when he left he stepped on a snake in my yard, and picked it up. leo, who was standing in his doorway across the road, saw it, and began to scream: "you're mean, you're cruel!" then slammed his door, pulled down all his shades, and curled up under his desk, and stayed there the whole afternoon, in a real fit of terror: no one, of course, had any intention of frightening him. but two workmen who were putting firewood in our studios saw the whole thing and reported it to Mrs. A, who promptly sent a little "blue note" (all communication is carried on through these blue notes) saying that Mr. Lerman had been made ill by our (howard's and mine) insistent persecution. i suppose it will blow over, but it's all too absurd for words. leo, of course, feels very badly that he got us into so much trouble. howard wrote a wonderful reply explaining everything (we felt like little naughty schoolboys, which annoyed howard, for he is a professor at Harvard, and 42 years old). otherwise everything is o.k.

carson has been sick in bed, that is the reason she hasn't written you. she is better now, though, and may be up today. we had breakfast together, and she seemed much better. i took a seconal last night and feel so damn dizzy i can hardly see the typewriter. katherine anne porter and i danced together till all hours last night. she must be about sixty, but oh how she can do the hootchy-cootchy. she tries to act like a southern belle of sixteen or so. she is so unserious it is hard to believe she can write at all. she is like a little new york debutante. she thinks i am a wonderful dancer, and makes me dance with her all the time: it is simply awful, because she hasn't the faintest notion of how to do the simplest steps. I love agnes smedley, marvelous person. but of all the people here i like howard doughty best.

oh my precious marylou, i love you, and i love barbara, and hope you both love me: you are both so dear to me. and I miss you so much that it is a real pain.

enclosed, please find violets: i know they will be dry by the time they reach you, but remember how beautiful they were, and that is the way i send them to you, my darling dearest marylou.

LEO LERMAN The first month Truman and I were there we had adjoining rooms and shared the same bathroom. At Yaddo they have a system of notes. You got notes if there was something they didn't approve of. One morning we got a note that neither of us understood: "Would Mr. Capote and Mr. Lerman stop committing nuisances on the bathroom floor?" I hadn't committed any nuisances, Truman hadn't committed any nuisances, but that was never explained.

One day I went into Truman's room and he was standing in front of the looking glass; he was naked. I never saw him naked before or since. I was astonished because from the hips down he seemed to be a truck driver. Hips up, he seemed to be almost a hermaphrodite. I never thought to look . . . I rather wish I had. I'm rather limited sometimes, I forget the essential part . . . I once wrote a piece about Vienna and I forgot to mention the Hapsburgs.

JOHN MALCOLM BRINNIN (*writer*) Small as a child, he looked like no other male adult I'd ever seen. His head was big and handsome, and his butterscotch hair was cut in bangs. Willowy and delicate above the waist, he was, below, as strong and chunky as a Shetland pony. He wore a white T-shirt, khaki shorts too big for him, sandals that fit as neatly as hooves.

LEO LERMAN We played Murder a great deal—that game where the ace of spades is the murderer and the jack of hearts is the detective and you mill around in the dark hiding and scared that the person next to you may turn out to be the murderer. One night at Murder . . . it was an extraordinary night, very full of clouds and a great moon . . . We were all scared because we were playing in this great hulking house where we weren't supposed to be. I was the murderer. I knew exactly what victim I wanted. Truman. Everybody flew from room to room screeching, hiding here, hiding there. Carson adored it. She gave screeches. We all screeched. She moved when she had to move. She wasn't sick in those days. Slightly ossified, but she wasn't sick. We hid here and we hid there and conjectured about who the murderer was. Being the sinister creature I am, I enjoyed every moment of it. Finally, I lured Truman into my closet. I strangled him. He screamed, "Oh, you, I'll get you for this! I'll never trust you again!" It was absolutely thrilling; his scream went up several octaves above and several octaves below: it was the full rage of Truman. It was the manly Truman, the female Truman, it was the *works*. I think the scream haunts Yaddo still.

JOHN MALCOLM BRINNIN He told me he was working on a novel, his first. He now had five chapters and a title. Did I like titles? What would I think of *Other Voices, Other Rooms*. His voice, odd and high, was full of funny resonances that ran a scale of their own: meadowlark trills and, when he laughed or growled, a tugboat basso. Before I could respond he asked me if I would care to listen to a chapter.

Led into a Gothic chapel-like tower room with tall windows on three sides, I sat on something that looked like a section of a choir stall while he read from yellow foolscap in a steady, barely inflected voice that seemed suddenly to belong to another person. His respect for every one of his nuances was contagious; I found myself listening with as much care as he took to read. With no preface to cue me in, I grasped only that a character named Joel was being put through a series of small adventures meant to test his courage and sense of reality. The story didn't matter. What did was the quality of a prose that mixed hard observations with extravagant fancy, without ever losing a grip on either. There were too many shimmering "effects" and too much poetic "atmosphere," yet his eye for detail seemed to me as exact as Faulkner's, and much less portentous, or lugubrious. Most, I was struck by his concern for rhythm; when a paragraph got off on the wrong beat, he'd stop and start over. Surprised, I said only that I'd like to hear more of it sometime.

JERRE MANGIONE (*writer*) He came up with a blanket and said he'd like to talk with me. He spread this blanket out on the lawn and we had this conversation to the effect that there was his group, which was very interesting and included Marguerite Young, who would one day—twenty years in fact—become famous, and that there was this other group that was rather dull. He was extending an invitation to me to be part of his group. I explained that I usually didn't "take sides," and I gravitated to people that I liked. Whatever, we became good friends. He saw something in me that he didn't see in the others, because when his parents came to visit him, he seemed embarrassed to have them there. I was the only one who was asked to meet them. He actually kissed my hand in gratitude.

JOHN MALCOLM BRINNIN When the Capotes—Joe and Nina—came for a visit, I was invited along with Newton Arvin to meet them. Frail, dark, and pretty, she seemed tense; he was outgoing, a bit brusque, anxious to please. We sat on the liturgical furniture and made conversation while Truman, edgy as a preppie on Parents' Day, stared from one window, then another.

Early evening, when the others had gone, he and I sat, lights out, to watch the rising of an enormous harvest moon on hills rolling toward Vermont.

"Well," said T., "that's my family—a bewildered woman and a man who doesn't know he's bewildered. You see why I count on friends—anyone. When my real father ran off, at least I had these aunts, these marvelous weird sisters. Then, for a long time, no one . . . until a schoolteacher. Miss Catherine R. Wood. She made me feel like an adult, we'd talk like adults, exchange books no one else ever read. She even knew who Sigrid Undset was. She wore pearls, little strings of them. She looked like the Duchess of Kent . . . at least I thought so."

There was a tap on the door. He wiped his eyes.

"Newton," he said.

PHOEBE PIERCE VREELAND Like Edith Wharton, Truman really was privately educated. The first teacher was Ms. Catherine Wood and the second one was Newton Arvin.

KARL BISSINGER (*photographer*) I first heard Newton Arvin's name
from Mary Garrison Grant, who had been his first wife. She'd been
in his class at Smith. At the time their marriage was breaking up and
she was getting over a nervous breakdown—it had all been pretty
traumatic to her—I remember asking her, "Well, didn't you *suspect*
that your husband was a homosexual?" She said that no, that she
hadn't. "Well," I asked, "was he totally dishonest about it?" She said
no, he had given her a lot of poems to read before they were
married; among many were Oscar Wilde's poems, poems about the
love that dare not speak its name.

Arvin had asked her, "Did you read the poems?"

She said yes.

"Did you understand them?"

She had said like a typical student, "Yes," when she in fact hadn't.
And that was that.

DANIEL AARON (*professor*) I knew Mary Grant very well. She was a
great Valkyrian figure. She could make ten meals of Newton. You
can imagine the incongruity. His problem was that he lived too early.
If he had just held on, he could have had an open marriage and
nobody would have said a thing about it. He came from a small
Indiana town; he was extremely conventional in his demeanor and
behavior in public and must have suffered a great deal of shame and
embarrassment. He was constantly going to doctors and
psychiatrists, although he despised most of them because he didn't
think they were very intelligent. He stayed in Northampton. He
would always talk about leaving, but he couldn't, because Smith was
the only place he felt safe.

What was true of his apartment was true of his office. Both were
impeccable. The volumes were always dusted. No dust jackets. His
desk was always immaculate, everything orderly, very careful of files.
I suppose you would describe his as an anal retentive personality.
Sometimes when he'd try to cook, things would get disorderly.
People would come over and cook for him. He was able to make
soup and an egg, but that's about it.

Newton was a very stylish but conventional dresser. He paid
enormous attention to his dress: many suits and many shirts, and he

always dressed elegantly. A great fetish for shirts, ties, and great stacks of things in his wardrobe. Not quite like Jay Gatsby's, but carefully put away. Most people seeing him would have seen him as a sort of decorous professor. He was prematurely bald. He was very slight of build. Wore owlish glasses. Very funny, rather dry wit. He was amusing and self-deprecating about himself. Lots of jokes about himself.

SYLVAN SCHENDLER (*professor*) I remember he had no car—he'd never had a car—and he'd say, "Sylvan, I'd like you to take me to Springfield this afternoon so I can get a new suit." And I, who used thrift shop clothes, the cheaper the better, would take him down to Springfield and he'd buy a suit for a hundred and fifty or two hundred dollars. It seemed to me very extravagant, but every year he'd do that. He was always well buttoned up, very precise in his dress.

DANIEL AARON He was enormously learned. The last year of his life he was translating Larbaud, Vittorini, Robert Musil, and Virgil. An extraordinarily disciplined, retentive, and refined mind.

JOHN MALCOLM BRINNIN I joined him one morning when, clerkish with gold-rimmed spectacles, he wore a dark suit to breakfast, sat like a furled umbrella, and buttered his toast to the edges. He'd been reading Melville, he said, while he made a game of pretending to himself he never had. "It's the only way," he told me, "otherwise you're apt to see the beard and the whale and the customshouse and miss the man."

"Amen," I said to myself.

BARBARA LAWRENCE Truman had a good eye for a kind of integrity and sincerity in people, and I think that's one reason he was so terribly drawn to Newton Arvin. But they were really an odd couple! Newton always looked to me as if he had too few red blood cells, a strangled artery somewhere.

DIANA TRILLING (*critic*) Newton was such a dried-up academic from his earliest youth that it seemed so strange for him to be involved with someone as feisty as Truman.

LEO LERMAN It had to do with varieties of glamour. Newton had the glamour of academe. Truman'd sit in a little old chair listening to Newton "reading things in the original Greek," as he said to me, listening to the quartets of Beethoven, and so forth. It was a world he hadn't known, a world that was so golden to him.

DANIEL AARON Newton wrote to me about how brilliant this young man was—what an extraordinary genius ingenue, a natural writer and an extraordinary person! It was the start of a great, great love affair. When he brought Truman back to Smith, it was as if a bridegroom were introducing his bride—Newton was foolish and bumbling with pleasure and embarrassed all at the same time. Actually, to bring Truman to Northampton at that time was like bringing some rare and very sultry tropical plant into a chilly climate . . . like bougainvillea to the North Pole. I'd known homosexuals before, but they'd always been of the very discreet variety. Truman behaved in the most outrageous way. I think he did it partly out of mischievousness, but it was a kind of camp I'd never seen before. Absolutely extraordinary. Mincing and fluttering and all these kinds of things. It was really an act of daring on Newton's part to bring Truman there. I was very taken aback. But at the same time Truman was very amusing. But after successive visits, he dropped all the gay mannerisms and became a simple Southern boy. Very funny. And very likable. Once he felt comfortable, he was as natural as an old shoe . . . enormously funny with wonderful stories to tell. He would tell them as if they were happening to him—spy stories, one about an old woman and a parrot cage on the train in Germany, dope inside the cage, things like that.

Newton had had a whole series of lovers before. He would break with them or they with him, and that would usually cause some kind of traumatic effect, sometimes a suicide attempt, carefully worked out so that he would be discovered, like leaving letters that were sure to be found. I put him in the sanitarium three times myself. He had a lot of electric-shock treatment, which apparently worked.

He was a terrible hypochondriac. Very sensitive and shy and yet the risks that he took when he would go cruising astonished me. His tremendous passion and drive underneath came out from time to time. But to most people at Smith College he was quiet, gentlemanly—a Caspar Milquetoast who never wanted to offend anybody. That was Newton's public manner, although he could be very spirited. He could be a savage reviewer. His handwriting was remarkable—bold and decisive. The hand of a man with great character and drive. In his relationship with Truman he was definitely the dominating figure.

SYLVAN SCHENDLER I was always sympathetic to Newton's anguish. You could tell by his eyes whether or not he was suffering, when he was going through a paranoid period, or he'd been drinking, his eyes glittered and I knew he was in trouble. Coming out of a very bad period and paranoid, afraid to leave Northampton, he decided he wanted to go into New York. I drove him down. He would go down and stay at the Hotel Latham on Twenty-eighth Street and then go down the street to the well-named Everard Baths on Twenty-eighth Street. Ned Rorem in his *New York Diary* speaks of the baths as one of the nine circles of hell—all the steam and the fungus and the smells, very creepy, very disturbed by it. Newton would pop over to the baths and after a couple of days, say, on a Sunday he'd come over to the little apartment I used to keep in New York and we'd take off and I'd drive him back to Northampton. I'd say, "Well, Newton, how'd it go?" He'd say, "Oh, Sylvan, I feel so clean." I would have thought he might have been repelled by it. He loved it there.

GORE VIDAL We went to the Everard Baths. Very grimy. Extremely grimy. It was a nineteenth-century building, which has since burned down. Cubicles, steamy places. A lot of activity. People wearing these white robes . . . like Fellini's film $8^1/2$. We were walking along a corridor—it was strictly voyeur time. Lights were dim. But each of us was sufficiently well known so that we did not particularly want to be recognized. As we were slinking along the corridor, I hear thumpety-thumpety-thump behind us and there's this splendid Southern queen, Peter Lindamood, the greatest gossip in town, who lived in the house where Capote was photographed on that round thing. "Ah see you! Ah see you!" he shouted as he came up to us. "Mah deahs, Tallulah was magnificent!" He was talking about the opening of *Private Lives*. That'll give you the exact date of when we were at the Everard Baths. The *one* person that you would not want to see you had come galloping up. So, that story must have been all over New York in twenty minutes.

PHOEBE PIERCE VREELAND Newton would come to New York. Poor Newton! He was terrified all the time. I mean he was terrified *all* the time. Small and gray and spectacles. I remember a wonderful conversation I had with him about the transcendentalists and Emerson and so forth and he was wonderful, but he was terrified, really terrified that Smith College would get wind of his private life. I said to Truman, "I don't know *why* he's so terrified of being discovered. Being discovered at what? Having dinner in a restaurant with a promising young author?" Well, we all went up to Harlem to see a famous female impersonator—the Celebrity Club, a great big barn of a place with a trellis all around the wall with a decor of little tiny artificial colored leaves. We all had a table. Suddenly these people in uniform appeared at the door. Newton thought it was the police coming for him! Actually it was the fire department. Remember the leaves? Anybody who put a match to one of those little imitation leaves, the place would have burned up. So they appeared at irregular intervals to get paid off. That's why they were there. Newton was crouching in a phone booth. It really took us hours to find him, he was down at the bottom. It's so awful. He was terrified all the time.

ALFRED KAZIN Love is very strange, and once in a while I would see Truman getting off the train, going to Prospect Street to see

Newton. I had nothing to say or do about the whole thing, but I was struck by the obstinacy and the integrity of what Truman felt about Newton. Newton, of course, didn't speak to me very often, so he didn't tell me what he felt about Truman, but it was sort of beautiful and tragic. At the end, it was terrible for Newton. Northampton, Massachusetts, though it's a charming place and has an excellent women's college, is no place in which to get into a sexual scandal, and there it was.

DANIEL AARON During Eisenhower's administration, the Postmaster General Arthur Summerfield, launched an anti-smut campaign: post offices added to the postmark, "Stamp Out Smut." People were encouraged to turn in anyone they suspected of receiving pornographic materials through the mails. Newton subscribed to some of this stuff, mostly photographs, I think. He was busted in a rather sensational way. The state police in Massachusetts were alerted, and they burst in on this shy quiet decorous man and tore his apartment to pieces. Newton did have certain pornographic books in his library. But what they seized upon and used as evidence were simply male pinups showing young, languorous men stepping out of shower baths, nothing you wouldn't find in Calvin Klein ads these days. What was so frightening was that Newton was kind of timid and rabbity, and you can imagine what it was to have these great fat-assed state policemen come smashing into your house. Enormous publicity. For someone like Newton, it was the worst horror he could have dreamed of. I sat through the trials with him. It was awful, just awful. I wrote to all his friends, and what a mixed lot they were. David Lilienthal, who had grown up with Newton in Valparaiso, didn't even know Newton was a homosexual. Truman, of course, was concerned. Many friends sent money and offers to help. But Newton was convicted, given a suspended sentence. Then, of course, two years later, a case like it was thrown out of court. It was unconstitutional. Nothing like that could ever happen now.

Smith didn't behave terribly well, but how many schools would have? I suppose that if everybody had gathered around him and said,

"Newton, we're going to stick by you. You're our colleague and by
God we'll go down the line with you," that would have been a fine
thing. But they were timid and frightened, always a bit
uncomfortable with his reputation. It was always kept very low, but
everybody knew about it. It took him a long time to recover. He
resigned from Smith.

SYLVAN SCHENDLER He said, "I'm glad not to have to talk to the
little tarts anymore." Of course, this was a kind of bravado, because
he liked a lot of the girls, and he'd speak to me of first-class minds
and be quite respectful. Then he wrote this very good book on
Longfellow, and I thought he was in the clear. But he developed
cancer of the pancreas; the oddity was that he was a frightful
hypochondriac, the kind of person who always wore rubbers, always
worrying about his health, doctoring himself, cautioning everybody
else, and we all thought he was going to live a hundred years
because he took such good care of himself. But that's what
happened.

Newton had on his bedroom bureau a nude bodybuilder pose of
Truman, who was maybe eighteen or so, which he kept there until
he died. He pushed Truman out into the world because he said
there's no future if you stay with me. So that was his version. It may
well be true, because Truman always held him in great affection. A
thoughtful, caring man, Arvin loved Truman very much, but he
didn't feel it was right in some way.

DANIEL AARON After Newton died, Sylvan Schendler and I were
putting together a collection of his essays when it occurred to me
that the obvious writer to draw attention to Newton would be
Truman. I wrote him and asked if he would do an introduction. I got
this very long letter written on foolscap paper in a large, round,
childish hand in pencil saying that he could not write something
about Newton in such a perfunctory way. He did say that Newton
had been one of the two people who had the most influence on his
literary career. I think that's true. Newton had been a literary mentor
as well as lover and had guided him. He was an extraordinarily good
critic and a writer himself of unfailing taste. I myself learned an

enormous amount from him every time we went over one of my manuscripts. There were certain kinds of expressions and mannerisms he detested. Usually he was right. He thought that Truman was this really great writer and that he was simply helping him a little bit. Apparently Truman felt he was a good deal more.

1947

CHAPTER FIVE *In Which TC Takes a
Train Ride, Meets the Trillings, and
Alarms the Island of Nantucket*

One of Truman's early manifestations of his impish side was to leap into the air and cry out, "I'm beside myself!" *(Cecil Beaton, courtesy of Sotheby's London)*

DIANA TRILLING I was in Grand Central Station with Lionel—we were going, I suppose, somewhere in Connecticut—waiting by our suitcases. I was standing there when a strange little creature came over to me and said, "Aren't you Diana Trilling? I'm Truman Capote." I knew his name, of course, because I had written something about him by that time. He said, "I recognized you from a photograph in Leo Lerman's house. I wanted to talk to you." Well, I was very glad to talk to him. He was going to Boston, and then to Nantucket, I believe, so we would have a little time together on the train. Lionel came from where he had bought the tickets. I introduced them. The three of us got on the train and we pulled the seat over so that we were facing each other—knees to knees, looking at each other in a very full car. Here was this little creature, odd-looking and with his extraordinary squeaky voice, very high-pitched and very resonant: it carried the length of the car. So he sat opposite Lionel and me and proceeded to ask questions about Lionel's book on E. M. Forster. Truman wanted to know why it was that Lionel had ignored Forster's homosexuality. Now this was not only a bold question to put at the top of his shrill voice in a very crowded car in those days. I remember having very mixed feelings. One: wishing he would shut up and go away, because I was embarrassed and I thought there was going to be a lynching in the car. I was afraid people would do something. I could see that they were uncomfortable, angry at him, very angry. Truman wasn't watching or if he was he didn't let on. But the other thing was that I was extraordinarily impressed by him. I thought, "Good for him, just going on, having this conversation and not caring about what the people in the car think." So I was absolutely in conflict, you know, in both my embarrassment and my respect for him. It was a very impressive first view.

He asked Lionel the question quite directly: "Why did you not treat Forster's homosexuality in the book?"

"I didn't know about it."

Truman said, "Well, didn't you *hear* about it?"

"No," said Lionel, "I had not heard about it. I know nothing about his life."

Truman said, "Well, didn't you *guess* it?"

Lionel said, "Yes, as I was writing my book, it began to dawn on me that probably he *was* homosexual."

"Then why didn't you write about it?"

Lionel replied, "Because it didn't seem to me to concern me very much. I wasn't very interested in it."

Truman simply thought that was *impossible*. Lionel said that it was exactly possible. So there they were, you know, having this very serious confrontation about this while I was going through, as I say, my emotions of both alarm and respect. Then Truman said that Forster had left a homosexual novel in the British Museum, and that at his death it would be found. Lionel said this would be interesting but he wasn't particularly concerned about it for his book, and that was it. We got as far as Truman was going and we got out and everything was all right—nobody had lynched either one.

Nantucket

TRUMAN CAPOTE [letter to Mary Louise Aswell]

Marylou, my beloved,

I cannot describe to you how pleased I am with the house: it could not be cleaner, larger or more comfortable. There is more space than you can imagine, and it is furnished most pleasantly. One thing, though . . . the stove, while very modern, burns wood and coal, and really I am having an awful time with it . . . however, I shall take a few lessons from someone around here, and so this difficulty should prove temporary.

Yesterday was terribly foggy, but today the weather is beautiful, and I have been riding around with the Marquis surveying things. It is one of the loveliest places I have ever seen.

You will not have to bring anything, unless it is an extra sheet or two, for the house is quite luxuriously equipped, and we are only about a five minute walk from the beach.

Newton is coming Tuesday.

My love to everyone. I miss you. I love you. Do not worry: someday

I'll write a bestseller and buy us all a castle in Italy (they're very cheap, I hear).

GWEN GAILLARD *(Nantucket resident)* They certainly left their mark in Nantucket for a few years because at that time the island was very closety and their style of living was not very popular. Moreover, I was disliked by him and his crowd. In the bar he didn't even wish me to carry a drink to the table or anything. I don't know why he disliked me so much. I was a New Yorker; I'd been to Parsons Art School, and stuff like that. I'd lived with a couple of the gay boys. I'd decorated Lord & Taylor's windows as a kid in art school. One time, somebody came into the bar—a new member of his entourage—when my husband Harold was tending bar. Truman was sitting at his table. He said, "The bartender is heaven but if you see that wife of his, she's a real bitch."

Truman was really rude. I think later on he was more clever, but then he was rude. He had to be in control of the whole scene. Nobody could be cleverer or get more of a laugh. I don't remember the people's names who were with him but they all seemed fairly intellectual. They must have had minds of their own but they were controlled by him. It was bizarre, because he was like a little nit. He was always the one at the head of the table who made the plan of the day, posted little things and chores. These guys could not be late to tea. If they were in shopping and there was a plan that was supposed to take place on the beach at 2:15, they were in terror of their lives out there. It was like a make-believe kingdom he'd created for himself. He was working on a book *[Other Voices, Other Rooms]* so I was told but I don't see how he had the time to write. He was always creating a play, a scene. Other people who knew him said he couldn't live in an everyday life. It had to be something different, planned, contrived.

They were making Jell-O in a bathtub out at the house. What they were going to do with it, I don't know. I don't know whether I *want* to know. But there was a shortage of Jell-O and Jell-O was very important in those days. Every kid had to have Jell-O. But Truman and his friends had gone around and gotten all the Jell-O they could . . . from the A&P, First National, and all the little stores like

Ryder's. There wasn't a box left on the island of any flavor. Nothing. Not even Knox gelatin. It turned out they were filling one of those big old bathtubs with claw feet with Jell-O. They made these little asides and comments around town about Jell-O. But heaven knows what went on with it.

He always went to the ladies' room at the Opera House and told everybody about it—which doesn't mean anything now, but in those days some little old lady having a sherry at the bar would be shocked by it. I remember one gal saying, "I have to go across the street to the bathroom 'cause since those people came I never know *who* is in the ladies' room nowadays." Truman's group would all start singsongy, *"We know where you're going . . ."* He'd say loudly, "We-ell, I must say it's much nicer in the ladies' room. It's got those ruffled curtains and . . ." and then they'd all clap around the table.

Truman showed a real dislike for women in those days, almost to being unbearable about it. Just rude and nasty. I was about twenty-six years old then. He wouldn't let anyone take an order from him except the waiter he wanted. He was very fond of my husband because Harold was very good-looking. Truman was "just crazy about the bartender, just crazy." He would always ask for four or five cherries in his Tom Collins and stab away at them. Stuff like that. He used to come in wearing a mask, a hospital mask. He didn't want any germs. He'd say, "Halloo!" and then he'd always go over to this old French chef who knew no English. Truman would say, *"Bonjour ma petite fille!"* or something like that. This French chef didn't know what this little thing was. But any entrance of Truman's always had a shock value.

We opened the restaurant in '46. There was nothing else here of that type. Before us, the restaurant on Nantucket served little bread baskets, creamed chicken on toast points, and lobster salad, cottage curtains, and the waitresses wore little white aprons. We opened— to quote some of the old-timers—the "first dreadful place." We had a piano player. We had the first stained-glass colored lampshades, because they were so cheap at that time. We had waiters in black pants and white jackets and ties. People thought that made it like a mini-bistro in New York. It's funny how people go away for vacations but they home in on a little bit of sophistication. Everyone stood

and sang around the piano. Truman's group used to come in. I think
they had a house in Quidnet on the beach, somewhere out by
Sesachacha Pond, but I'm not quite sure. I know the women would
get the children out of the way when Truman's group had beach
parties out there—the antics on the beach, fans and hats with roses,
and very few clothes, feather boas, Isadora Duncan dances.
Nantucket was always a few years behind Provincetown, which was
really wild then. My guess is that they all made a stop there
beforehand.

1948

CHAPTER SIX *In Which TC's Other Voices, Other Rooms Is Published and Given the Critical Once-Over*

Certainly the most famous book-jacket portrait of contemporary letters. Taken by a photographer friend, Harold Halma, it caused almost as much commotion as the book itself. Truman, dismayed by the negative comments, said he had been cajoled into the languorous pose, which in fact he had suggested himself. *(Harold Halma/Random House)*

PHOEBE PIERCE VREELAND He sent *Other Voices, Other Rooms* to me in galleys. I can still see myself reading it. I was so thrilled I called him at 1060 Park. He tried to be blasé, but he was absolutely, just like every author with their first book, just in ecstasy. We went to the White Turkey over there on Fifty-seventh Street and Second Avenue, sat there and had terrific cocktails. We drank Manhattans and talked about the future and everything and then staggered in for a turkey dinner. He was really thrilled. I think he was rather sensitive to the reviews that came afterward, but not too, because Truman had a very sure sense that he would always write no matter what . . . that was the golden thread in his life. He was no Virginia Woolf who sat and brooded over bad reviews. Besides, at that time he had a tremendous natural ebullience, and then the fun of being a celebrity . . . going out all over New York and everything.

JANE GUNTHER (*friend*) I met him at the Cerfs'. I remember it very well because *Other Voices, Other Rooms* had just come out with that incredible photograph of him on the back cover. He seemed tremendously young and vulnerable. He looked about twelve at this party. People looked at him as if he were a sort of freak. When I talked to him, I liked him right away.

ROBERT FIZDALE Arthur Gold admired the beautiful photograph of him reclining and he asked, "You look so beautiful, how do you do it?" Truman said, "All you have to do is think beautiful when you're being photographed—that's the secret—and then you are beautiful."

NED ROREM (*composer*) It's possible if you have a strong enough personality. The greatest courtesans in history have never been great beauties. Lillian Hellman offered herself as a beauty—very coy with men, very cute: she was a battle-ax in fancy clothes.

BABS SIMPSON (*editor*) Terribly vain. I'm sure he always saw himself for his entire life lying on that sofa. I'm sure he thought he was a beauty till the day he died.

PHOEBE PIERCE VREELAND Ah, the photograph! On the back cover—Truman lolling on the sofa, a lost elf. I knew Harold Halma, who took it, very well. He and Andrew Lyndon lived together. Very interesting guy. Among other things, an absolutely marvelous cook. He was from California. Started off to be a pianist, but wasn't good enough, so he became a photographer. They had a place way east in the Fifties. It wasn't a cold-water flat, but well kept up. That's where they had their parties with this marvelous cooking. I think that photograph was done at the house because of the sofa. It's a French Provincial sofa, isn't it? Well that was Harold's passion, collecting French Provincial furniture. I think they did it really as a kind of a lark together. I don't think they had any idea that it could cause such an uproar.

BRENDAN GILL Truman had been just an apparition in the corridor of *The New Yorker* as far as we knew. Then it turned out to our astonishment that he was a real writer and better than most of the people on the magazine. Tradition at *The New Yorker* was nonintellectual, even anti-intellectual. The editorial attitude was one of profound skepticism about every writer. It was a kind of tough-guy attitude Harold Ross, who had been a reporter and was suspicious of writers who hadn't been, believed in. When *Other Voices, Other Rooms* came out, Wolcott Gibbs who was a homophobe of course   almost everybody was in those days—walked up and down the corridors jingling coins in his pockets and saying, "The boy can write! The boy can write!" He was in awe of the fact that somebody he had felt nothing but contempt for, a messenger boy in the corridors of *The New Yorker,* was in fact a genius! Gibbs could not fail to acknowledge this, pretty unwelcome news, but there it was.

DIANA TRILLING [in *The Nation,* January 31, 1948] It is seldom I have so double a response to a book as I have to Truman Capote's *Other Voices, Other Rooms*. This is a first novel—or, more accurately, long novelette—by the twenty-three-year-old writer whose short fiction has already brought him much notice from the advance talent scouts. I can well understand what the shouting has been about: not since the early work of Eudora Welty has there been an instance of such striking literary virtuosity. Even if Mr. Capote were ten or twenty years older than he is, his powers of description and evocation, his ability to bend language to his poetic moods, his ear for dialect and for the varied rhythms of speech would be remarkable. In one so young this much writing skill represents a kind of genius. On the other hand, I find myself deeply antipathetic to the whole artistic-moral purpose of Mr. Capote's novel. In Mr. Capote's case, as in the case of so many of the gifted contemporary artists, I would freely trade 80 per cent of his technical virtuosity for 20 per cent more value in the uses to which it is put.

In some respects *Other Voices, Other Rooms* can be read as a perfectly realistic story. Set in the rural South, it is about the miseries, fears, and loneliness of a thirteen-year-old boy who on the death of a beloved mother comes to live with his unknown father— only to discover that the father is a hopeless paralytic, the father's newest wife an imbecile, and Randolph, the remaining member of the household, a middle-aged degenerate aesthete. We can even include in the general realistic pattern certain of the other characters that surround the young Joel in his new environment: the tomboy Idabel, who is incapable of the tender girlishness that Joel needs in a friend; the century-old Jesus Fever, the Negro mule-driver; Zoo, the colored housemaid whose native warm-heartedness we watch disappear in a developing religious hysteria. But this realism, already sufficiently weighted in the direction of nightmare, is overlaid with so many trappings of symbolic horror that the book as a whole has predominantly the air of a work of surrealist fantasy. Thus, as if it were not bad enough that Joel's father is a paralytic whose only means of calling for aid is to drop red—not even white—tennis balls from his bed, which bounce slowly down the stairs to the lower floor of the house—though there is no reason why he should not simply ring a bell! Or Miss Amy, the father's wife, in addition to being feeble-minded, must have a wooden hand on which she always wears a glove! Or Cousin Randolph, in addition to his other pleasant habits, must collect the wings of bluebirds which Miss Amy has killed for him with a poker! This claptrap, however skillfully set on the page, paradoxically enough changes what might be a valid symbolic statement of the loneliness and decay of modern life into merely the latest chic example of Southern Gothic. In large part it transforms a sincere if ambiguous psychological study into a self-conscious titillation of the nerves of the reader.

But happily for Mr. Capote's future as a novelist, the transformation is not complete. Despite its surrealist paraphernalia, *Other Voices, Other Rooms* does manage to convey a serious content. At the end of the book the young Joel turns to the homosexual love offered him by Randolph, and we realize that in his slow piling up of nightmare details Mr. Capote has been attempting to recreate the emotional background to sexual inversion. What his book is saying is that a boy becomes a homosexual when the circumstances of his life deny him the other, more normal gratifications of his need for affection.

Well, I am not equipped to argue whether or not this is a sound explanation of the source of homosexuality. Nor does the question interest me here. Much more interesting, it seems to me, is the implication of Mr. Capote's book that, having been given an explanation of the cause of Joel's homosexuality, we have been given all the ground we need for a proper attitude toward it and toward Joel as a member of society. For what other meaning can we possibly draw from this portrait of a passive victim of his early circumstances than that we must always think of him in this light—that even when Joel will be thirty or forty, we shall still have to judge him only as the passive victim of his early circumstances? But this is surely a very dangerous social attitude, since, in exactly the same sense in which Joel is formed by the accidents of his youthful experience, we have all of us, heterosexuals no less than homosexuals, been formed by our early experience. Is no member of society, then, to be held accountable for himself, not even Hitler?

Let me make myself unmistakably clear. I do not oppose the attitude set forth in Mr. Capote's novel simply as it refers to homosexuals but as it refers to all mankind. For it seems to me to create an adult world of passive acceptance in which we are rendered incapable of thinking anybody responsible for his behavior in any department.

And I dwell on it because this blanket endorsement of the

deterministic principle is frighteningly current in contemporary fiction. With startling regularity our most talented young novelists present us with child heroes who are never permitted to grow up into an adulthood which will submit them to the test of *conduct*. Or even in novels which have grown characters we see the almost total disappearance of plot; we see, that is, the disappearance of the kind of action in which moral attitudes are properly assessed. Our fiction, in other words, is taking the lead in opting for a world of irresponsibility.

The problem is of course a very complex one. Obviously, in standing against this absolute of determinism, I do not mean to close out all social or personal causality but merely to ask for a mediation between the extremes of causality and freedom. But is this not, after all, what fiction is peculiarly suited to do, to mediate between extremes? Surely the novel, compounded as it is or should be of both psychological insight and dramatic action, is par excellence the medium for bringing both sympathy and moral-social discrimination to bear upon the individual human plight.

But I am afraid that this is not the function of the novel as Mr. Capote sees it. Nor as a large percentage of present-day readers see it; else most of the new writers whom we regard as distinguished would not be found so interesting. Were we to ask of fiction, as we once did, that it base its claim to artistic stature on its moral stature, most of the writing gifts which we celebrate today would fall into their proper place as merely feats of literary athletics.

TRUMAN CAPOTE *Do you remember the young boy who goes to a crumbling mansion in search of his father and finds an old man who is crippled and can't speak and can communicate only by bouncing red tennis balls down the stairs? Well, I suddenly understood that, of course, this represented my search for my own father, whom I seldom saw, and the fact that the old man is crippled and mute was my way of transferring my own inability to communicate with my father; I was not only the boy in the story but also the old man. So the central theme of the book was my search for my father—a father who, in the deepest sense, was nonexistent. This seems so clear and obvious today that it's hard to understand why I never grasped the fact at the time; it was a classic case of self-deception. I now realize that what I was attempting in* Other Voices, Other Rooms *was to exorcise my own devils, the subterranean anxieties that dominated my feelings and imagination: and my ignorance of this was probably a protective shield between me and the subconscious wellspring of my material.*

PHOEBE PIERCE VREELAND When he was living on Second Avenue, his father sent him a family ring. The only time Truman ever really talked to me about the South was in connection with his father, Arch Persons, a highly romanticized version . . . that he was a riverboat gambler, wore a white linen suit, you know, all that kind of thing. Truman said to me, "Well, you know, Persons"—he always called him Persons, never Arch—"Persons is going to send me a ring, a family ring or something." That meant a lot to Truman. Truman never was a big possessions person, but this was something that interested him a great deal. It came in the mail. I knew he was looking forward to it. It was the most god-awful thing you've ever seen. It was a piece of junk, like it was out of a Cracker Jack box, rather gaudy-looking, and I could see that Truman was terribly disappointed. We were sitting around talking about it. I mean, this is what a father gives a son? I was terribly upset. Truman finally said, "I'll tell you what we'll do. We'll go to the Gimbels jewelry department." Or was it Macy's? I forget. "And we'll sell it. We'll pop it." So we got some money for it, and we went to the White Turkey and drank Manhattans and had a turkey sandwich.

1948

Embarks on the Grand Tour and Visits the

Salons of Paris

(Truman Capote Papers, The New York Public Library)

France

ANTHONY HAIL *(decorator)* Le Boeuf sur le Toit was where everybody went late, late at night after other people's dinners and balls and parties. Truman was involved in everything. Le Boeuf was in full force: the Windsors and Jimmy Donohue . . . it was very, very snappy. There was always a cabaret with somebody singing and playing the piano. I think the duchess even sang at one point. Truman was in all of that.

DANIEL AARON He took us to Le Boeuf sur le Toit. It was when he was beginning his great international career and meeting everybody and telling very funny stories and making fun of his ignorance of foreign languages. Going past the hotel in a taxi he'd call out, "Stop-po! Stop-po!"

GEORGE PLIMPTON As soon as he landed in a town—Paris, say—it didn't seem to take him more than a minute to be at the center of things. I suppose he was supplied with names, and then of course he had the brass and charm to make use of them, barging into the most sacrosanct of places with enviable ease. In Paris in the early fifties there were two weekly literary salons, one officiated over by Marie-Louise Bousquet, the foreign editor of *Harper's Bazaar*— mostly frequented by visiting American celebrities, movie stars, though once I saw Jean Cocteau there with Jean Marais, the French movie star who lived on a houseboat on the Seine—and then the other was Natalie Barney's, a rather more highbrow affair, very much more French, often with elderly members of the French Academy on hand.

EUGENE WALTER Natalie Barney, who'd come from Ohio around the turn of the century and stayed on (Rémy de Gourmont addressed *Letters to the Amazon* to her), had a marvelous weekly salon. One entered a dim, cluttered hallway, received by an ancient servant, was led back to a huge room with a big round table in the middle loaded with sandwiches and pastries, a great divan in each of the four corners. Some major personality or beauty presided over his or her court from the center of each divan. Natalie wandered around beaming, looking very much like Benjamin Franklin. She even wore squarish glasses.

The past seemed so recent in the chatter. Many of those present had known Proust, some were angry at having been used as models for characters in his novel. Some were angrier still for not having been used. They had all seen Bernhardt, and spoke of Maggie Teyte's Mélisande as if they'd seen her a week before. Once Colette was there, had brought her scrapbook covering her vaudeville days. She sat on one of the four sofas preening like a great pussycat. I'm certain she flung her mascara on with a tablespoon, then took a toothpick to pry out a peephole.

GEORGE PLIMPTON We did a feature on Natalie Barney one year for the *Paris Review*. We had asked Truman if he would reminisce about the Barney salon, and he had obliged. I have often thought that what he told us was Truman at his very best as a storyteller—the buildup, the suspense, the vividness of character. We had a tape recorder. What follows is exactly as it came off the tape, starting with the long-drawn-out "We-lll," which is how Truman began a story he especially relished:

We-lll. Natalie Barney was a small chirpy woman who dressed very conventionally. She loved the color gray. She had a gray car and a chauffeur dressed entirely in gray. She wore smart little gray suits. To look at her, and until you got into conversation with her, she seemed like a lady from Shaker Heights, but she wasn't that at all. She had a party every week. I can't recall what day of the week. But it was arranged so it didn't conflict with Marie-Louise Bousquet, who was the Paris editor of *Harper's Bazaar* and had her salons on Thursday. I don't think the two ladies were particularly friendly.

At Miss Barney's, everyone met in a room with a huge domed ceiling of stained glass. The decor was totally turn-of-the-century, with a slightly Turkish quality about it—kind of a cross between a chapel and a bordello. There was always a big buffet on the side, with the most marvelous things—I mean the most delicious kinds of strawberry and raspberry tarts, in the dead of winter, and always champagne. The guests stood, or sat on all sorts of couches and hassocks. Sometimes she had rather curious or unexpected people—the publisher of *Botteghe Oscure,* Marguerite Caetani; Peggy Guggenheim; Djuna Barnes (they always spoke of her as the "redheaded bohemian")—but it was always very proper . . . talk about this concert or that concert, or so-and-so's paintings, or "Alice has a fabulous new recipe for eggs." The only shocking thing I ever remember was when Carl Van Vechten came for tea and peed on the sofa by mistake. Everybody said, "Oh-oh, wait a minute," and then they turned, and down the line Esther Murphy, with the same problem, had lost control of *her* bladder and was peeing on *her* sofa.

Miss Barney's circle was not limited to lesbians . . . though certainly all the more presentable dykes in town were on hand. She had *tout Paris.* Many of them were friends of Proust's who had been characters in *Remembrance of Things Past*—like the Duchess de Clermont-Tonnerre. Miss Barney would say to me very specifically that she wanted me to meet somebody because that person was so-and-so in Proust. She was trying to give me some sense of her particular time—which was typical of her generosity. She was certainly interested in celebrities—that was one of her hang-ups—but, on the other hand, she was not exploitative. She was one of those people who are always trying to bring people together.

One day Miss Barney came by—I was living at the Hotel Pont Royal—to take me to luncheon, after which she wanted to show me something very extraordinary, something few people had ever seen. She didn't tell me what it was. So we went to a curious little neighborhood near the Arc de Triomphe—not the sort of restaurant you would associate with Miss Barney—and afterward she had the gray chauffeur park the gray car somewhere, and we started out walking. We walked for the longest time, and finally we came to an ordinary pension (at least from the outside), and inside we went up in the cat-smelling, creaky elevator. Out on the landing, she rustled around in her bag and came up with this huge, mysterious key. She put it in the door, and she looked like a burglar at a safecracking. She said, "Now you stand out here because it's all darkness inside, and I have to go in and open the curtains a bit." So I waited and waited until it seemed like fifteen minutes had gone by when she came back out on her stubby-heeled, gray silk shoes, and she led me in as if we were going into Ali Baba's cave. We walked into an enormous room. I mean *really* enormous—like sort of a superloft. The whole room was well kept, but it had the quality of desertion, as if no one had been there for years. In the middle of the room was an easel with a half-finished painting on it and beside it a table covered with tubes of paints, but all of them were rather dry and desiccated-looking. Around the room the walls were covered with paintings shrouded with cloth, each of them with a little pull cord next to the frame so you could pull it and the cloth would fold back and you could see the picture. I remember it was about four o'clock in the afternoon, a Paris winter afternoon, with that strange, gray, pearly light.

And Miss Barney said, "This is the studio of my beloved friend, Romaine Brooks"—and I'm quoting that just exactly—"my beloved friend, Romaine Brooks," and we began moving around the room and she would pull the cords and the cloth would slide from these paintings, and there they were: Lady Una Troubridge with a monocle in her eye; Radclyffe Hall in a marvelous hunting outfit with a terrific hunting hat. It was the all-time ultimate gallery of all the famous dykes from 1889 to 1935 or thereabouts. The paintings were wonderful, they really were . . . with terrific quality and style, and we looked at them, one after the other, and Miss Barney described who they were, many of them people I'd never heard of before: Renée Vivien; Violet Trefusis; and, of course, Miss Barney herself, with a pair of gloves here and a whip in the foreground. That's what made the whole thing so eerie.

Because it had so little to do with the Miss Barney I was standing with, this cozy little Agatha Christie–Miss Marple lady . . . and it was not that she was thirty years younger in the picture but that on the canvas she was this wild thing wearing a cravat, with her hand on her hip like *this* and a *whip* over there . . . and I said, "Miss Barney" (I never called her anything but Miss Barney because, well, I was about twenty-five years old and anyone who was older than me I called Sir or Ma'am, and with her it was just automatic) . . . I said, "Miss Barney, my goodness, really, is that really *you?*"

GEORGE PLIMPTON At the other end of the scale of Truman's acquaintances in Paris—at least as far removed from Natalie Barney's French Academicians as one can imagine—was Denham Fouts, a fascinating figure, a male whore, a kind of dark angel of the Paris nighttime streets, and who had been—as rumor had it—so entranced by the famous book jacket photograph of Truman reclining on the sofa that he had sent him a blank check with the single word on it: "Come." Truman went to see him a few times in a darkened bedroom in his apartment on the Rue du Bac. The relationship was apparently asexual, Fouts's libido having been destroyed by drugs, opium in particular. Truman read to him, and listened to his stories. He was eventually to use him as the model for the character Jonesy in *Answered Prayers*. He also turns up in Christopher Isherwood's *Down There on a Visit* and in Gore Vidal's "Pages from an Abandoned Journal."

GORE VIDAL Denham came from Jacksonville, Florida. He'd been picked up by a German baron when he was about sixteen. He looked like an American Indian—with an asymmetrical face. Good-looking in a cadaverous way. Like many drug addicts he had a medicinal, acrid odor. He looked like a boy with straight black Indian hair, black eyes. Fouts's own sexual taste was for small boys. But he put up with older gentlemen as that was his occupation. He fell out with the German baron and hitchhiked from Berlin to Venice. A Greek shipping magnate stopped and picked him up. They drove on to Venice and the magnate's yacht. At Capri, he and a sailor skipped ship, taking as much of the Greek's money as they could find in a strongbox. They moved into a suite at the Quisisana Hotel on Capri. When the money started to run out, the sailor vanished. Denham dressed every night for dinner in his beautiful evening clothes, sitting at smaller and smaller tables as he was not paying his bills. Finally, when it became apparent to everybody that he had no means of support, the police came. He was being led across the lobby of the Quisisana when Evan Morgan, the Lord Tredegar, entered and called out, "Unhand that handsome youth, he is mine." Or words to that effect . . . So Denham went off with Evan Morgan, whom I met in Rome, 1948. For various high-jinks Evan could not go back to England. I think he had set fire to his wife. I've forgotten the details, but it made a bad impression.

Evan had a papal passport and a big attaché case with the Tredegar coat of arms, more elaborate than the Queen of England's, and some sort of diplomatic thing stating that he was a chamberlain of the Pope. He was a birdlike sort of man. Possibly because his mother, the dowager Lady Tredegar, had built the largest bird's nest in all the world; it had taken her twenty years and can still be seen at Tredegar Castle. Yes, a bird's nest. She apparently hatched nothing in it except—who knows? Evan?

For a time Denham moved in the glamorous Mountbatten world, which was, contrary to what you may read in all the biographies, boldly bisexual. Bloomsbury with coronets. And everybody got married. In that world, Denham was extremely popular. In due course, he was passed from Tredegar to Prince Paul, later King Paul of Greece, who had not yet married Frederika. There was a whole group around Mountbatten—Paul of Yugoslavia, Paul of Greece, and various others, with Chips Channon darting in and out. Mountbatten was a kind of master of the revels.

Denham never lied, as I discovered. I read in the Paris *Herald* on my way to meet Denham for dinner—a hot summer night— that King Paul of Greece was ill with pneumonia. I told Denham. He said, "I must send him a telegram." There was an all-night Western Union open on St.-Germain. We went there together. The next day Denham showed me the reply: "Darling Denham, so wonderful to hear from you. Why haven't I heard from you before? Much exaggerated about my illness . . . Love, Paul." Unlike Truman he had not made it all up. I saw the telegram go, and I saw the return.

Denham lived in the Rue du Bac in an apartment with only a bed and six Venetian chairs. He was on opium. He was being kept by Peter Watson, the oleomargarine king of England, who'd given the money to Cyril Connolly for *Horizon*. Watson was a charming man, tall, thin, perverse. One of those intricate English queer types who usually end up as field marshals, but because he was so rich he never had to do anything. Actually he didn't really see that much of Denham because he couldn't put up with Denham's drugs and so on. The life was too much for him. But he was still paying for the apartment and helping him out. I never saw them together.

Denham had this large bed with a magnificent Tchelitchew painting hanging over it. Denham stayed in bed all day, smoking his opium. He had a big, fluffy white dog, a sheep dog I think it was. At sundown, like Dracula, Denham would appear in the streets leading his dog down St.-Germain-des-Prés.

I smoked opium with him once. It made me deathly ill and I never tried it again. He had a long pipe and this little piece of gunk that he would light and put in the pipe. It was a solemn ceremony. Bright lights hurt his eyes. Narrow eyes—tended to blink quite a lot. He only went out at night. He was caught in the drug bust of '48 or '49. Moved to Rome with a friend. Just before they were to go out to the opera, he went to the bathroom and dropped dead. Autopsy revealed what they called a "malformed" heart. Could've died at any moment. Wasn't forty.

NED ROREM Denham Fouts, according to Truman, went to bed with the Shah of Iran and all the usual people. But the cute part about it was how Truman said if Fouts had slept with Hitler, as Hitler wished, he could have saved the world from the Second World War, and that's really rather amusing.

GORE VIDAL We met Camus at about the same time, I think at a party given in Paris in the summer of 1948 by Gallimard, who were the publishers of Capote. Camus and Sartre were there. Toward the end of the summer Capote said that he'd had an affair with Camus. Now, Camus was chasing every actress in Paris. He had never been known to have any interest at all in men or boys. Besides, I'd already caught out Truman that summer when he said he'd had an affair with André Gide. He said Gide had given him a gold-and-amethyst ring. I saw Gide about two weeks later. I said, "Oh, how do you find Truman Capote?"

"Who?"

I repeated the name. He said, "Oh, I know who you mean." He picked up the photograph of Truman on the sofa and said, "Is he in Paris?"

I said, "Yes. He said he had such a nice meeting with you."

"Oh," he said, "I have not met him. But I have received at least ten of these photographs in the mail!"

NED ROREM Marie-Louise Bousquet told me that she had both Cocteau and Truman at her salon. Truman couldn't speak French, but he wanted to be the center of attention, which would be very difficult for the Queen of England if Jean Cocteau were around. She said that Truman got up and walked around the room, showing everybody his new clothes.

ARTHUR GOLD Peggy Bernier gave an immense party for us in '49 when we were in Paris working our debut. In walked Truman Capote. Janet Flanner was there and he sat on her lap, like a little baby. Janet loved it. The wonderful lesbian and the wonderful homosexual sort of "wedded" for the moment.

MARGUERITE YOUNG I introduced Truman to Djuna Barnes. I don't think Djuna paid any attention to him, because she's all wrapped up in her own world. She was wearing a chinchilla fur coat.

KARL BISSINGER Paris at that time was jammed with young Americans living there. They were everywhere that summer. Sometimes you wouldn't even hear French spoken in a restaurant. So that evening, after spending some time at a vernissage, we went to this little restaurant on the Rue du Dragon to get as far away as we could from the constant chatter of American voices.

Truman was in high spirits. He was everybody's darling. Sporting that long Bronzini scarf he wore whatever the weather, he swept into the restaurant, and we took the table in the back. Truman had begun telling stories—and telling them very well—when suddenly, from the front of the restaurant, some guy, a red-faced, very drunk American, called out something to the effect of: "For Christ's sake! Wherever I go I hear that American faggoty pansy voice! Can't I ever get away from you guys?" He must have been kind of half-assed educated, because I remember him saying, "What the hell kind of Dorian Gray voice is that anyway?"

The usual thing, then at least, was to ignore such people, but not Truman! He bristled and got up. He started shaking his finger at the man at the bar, shouting at him in that high, crazy voice: "Just you shut up! Wherever you go you cause fights and trouble . . . fights and trouble. Just you shut up! Don't wreck people's lives. Stop calling people faggots . . ." And so on, this bantam rooster! What was interesting was that there was this general swell of approval from the French, quite solid, and though they probably had no idea what was being said, they supported Truman's performance, you could tell. It worked! The guy hopped down off his stool and slunk out of the restaurant.

Then Truman sat down and continued his story exactly where he had left off. No comment on what had happened. He just was not to be troubled by the philistines! He had a marvelous sense of justice. I don't actually know whether it was a form of gay pride before there was such a thing, but it certainly was a form of courage and a demonstration of his own convictions.

1948

Truman and Jack Dunphy lying on the Palatine Hill, Rome, in 1949. (*Photo by Jared French,
private collection*)

ELEANOR FRIEDE He hung his hat at 1060 Park
Avenue for a time, but it was Nina's apartment. His
room had a great big bed and the usual reasonable
chest of drawers, all very clean and neat and nice.
But it wasn't Truman.

LEO LERMAN One middle of the night there was a
great clattering up the steps where we were living

and there was Truman with his enormously long scarf, wailing away as he came up the steps, banging at the door. He said that Nina, his mother, had really gone berserk and thrown all these letters from Newton Arvin out, and so forth, and so on. Dozens and dozens and dozens. She'd thrown them out the window and he'd gone down into the street and collected them. Would I keep them for him? To the best of my knowledge, they're still in a little trunk sitting in my bedroom.

DORIS LILLY Truman moved and had a little apartment, a walk-up on Second Avenue. He was living with a young man named Johnny Nicholson—who had the Café Nicholson and still does. Nice fellow. Couldn't be nicer. The apartment was decorated in battleship gray and purple and black. The reason I know that is when I finally got an apartment at 952 Fifth Avenue, I decorated it in battleship gray and purple and black. Salvador Dali came in and said, "My God. This is like a funeral. I love it."

GRAY FOY Leo and I had a visit from Todd Bolender, an old friend, who was with the New York City Ballet, one of their really greatest character dancers as well as a choreographer. He was living with a man called Jack Dunphy. Jack Dunphy had been married to a dear friend of ours, Joan McCracken. They had been together in *Oklahoma!*—Jack in the chorus, a cowboy I suppose, and Joan was the girl "who fell down"—that was how Agnes de Mille referred to her, because that was what she did in one of the scenes. We were just sitting around—Leo, Todd, and Jack Dunphy—and the telephone rang. It was rather late, probably around nine o'clock or so. It was Truman. He said, "What are you doing?" Leo said, "We have a couple of friends here." "Well, could I come over?" Leo said, "Certainly, come over," and so about half an hour later Truman trundled in. We had been given a big red satin brothel-type sofa by Carmel Snow—we had very little furniture in those days, mostly accumulated over the years, from junk shops or generous friends— and Jack was sitting on one end. Truman came in and sat down on the other, and it was really like one of those scenes in which "their eyes met." I think they both saw something that they fancied. We sat around talking rather desultorily for quite a long time until Truman said, "Well, why don't we go around to my apartment?" With nothing better to do, and all curious because we hadn't seen it, we went over to his place on Second Avenue—a little apartment on the second or third floor, very small. He had a little rocking chair in which he sat.

LEO LERMAN Freezing cold outside, still frost and ice and snow on the ground. It was only one room. One wall had photographs of children. There was a record player. He put on Bessie Smith. We sat. I don't think he had anything to drink. Very cozy, and he did his routine trying to be a tap-dance artist. He got up from his rocking chair in front of these two dancers and did this. He wasn't very good. There was lots of esprit, not esprit de corps exactly, but esprit. Being amusing and funny and lovable and everything. Except in hindsight it didn't occur to me that he was putting on a show for any purpose.

It got to be about two o'clock in the morning. We all said we've got to go home now. Truman said, oh, he'd come out with us, he had to go someplace or something. His voice got a little bit higher. We went to the left on Second Avenue at the corner. I remember turning around, and there was Truman at the other corner looking after us. The next morning Todd called and said, "Jack's gone! He's gone to live with Truman!"

GRAY FOY They never seemed a pair to me at all, though Truman was absolutely mad about him, absolutely. "This is the most beautiful man I've ever seen in my life." Well, it took a bit of peering, I would say, to see *that*. I mean, he was a perfectly nice-looking, redheaded man, freckled, and kind of pale-eyed. I was never conscious of his body at all. Usually in a dancer you are. Truman was the one who had an extraordinary body. The lower part of him was like a truck driver—sturdy legs—and the upper part was like a little boy.

GERALD CLARKE (*biographer*) Truman wasn't interested in men most people thought good-looking guys. Wyatt Cooper, Gloria Vanderbilt's husband, described Truman's ideal for me. He was a character actor. Lloyd Nolan. No one else, including Mrs. Nolan, would ever think Lloyd Nolan was good-looking. But Truman told Wyatt, "Well, he's my ideal. I think he's just wonderful."

I remember sitting in Bobby Van's in Bridgehampton and a handsome guy in his twenties, the hunk type, came over to our table and began putting the make on Truman, who wasn't interested at all. He was in fact barely polite, and when he turned those frosty blue eyes on him, the poor fellow just scurried away. I think he thought Truman would drop dead for him, but he had the wrong man. Truman was attracted to straight, ordinary-looking men. It thrilled him to think he had such appeal that he could take a man away from his wife and family. And he did! Jack Dunphy was one of those married men—actually, Jack was separated—to whom he was attracted. Jack wasn't handsome in the conventional sense, but attractive in a sort of surly way. Truman said to himself, "I want this man. Other people can get somebody like that, why can't I?" He set himself to get him. And he got him. "I'm convinced that if you really set your mind to it, you can get anybody you want in the world," he told me. "You just have to be very persistent; you really have to go after that person, think about it constantly."

PEARL KAZIN BELL He [Jack] wasn't very handsome, but a wonderful Irish face and reddish hair and freckled . . . He had a marvelous smile and a charming dog named Kelly, who was a Kerry blue who never turned blue. Jack used to identify with this dog: the dog who never became what he was supposed to become. I often thought Jack used to say to himself, "Why did I never become the writer I was supposed to become?"

MARELLA AGNELLI (*writer*) I never met Jack. He adored Jack. Love of his life, he was always referring to Jack. I remember a very touching photograph he had in New York of Truman and Jack lying on a field and Truman had his head on Jack's shoulder. I asked, "Who's that?" He replied, "You don't know him. He's a great friend of mine—Jack."

JOHN RICHARDSON (*art critic*) I don't think I'd recognize him if I saw him again. I remember him as being nice and quiet, but that's about all. Truman certainly never stopped talking about Jack. He always seemed to refer to him as the one and only . . . The rich people, the grand people, the fancy people were all very well, but thank God there was always Jack Dunphy. He could touch base with him. If Jack Dunphy didn't warm to most of his friends and, equally, if most of his friends didn't warm to Jack Dunphy, that was fine with Truman. He rather liked to keep things that way.

NED ROREM At Marie-Laure de Noailles's salons, Jack Dunphy didn't even come around when Garbo was there. He missed out on a lot of things that most people would think would be fun. When Truman came to Marie-Laure's, he would just as soon have taken Jack along, but it would have meant that Jack would sit around being jealous. How could he not have been, also being a writer? He had written a play that Shelley Winters was in called *Saturday Night Kid,* which opened in Philadelphia and was a mild success, though it never opened in New York. He did another play called *Light a Penny Candle.* He also wrote a pretty good book called *Friends and Vague Lovers.* He didn't want to coast on Truman's fame.

PHOEBE PIERCE VREELAND I was so terribly pleased that Truman had found someone. He was very much in love with Jack. Jack was a very amusing, charming person to talk to and so forth, but he did not like women. Many homosexuals are divine with women, but Jack never was. I think he treated his wife ridiculously. I could see why Truman cared so much about him, but I could never feel very warm about him. He liked Truman's friends, the people he called the "Real Friends," you know, Andrew Lyndon, Harold Halma, Bob Linscott, Truman's editor at Random House, Mary Louise Aswell, because he felt that they were people who had Truman's best interest at heart. He feared right from the beginning not so much the influence high society people might have on him but the undue time and energy Truman would spend with these people. That was the only cloud on the horizon—that Truman would lose himself in these various worlds. We agreed. We'd take the Mickey out of him. "Don't come in here trailing your train."

PEARL KAZIN BELL But Jack was a very, very strange man. He came from a working-class Irish family in Philadelphia, a rather large family. He was a rough diamond, with emphasis on the rough. I stopped inviting him to my dinner parties after a while because at some point he would always stand up and insult someone at the table in resounding terms and stalk out. This got to be too much. He could also be very tenderhearted, very sweet. He wrote a number of books, very strange books which never had much success. I often wondered whether he minded being associated with somebody who had such enormous success. He never showed it actually, because he really did love Truman very much.

CAROL MARCUS MATTHAU I was in false labor in Paris and Truman came up to see me. He had just come back from Switzerland. He said, "Goddamnit! Jack just did the rottenest thing you ever could have done!"

I was very surprised. Truman always said the most loving things in the world about Jack Dunphy.

"Well, the Guinnesses have really entertained us royally, particularly me. Not really Jack, because he doesn't like them and they know it. So when they came to Verbier in Switzerland I made the perfect dinner for them at our house and we had the perfect wine and the house was beautiful. Everything was perfection. Suddenly, Jack looked at Loel Guinness and said, 'What the fuck are you doing here, you big fat Nazi?' After that, there's nothing you can do. You can't excuse yourself. You can't excuse him. You just have to sit there and *die*. Can you *believe* he would do that?"

I said, "Truman, get down on your hands and knees and kiss Jack's feet every morning. He's the only decent human being near you."

Truman said, "Oh, well, I know you're right, but really . . ."

GERALD CLARKE Jack was a very strange man. I saw him independently—we used to have dinner together once in a while. I'd have him over or sometimes he'd have me over. One time I was out here by myself. I called up Eleanor Friede and invited her to dinner. "I know it's short notice," I said, "but would you like to have dinner tonight?" She said, "Well, I'm having Jack over for dinner and I'd love to have you come, but Jack is so strange. Are you good friends?" I said, "Well, yes, sure. In fact we have a date for dinner at my house next week. I don't think he would mind."

Eleanor had a house right on the ocean. I arrived there before Jack. Eleanor had another friend there, a woman whose name I can't remember. I was standing inside as Jack came in the door. He looked at me as if he had seen some terrible apparition. "Oh, I didn't expect to see you here," he said and kept on walking; he walked straight through the house, out the other door to the beach, turned to the right—and kept on walking. The three of us stood there nonplused. Totally nonplused. We didn't know what to do. And of course I felt awful. I had ruined the dinner. When we got ourselves together, Eleanor's friend and I started to follow him, calling out, "Jack, Jack, Jack, please come back!"

But he had gone pretty far by that point and he didn't come back. So Eleanor's friend and I went back and the three of us had dinner. While we were at the table, Jack sneaked quietly back, got into his car, and drove away, drove home. Okay. We still had this date for dinner at my house the following week. I had no idea what to expect. But at the appointed time, Jack showed up in his red Mustang and we had a very pleasant dinner. That was the end of it. I never asked him what had happened. He never said a word to me about it.

PIEDY LUMET *(editor)* He's the swellest swell you ever saw. Mostly he had bare feet and some wonderful old pants, very soft and fine. Either a shirt or no shirt. His body is beautiful and it's a wonderful color, sort of red-gold, his body in the summertime, and it just looks perfect inside his clothes. A pure pleasure to look at. You see him on a bicycle with almost no clothes on at all; he's now, what, seventy-two, and he looks terrific.

At a cocktail party? Oh, please! Never! He can't get in and out of a room. He said to me only two weeks ago, "If only I could get in and out of a room." I remember his coming at Christmas time to a party for children and old relatives and everything. We were having dinner in the dining room—maybe twelve people. Jack came in and he was in one of his elegant suits. He looked at us, then went right into the living room, crossed his legs, and sat there with his face in the corner. My mother-in-law went out there and struck up a conversation and was never more charmed. But he couldn't negotiate people . . . how to sit down with us.

Jack was the one true, honest-to-God, stable thing in Truman's life. There was a very real formality about their connection. It was rather grand and reserved. A familial formality. It was very correct. You must keep to the construction of your own life. Jack knew this intuitively. He'd be asleep and the doorman would bring Truman up in his underpants, returning him to the apartment. But Jack just kept his steady focus and that was probably better than anything else, because that was one life that Truman could not alter. His feelings never wavered; he never didn't love Truman.

JACK DUNPHY (*writer*) Joan left me. Some of my dearest friends, who I think may know every hair on my head, have turned the whole thing around: "I thought *you* left her." I adored Joan. You can't explain it. And then I adored Truman . . . the adoring kind. It's rather wearing. I came through the wars with her and I thought I would rather kill myself. She was very full of herself because she'd become a stage star. So I knew before I met Truman what success can do to a person inside. Therefore I could be silent about an awful lot of things with Truman.

1949

CHAPTER NINE *In Which TC and*
Jack Dunphy Leave for the Expatriate Life
of Europe

Jack Dunphy photographed aboard a yacht—an unfamiliar setting,
since he disapproved of Truman's high society friends and could not
abide their company. *(William S. Paley, collection of Kate C. Paley)*

Ischia

TRUMAN CAPOTE *It was being very much talked about,*
though few people seemed actually to have seen it—
except, perhaps, as a jagged blue shadow glimpsed
across the water from the heights of its celebrated

neighbor, Capri . . . Islands are like ships at permanent anchor. To set foot on one is like starting up a gangplank: one is seized by the same feeling of charmed suspension—it seems nothing unkind or vulgar can happen to you; and as the Principessa *eased into the covelike harbor of Porto d'Ischia it seemed, seeing the pale, peeling ice-cream colors of the waterfront, as intimate and satisfying as one's own heartbeat. In the wrangle of disembarking, I dropped and broke my watch—an outrageous bit of symbolism, too pointed: at a glance it was plain that Ischia was no place for the rush of hours, islands never are.*

JAMES SCHUYLER (*poet*) In 1949 I was living on Ischia in Auden's house with Chester Kallman. In the very early spring one evening, Jack Dunphy and Truman came up from one of the pensiones, both with shawls draped over their shoulders. They spent most of the spring there. Once we were sitting with Auden having a little aperitif before lunch at Maria's café and I asked Truman what he was reading. It was Stendhal's *The Red and the Black.*

I said, "Well, what do you think of it?"

"I'm rather disappointed, the transitions are so clumsy." Auden had very authoritarian ideas about who was who in the world of art; he didn't say a word. But on the way back to the house, he started saying, "The cheek, the cheek!" Auden had trouble with Truman's ways.

Truman had a cocktail party and served martinis made from a bottle of something called "Old Lady Gin," which was made in Trieste. He'd brought with him a windup phonograph. At one point he put on Ethel Merman singing or shouting "Life Is Just a Bowl of Cherries." Auden, who was sitting in a rocking chair, said, "Take it off, take it off. It's the jungle!"

Truman wrote a piece called "Ischia" that's in *Local Color.* Talk about being a *romancier, nothing* in it's true. The piece came out in *Harper's Bazaar* and then eventually in one of those big Italian weeklies. Truman wrote that Maria, who ran the café, watered her wine. It was obviously untrue. The wine was so bad and so cheap it was pointless to water it. Maria read it and the whole village exploded.

They loved each other very much; they were very harmonious. I like Jack, but he has a sort of dour Irish side. The opposite of Irish good humor. He was stern with Truman and I think Truman liked that. Later that summer I saw them in Paris with Joan McCracken. Jack had been musing over whether the thing to do was leave Truman and go back to Joan. I gathered from Truman in Ischia that Newton Arvin had given him a rough time. Once they had gone to see *A Room over the City,* which Newton partly for leftist reasons liked very much. Truman apparently exploded in a hatred of the movie and Newton shoved him down a flight of stairs. After they broke up, every morning for a year Truman played Billie Holiday singing "Good Morning Heartache"—his way of self-dramatizing things.

JACK DUNPHY *Best about Ischia were its cliffs, its few fields, its vineyards. I liked to walk to and from the cove where I swam every afternoon. The light would be golden as I faced back into town, everything would be etched against the superb blue of the sky—a proud, cruel blue if you had no shelter against it. The late afternoon shade of the narrow streets felt soothing as I walked to the pensione where Truman and I had rooms. Bougainvillea flopped over balconies everywhere. The floors of our rooms were paved with blue and yellow tiles. Boys lazied on the seawall in the evening as we drank martinis. Soon the white shirts of their uncles and fathers would gleam like lamps in the dusk. We had little red fish almost every night for dinner. Truman was writing a novel called* Summer Crossing *that came to nothing. I wrote a short story that has disappeared in the wash of time. The truth was we were too new to each other, and perhaps too happy, to do anything about writing except to keep our hand in.*

Morocco

PAUL BOWLES *(writer)* Truman came because he knew Cecil Beaton was going to spend the summer in Tangier. We had nothing to offer him. Cecil Beaton did. He was known to high society, to the royal family. That's what interested Truman.

Truman called him "honey" and "darling" and such. Cecil Beaton didn't react at all to this Southern talk. However, he didn't throw him out. He found him amusing.

In Paris I mentioned to Gore that Truman was coming down to Tangier on a certain date. He said, "Ah, well, I'll be there three days before." I said, "Oh, fine." So Gore did come and he stayed about a week. Gore didn't really approve of him. There was hostility. Gore came all the way from Paris to Tangier that summer in order to, as they used to say, "bug" Truman. He succeeded because we went down to the dock when Truman's ferry came in—he was coming over from Algeciras. He was standing on the deck with a Bronzini scarf ten meters long. He looked like a real-life Isadora Duncan. He was standing in front of one of those fan ventilators, waving and waving. Then he suddenly saw Gore on the dock, looking. He put his hands over his head and disappeared, fell backward and didn't come up. It was as though he'd fallen into the water or into the ventilating shaft.

GORE VIDAL It's partly true. I came to see Paul. Capote and Dunphy announced that they were coming, so Paul and I went down to the dock to receive the ferry coming from Algeciras. There was Truman on the deck. "Oh, my Goddd . . ."—the scream went up. He waved his paws in the air.

DAVID JACKSON (*writer*) Truman and Jane Bowles were great pals. You couldn't resist Jane, she was the most enchanting creature. Not of this world. Once Jimmy Merrill was with Tennessee for dinner at Jane's. Just the two of them. Jane was cooking a lamb roast. They sat down and had their martinis. More martinis, talking. Jane was talking about the English actress in *Summer House* who was a great lesbian and whose groupies were these really tough girls in motorcycle jackets. Anyway, they all had about ten martinis. Very drunk. Finally Tennessee said, "Janie, we are getting to be the consistency of Miriam Hopkins's breasts: we are dead drunk." Janie realized she hadn't turned the oven on. The roast was in there and she'd forgotten. Alice Toklas once said that to understand Jane, you had to see her from a second-floor window and watch her trying to cross the street below. This funny little creature, staring up and down.

NED ROREM Paul Bowles was the first grown-up composer I'd ever known. I'd met him ten years earlier in Mexico when I was sixteen. In '49 I was living in Morocco, in Fez, the ancient capital founded by Mohammed in 800 A.D. I stayed there for two and a half years. We drove up to Tangier to see Paul. Paul said, "By the way, Truman Capote and Jack Dunphy are here." Cecil Beaton had given a costume party and Truman and Jack had gone as Topsy and Little Eva.

PAUL BOWLES Cecil Beaton designed Truman's costume. They were busy working on this ridiculous party for a week. All the furniture and the Aubussons were taken out of the ballroom and then a miniature Berber village was put in—all mats and fires. There was a snake charmer. People beating their drums. It was a very strange ballroom. Truman looked rather like Little Bo Peep—all tulle and organdy and rosebuds and glue. He looked as though if he went near a candle he would go up like a moth. I suppose it was very chic; after all, Cecil designed it. Ada Greene was there. Her husband had been the governor of Nyasaland, which Truman mispronounced "Nicey-land." Everything was exactly as it had been down there in Nyasaland—black servants about eight feet tall, peacocks wandering around the house. At the entranceway to the costume party Ada saw Truman arriving, and towering at least a foot or more above him, she asked, "And . . . what are you?"

"I'm the spirit of spring!"

She said, "Well, you don't look like it."

Then for Jack Dunphy's thirty-fifth birthday, Truman was supposed to give a party inside the Caves of Hercules. Cecil Beaton spent a long time decorating the cave with draperies and lanterns. He really did a fantastic job. Truman said, "There'll be nothing but champagne and hashish." And that's all there was! Nothing to eat. It was on the beach. Very beautiful under a wonderful moon and the waves broke. People took off their clothes and rushed into the breakers. There was nobody on the beach, of course, absolutely nobody. There was an orchestra playing inside the caves, an Andaluz orchestra. It was a really fancy affair, except to get there you had to climb down a rather steep cliff. There was a little restaurant at the top where the cars could park and you wound your way down the side. Truman decided that he wouldn't do it. No. He said there were scorpions in the rocks and he wasn't going to take the chance. So they hired four stalwart Moroccans and they had a litter on which Truman sat cross-legged. He started down this perilous path, sitting there and waving, "Goodbye! Goodbye!" as he went down the cliff. A scene I haven't ever forgotten. They had to wait around and carry him back up at the end of the party too. He was *not* climbing up or down that cliff.

NED ROREM The minute I met Truman I liked him. His "thing" was that he was interested in you—at least he was in me. He would ask questions and was actually interested in the answers: "How do you write a piece?" Despite his exhibitionism, he was probably a pretty good listener all of his life. I stayed a couple of days. Tangier was a good place to change money in those days. I saw Jane and Paul. Jane, if you hit it off with her, was irresistible. There was only one of her, just like Truman. The two of them together! They were all staying in a place called El Farhar, a hotel in the form of about a dozen little cottages. Jane had a tiny kitten that had the flu. A Spanish doctor who was about six feet had been called in. Here was this huge doctor, used to dealing with people having twins or being knifed in their backs, crouching over this tiny kitten.

PAUL BOWLES Truman was a very interesting conversationalist, which is why I could listen to him talk about himself and his plans and what he was going to do. He was writing at that time a book which turned out to be *The Grass Harp*. Then he said he was going to write a travel book, which he did: *Local Color*. He was going to do a really good picture book, which he did, and then he was going to write some plays. He had all this planned, and he did them, and— the strange thing—in more or less the order he had announced them to me back in '49. It was like a carefully planned military campaign.

Sicily

PEARL KAZIN BELL I was on a leave of absence. I had taken a year off from *Harper's Bazaar*. I was on my grand tour. Somehow Taormina seemed awfully far away but I thought, Well, why not? It sounded very interesting. Jack Dunphy, of course, was there, and it turned out Peggy Guggenheim had arrived, an old friend of Truman's. He loved to spend time in Venice and she, of course, put him up when he wasn't staying at one of the ritzier hotels there. It was October. Venice had become quite cold, so she was searching out all her friends in warmer climes. She was really an impossible woman with a kind of rich, worthless quality about her that I just found very disconcerting.

The house was absolutely marvelous—a villa called La Fontana Vecchia (the Old Fountain). It was the house that D. H. Lawrence and Frieda had lived in, which Lawrence describes at the beginning of *Sea and Sardinia*. The landlord told us, "Oh, this Lorenzo—a very peculiar man." He said that Lawrence would take off all his clothes to clean the house because afterward it was easier to clean himself than to clean his clothes. Every time Frieda lit a cigarette Lawrence would dash it out of her mouth because he disapproved of smoking. It was an oldish house with a wonderful deck, as we call it now, which looked out toward the sea and toward Etna. Toward the end of my stay, there was a big eruption. We could see the red rim around the crater. It was really quite extraordinary. What shocked me was that the Sicilians took it as a sort of holiday and they would organize these picnic parties going up to the rim of the crater.

In the morning Graziela, the maid, would usually give us breakfast, and then we disappeared into our separate quarters to write. At about five o'clock in the afternoon, Truman and I would go into town to do the marketing. He would get the mail, which was *terribly* important to him, and we would sit in a bar on the piazza and read. Then we'd go back and cook dinner. And so it went. It was such an incredibly beautiful place. It was a great refuge for British homosexuals who had been hounded out of England. One of them was always doing things like giving a new football stadium to Taormina if they would give him a number of their boys. Nobody seemed to think there was anything wrong with that. Sicilians— they're hot-tempered and rather open-minded.

THOMAS QUINN CURTISS (*writer*) There was a hotel right there on the beach run by an old Englishman who'd married an Italian woman. You could go swimming in the middle of the night. It was such a warm and beautiful place. Truman would be at the beach in the morning and sometimes have lunch there, then go in. The siesta thing came along and they'd all go to bed. He worked very early in the morning. That was a habit, probably a very good habit. I've never been able to do it because I'm a night man, a journalist.

JACK DUNPHY *At Fontana we used to go down to the water after lunch to a small beach covered with white pebbles that were so hot that Kelly [Jack's dog] could not bear it until he had reached the water, nor could we. We swam from an old rowboat, each of us taking the oars while the other swam, Kelly barking all the time. But he was quiet in caves that were dark, green, and full of the musical sound of gurgling sea water. There we snorkled, and all he could see of us was the pipe through which we breathed. We took turns with the mask, since we only had one between us. Truman did not like me to stay underwater long. He said it bothered Kelly. "Imagine thinking someone you love has turned into a fish," he said.*

THOMAS QUINN CURTISS Gayelord Hauser lived up in a castle on a hill. He was the famous nutritionist who talked a lot about "you are what you eat" and who promoted blackstrap molasses, buckwheat, and yogurt. He said the most poisonous food was Italian but I always saw him eating a lot of pasta. Certainly he wasn't eating blackstrap molasses. He was quite an amusing man. So he was one of Truman's neighbors. Then there were these old English queens who had been there since Edwardian days . . . right through the two world wars. They wanted to talk about the theater, but the only theater they knew about in London was all about Lillie Langtry . . . interesting in the Age of Samuel Beckett but hardly of the moment.

Oscar Wilde went to Taormina in 1889, I think it was. Von Gloeden, the famous German photographer, was there, who took all these pictures of naked boys, dangling in robes, 1890s stuff, the whole thing so period, all posing in classic positions, and Oscar Wilde had bought a pack. The Edwardian queens showed me the pictures. Von Gloeden shot himself there. There's a very good book, a wonderful novel, by Hermann Broch, called *The Sleepwalkers*, which describes all this.

PEARL KAZIN BELL Truman and Jack were writing, of course. Truman was working on *The Grass Harp*. I was trying to write some fiction at the time—without any great success. Peggy Guggenheim was just gallivanting around. She made it difficult for us to sit down and work because she talked incessantly. She also fancied herself a very great cook; so she would cook up things like chicken mole, which is chicken with chocolate sauce. It's apparently a great Mexican spicy dish, but I found it inedible, or maybe it was just the way she cooked it.

THOMAS QUINN CURTISS They liked peace and quiet. They were very eager writers. He was writing books then, finishing *Local Color* and beginning *Breakfast at Tiffany's*. He'd also written a play, *The Grass Harp*. Jack, as usual, was writing a novel. They had very early hours. They'd leave the dinners early. It was a very quiet life and apparently very productive. He wasn't dissipating in Taormina. I think he probably did some of his best work there.

Dunphy wrote plays. He wrote a play called *Light a Penny Candle*. It wasn't bad. About the Irish in Philadelphia. In Taormina he was very standoffish and shy—sort of balding with his strawberry hair. There was a great bond between him and Truman. They discussed their own work. Truman read to him and they would talk about passages. They had their secrets, a very closed circle. Truman never read his work to me. Probably a sensible thing for a writer. George Moore said a sensible thing about that. He said, "If a man says he's going to write a book, you may see that book one day. But if he tells you how he's going to write it, just forget about it." That turned out to be something Truman could have thought about later on.

JACK DUNPHY . . . *a little town near Taormina up off the beautiful road to Catania. Orange trees, lemon trees, but mostly orange trees. Blood oranges. It is night and I'm standing alongside the bandstand. The musicians are playing things from operas of Bellini, Donizetti, Verdi in a charming thump-thump sort of way. Truman is looking down on all of us in the square from a balcony of one of the surrounding houses. There are colored electric lights strung across the square, some of the bulbs half-hidden by tree leaves. People are eating gelati, dining al fresco. Sunburned farmers in gleaming white shirts stroll around with their brown hands buried in their pockets. The instruments of the musicians shine, some silver, some gold. Truman calls to me to come join him. "Jack . . . ! Jack . . . !" He still has the same way of calling to me, as if I'm still new to him, as if he has yet to get over me.*

1954

CHAPTER TEN *In Which TC Receives*

Sad News

PHOEBE PIERCE VREELAND His mother never liked
me. Truman always said it was because she felt I was
the one woman to whom he was drawn emotionally.
For whatever reason, we never did get along. One
day when Truman was in Taormina, she called me
out of the blue and invited me to lunch. I thought to
myself, "Well, this is really peculiar."

So we went out to lunch and she was sort of
rambling on, not drunk or anything, and I realized
that what she was trying to do was to apologize to me
for having been unpleasant.

A bit later, when I was working for *Gourmet,* Leo
Lerman called me at the magazine and said, "Did
you know that Nina has died?"

Nina was young; she certainly wasn't fifty, because
she was married at no age at all, dumped Arch at no
age at all, and so I said, "Did she have a heart
attack?"

"No, worse than that."

"Oh God, cancer?"

"Worse than that."

Nina Capote with her husband, Joseph Garcia Capote. To support her extravagant lifestyle, Capote played the textile commodities market and fell heavily into debt. He embezzled $100,000 from his company—a crime for which he would eventually spend fourteen months in Sing Sing. *(Truman Capote Papers, The New York Public Library)*

"You mean—she's killed herself?"

"Yes. Get ahold of Truman."

I wrote him a long letter, which I sent to him at 1060, which was the only place I knew. I guess for public consumption they had said that she died of something else. Heart. There were different stories.

I'm not trying to tell you my troubles, because I hate that, but a couple of years later my mother killed herself. Truman called me. He said, "You know Nina killed herself." I said, "Yes, I do know that." We couldn't even talk to each other about it. People who were raised in the Depression and went through the war are not expecting the rainbow trail to stretch, but the most devastating thing is to have your mother kill herself. What's so awful is when a person kills themself you can't say wonderful things about them; you can't talk to your friends really. Everybody is very polite, and they don't talk about it, and they try to cheer you up. It almost dragged me down. Twenty years to get over it. Truman never broke stride, but I think that's the major unhealed wound in his life. There's nothing you can do about it. There's nothing *anyone* can do about it, except rent a soundproof room and take a whole bunch of plates and throw them at the walls and scream and yell and do it every day for a year.

I think in her case it was just despair. She was never someone with a terribly strong hold on life. She didn't know what she wanted. She was the kind of person you could have given anything, I mean anything—a big apartment—but who had no idea of what could please her. Nothing. It's a question of once you lose the appetite for life you can't be told, "Well, buck up, it's a great world." There's something in most of us that enables us, a vitality, a wellspring, something to keep us going. But once you lose that . . .

Like a crack in the foundation of a house that is not apparent, that whole thing of Nina's suicide affected Truman. I think it was central. He was an only child. He'd been in a way responsible for Nina and failed. In many ways Truman was the parent and she was the child. Perhaps her death paved the way for Babe Paley and so forth. I hate pop psychology. I don't think he was looking for a mother. I don't know what he was looking for. Some woman, somebody glamorous, somebody wonderful, somebody perfect.

ELEANOR FRIEDE I happened to be in Florida at the home of MacKinlay Kantor. My husband was his editor. Truman called and said Nina had died. It was Thanksgiving weekend. I'd had lunch with her just before, and at that time things were very bad. She'd given up drinking, but she drank coffee, coffee, coffee, coffee. She was shaking. She was very nervous. She was very ragged. We used to love to have a drink. We'd have a drink before lunch, but this day she had coffee first, and coffee, coffee. Then she put on her lipstick. She used bright red lipstick, which everybody did in those days. She had a brush with it. She was poking into the bottom of the lipstick with it. She said, "We have no more money left, and I'm using the last of my lipsticks." She wouldn't buy a lipstick, which I thought was very funny, because even I could afford a lipstick. But she wasn't herself, there's no doubt about it.

JACK DUNPHY *I came back to the hotel Choiseul on the Rue St-Honoré from the dentist one day to find Truman putting down the phone in the bedroom. Nina was dead. I felt she killed herself but refrained from saying so. Truman was not sad, only stunned. He flew home alone. She had him, even if she did not know it. She had got him home, brought him down! She fixed it so he would have to sit by her coffin shaking hands and getting his full of banalities for hours, as she, let it be remembered, had never sat by him, not when he was little, not when he was growing up, never.*

He would do it for her, he would do it for other grown-ups who thought he should. He would do it because he felt it was expected of him. He did it despite the price he had to pay, as he did everything that he should not have done, because the price he paid was too great. He was not like other sons. He was better. He was this instrument, this finely tuned thing made of nerves that helped him catch the nuances of things and record them. His sitting there beside Nina was a waste. He could never talk about it. It was too black a farce he played, the homecoming son who sat remembering how he came near to pushing this dead mother he was now dutifully burying out the window of their ill-furnished, nearly empty Park Avenue apartment. Dying she pulled him back to her, dragged the phoenix down to her level, but of course he would rise again. That was the beauty of it. I came home. Joe went to Ossining, where Truman visited him, but it was the end. When he came out, he married a mad woman, then died, swearing eternal love to Nina. The phoenix soared free, his wounds invisible to all but me.

ANDREAS BROWN Truman was just starting to make a lot of money. If what he said is at all accurate, he literally turned over most of his money to his stepfather in a desperate attempt to bail him out. But it was too late and it was very clear that Joe Capote would be indicted by the federal government, convicted as a felon and would have to go to prison. The anticipation of this terrible disgrace to Truman's mother was evidently more than she could bear and she committed suicide. A traumatic shock to Truman. He had to rush back from Europe and make all the arrangements.

It seems reasonable to conclude that this suicide was so devastating to Truman that it became an obsession, a focal point in his life. He adored his mother who—as difficult as she was, and as cruel as she had been to him, in effect, abandoning him as an infant—was glamorous, larger than life, a survivor. She had succeeded in her dreams. She'd found a rich man, aggressively achieved an elegant lifestyle, been accepted by Café Society. Though her dream had come true, she was still vigorously pursuing it, as some people do. Compulsively. You can see examples today right here in New York—many of the very people Capote socialized with. Go to the so-called jet-set restaurants on any given day and here are all the current Mrs. Capotes. In effect, her obsession with being accepted by these people, her addiction to their lifestyle, is in all probability what destroyed her and in turn her husband.

These circumstances and events would seem to provide Capote's motivation for writing *Answered Prayers*. It's a kind of retribution, or at the very least, an exposure of the foibles and the foolishness of their lives . . . that this world of glamour and superficial values can easily dazzle and confuse and mislead impressionable, naïve younger people to want all of these things and to pursue them with a desperation almost like an addiction to a drug; it can end up very easily destroying people. And it does. And seems to have done just that in the case of Nina and Joe Capote.

It certainly would explain why Capote had this long-term motivation to write his great Proustian novel about contemporary wealth and café, jet-set society. His archives reveal that he began to think about such a book very early on, very soon after his mother's death. So, it fits. Capote got sidetracked doing *In Cold Blood*, but he continued to take notes and to talk and think about *Answered Prayers*.

Capote's whole life was haunted by abandonment. One visualizes this sensitive, precocious child waiting for his mother to come home to rural Alabama for one of her rare, brief visits, and watching her leave that same day or the next day, never knowing when she was going to come back. His mother was always interested in something else: he wasn't important to her and he knew it absolutely. And yet he needed her desperately. I think that's why her suicide emerged as an event of immense importance . . . somebody destroyed his mother—that had to be his feeling. She didn't kill herself because she was bored, or because she didn't like herself: his mother was enjoying her lifestyle. "Somebody killed my mother. Something took her away. Who did that? Who did that to me?" That would be the question he must have asked himself almost on an unconscious level. So he had to be filled with bitterness and a need for retribution, or at least some kind of redirection of those anxieties and those angers and frustrations. And I think he channeled it into *Answered Prayers*.

1952—1954

CHAPTER ELEVEN *In Which TC Tries*

His Hand at the Theater

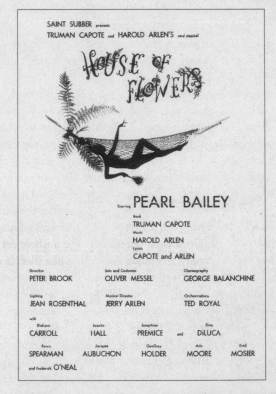

SAINT SUBBER presents
TRUMAN CAPOTE and HAROLD ARLEN'S new musical

House of Flowers

Starring PEARL BAILEY

Book
TRUMAN CAPOTE

Music
HAROLD ARLEN

Lyrics
CAPOTE and ARLEN

Direction   Sets and Costumes   Choreography
PETER BROOK   OLIVER MESSEL   GEORGE BALANCHINE

Lighting   Musical Director   Orchestrations
JEAN ROSENTHAL   JERRY ARLEN   TED ROYAL

with
Diahann   Juanita   Josephine   Dino
CARROLL   HALL   PREMICE   and   DiLUCA

Rawn   Jacques   Geoffrey   Ada   Enid
SPEARMAN   AUBUCHON   HOLDER   MOORE   MOSIER

and Frederick O'NEAL

(Photofest)

The Grass Harp, 1952

VIRGIL THOMSON *(composer)* Truman asked me to work on *The Grass Harp*. I'd often done music for Broadway shows, and besides, he had a producer who had lots of money and would give him anything he wanted. He had a funny face, half frozen. Saint-Subber. He'd had some kind of motor accident, which had left half of his face motionless. Truman knew what he wanted. He wanted Peter Brook to direct and Cecil Beaton to design the sets. Cecil and I said yes, but for some reason he couldn't get Brook. The set which Cecil designed, particularly the one with the big tree, was so large and heavy that nobody ever saw it until the opening in Boston. There was no point in setting it up in New York for rehearsals. It was a sweet show, good cast, and on the Sunday afternoon before we left for Boston, there was a professional matinee. We invited a lot of actors and theater people. The cast played in street clothes with just one work light. It was a wild success. Everybody wept buckets. Then we moved up to Boston, and, once we got into the set, nobody out there in the seats ever wept anymore. The set was too large and complicated—very grand, something for the Metropolitan Opera. It was overpowering. The interior set where the two old ladies lived was loaded down with Victorian furniture and antimacassars. At the last moment, Cecil went out and bought a whole set of china for it. Too much scenery, too much everything like that. It was a sweet and tender play about young people and . . . it did not work. I'd have said, "To hell with the scenery." Without the scenery, everybody wept buckets. This hard-boiled professional audience just loved it.

It didn't get good reviews in Boston. I don't think the play ran more than six weeks. Later, he put on that play about the whorehouse, *House of Flowers*. I never saw it, but it didn't work either. Truman was a storyteller and he could tell stories very sweetly. He was not really a stage man. He was always trying to get big international names in the production to save him, which they didn't do.

House of Flowers, 1954

GEOFFREY HOLDER (*dancer*) Mr. Capote came in for the first reading of *House of Flowers*. The principals were gathering around. Truman came in with an enormous bouquet of red roses. Hopping, skipping, jumping around the theater to give each one of us a rose. "Pearl, a rose for you . . . Diahann [Carroll—pronounced Dah-hanne], honey, a rose for you . . ." It was so sweet. Like a little elf.

JAMES SCHUYLER When *House of Flowers* was in rehearsal, he used to drop into the bookshop. I think he was on his way back from Dr. Feelgood, probably, and had gotten some vitamin B_1 amphetamines shot in his butt. He'd tell me never get mixed up in the theater, it was such a nightmare.

JOE HARDY (*producer*) It wasn't a successful collaboration. Truman came to the first rehearsal with dark glasses on. He'd just had his eyes done and he said one of his dogs was very sick; he had to take him to Palm Springs because the only vet was in Palm Springs and anyway, he'd had his eyes done and he didn't want anybody to see him. He said hello to everybody and I never saw him again until opening night. He really didn't have much interest in it. He made minimal changes. He said, "Go ahead and do whatever you want."

He was not a dramatist by any means. I don't think Truman ever listened to anybody else much. So how would he know how people talk to each other?

JOAN AXELROD (*friend*) Truman had given Saint-Subber a bell to wear around his neck. I don't know if you've ever seen Saint-Subber, but when he was healthy, you could hardly find him. In the peak of health he was so skinny that you saw every bone of his chin. He was tiny. He had this very thin little voice, you could hardly hear him. In a typical Truman kind of naughty thing to do, he got the cowbell and he tied it around Saint's neck and he said, "You have to wear your bell so I know when you're coming."

That was Truman in the best of health, in the best of form, who was then really just trying out his humor on others. But his humor turned against himself. That whole thing at the end with the black hat and the great big black cape, falling down. It was just a nightmare. When you saw him doing that to himself and then you would relate that to "the Saint wouldn't wear his bell," you'd just see the other side of that coin.

JOHN BARRY RYAN (*friend*) What a cast of characters. You had personalities in each other's face all day long. The gay gentlemen who had gotten together to turn this fragile story into an even more fragile musical. You had Harold Arlen being nursed by Marlene Dietrich, you had George Balanchine being replaced by Herbie Ross, you had Peter Brook telling the cast (they were all, of course, black) that if they didn't learn how to behave he'd send them back to Africa. The whole show was going to be closed down in Philadelphia by Actors Equity, who said, "Mr. Brook, you'll have to publicly apologize to the cast before we'll allow another performance . . ." Truman thought this was all absolutely fabulous. But every night he went to his room and he wrote—he must have rewritten *House of Flowers* four or five times. I never thought you could minimize the importance of Truman as a dedicated worker.

JOAN AXELROD I loved *House of Flowers*. I loved the music. I loved the whole fantasy of it. That piece embodies so much of the fantasy world that Truman brought to a lot of us—a lot of us Northern girls who were not brought up in English country houses where you had nannies who told you stories, or in the South where you were brought up by big black mamas. For us Northern, slightly more intellectual ladies, Truman was a shot in the arm of fantasy. A shot in the arm with all that—the way he spoke, the way he turned a phrase, the way he was quick to tell you—whether he made it up or not, it never mattered—things about his childhood. Men have such trouble communicating anyway, so that women are absolutely enchanted when they meet a man who has the ability to really talk about remembrances of things past. I'm sure that's what he was for Babe Paley and for Carol Marcus Matthau, and Gloria Guinness.

JOHNNY NICHOLSON I went to the opening night of *House of Flowers* with him. He had been telling me the trouble he was having with Pearl Bailey. He told me how much he hated her, how she was taking over the show. Afterward, he turned to me and asked, "What did you think?" I told him the truth, "It's a terrible show. She ruined it." He was very pissed off at me for that. I always found him forthright about things, but he didn't care for my telling him the truth at all.

VALENTINE LAWFORD (*friend*) At a dinner party in New York, given by Joseph Cotten and his wife ostensibly for Noël Coward, Noël sat down and played after dinner—a lot of his old songs, all about "mad dogs and Englishmen." I wrote in my diary that it all seemed very boring compared with Harold Arlen's music for *House of Flowers*. He played that night. It was absolutely charming. I remember Truman getting up and singing "My house is made of flowers. And fireflies climbed into my dome."

1954

CHAPTER TWELVE *In Which TC Returns to Europe, Teaches a Large Bird Epithets, Writes* Beat the Devil *amid Bedlam, and Arm-Wrestles Humphrey Bogart*

Truman in Ravello, Italy, on the set of *Beat the Devil* with Jennifer Jones, at the time married to David Selznick. *(Robert Capa, courtesy of Magnum)*

Italy

MARGUERITE YOUNG There were all the people from the midnight watch on the *Queen Mary*—the sailors, the stewardesses, the star watchers—and Carson McCullers invited them to join us. She got up and said, "Ladies and gentlemen, I want to introduce you to America's most beautiful of all prose writers . . . she is angelic." She turned to me and said, "You know, I can praise you when I know I'm talking to people who do not read." That's the kind of person she was. Competition incarnate.

Originally, Truman worshipped at her feet, but when she emerged as a writer the feud began: She felt that he took "his eye is on the sparrow" from the song that Ethel Waters sang. It's an old song and I don't know why more than one person couldn't have heard it. The image of the butterflies floating in and out of the windows of a slow-moving train—a line out of *Local Color*—was another "theft." So they had this great feud. I was in Rome during it. She and her husband stayed for one night at the same place—the Casa Linguatera, the beautiful old hotel where Henry James had stayed, and the Emperor of Brazil and Lord Byron. She decided it wasn't fashionable enough for her. The next day she moved to a more expensive hotel. She said, "It's just not fashionable enough for me." I said, "Well, you were sleeping in Lord Byron's, in the Emperor of Brazil's bedroom, isn't that enough?"

"I was?"

She asked me if I had been invited to Princess Caetani's Sunday-night soiree. I said, "No, I don't believe she knows I'm here."

"Well, I have." She would not let Reeves, her husband, go. Reeves told me, "Sister says I'm not fit to be invited to the Princess Caetani's salon. Let's you and me spend the day together." We got a horse and buggy and we went almost to Naples! We had the most divinely beautiful day I'd ever spent in my life. I loved her husband; he was a real folklorist.

Then Princess Caetani did hear that I was in Rome and she

invited me to the next salon. She was worried about the Truman-
McCullers feud. She said to me, "Word comes that Truman Capote
and his forces have reached the outskirts of Rome; I'm waiting for
the withdrawal of Carson McCullers."

She was supposed to have left town—to live in the Pope's garden,
Castel Gandolfo. Truman arrived. He was driving me along and
suddenly we saw Carson on an island in the middle of traffic,
leaning on her silver-headed cane. He said, "Ahhhh, now I can get
her! I can just brush past her and knock her down, kill her!"

I said, "Oh, Truman, don't be ridiculous, everybody will know."

GRAY FOY In Rome they had a beautiful little apartment on Via del
Babuino which belonged to one of those ubiquitous Italian
contessas—I mean, who knows, but she was *reputed* to have been a
contessa. It was a charming apartment. It was elegantly furnished,
and between Kelly, Jack's dog, who was a Kerry blue terrier, large,
just an awful dog, and a crow or a raven named Lola, I can't
remember which, but a very large black bird, which would sit on the
furniture and pick the stuffing out, I'm sure that the contessa who
owned the apartment, once she repossessed it, must have had a
stroke.

Almost daily Truman would come over and he'd say, "Do you want
to go shopping?" He would almost always buy either a bottle of vodka
or a bottle of gin. He was drinking a lot. He would buy groceries or
household supplies in the smallest quantities imaginable. He'd go in
and say, *"Due cipolle per favore,"* or something like that and he'd get
two little onions. He would take them home to a cook who mostly, as
far as I could make out, cooked only pasta . . . that was about it. The
interesting thing was that no one ever made fun of him, the
shopkeepers or anybody, and he was really not like anything else you
saw in Rome and God knows you could see a great deal. But with his
great trailing scarf and all that, you know, they were all somewhat
awed by him and respectful, sort of wide-eyed at this precocious little
boy who had suddenly become a housekeeper. He was really very
generous with his time with me. He'd drive me around Rome on
errands or, as we would say, "joyrides." He was a dreadful driver,
terrifying. In those days there were very few cars, mostly Vespas—

very noisy, so the traffic was usually motorcycle traffic rather than automobiles. He had a very small car, and I had the feeling it was the first car he'd driven. I'm not sure that it was, but by the way he drove, you had that feeling and it was an experience just to go tooling around the seven hills or wherever.

WILLIAM STYRON *(writer)* When I went to Rome I got a letter put in my box at the American Academy from a Rose Burgunder, whom I really didn't know, saying, "I met you in Baltimore." I remembered seeing a very good-looking girl in Baltimore a year before when I'd gone down to lecture at the Johns Hopkins writing class. I didn't connect the good-looking girl with the name, but having nothing better to do, and being frankly sort of eager to meet any female, I thought I'd give this a try. Then I realized that I had a conflict that same night. I was supposed to meet Truman, whom I had never met before. A painter at the Academy named Stephen Green, who had known Truman, had arranged it. The three of us would have a little get-together—have a drink or something at the Excelsior. So I told Steve, "I'll tell this Rose Burgunder to meet us there too. I'll size her up, get rid of her early, so the three of us can go out afterward." So Steve Green and I went to the bar of the Hotel Excelsior, where Rose was, and I saw this extraordinary creature; there was no possible way I was going to get rid of her that evening. I was going to the john when Truman showed. He was an absolute sketch. He wore this strange little sailor suit—like a costume, like when you dress up when you're seven years old—and he had this damn bird on his shoulder called Lola. Truman had this little whistle. I don't think he blew it. The bird made the noise. Truman had taught it a few obscenities like "screw you" or something like that. That was all. It sort of sat there and clucked and suddenly it would come out with "fuck you" every now and then throughout dinner.

Rome at that time was a kind of movie capital—Hollywood on the Tiber. Carson McCullers had been in Rome, I believe, working on a movie script for David Selznick (it may have been an early discarded draft of *Beat the Devil),* and Truman, who could be very bitchy, did a riotous imitation of Carson McCullers drunk, hunting for a script in her room that she was supposed to have finished, with

Selznick at the door saying, "Carson, we've got to have the script," and Truman imitating Carson's Georgia accent and saying, "Well, just a minute, David, Ah seems to find, Ah'll hunt under the bed . . . it's around heah somewhere . . . daggone if Ah know where that script is." Truman was just laying it on, one Southerner imitating another . . . and in this case rather cruelly since Carson was constantly drunk and had a withered kind of arm. He took great joy in laughing . . .

TRUMAN CAPOTE *The last few weeks have been filled with peculiar adventures, all involving John Huston and Humphrey Bogart, who've nearly killed me with their dissipations . . . half drunk all day and dead-drunk all night, and once, believe it or not, I came to around six in the morning to find King Farouk doing the hula-hula in the middle of Bogart's bedroom. Jack [Dunphy] was disgusted with the whole thing; and I must say I breathed a sigh when they went off to Naples.*

JOHN HUSTON *(director)* I had met Truman Capote at a party at Bennett Cerf's. Bennett was the party giver of New York at that time. Truman's picture had appeared in various magazines—the famous one of him reclining on a sofa looking very feminine. Sure enough, when I met him, he was the only male I'd ever seen attired in a velvet suit. It would have been a very easy thing to have laughed at him had it been anyone except Truman. I immediately fell for him—it didn't take me five minutes to be won over completely, as he did with everyone I ever saw him encounter. He had a charm that was, to coin a phrase, "ineffable." He exerted this charm freely. We planned then and there to do a picture together "one day." I hadn't read his book—I didn't get it the same night because there were no bookstores open—but I had one the first thing the next morning.

Next, I met him in Rome. I was there to do *Beat the Devil*. I didn't have a very good script, well, practically no script at all. It occurred to me to get Truman to write on it with me. I said, "Truman, we spoke back in New York about our one day doing a film together, here's the big chance." He agreed.

STEPHEN SONDHEIM (*lyricist, composer*) I went with Johnny Ryan, who was going over to be John Huston's assistant. We were great friends. I'd never been to Europe. I had seven hundred bucks in the bank, and so I took it and accompanied him.

JOHN BARRY RYAN Before moving on to Ravello, we all arrived at Rome. There was no script. We would go out every night to the Café del Orso, already two weeks after the start date of the movie: Humphrey Bogart, Jennifer Jones, Huston, Peter Viertel, who had written the original script, which no one liked, and Jack Clayton, who was the production manager. It was the hottest place to go in Rome. It had a bar on the ground floor, a restaurant on the second, and a dance floor. It is indescribable how much we all drank. One night we were leaving and Huston grabbed Jack Clayton and said, "See that piano player over there? He would be great as the purser in the picture." So Clayton went over to this piano player and asked, "Do you speak English?" The piano player said, "Yes." Two and a half weeks later when we all got down to Ravello we discovered that that "yes" was the extent of the piano player's English. But Huston decided his face was so perfect for the part of the purser that he got the dialogue director to train him to speak enough English in the next few days to deliver his line. Truman was writing the movie in a sequential order. Well, the first scene in the movie is a shot of Bogart sitting outside the café and the purser comes to see him. Truman wrote a line for this purser who spoke *no* English at all which I will remember to my dying day: "Mr. Danruther, the captain of the S.S. *Niagara*, presents his compliments and wishes to inform you that owing to failure of the oil pump, the sailing will be delayed." I swear to you that Truman did this intentionally. If we had stayed in Ravello for five *years* the piano player never would have been able to say these lines! So we spent three days in the square of Ravello with John Huston listening to the purser repeat his lines: "Mr. Danruthah, the captain . . . compliments of the S.S. *Niagara*." And then we would start all over again.

PHOEBE PIERCE VREELAND They finally wind up on the coast of Africa with Robert Morley, who has never been better, trying to explain to the official what they're doing, that they're selling vacuum cleaners to the natives, and the man looks up and says, "Hut to hut, no doubt?" That's pure Truman. If John Huston wrote that I will eat that poster on the wall. Then, when Bogart is conning the same official, the one with the glasses and the fez and the hookah, trying to get out of this terrible pickle they're in, he says to him that if they get him to Paris they'll introduce him to Rita Hayworth. Which is a terribly funny idea. "A man like you," he says, "darkly handsome." And the man says, "You're sure the peerless Rita will like me?" I love that. He says, "Oh, beyond question." Just wonderful. The captain is divine, everybody is divine. The more you see it—I've seen it, I guess, about ten thousand times—the more you love it. "In point of fact." That's Jennifer's line. When she starts to tell a lie she always says, "In point of fact." All Truman. Robert Morley has this ragtag band of rapscallions walking along the ship's deck and he says, "Take deep breaths!" He says, "This air! Every breath is a guinea in the bank of health."

JACK CLAYTON *(director)* It was bewildering to work on the picture. The pages for the next day would arrive at ten-thirty at night, if we were lucky. More often, seven-thirty the next morning. David Selznick, who was in Italy because his wife, Jennifer Jones, was in the cast, used to send me at least five letters a day. I wish I had kept them. All on yellow pages. They were absolutely brilliant. He knew more about producing a film than anybody I've ever met in my life. He kept complaining about the things that were wrong but could not be helped because without a script you can't plan. He was always complaining about how Jennifer's dress didn't suit a particular scene. So I would reply, "David, if I knew what the scene was going to be . . ."

I kept pleading with Huston, saying, "Listen, give me an idea, even if the scene is not set yet. Just give me an idea where exactly it's going to be—the boat, or the palace, or the grounds, just so I can prepare."

JOHN HUSTON Truman and I worked on the script. We tried to stay ahead of shooting. If it caught up to us, I'd give the crew a very complicated setup—to put together dolly tracks, take out walls and such . . . While this was going on, Truman and I would go back to the hotel and write a scene. We hoped the company wouldn't know of our desperation, how close the dragon was breathing on our necks.

STEPHEN SONDHEIM Huston did a lot of standing around musing. This was not a serious movie in any way, shape, or form. Huston took a liking to me. I was trying with my little sixteen-millimeter camera to shoot a documentary on what happens to a small town when it gets hurricaned by a movie company, but I didn't have enough film or money, enough time, that sort of thing. But Huston acted for me. I wanted a shot of Huston pondering. So he walked back and forth in front of the camera pondering . . .

JOHN BARRY RYAN There was this big poker game associated with *Beat the Devil*. Selznick, Huston, Bogart, Jack Clayton, occasionally, and Truman. Truman didn't know three of a kind could beat a pair when he sat down. He'd never played poker in his whole life! He thought it was hilarious to sit down with these people. Then Selznick's lawyer came to town and took everybody's money for three nights until Bogart and Huston went to Selznick and said, "Get this man out of town, or we'll find some nice mafioso to take care of him."

STEPHEN SONDHEIM It was a very macho game—Huston, Bogart, Selznick, and the lawyer. The stakes were very high—fifteen hundred, two thousand dollars a pot at least. Truman asked to play though he didn't know how. I remember the first night, I sat on the outside. Obviously they were playing for stakes I couldn't afford. At one point Truman said, attempting to bluff with bravado, "I'll match the pot." Somebody said, "You can't do that. You don't have enough money." Truman said, "Oh well, then I'll fold."

JOHN HUSTON Truman was a little bulldog of a man. One night, he and Bogie were arm-wrestling. Funny picture, Truman and Bogie arm-wrestling! Truman put Bogie's arm down! And the next thing, they were wrestling on the floor, and Truman again put Bogie down!

Bogie wasn't all that husky a number, but you don't see Truman in the role of a wrestler. A little bulldog. His effeminacy didn't in any way affect his strength or his courage.

There were only a few interruptions. One was when Truman hurried back to Rome to see his bird Lola. He said that his bird—I think it was some kind of crow or raven, black in any case— wouldn't talk to him over the phone. It was either ill or sulking. It turned out it was neither: it had flown off the balcony and disappeared . . .

Two weeks into shooting the picture, I came back down one day. Truman was staying in his room writing, trying to keep up with my shooting. This evening, Truman's face was twice its normal size. He had an impacted wisdom tooth; it was frightening to look at him. I said, "You've got to get to the hospital."

He said, "But, John, we have work to do . . ."

When Jack Clayton saw him, he sent for an ambulance. We helped Truman down the stairs. He must have been in dreadful pain. Typical of Truman: he said, "Bring me my shawl. Don't forget my shawl." Jennifer Jones had given him a Balmain shawl; he needed his shawl to go to the hospital? That night he worked in the hospital. That's Truman.

JOHN BARRY RYAN Only Truman knew what he was going to write. John had no idea. Selznick had no idea. You should see the script, if there is such a thing. Drink had a lot to do with it.

JACK CLAYTON Truman had the gift of dialogue. Narration doesn't really come into films because the narration part is done with the camera. The story was there, and all that had to be filled in was the dialogue. He had absolutely a brilliant sense of dialogue. You may not think it from *Beat the Devil* . . . he did a wonderful script for me on *The Innocents*. Although he only got half credit, he wrote the whole script, really . . . It was a very difficult script to do, because you had to keep the Victoriana and at the same time bring the dialogue up to date. It was brilliant.

JOHN HUSTON *Beat the Devil* came out to absolutely wretched reviews. No one came to see it. But the other day I saw Jennifer Jones and she said, "They don't remember me for *The Song of Bernadette*, but for *Beat the Devil*."

JACK CLAYTON I am one of the few people who is not attached to that clique who think *Beat the Devil* is a masterpiece. I view it with enjoyment, but only the enjoyment that such a thing could happen. It's a film that shouldn't have been made.

JOHN HUSTON But afterward Jack Clayton gave him a bulldog that he adored. Truman had expressed his liking for the breed and I don't wonder at that, because, as I say, Truman himself was one.

LAUREN BACALL *(actress)* He swam into my life after *Beat the Devil*. I had been making *How to Marry a Millionaire* in California and when I was finished I met Bogie in London. He told me about Truman. "When you meet him, you can't believe that he's real. And then after a while, when you get to know him a little bit, you just want to put him in your pocket and take him home." He said he'd never seen anyone who worked harder than Truman. In those days he was really nose to the grindstone. Then I finally met him when he came to California. He came to the house. And of course I *didn't* believe him. That little voice: "Hello, dear." He was totally infectious because of his incredible brain and his wit. This was before any of the bad stuff happened. We developed a great friendship. He adored Bogie. The unlikeliest couple in the world were Bogart and Truman Capote.

The Faulk Millinery Shop in the Monroeville town square, c. 1920s–1930s. Truman's aunts Jennie and Callie are standing fifth and sixth from the left. *(Courtesy of Aaron White)*

The three Faulk sisters: Mary Ida, Marie, and Lillie Mae.

The main square of Monroeville, Alabama, in the 1940s. *(Courtesy of Aaron White)*

Lillie Mae and Marie (Tiny) Faulk at Mardi Gras in New Orleans. (*Truman Capote Papers, The New York Public Library*)

Truman and his Aunt Sook. (*Truman Capote Papers, The New York Public Library*)

A photograph of Truman's father, Arch Persons, and a steamboat captain taken July 5, 1968, in St. Louis. Persons was a born entrepreneur and salesman, known as the Streckfus Steamship Line's "Prince Charming." He spent some time in jail for writing bad checks ($1,800 worth); for forging a postal money order he was sentenced to three years in the federal penitentiary in Atlanta. (*Truman Capote Papers, The New York Public Library*)

Phoebe Pierce Vreeland, Truman's best friend at Greenwich High School. *(Harold Halma)*

Catherine Wood, Truman's English teacher and mentor at Greenwich High School. *(Truman Capote Papers, The New York Public Library)*

Carol Marcus Matthau, one of Truman's earliest Manhattan friends. *(Courtesy of Carol Matthau)*

Newton Arvin, a professor at Smith College, bespectacled, short, balding, shy, became Truman's lover when the two met at Yaddo in the spring of 1946. Arvin was a distinguished literary critic (in 1951 he won the National Book Award for his biography of Herman Melville), and his importance to Truman's intellectual education was considerable. Truman said of him, "He was my Harvard." His first novel, *Other Voices, Other Rooms*, was dedicated to Arvin. *(Courtesy of Yaddo)*

Truman at Yaddo, working on his first novel, *Other Voices, Other Rooms*. *(Lisa Larsen/Life magazine)*

Elizabeth Ames and Carson McCullers at Yaddo. McCullers's reputation had been established in 1940 with the publication of *The Heart Is a Lonely Hunter*—an astonishing portrait of a deaf mute. McCullers, left partially paralyzed by a series of strokes suffered in her twenties, was a strange figure on the literary scene. Her younger sister, Rita Smith, Truman's editor at *Mademoiselle*, introduced the two of them at the Smiths' Nyack home. Truman described the meeting in a eulogy written in 1967: "The first time I saw her—a tall slender wand of a girl, slightly stooped with a fascinating face that was simultaneously merry and melancholy—I remember thinking how beautiful her eyes were: the color of good clear coffee, or a dark ale held to the firelight to warm. Her voice had the same quality, the same gentle heat, like a blissful summer afternoon that is slow but not sleepy."
Not long after they met, the two had a falling-out due in varying degrees to professional jealousy and accusations of "poaching" from each other's work, a serious enough rupture to cause McCullers to form a Hate Capote Club, which, among other writers, she tried to induce Tennessee Williams to join. *(Courtesy of Yaddo)*

Truman and John Malcolm Brinnin in New York in 1950. *(Rollie McKenna)*

Truman and his friend author Donald Windham in Piazza San Marco, Venice, July 1948. *(Courtesy of Donald Windham)*

While abroad, Truman kept in close touch with his friends, especially his Random House editors Bob Linscott, Joe Fox, and Bennett Cerf. *(Truman Capote Papers, The New York Public Library)*

Truman's likeness by three famous photographers: Carl Van Vechten (top left), Cecil Beaton (top right), and Henri Cartier-Bresson (above). *(Private collection; Sotheby's London; Magnum)*

Bennett Cerf, Truman's editor at Random House for many years. *(Courtesy of Phyllis Cerf Wagner/Chris Cerf)*

Truman kept a pet raven. This specimen is "Ole Crow," a professional, who lost his chance for a Broadway career when Pearl Bailey proved allergic to birds at rehearsals of *House of Flowers*. His part was written out. *(AP/Wide World)*

Humphrey Bogart and Gina Lollobrigida on the set of *Beat the Devil*. *(Photofest)*

On the dance floor with Marilyn Monroe. By his account Truman was an accomplished dancer from his earliest days—a childhood tap dancer on the Mississippi River's Streckfus Steamship Line. (*UPI/Corbis-Bettmann*)

Truman with one of his favorite breed, a bulldog, Charlie J. Fatburger, here in Verbier, Switzerland. (*Truman Capote Papers, The New York Public Library*)

Truman and Gloria Vanderbilt. (*UPI/Corbis-Bettmann*)

1956

Truman relaxes in his Brooklyn apartment. (*Library of Congress*)

GRAY FOY Truman moved into the basement of Oliver
Smith's house on Willow Street in Brooklyn. He
often made it sound as though the house were his
own, which was rather galling to Oliver. I think
Truman was fairly happy there. It was an absolutely
beautiful house with a great spiral staircase, a grand
merchant's house, a rich sea captain's or something

of the sort. Perfectly beautiful with a veranda across the back of it. Oliver's mother had a room that looked as though it came out of Canton, Ohio. It had his mother's favorite furniture—old beaded lampshades, rocking chairs—very much like a stage set of authentic eighteenth- and early-nineteenth-century furniture. It was so extraordinary to go in and see this room settled in the middle of this rather grand house.

DONALD WINDHAM (*writer*) Lovely place. I went there one day with Sandy Campbell when Truman was showing a journalist from Kansas around. He took the journalist from the top to bottom and said that it was his house, all his, and how he had restored and decorated it all. At the time Jane Bowles was living on the top floor. How did Truman dare to say such a thing when he knew that both Sandy and I knew it wasn't so?

JOHN KNOWLES He had ceramic dogs and cats and leopards. Paperweights, a tremendous collection of paperweights. Supposedly very valuable. He showed them all to me one night when he was really drunk. "Now this one was given to me by Jean Cocteau. It's priceless. Colette gave me this . . ." I don't know if he'd bought it at the corner store, but he had stories like that. I have a beautiful one he gave me, beautiful monarch butterfly. Golden. That was one of his signs of friendship, when he gave you a paperweight. Then he gave me a marvelous present. I think Bill Paley gave him a couple of bottles of bourbon which had been made during prohibition. Like a certain amount of bourbon for "medicinal purposes" in this country. They were collector's items. Truman didn't like bourbon, so he gave them to me. I drank it with an eyedropper; it was wonderful. It was just the *essence* of bourbon, all the impurities had been filtered out with time.

PHOEBE PIERCE VREELAND I went to the Brooklyn place two or three times. I remember his apartment very well. It was quiet. It was one of the quietest places I have ever been in my life, and that's what Truman was looking for. I said, "Oh, you must love this, T, because there's no one to disturb you," and he said, "Isn't this wonderful, isn't this marvelous, isn't this quiet?" Because 1060 Park was a very small apartment and any apartment was small with Nina in it.

PIEDY LUMET It was a great old parlor floor of a great old Brooklyn house with a big grape arbor outside that you could eat under in summer. A big yard. It looked almost Southern. Downstairs below the sidewalk level were two whitewashed rooms or maybe three but they were definitely sort of cellarish, but with higher ceilings than if it would be in a cellar in a New York City apartment and there were copies of Truman's books in strange languages, a bicycle for Jack in the hall, and rather spare inside, a little bit austere. I once went there with Darryl Zanuck and some beautiful girl, Christian Marquand, and also Salvador Dali. Afterward we went to a twist place called Trudy Heller's. Dali said, "You see the beautiful girl?" I said, "I do." He said, "Is a boy. Is a boy. I paint him all afternoon." He just said that to scare the living lights out of me and he did. I mean it may or may not have been true but this girl-boy was twisting up a storm and was very beautiful and lissome and he said, "Is boy." Isn't that too sophisticated? I was just not up to something like that. That was too cool for me. Afterward I said to myself, Hmm, what an evening. Salvador Dali was a very strange companion for anyone. My mother would not have approved. Especially of the boy-girl. But she had a lovely sweet little lemon-yellow chiffon dress; it was so pretty.

NATALIA MURRAY I went there with Janet Flanner for dinner with Oliver. Later we went downstairs to see Truman. He was crawling around on a great big sofa with lots of pillows. He was so small, so . . . pixilated, you know? Funny, witty. He became bitchy later. Once we went downtown with Truman and Cecil Beaton. Cecil was very tall and wore a three-quarter coat—one of those dark English coats. Very chic. Truman had a cape. Those two were very funny walking in the streets of Greenwich Village together. We went to all the little bars. In and out. They didn't like anything they saw. They'd go in with us trailing behind them, and we'd come out again. Through the entire Village!

NORMAN MAILER (writer) I used to have a workplace in Brooklyn at the Ovington Studios on Fulton Street about three blocks from where Truman lived. When I moved back to Brooklyn, Truman and I lived a block away from each other. We were like neighbors—we'd see each other six or eight times a year, run into each other on the street. On one occasion, in 1958 I think, we went to the first bar we could find, which was down on Montague Street near Court—a big Irish bar with a long brass rail at which were lined up fifty reasonably disgruntled Irishmen drinking at three-thirty in the afternoon. We walked in. Truman was wearing a little gabardine cape. He strolled in looking like a beautiful little faggot prince. It suddenly came over me: My God, what have I done? I've walked into this drunken den of sour male virtue with Truman! I walked behind him as if I had very little to do with him. And Truman just floated through. As he did, the eyes—it was a movie shot—every eye turned automatically to look at him with a big Irish "I've seen everything now." He was used to it, obviously. He walked right through to a table in the back, sat down and drank, and we talked for about an hour. Nobody bothered us. It took me half an hour for the adrenaline to come down. I figured people would get rude and I'd get into a fight. My system was charged with adrenaline. It all proved unnecessary. Afterward, I thought, "My God, if I were that man, I couldn't live, I'd die of adrenaline overflow." I was very impressed with what it cost him to live. That quality—that he had a special life and was going to live it in a special way—is enormously exhausting.

JOHN KNOWLES I was an editor of *Holiday* magazine in the late fifties. It was a quality commercial magazine. It aspired to be another *New Yorker* except that it didn't print fiction. Many of the *New Yorker* people wrote nonfiction for *Holiday*. Though I had never met him, they asked me to get Truman for them. They also asked me to get Jack Kerouac, who had just published *On the Road*. I got them both the same night. Truman met me at the Oak Room at the Plaza. He came in from Brooklyn . . . this incredible little person in a black velvet suit with blond bangs swinging, looking this way and that to see where I was. He took to me instantly. He decided to annex me, to add me to his friends. Once Truman made up his mind to do that, that was it. That night he was going on to read his work in progress, which was *Breakfast at Tiffany's*. I said, "Mr. Capote, shouldn't we be leaving? It's almost time for your reading." He said, "Let them wait, the hell with them!" He had another drink, of course. We got to the Ninety-second Street Y late and he read in that extraordinary voice of his, which was like nothing on earth.

From there I got in a taxi and went down to the Village Vanguard, where Jack Kerouac was reading from his verse . . . let's not call it poetry, let's call it *verse*. He had on a green, white, and blue striped sailor's jumper and he was parodying himself in his readings because he felt the audience wasn't taking him seriously. He tried to read, but his audience was half drunk and, this being the Village, he would sort of mock himself. He was very gifted in his way, but it wasn't poetry. I told Kerouac I had been with Truman. Kerouac wanted to meet Truman, but Truman scorned Kerouac as a typist and he refused to meet him. Never did meet him. It probably would have been a disaster. Truman would have been terribly supercilious and condescending and cutting and Jack would be very impressed. Both wrote for *Holiday*. Jack wrote a number of pieces. He wrote in a stream-of-consciousness style which he thought was the way to write; then I had to curb it a little bit to get it past the other editors at *Holiday*. That's the way he wrote at that time. He liked the money, liked the exposure, pretended to object to stooping to commercialism, but he managed to force himself to do it. I liked him very much. He was a warm, touching person, though he was pretty far gone on alcoholism by this time. Best work behind him. I was awfully young at the time and took it all in stride, the way one does.

Truman wrote a beautiful piece for *Holiday* called "A Neighborhood in Brooklyn" about his home at the time down on Willow Street in Brooklyn Heights. It was an evocation of Brooklyn Heights and Brooklyn in general. It was in his best vein, really very special. It had this unique ending which is beautifully written.

We kept having dinners, on *Holiday*, only Le Pavillon and the Colony. The next night after dinner at the Colony, he wanted to go to this male dancing palace up on the West Side . . . in the back of a bar through swinging doors. Truman told me it was where the convicts would come when they got out of Sing Sing. First place they'd head for. I went along with him. After all, I was trying to land this writer for *Holiday*. I remember dancing with this little tiny person . . . So I recruited him successfully . . . all the time, in my mind's eye, seeing the Curtis Publishing Company board of directors speculating on what their editor was doing to get this author for them.

JENNINGS FAULK CARTER Around this time Truman only came back to Monroeville in the summer and at Christmas or something like that. He had changed. That distinctive high voice of his developed when his lifestyle changed. When he was young he had a child's voice, just like all of us. When his voice changed he talked sort of like Arch Persons, his father. But then with his lifestyle he started this effeminate inflection in his voice that was hard on all of us.

After he got successful and had money he wanted a little vacation place back in Monroeville. Daddy had told him about a piece of land across the woods, thirty acres, with a small house on it, for sale. Truman immediately wanted to buy it. The jeweler in Monroeville owned it. They almost closed the deal. But Daddy got to thinking, he and Mother talking about it, and Daddy came to the conclusion that if Truman bought that little piece of property, all these strange people from the North that wrote and did movies would come down. And Daddy could just see all those people climbing over the fence and coming to visit Mother, you know, and leaving the gate open for the cows to get out, and all this. And so, he just took it upon himself to tell Truman that Mr. Jones, the jeweler, had decided not to sell. It wasn't six months after that that Truman came up to Mother's in his red Jaguar. He had this funny boy in there with him, a nice-looking young man. I didn't know that anything was going on, but Mother saw right through it and she just had this screaming fit. She got that broom and ran the boy off. I never really suspected till Truman came up in the red Jaguar with his funny fellow in there. Well, after Mother had the fit, we all knew.

Interlude

CHAPTER FOURTEEN   *In Which TC Speaks About His Working Habits, His Mentors, and His Aversion to Nuns Traveling on the Same Plane*

A manuscript page of the preface to *Other Voices, Other Rooms*. *(Truman Capote Papers, The New York Public Library)*

TRUMAN CAPOTE I am a completely horizontal author ... I can't think unless I'm lying down, either in bed or stretched on a couch and with a cigarette and coffee handy. I've got to be puffing and sipping. As the afternoon wears on, I shift from coffee to mint tea to sherry to martinis. I don't use a typewriter. Not in the beginning. I write my first version in longhand (pencil). Then I do a complete revision, also longhand. Essentially I think of myself as a stylist, and stylists can become notoriously obsessed with the placing of a comma, the weight of a semicolon. Obsessions of this sort, and the time I take over them, irritate me beyond endurance. Then I type a third draft on yellow paper, a very special certain kind of yellow paper. I don't get out of bed to do this . . . I balance the machine on my knees. It works fine . . . I can manage a hundred words a minute. When the yellow draft is finished, I put the manuscript away for a while, a week, a month, sometimes longer. When I take it out again, I read it as coldly as possible, then read it aloud to a friend or two, and decide what changes I want to make and whether or not I want to publish. I've thrown away rather a few short stories, an entire novel, and half of another. But if all goes well, I type the final version on white paper and that's that.

I invariably have the illusion that the whole play of a story, its start and middle and finish, occur in my mind simultaneously—that I'm seeing it in one flash. But in the working-out, the writing-out, infinite surprises happen. Thank God, because surprises, the twist, the phrase that comes at the right moment out of nowhere, is the unexpected dividend, that joyful little push that keeps a writer going.

At one time I used to keep notebooks with outlines for stories. But I found doing this somehow deadened the idea in my imagination. If the notion is good enough, if it truly belongs to you, then you can't forget it . . . it will haunt you until it's written.

I've never been aware of direct literary influence, though several critics have informed me that my early works owe a debt to Faulkner and Welty and McCullers. Possibly. I'm a great admirer of all three; and Katherine Anne Porter too. Though I don't think, when really examined, that they have much in common with each other, or me, except that we were all born in the South. Between thirteen and sixteen are the ideal, if not the only ages for succumbing to Thomas Wolfe, though I can't read a line of it now. Just as other youthful flames have guttered: Poe, Dickens, Stevenson. I love them in memory, but find them unreadable. These are the enthusiasms that remain constant: Flaubert, Turgenev, Chekhov, Jane Austen, Henry James, E. M. Forster, Maupassant, Rilke, Proust, Shaw, Willa Cather . . . oh, the list is too long, so I'll end with James Agee, a beautiful writer whose death was a real loss. Agee's work, by the way, was much influenced by the films. I think most of the younger writers have learned and borrowed from the visual, structural side of movie technique. I have.

I don't know if it's art, but I was stagestruck for years and more than anything I wanted to be a tap dancer. I used to practice my buck-and-wing until everybody in the house was ready to kill me. Later on, I longed to play the guitar and sing in nightclubs. So I saved up for a guitar and took lessons for one whole winter, but in the end the only tune I could really play was a beginner's thing called "I Wish I Were Single Again." I got so tired of it that one day I just gave the guitar to a stranger in a bus station. I was also interested in painting, and studied for three years, but I'm afraid the fervor, *la vrai chose,* wasn't there.

The first person who ever helped me was, strangely, a teacher. An English teacher I had in high school, Catherine Wood, who backed my ambitions in every way, and to whom I shall always be grateful. Later on, from the time I first began to publish, I had all the encouragement anyone could ever want, notably from Margarita Smith, fiction editor at *Mademoiselle,* Mary Louise Aswell of *Harper's Bazaar,* and Robert Linscott of Random House. You would have to be a glutton indeed to ask for more good luck and fortune than I had at the beginning of my career.

I have my superstitions, though. They could be termed quirks. I have to add up all numbers: there are some people I never telephone because their number adds up to an unlucky figure. Or I won't accept a hotel room for the same reason. I will not tolerate the presence of yellow roses . . . which is sad, because they're my favorite flower. I can't allow three cigarette butts in the same ashtray. Won't travel on a plane with two nuns. Won't begin or end anything on a Friday. It's endless, the things I can't and won't. But I derive some curious comfort from obeying these primitive concepts.

Truman's apparel tended to catch the eye—bathing suits with novelty slogans on them, black velvet suits, floor-length overcoats, siren suits, a variety of hats, and invariably in wintertime long designer scarfs. (*Jill Krementz*)

1956

CHAPTER FIFTEEN *In Which TC*
Alarms the Town of Stonington,
Connecticut

JAMES MERRILL *(poet)* One summer he rented a
house in Stonington—the top floor of a strange little
clapboard box with a lot of glass around it
overlooking the harbor. It was the same house that
David Jackson and I first rented two years earlier. He
was just back from Russia. The refrigerator was full
of caviar and he was reading the galleys of *The Muses
Are Heard.* Jack Dunphy was with him, though we
rarely saw him. They would go out on picnics to the
sandbar in the harbor—a crowd of them, picnic
hampers, and the terrible dog, lowering all of this
into a boat. They had their own friends. Joan
McCracken, the dancer who was married to Jack.
She came up. David remembers going down to the
little beach at the end of the town with her and
Truman—Truman so busy talking as he changed out
of his pedal pushers that he forgot that he hadn't
anything on underneath. Portuguese grandmothers
shielding their children's eyes. He got the pants
down to mid-thigh, and Joan said, "You're not going
to get away with it, T."

JAMES SCHUYLER Instead of wearing bathing trunks at the beach, he wore undershorts. One pair had a pattern of large ants on it: Ants in My Pants. Another: Don't Open Until Christmas. Otherwise, he dressed rather chicly. More chicly than other people dared.

DAVID JACKSON He had a blue T-shirt that kept riding up on his trunk, not tucked in his pants. The village had never seen anything like that, a bare midriff. The shopkeepers edged toward the door and peered out. His beach clothes had been designed for him by Schiaparelli. It was a sort of faux baseball suit. He was very amusing that summer, we all adored him. If you had him for dinner, an evening of talk—he had these glasses he'd bring along: a clear pair, a slightly shaded pair, and a really dark pair. It was quite apparent that he couldn't lie properly unless his eyes were covered. So he would change glasses. When they were really dark, you knew a huge exaggeration, a lie was coming. We called them "the shades of truth." The Du Ponts have a house over there on Fishers Island, and when they gave a lunch, they sent over this massive boat for Truman. He was very pleased with himself. When he came back he said that there had been one hundred for an outdoor lunch. (Medium-shaded glasses.) There had been a young girl there, in her teens. Hundreds of gulls—it was the mating season—were circling around the dock. As lunch went on, this girl was dying to go down to the dock and look at the gulls. Everyone said, "No, don't. They're very vicious at this time of year." (Darker glasses.) Finally, she went with an umbrella to watch them. On the docks, the umbrella collapsed in the wind and the gulls tried to peck her eyes out. (Darkest, darkest shades.)

JAMES MERRILL He'd put on these shaded glasses and tell these perfectly absurd, exaggerated stories. The lying was beginning even then. I remember one story about somebody who had her nose eaten away on a Greek island by rats. She and her son had paid a fisherman to take them to this little island. The boatman was coming around to get them the next day. They were going to have a quiet evening with nature—their fishing, their sleeping bags and cans of pâté, and so forth, and at dusk—in the light of their fire—

they saw hundreds of little beady eyes around them. The son made it to the sea and stayed in the water all night long. I think the mother finally got in the water with him but not before her nose had been eaten away. You know, she always had to wear a little face veil. He loved stories like that.

ELEANOR PERÉNYI *(editor)* The town—it's now much more sophisticated than it was then—was both dazzled and horrified by Truman. He was followed by troops of children shouting rude things. He had a whole bunch of little outfits, white cotton with red piping, that were made for him. Very elegant, really. I asked him about these things once, and he said that Dior had made them for him. Well, I don't know. Maybe and maybe not. The town was not accustomed to the sight of anyone looking quite the way Truman looked, flouncing around. He had this huge dog, one of those dreadful boxers, that he subsequently came to resemble but he didn't in those days. He was teased and annoyed. There was a boat that went with his rented house, and somebody sank it. Pure malice. No, Stonington wasn't ready for Truman. He didn't have a good time here and he never came back. One of the reasons he hated Stonington was that there weren't enough "magnates." Just across the Sound is Fishers Island. He kept saying, "I have to go over to Fishers and see my magnates." "My magnates," he always used to say. "My magnates." We all got rather tired of it.

Interlude

CHAPTER SIXTEEN *In Which the*
Reader Is Introduced to the Swans and TC
Is Seen as Counselor and Confidant

GEORGE PLIMPTON He called them his "swans"—for
their beauty, their elegance, their charm, and not
unsurprisingly because they all seemed to be
endowed with long necks—Babe Paley, Marella
Agnelli, Gloria Vanderbilt, Gloria Guinness, C. Z.
Guest, Lee Radziwill, Slim Keith. Baby Paley was, to
use a completely inappropriate term, the leader of
the pack. Slim, elegant, a remarkable beauty, she was
surely the most undisheveled person imaginable—so
groomed, everything perfectly in place whether she
was sitting in a cabana on the Lido or hosting a fancy
dinner. It would be difficult to imagine her being
tossed about by a strong wind: she would remain as
unruffled as the figurehead on the bow of a ship.
Billy Baldwin, the society decorator, once said of
Babe, "So great is her beauty that no matter how
often I see her, each time is the first time."

SLIM AARONS *(photographer)* I am always asked who
the people are that I most liked to photograph. The
two who come immediately to mind are Babe Paley

Two of Truman's "swans"—Gloria Guinness (foreground), the Mexican-born wife of Loel Guinness, of England's great banking family, and Barbara Paley—or Babe, as everyone called her. She was one of the three fabled daughters of Harvey Cushing, a distinguished Boston brain surgeon. Each of the daughters married twice—Betsey to James Roosevelt, FDR's son, and then to John Hay Whitney, a great sportsman (polo, horse racing) and owner of the *New York Herald Tribune*; Minnie married Vincent Astor, the New York real estate tycoon, then James Fosburgh, an artist and member of an old New York family. Babe was first married to Stanley Mortimer, Jr., New York socialite, scion of a Standard Oil family. *(William S. Paley, collection of Kate C. Paley)*

and C. Z. Guest. Babe was the queen, gracious, utterly charming. Once when I was at lunch in Acapulco I was asked the same question and I replied that Babe Paley was what I thought every woman in America wanted to be. One of the ladies at the table got up and left—she was really livid. But I still maintain that everybody wanted to be either a Babe Paley or a C. Z. Guest, and it all worked down from there.

NAN KEMPNER (*socialite*) Babe was so beautiful. The most beautiful woman I think I've ever known. I think there was so much more to her than was ever allowed to come out. I think her self-control was admirable, she was very fragile, and I thought the most endearing feature was that she was never full of herself. This wonderful sort of incompleteness was devastatingly attractive.

I stayed with Gloria Guinness once in Acapulco. I was just charmed beyond words, the mouth hungeth open. It was such a pretty house, and she always looked so meticulous, wonderful, always had on the right thing at the right time.

In the end, neither Gloria nor Babe lived long enough to become messy. I remember at the end when Babe was the weight of a feather, little Freddie Melhado picking her up and carrying her into bed after lunch at Lyford Key. A wonderful blue caftan. She never let the side down, even when she was ill. I remember Robin Hambro telling me when she stayed with Babe, Babe was up at seven putting her lashes on and everything to present the perfect face to the world early in the morning. I think that's beyond the line of duty. For some people, less is more. If I get all done up, I look like a female impersonator. It's true, it's so awful. I guess the answer is that after a certain age, you stay home. Lock yourself up. That's the wonderful thing about never having been a great beauty. If you've been one, it must be perfectly disastrous. It's bad enough if you're just normal looking. I've painted my bathroom pink, because it helps in the morning not to have a white bathroom. Try painting your bathroom pink. It's amazing what it does to your skin tone. Don't do anything tomorrow that you can do today. Rush and get pink paint. It'll change your life.

BABS SIMPSON (*editor*) Babe's mother, Mrs. Cushing, was such a dragon. She was just determined that her three daughters were going to marry three of the richest men that she could find, and they did. Betsy first married Jimmy Roosevelt and that was a disaster. Then she married Jock Whitney. Minnie married Vincent Astor, and Babe married Bill Paley. They were all charming. But the real beauty was Babe. A Gibson girl, that kind of beauty. Extraordinary skin, beautiful hair, beautiful figure, and dressed better than anybody I've ever seen. She was fun and lively and cozy and I think probably a quite lonely person. So Truman must have been a big help in that way.

GEORGE PLIMPTON Babe Paley came into his life in the mid-fifties. The story was that the David Selznicks, invited down to the Paleys' place in Round Hill, Jamaica, by private plane, had asked if they could bring "Truman" along. The Paleys said, "Absolutely, it would be our honor," thinking that the Selznicks were referring to Harry Truman. One can imagine the Paleys' surprise . . . expecting the former President to walk through the door and getting instead a squeaky-voiced personage trailing a long scarf, his mischievous face under a wide-brimmed straw hat. But, of course, they all got along famously. I doubt it took more than a few minutes for Babe to be absolutely enchanted by him.

Slim Keith was one of the major swans. Apparently, William Powell, who became sort of a father figure to her when she was a teenager, called her his "Slim Princess." The "Slim" stuck with her for the rest of her life (Hemingway called her "Slimsky"), but later on, though enormously attractive, she was hardly a sylph. Truman called her "Big Mama." She called Truman "True Heart."

SLIM KEITH (*socialite*) I was married to Leland [Hayward] when I met Truman. I met him at the Vreelands'. They had a tiny little apartment which was the chicest thing you ever saw, with ten-cent chintz and everything. I found him absolutely spellbinding. He was quick and funny. When he was away from you, you thought about him, but when he came back, you had to readjust again. You had to start at the beginning as though you'd never met him before. Get used to that squeaky voice.

He'd see somebody at a party who wasn't doing very well, and he'd really make an effort—go and talk and jabber, or do something silly. "I'm beside myself!" He'd jump in the air and call out, "I'm beside myself!" But he was a shit-stirrer. He wanted to start some kind of turmoil . . . because there would be a tangible result that he could use. A different kind of juice. Lillian Hellman had a little bit of that. She wrote best when she was furious . . . at Bill Styron because he didn't cut the ham the right way or something. She'd be furious for two or three years. It would drive her. It was like a motor. Truman's motor was driven by gossip and knowing things he shouldn't know. Personal things. "How dare you ask me that? I wouldn't think of answering that!" . . . though, of course, some of us did.

MARELLA AGNELLI I had always thought that before being a writer, Truman was a human being who had the talent to get close and intimate and warm and kind and amusing. So I didn't think of Truman as a writer. When I met him, I had read his two first books and for me he was this baby genius. But that wasn't as important to me . . . because our relationship came immediately on a human basis. For me. For him, no. For him I remained Mrs. Agnelli. The wife of a tycoon.

GEORGE PLIMPTON Truman thought of Gloria Guinness as one of the three great beauties, the others being Greta Garbo and Babe Paley, of course. Gloria, born in what were referred to as "reduced circumstances" in Mexico, had married an Egyptian diplomat dispatched to Germany, had danced with Goebbels in Berlin, married a Fürstenberg and eventually ended up with Loel Guinness, a banking scion, former member of Parliament, who had a "splendid war" with the RAF, and to escape taxes (I believe he could only return to England for one month out of the year) had residences in France, Palm Beach, Acapulco, as well as a large yacht on which Winston Churchill often came in his declining years for a cruise, sitting heavily bundled up on the afterdeck. Gloria always reminded me of a flamenco dancer gone "cool"—a touch of Spanish in her accent, slim, vivacious, and always beautifully groomed. In New York she was known as "the Ultimate" and wore a ring so large she couldn't fit a glove over it.

Truman invariably spent part of his winters with the Guinnesses in Florida. They lived south of Palm Beach in the David Lambert house in Manalapan, originally owned by the inventor of Listerine . . . absolutely unique in that it was built under Route A1A. It was called Gemini because it fronted the ocean on one side and Lake Worth on the other. Marble steps led out to the beach and the sea on one side and on the opposite side to a lawn that sloped to the lake. Quite astonishing! The living room in the center of the house was literally under the traffic, though it was completely quiet—that is, unless Gloria had put on the Chubby Checker records. Everyone was doing the Twist then, and after dinner the younger guests danced on the marble floors. It was all quite grand . . . a Palm Beach decor: white wicker furniture, one or two pillows with funny slogans on them, always a faint scent of lily. The Guinnesses entertained the Duke and Duchess of Windsor when they paid their annual visit to Palm Beach. Out on the lawn, Loel kept his helicopter, a two-seater Bell, as I recall, which he flew himself. He had flown in the war, Spitfires I believe. The oldest active pilot in the RAF. Once, I went up with him, flying up the coast to Seminole to play golf, and I remember looking down and seeing the cluster of sharks at every inlet mouth, waiting for what came out with the tides. They were thresher sharks, which aren't dangerous, but it was startling to look down and see people swimming completely unaware not more than twenty feet or so away.

Truman had his dog with him, one of the bulldogs, but the animal of the house was a Pekinese named Mister. My God, that dog was fussed over. At mealtimes he had whatever their superb chef had provided for dinner, absolutely four-star stuff for Mister. Inevitably Loel would ask Mister if he approved of what he was being fed, leaning over and murmuring to him as if to a dinner partner.

LOEL GUINNESS (*financier*) Truman's dog came to stay at Gemini. It was a bulldog. Never had any problems with Mister. At the end of dinner, Mister came to get his peppermint. He never went around asking people for anything. That he wasn't allowed to do. But the end of dinner when the peppermint time came, I'd pick him up, put him on the table and give him his peppermint. Sometimes, if people were very nice, he used to walk about the table and have a drink out of their water glasses.

GEORGE PLIMPTON That winter Truman was helping Gloria with an article she was writing for *Harper's Bazaar* . . . which, as I recall, he had suggested . . . a totally weird idea in which she was constructing a composite man. It had the brain of Einstein, the legs of Muhammad Ali, that sort of exercise. Its torso was Jesus Christ's. I remember there was quite a lot of discussion as to whether Jesus's torso was appropriate. Truman thought it was a grand idea. Poor Gloria suffered a lot of criticism when the article came out.

ALICE MORRIS (*editor*) Gloria Guinness had written something for *Harper's Bazaar.* It was a piece about beauty, a kind of composite. It was a piece of utter nonsense. The brain of Einstein, the body of Jesus Christ—something like that. We were told not to change a word. Truman Capote had told Gloria Guinness never to change anything. Truman was just being wicked, because he must have known it was just laughable, but she was a very pretty, very social woman. Anyway, it was published as she wrote it. We got hundreds of letters. The body of Jesus Christ! Ludicrous!

LOEL GUINNESS Gloria loved Truman. He stayed with us a lot. When he was staying with us, I used to say—because he talked to us all night—"Bedtime, off you go." "Yes, Pa," and off he'd go to bed. Gloria and he would bellyache and say, "We don't want to go to bed yet, it's only half past eleven," and I'd say, "Well, I do, and off you go!"

We gave him the guesthouse. David Lambert had built two studios: one for himself and one for his wife, because both were painting at that time. I turned one of those into a little house for someone like Truman who'd come to stay for a week or so. He spent most of his time writing there. He was a very good houseguest.

I assure you, he was no problem. He wouldn't have stayed very long if he had been. You could turn him loose on the other guests and he'd keep them busy.

When he was living in the guesthouse at Gemini he was writing *In Cold Blood*. He used to give me bits to read and ask what I thought. I told him quite blankly when I didn't like something and he'd say, "I must say, I agree with you," and he'd take it out. Wasn't difficult at all in that way. He didn't mind at all your saying, "I hate that," or "Why'd you do it that way?"

Whether Truman spoke the truth or not, I haven't a clue and I didn't care. He was a very good conversationalist. And storyteller. I have been told that he used to tell a story about President Kennedy coming down to Gemini and swimming naked in the pool. Well, that's not the truth. He never came to Gemini. Bobby Kennedy did. He was bad news. I thought he was much too pugnacious and much too arrogant compared with his brother, who I thought was a lousy President, but probably the most attractive man I'd ever seen in my life.

I liked Truman. I liked him very much, got on with him very well because he was never unpleasant to me.

KAY MEEHAN (*friend*) He was always very good to me. He always was very gentle, very protective. I met him at Rocky Cooper's house at a dinner for him. We went to a party at the St. Regis. Joe, my husband, was away on a trip and the man I had taken wanted to go home. Truman, in that squeaky voice of his, said to me, "Don't go home. I'll take you home." I remember saying, "But you live in Brooklyn." He said, "We'll get something to eat." I thought he meant the buffet at the St. Regis party, but off we went to El Morocco. The next thing I knew, they were putting the chairs up on the tables. He was such good company. When he let me off about five o'clock in the morning, he said, "Now you're my friend. A friend is someone you don't have to finish your sentences with."

HERB CAEN (*newspaper columnist*) We had a drink at the St. Francis and he was really on. I was fascinated, as everybody is when they first meet him. The bar at the St. Francis was full of men for some reason at that point and they started crowding around listening. He did a sort of performance. The more they listened to these wild stories of his, the more he was on. He was a real performer. His voice was unlike any I'd ever heard. A reporter for the *San Francisco Chronicle* interviewed him and described it as "a high, expiring voice," which I thought was a pretty good description. He was beguiling and sly and insidious and irresistible. He did his usual trick of captivating my wife. In fact, he captivated two of my wives. That was a trick of his—getting the wife in his pocket. The husband didn't really matter; we'd just sit there and listen to him anyway. My first wife, Sally, fell madly in love with him. He'd say, "We must go on a trip together, darling. Get rid of this old bore you're married to. Let's go to Tangier."

She believed him! I said, "He's just kidding. That's the way he talks. He's not going to take you to Tangier." She was so sure that he was. Of course, she never heard from him again for about a year. My second wife, Maria Theresa, she was mad for him too. He sort of resented me, I think. He used to come over to the house a lot with Saint-Subber. They kind of berated me. I didn't deserve anybody as wonderful as Maria Theresa . . . you're just too lucky for words . . . what does she see in you? They were awful to me.

JUDY GREEN *(writer)* His plans were punctuated with this daredevil . . . Maybe it was because he wanted to seem macho to his friends. He'd say, "There's this fabulous whorehouse that runs out of Seventy-eighth and Park. There's a man who sits behind a desk in the most beautiful duplex in New York. You pay on the line." He would say, "We're going to go there someday." He would tell me fabulous stories about Madame Claude, the famous Paris madam, and how she was a great friend and how he would visit her in San Francisco. As drunk as he might be, he was filled with plans— whether to visit whorehouses and madams, take *Porgy and Bess* to Cuba, or see Saint Laurent in Marrakesh. It was as if he weren't going to let today stop without starting tomorrow. It was like the way Hemingway wrote, never ending a chapter when he ended his day. That was how Truman would leave you—always with the promise of something to come, something that he would want you to appreciate and see through him.

JOHN RICHARDSON The trouble with Truman was that he was the *Spielmann*—the manipulative court jester. With his wit, shit-stirring and conniving ways, he was able to twist these rich people round his finger. It was very important for Truman to feel that people preferred him to their husbands, wives, or children. And quite often they did. They'd choose Truman because he was so beguiling and then they'd become addicted to him. Intentionally or not, he broke up Slim Keith's marriage to Leland Hayward. Truman had said, "Come on, Slim, let's go off somewhere." And Slim got Pamela Churchill, who was at loose ends, to look after her husband. The next thing she knew, Leland and Pam had gone off together.

KARL BISSINGER Anybody would be impressed with his conquest album. I think he probably loved changing their lives, becoming the most important person in their lives.

BARBARA ALLEN (*photographer*) Every now and then, out of the blue he'd call me up and say, "I've got the man for you to meet." I was always intrigued. He would set up the whole thing, and it was always very theatrical, almost like being in a novel. I remember once it was this man . . . he thought we were just perfectly matched. He said we'd have lunch. "You, me, and him at Quo Vadis." I think it was his lawyer. I can't remember his name. Really intelligent, very nice. He did a lot of things with the movie business, and he's probably very well known.

I remember when Norris Church and I met him for lunch. He had said to me, "I want to meet the girl that's going to marry Norman Mailer because I want to warn her." So Norris came—six months pregnant or whatever—and the three of us had lunch. TC started to tell Norris about Norman with other women. Truman said, "I realize you're going to marry him anyway, but I just feel I ought to tell you."

NORMAN MAILER He warned Norris not to marry me. That was the measure of his vanity at the end. He really had this notion that he could tell her whether to get married or not—and she would listen.

It wasn't like "I'll put in my opinion with a hundred others." I wasn't even furious. I was amused. I thought, "My God! He sure doesn't understand Norris!" It reminded me of that joke: What's the epitome of vanity? Answer: It's a guy floating downstream on his back with a hard-on. He approaches a drawbridge and yells that it's got to be raised.

PEARL KAZIN BELL Truman knew the man I had decided mistakenly to marry and go to live with in Brazil. At one point Truman sent me a postcard when he knew that I was leaving in a few days. It said, "If I weren't such a coward, I'd throw myself in front of the plane!" He felt that strongly. He was very right. He had a certain wisdom. He was an uneducated person, but he picked things up from the air. Oliver Smith once said to me that he thought Truman was the smartest person he had ever known. He had a way of adding things up very quickly and coming out at the right point.

JAN CUSHING (friend) The only time he ever tried to do something funny was when someone came in that I rather fancied at the time. TC said, "Let's make him jealous." He lunged over and gave me this gigantic French kiss. I said, "Truman, honestly," and moved away. He was joking.

I met TC at a dinner that Lester Persky was having at Four Seasons. I was seated next to TC. We started talking about psychiatrists. "Are you going to a psychiatrist?" Truman asked me. I said, "Yes." He asked me the psychiatrist's name, and Truman said, "Oh, I know him well. He's terrible. Let's play a trick on him."

"Well, what type of trick?"

"I'll set it up. When you go to the office tomorrow, you say to the doctor, 'I have finally found the man of my dreams. I don't need you anymore.' That's all you have to do. Do it about eleven o'clock."

The next day I walked in and sat down and said, "Doctor, I have finally found everything you told me to look for in life. I have found the man of my dreams!"

The doctor said, "I'm so happy, Mrs. Cushing, that you have. I'm so happy that you've listened."

At which point in walks the nurse—dead-white and ashen—and she said, "Doctor, Mrs. Cushing's fiancé has arrived."

Two seconds later, in walks Truman outfitted with a cape and he screams, "Darling, you snuck out of bed without waking me. I'm so unhappy. I miss you so!"

The doctor almost went into a faint; he dropped his pencil. Truman said, "Bye-bye, Doctor," and he walked out with his arm around me. That was my first experience with Truman. And the last time I ever saw that psychiatrist.

SLIM KEITH He could play it either way. He could play it like a very strong-minded man, who was wise, full of advice, and full of what seemed to be wisdom, and in many instances, as it turned out, *was* wisdom. Or he could say, "That's the wrong color lipstick. Now, I've got one on me that's just the right color. I also have some ooey-gooey."

I said, "What in God's name is that?"

"That's the stuff you put on after the lipstick. The ooey-gooey."

For a woman, that's kind of fun—interested in the things that you're interested in. Shoes, or your dress, or whatever.

MARELLA AGNELLI I got so intimate with Truman because he had a very special quality. He would observe people and see their soft spots; he became the father confessor. I found myself telling him things I never dreamed of telling him. Absolutely. He was waiting like a falcon. He created a very deep sort of intimacy. Very deep, very tender intimacy. Little did I know . . .

The first time I was a little bit disappointed with Truman—because I thought we had this very special relationship—was at a luncheon he gave at the Colony. Beginning of the sixties, maybe middle. He invited a lot of friends. C. Z. Guest was there, Babe Paley. He invited us all. We found ourselves suddenly with a big bunch of friends who all had more or less the same relationship with him. He called us swans. In a way, I was a little disillusioned. Too many swans. Some of the swans I didn't like so much at all. For some I had an enormous admiration, so on one side I was flattered, but on the other, there were too many. My relationship with him was enormously personal, unique and special . . . The intimacy, the laughs, the giggles: I thought it was a special relationship between Truman and me. I didn't think he was giggling and laughing with Babe or Gloria or Slim. I said, "Well, I thought I was the only swan." He said, "Oh, well, darling . . ."

I must tell you frankly that he did not adore us for ourselves, though he made us believe he did. We always think that when the intimacy comes it is because of ourselves. But with Truman, it was the situation in which we lived that interested him. This is why I didn't like that lunch. We only had one common denominator—the kind of life we lived. He was the only man at lunch. There were photographs taken before and after.

SLIM KEITH Babe Paley really did confide deeply in him. She considered him her best friend. I was always appalled when she'd talk about it. I said, "How can you tell him anything? You mustn't. You don't understand this, but I do. It's bad news. He's going to rat on you."

"Oh, he wouldn't do that to me. Our friendship is deep and binding. We love one another; we trust one another."

She was so good to him. My God, she was good to him. He'd go and stay at Kaluna, the house in Manhasset. He spent a lot of time pumping the butler, who was as queer as he was. "How can you tell if Mr. Paley comes home right from the office?" He was getting information from anybody who'd ever been houseguests. What he was giving the butler, I don't know. I always thought a little more than met the eye.

He was very brave in many ways—brave to expose that he was as he was. One night when we were traveling together in Copenhagen, Truman said, "I'm going to tuck you in. Kiss my baby good night. Say a little prayer, tell you a little story, and then you'll go to sleep." He treated me like I was some little baby. He said, "I love you very much, Big Mama."

And I said, "I love you too, Truman."

"No, you don't."

"Yes, I do. How can you say that?"

"People don't love me."

"Certainly they do."

"I'm a freak. People don't love me. People are fascinated by me, but people don't love me."

"Well, I love you."

"You don't know what it's like to be me."

"What do you mean?"

"Well, when you walk into a room, there's a shock on people's faces. I see it; they don't see how they look; I see how they look. Why I'm so outrageous, so ridiculous and so squeaking and so carrying on is simply to relieve them of the sudden embarrassment. I do something so outrageous that all they can do is laugh and then it's okay. I have to do that every time I walk into a room or meet somebody."

He used to say, "You never confide in me, Big Mama."

I'd say, "No, I don't, darling, you're right."

"Why don't you confide in me?"

"Well, it's very simple, I don't trust you."

LEE RADZIWILL (*friend*) I met Truman in the late fifties. It must have been at a dinner, I don't know whose or where. Then he became a part of my life. I was interested to meet Truman because of his accomplishments. He was an original. I was a little leery, but I was interested to meet him. He felt that he was there to amuse, to be "on" and entertain. In a way, he was like Holly Golightly in that he felt he had to give the equivalent of what she gave—that he not only had to amuse but to story-tell and invent. Of course, each time he told the story, the next time it was more elaborate, the next time even more so until you wondered if he still could believe it himself. The stories, with time, became more and more exaggerated, until it was total *folie d'imagination*—sort of looking at another world.

I never thought he was a dangerous person to know, even though the exaggerations got far out of hand. If he'd tell you that you were there when you knew you had not been there, then I was no longer interested in the story.

Perhaps he wanted to please too much. He not only wanted to please you by storytelling, but also by gossip. I've never been very interested in gossip, and I think that was a disappointment to him.

In the beginning the stories were more about his family, his childhood. In the end, they were much more superficial, about his society friends—his lunches and dinners. About so-and-so's jewels and how she spread them all out . . . stories like that. It was odd, because it was so different from the purity of his work . . . that he could be so intrigued by what would seem to me so meaningless. It's important to say that he did appreciate himself as an artist, but he didn't understand that he was being treated like a toy.

MARELLA AGNELLI We went to see an *antiquaire*. One of the best in Europe, run by an old man. It was a huge, rambling place. We went there in the middle of winter, a very foggy day, I remember. In this huge, wonderful place full of dust and beautiful pieces of furniture, while bargaining for an extravagant red English lacquer piece, he began saying these horrors to me about someone I cared for a lot, passing them off as little asides as he bargained with the old man. It was a nightmare. What a scene. It was the end for me. *J'étais blessé à mort* . . . suddenly I looked at him and saw my enemy . . . this man is dangerous, you should run away. Suddenly I connected. I thought that only somebody very strange or mad could have a very intimate, kind, warm relationship and at the same time stab.

Three days later I asked Truman why he had said what he did. "I thought it was better that you knew," he told me. "Everybody knew and you didn't." And then, talking about something else, he said, "Some people kill with their swords and some with words." I did not know how long it took, but one day I realized that I didn't care for Truman anymore. He was out. I was not even curious, not about his books nor his life. Not even curious about whether he was right. For me he died that morning at the *antiquaire*. Then he left Turin and I never saw him again. Well, I saw him once. I came to dinner at Lee's, and to my astonishment, there were only three of us. Truman, Lee, and me. We had a totally normal dinner, as if we had seen each other the day before. He took me home. We were talking as if nothing had changed. It was just before midnight. He asked, "Why don't you want to see me?" I said, "But, Truman, it's not true, I want to see you. But you know how things are, you live over here, I live over there . . . we travel all the time." I lied, in the most cowardly way. I didn't want to straighten it out because I had no confidence in him anymore. I knew this man would stab me again . . . *aucune confiance*. I never saw him again. It was a pity because he had been really a great friend. With a great friend, one has the deepest intimacy. He told me so many things about his childhood. I told him many things. He knew at that time many more things about me than probably anybody.

ALAN SCHWARTZ (*TC's lawyer*) Of course, he was capable of being incredibly supportive of people he felt close to. When I split up with my former wife, Paula, there was one point when I wanted to get back with her. I was really desperate. Truman insisted I come up to his apartment. He counseled me in the writing of a letter to her which became a forty-eight-page letter. It was like drafting the Constitution. As I finished a page I would hand it to him. "Very good, very good." Finally, he said, "Sign that letter right there. Now fold it up. You go right to the apartment. Give it to the doorman. Don't take 'No' for an answer."

Paula was very touched by this letter, though it didn't help, obviously. Thank goodness, because we're both happily married now, though not to each other. But it shows that even throughout all this nonsense and his really deep illness he could be very supportive of certain people. We know how bitchy he was to most people, but if you were his friend, his real friend, he was a great friend.

JOANNE CARSON (*friend*) Before Johnny and I separated, Truman said to me, "My dear, women always have problems. Just tough it out." He gave me the same advice he gave Babe Paley. "Consider yourself a very expensive personal secretary. Executive secretary. Just hang in there and take all the perks, go to all the parties, buy all the clothes, enjoy your life." I can't do that, that's not me. If I'm not happy, I can't stay married to someone I'm not happy with. Actually, it wasn't that I wasn't happy with Johnny, but that I had hypoglycemia; when you have hypoglycemia you're depressed a lot of the time because your blood-sugar level is low and you cry easily. But anyway, when I separated from Johnny, Truman was the first person to know. He stood by me like glue. After I moved from UN

Plaza to stay with Henry and Shirlee Fonda in their town house, Truman got me out of there because he thought it was too depressing—black and red flowered needlepoint rugs, walls covered in black burlap. Very chic, but right across from a funeral home. All I saw were bodies going in and out every day in black sacks. Truman said, "This is very depressing, I'm getting you out of here."

He took me over to the Navarro Hotel and got me the penthouse suite. I was not in very good shape, so he would come up every morning. He'd sit in the living room and write. I was staring out the window or whatever, and he was just there. He would call room service. He couldn't get me to eat even pork chops and applesauce, which was my favorite. He said, "I know what is perfect for you." He disappeared for a while and came back with his arms loaded with grocery sacks. He unloaded them. He'd gone to Hammacher Schlemmer and got a blender. He'd gotten ice cream from Rumpelmayer's downstairs, and strawberries and bananas and peaches . . . to make me a fruit milk shake. He put the ice cream in, then the peaches, more ice cream and bananas and strawberries. He turned on the blender, but he'd forgotten to put the top on. So suddenly ice cream, peaches, and strawberries were splattered all over the place. Truman turned around—ice cream, a slice of strawberry on his blond hair. And he said, "My dear, I think I'm going to take a shower. You call Rumpelmayer's and order up a milk shake." I sat on the floor and laughed for the first time in weeks. I wondered if he hadn't done it on purpose.

1958

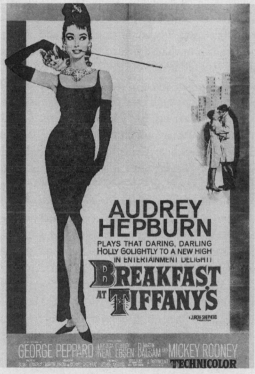

Holly Golightly, the captivating heroine of *Breakfast at Tiffany's*, was
immortalized in film by Audrey Hepburn, though Truman felt she
was wrong for the part and would have preferred Marilyn Monroe.
The curious title came from a story Truman had heard about an out-
of-town lover, ignorant of New York, who upon being asked to which
of the fanciest, most expensive restaurants he would like to be taken
for breakfast, picked the only place he'd heard of: "Well, let's have
breakfast at Tiffany's." *(Photofest)*

ALICE MORRIS We were going to publish *Breakfast at Tiffany's* in *Harper's Bazaar*. The layouts had been made to run with it. Alexi Brodovich was the art director. He had these wonderful photographs taken that had nothing to do with the *Breakfast* story, but with Holly Golightly's cat. A cat in a window, mysterious-looking, slightly shady and misty. I saw a lot of Truman during this because a man at Hearst called Dick Deems—originally a space salesman at *Harper's Bazaar* (very nice, affable fellow, tall)—had become a sort of manager of all Hearst publications. He began objecting to *Breakfast at Tiffany's*—specifically every word that he didn't think was absolutely elegant. My editor would come to me and say, "We have to get Truman to change this and that word." It was so idiotic. Truman was always sitting there laughing. We did change some of the words. I mean, some of Holly Golightly's friends were slightly raunchy characters and they might say a phrase like "fuck it." It always appeared to be right for where it was, never seemed vulgar at all, though, of course, it did to Dick Deems. We changed all these things painstakingly and tried not to ruin the flow of the story. When it was all done, the layouts and everything—all these cats roaming in and out—Truman brought me a beautiful blue Tiffany box and in it this beautiful rose with green leaves, just a perfect replica of a rose.

Truman was leaving for Greece that summer. One weekend after he'd left, my editor called me at home and said Dick Deems had called her to say we cannot run *Breakfast at Tiffany's* in *Harper's Bazaar*. Can't run it; not suitable. She was absolutely outraged. She suggested we run it in one of the other Hearst publications—*Good Housekeeping* perhaps. Or *Redbook*, just as long as it was kept in the Hearst empire. She was distressed because they never paid very much in those days for stories—$700 tops—and I had paid $2,000 for *Breakfast at Tiffany's*.

I said we couldn't possibly do that—*Harper's Bazaar* was very different than *Good Housekeeping* or *Redbook*. By then, word had gotten around and the editor of *Esquire* called and said, "We'd like to buy it." I told them I couldn't sell it; they'd have to go to Truman. He asked, "Do you think if we offered what you paid him he'd accept?" I said, "No, you'd have to offer at least a thousand more."

5 8

So they did. They cabled him and telephoned him in Athens, and offered him $1,000 more than we paid for it and he accepted. I have this postcard from Truman from Paris, where he'd gone from Athens. "Don't you think I'm making a mistake to appear in *Esquire*?"

ELEANOR PERÉNYI Nancy White, who had taken over from her aunt, Carmel Snow, at *Harper's Bazaar,* was afraid that Tiffany's—probably an advertiser—would be offended if *Breakfast at Tiffany's* was serialized in the magazine. Nancy had none of her aunt's taste or flair. I mean, Carmel would have published it in a minute. Wouldn't have even worried. But Nancy got agitated. It seems almost impossible to believe today, but she considered it a little too racy. We were so much more prudish in those days. Anyway, she dragged in this business about how Walter Hoving, the head of Tiffany's, would be offended. I think the contrary. He would have been enchanted by the publicity and probably would have put copies of the book in the window. But Truman never forgave us, and I don't blame him.

CLAY FELKER *(editor)* One day I was going to lunch and I picked up a copy of the *New York Post* on the way. I read in Leonard Lyons's column that *Harper's Bazaar* had turned down *Breakfast at Tiffany's* because the publisher had complained about the term "bull dyke" in the piece. Actually, I think it was a smoke screen. After all, Tiffany's was a major advertiser and they may have objected. Or maybe the publisher, really the chief advertising salesman at the magazine, was afraid of Tiffany's reaction. In any case, at the time I was an editor of *Esquire* and we called up and said that we'd like to buy this story. We ran it in the November issue. It had a dynamic effect on the sales. The book had come out in the middle of the newsstand sales to wonderful reviews and you could buy the whole damn novella in *Esquire.* The sales did something that I have never seen in a magazine since. Normally a magazine's sales are the highest on the first day it's out and it goes down geometrically from then. In this case, once the reviews came out, the sales took off once again.

DORIS LILLY There was a lot of wondering who the original Holly Golightly was. Pamela Drake and I were living in this brownstone walk-up on East Seventy-eighth Street, exactly the one in *Breakfast at Tiffany's. Exactly.* Truman used to come over all the time and watch me put makeup on before I went out. He was like a little boy. We used to go to the drugstore around the corner and get hamburgers. The man at the drugstore always said to me, "How's your little brother?" Anyway, Truman was in the apartment a lot. There's an awful lot of me in Holly Golightly. There's much more of me than there is of Carol Marcus (who is now Carol Marcus Matthau) and a girl called Bee Dabney, a painter. More of me than either of these two ladies. I know.

JOHN MALCOLM BRINNIN A little bit of Anky Larabee; a little bit of Phoebe. Beyond that, my gate closes. We all knew girls somewhat like that but the difference was that she really was a kind of high-class hustler. The girls we knew might have been amused about sexual associations and so on, but they weren't into the big time like Holly.

JOAN AXELROD Truman had sent me *Breakfast at Tiffany's* in galleys and I was enchanted by it. I told my husband, George, that he just had to read it. He read it and said, "What a fabulous character for a movie." As very often happened with him, about two months later, at three o'clock in the morning, he woke up and said, "I've got it! I know how to do *Breakfast at Tiffany's* as a movie." He had the love story all worked out . . . because he was wise enough to the wicked ways of Hollywood to know that you had to do certain things. Buddy Adler at 20th Century Fox said it sounded tremendous. But then the people assigned to the movie said to George, "Oh well, we can't use you to do the script, we need a serious writer."

George reported this to Truman, who was marvelous and said, "Well, bullshit. They don't know how to do it, *you* know how to do it." But Truman had nothing to say about it. They hired some writer who fell on his ass with it. They came back to George and said, "We're in terrible trouble. Would you like Rhode Island and a piece of the gross?"

In fact, it became a slight bone of contention between Truman and George, because I think George ended up making more out of writing the screenplay for the film than Truman did in terms of selling it. When the picture came out—I think this was at Bennett Cerf's house—Truman was there and curious about how George felt about it. George said, "I'm very happy with it, but I don't know how to break this to you . . ."

Truman said, "What? What?"

"They're not going to stick with the title."

Truman said, "What?"

"They're not going to stick with the title . . ."

Truman said, "What? They're not going to use the title . . . ?"

"I pleaded and begged but, Truman, there's nothing I can do about it. They're calling it *Follow That Blonde.*"

Truman fell for it hook, line, and sinker. George caught him at his own game. The moment Truman got it, he turned bright red. I've never seen him be so embarrassed, because this was something he thought he was beyond. Nobody could play a joke on *him,* nobody could lead him down that sort of garden path. He was totally furious.

He always liked George, but he was never really friendly with him after that and I think it had to do with that story. But it's such a likely Hollywood story: you get a fabulous title like *Breakfast at Tiffany's* and then those people will change it to *Follow That Blonde.*

1959

CHAPTER EIGHTEEN   *In Which TC*

Decides to Go to Kansas

SLIM KEITH He called me up one day. "*The New Yorker*'s given me a choice of assignments. I can either follow a day lady around New York who never sees the people she works for and write portraits of them just by what I see; or I can go to Kansas where there's been some murders. Which one do you think I ought to do?"

"Do the easy one, go to Kansas."

BRENDAN GILL There was never a real assignment. Shawn [*The New Yorker*'s editor] would always say, "Well, that sounds interesting." It was never as cut-and-dried as a contract you'd get with a book. I think Shawn told Truman that he was interested in seeing the effect of a murder—a story of a small Midwestern town responding to an unprecedented catastrophe in their midst. That would have appealed to Shawn. Gore, blood, the criminal mind, or whatever would not have appealed to him. He would have been reluctant to say go ahead to Truman if he had known what, in point of fact, *In Cold Blood*

Nelle Harper Lee and Truman standing in the Alvin Deweys' kitchen in Garden City, Kansas. (*Truman Capote Papers, The New York Public Library*)

proved to be. I suspect both Shawn and Truman himself were surprised to find what the piece became.

JOHN KNOWLES He went into outrageous detail at dinner . . . at Le Pavillon, of course, where else? He drew the house and where the bodies were found. At the time, the murderers had not been apprehended. It was believed that it was a local crime because these people knew the house. So I said, "Truman, if they find out you're out there nosing around, don't you think you too might . . . I mean, they've already committed four murders, how safe do you think you'll be?" So he went out there with Harper Lee as an assistant and I called him up in the first couple of days and I asked, "Truman, do you feel safe?" And he said, "Reasonably . . ."

JOHN BARRY RYAN Harper Lee was a fairly tough lady, and Truman was afraid of going down there alone. I've been told the situation there was fairly tense. People wouldn't be happy to have this little gnome in his checkered vest running around asking questions about who'd murdered whom. He asked Harper if she would go, and once she agreed, he said, "Would you get a gun permit and carry a gun while we're down there?"

CLIFFORD HOPE (*lawyer*) I met him on his first visit here, he and Harper Lee. I was the lawyer for the Clutter estate, and he wanted to visit the house. So I talked to the administrator, whose name was Kenneth Lyon, and Mr. Lyon and I went out with Truman and Harper Lee to look it over. By that time some furniture had been removed. We went down into the basement. Mr. Clutter and his son Kenyon had been tied up and both killed down there. We looked into two of the upstairs bedrooms, the one where Nancy was killed and then Mrs. Clutter. We went all through that. My recollection is that Truman didn't say very much.

That was around the middle of December. Both he and Harper Lee were here over Christmas, so my wife and I invited them to Christmas dinner. They graciously accepted and we had a nice, very leisurely sort of dinner. Truman always brought along his bottle of J&B scotch. I think he did on that occasion. I know he did when he went to other people's houses. After he became known here and various people started having parties for him, it greatly increased the sale of J&B scotch.

As for first impressions, he was much thinner than in later years, small, and of course his voice seemed unusual. But after talking to him for a few minutes, why, you just forgot about that.

HARRISON SMITH (*lawyer*) Nature wasn't kind to him when they gave him his voice . . . just like they used to say about Eleanor Roosevelt: that she was the only woman in captivity who could eat peanuts through a fence. But if you knew her and visited with her, you overlooked her homeliness. And that's the way it was with Truman. Once you knew him, the voice never even hurt him.

DUANE WEST (*prosecutor*) I don't think there was any indication at first that Truman was working on a major book about the Clutter murders. Just that he was an Eastern writer and that he was going to come in . . . He was an interesting little fellow. He'd make a kind of deliberate effort to play the part of the kook. In the wintertime, when he came out here, he ran around in a huge coat and with a pillbox hat on his head. It made him look extremely . . . "funny" is the term that comes to mind.

Alvin Dewey was one of the detectives on the case . . . His first reaction when he heard about Truman coming out to Kansas was very, very negative because news of Truman's proclivities, I guess you would say, had preceded him. Then Dewey started reading his books and, of course, they became good friends.

ALVIN DEWEY (*detective*) I first met Truman at the courthouse here in Garden City. It was within a week or ten days after the crime, which had been committed on November 15, 1959. Truman and Harper Lee showed up at the courthouse. They introduced themselves and I had a little visit with them. The first time I saw him he was wearing a small cap, a large sheepskin coat, and a very long, fairly narrow scarf that trailed plumb to the floor, and then some kind of moccasins. He was dressed a little different than our Midwest news reporters. I'd speak to him in the hall there just as I would with the other news media, but as far as becoming fast friends or anything like that, it didn't develop then. At that time, the investigation was going full tilt and I really didn't have a lot of time to spend with them.

I'd never heard of Truman or Harper Lee before. We were literally besieged with news media. I asked to see his credentials. He didn't have any, which threw Truman for a loop. He'd never been asked for such a thing before. But he said that he did have his passport, which he brought to show me the next day.

MARIE DEWEY (*friend*) Alvin told Truman he could sit in with the rest of the reporters. He complained to Alvin, "But I'm not a reporter. What I'm going to write won't be published for years." But

Alvin said, "I'm sorry, that's the way it is." So Truman started to call him "Foxy," because Alvin would not cooperate.

ALVIN DEWEY He told me he came out here to do a story about the Clutters, just about the family, and that it really didn't matter to him whether the case was solved or not. I told him it sure in hell made a difference to me.

MARIE DEWEY He got off on the wrong foot there!

ALVIN DEWEY I think when Truman first came out here he thought of us all as a bunch of hicks.

MARIE DEWEY And some people probably still do.

HAROLD NYE (KBI agent) Al Dewey invited me to come up and meet this gentleman who'd come to town to write a book. So the four of us, KBI agents, went up to his room that evening after we had dinner. And here he is in kind of a new pink negligee, silk with lace, and he's strutting across the floor with his hands on his hips telling us all about how he's going to write this book. Nelle Harper Lee was there. She had the room next to Truman. Absolutely fantastic lady. I really liked her very much. But I did not get a very good impression of that little son of a bitch. We go up there and he's parading around in his negligee, it was not a good impression . . . and that impression never changed.

I got to say this much, that when he was in business, he was 100 percent getting information. But he kicked loose at the odd hours . . . Well, there is one thing I'll throw at you which will kind of give you why I feel the way I do. My wife is a very strict individual, always has been. She's straight as an arrow. Usually she went with me down to the Muelbach Hotel downtown where we had dinner, talked. Okay. One time when he came, Truman asked us if we wanted to go out and look at Kansas City, go out for the evening. Sure, you don't turn him down. First we get a cab, and just off the main street, about a block and a half off Thirty-fifth and Thirty-sixth, we go up there and there's a discussion where he pays a

hundred bucks to get us into a place above a gallery to watch what's
going on in a lesbian bar. Now here was what it was: they were
eating, tables, dancing, probably a hundred people in there, female
couples doing their thing. This was horrible to my wife. She tried to
turn away from it, but she didn't dare say anything to Truman. We
leave and he takes us over to a male gay bar, and we go in there. We
sit down at a little table and order a drink, and it isn't three minutes
until some of these young bucks nail him, talking to him, playing
with his ears, just right in front of my wife. But how the hell do you
say anything to a man as famous as Truman Capote that you don't
like what he's doing. This went on for a little bit and we finally tried
to excuse ourselves and leave. But Truman gets us to go on to the
Jewel Box, a little theater, and you know, I expect there must have
been thirty female impersonators in there . . . and they're damn
good. I mean they looked as good as any beautiful babes in New
York. But at the end of these little skits they revealed that they were
males. Now, to take this lady, my wife—and Truman knew what
kind of a lady she was because he had been to my house—and
subject her to this . . . well, his stock went down for us from sixty
percent to about ten.

ALVIN DEWEY But the more he stayed here, the more he became
more like us, as far as dress and actions were concerned. He got so
he looked comfortable walking down the street. He got rid of that
scarf blowing in the wind. He even bought a pair of boots eventually,
and a cowboy hat. He found out a thing or two that I was surprised
he found out. After we had developed Perry Smith and Dick
Hickock as suspects, we kept it pretty much of a secret, or we tried
to, and several days after that he came up to me saying to the effect
that he'd heard I had a pretty good suspect. I said, "No."

I never treated Truman any differently than I did any of the other
news media after the case was solved. He kept coming back and we
naturally got better acquainted. But as far as showing him any
favoritism or giving him any information, absolutely not. He went
out on his own and dug it up. Of course, he got much of it when he
bought the transcript of record, which was the whole court
proceedings, and if you had that, you had the whole story.

MARIE DEWEY I'm a great one to have people for dinner, so I invited Nelle and Truman. I love to cook Southern dishes, so I made red beans and rice and shrimp and things. Alvin refused to talk about the case. We just visited, that's all. Our friendship developed in that way, but the investigation wasn't talked about. We talked about the South, about people he had met here and elsewhere. Nelle returned with him two or three times. Neither one of them took any notes when they interviewed people, but then they would go back to their rooms and write down their memories of the day. Check one against the other.

HARRISON SMITH Tape recorders weren't too prominent in those days. As I look back on it, I'm just wondering how in the hell you can have a conversation like we're having now for an hour or better and then sit down and write it down. He told me the way he learned it when he was a kid: he'd get the New York telephone book and memorize a page. Then he'd have somebody ask, "On line so-and-so, what's the name there and what's the telephone number?" That seems a little far out but that's what he told me. I had no reason to say no.

ALVIN DEWEY He got information nobody else got, not even us. But to be right damn truthful about it, I didn't really care about all the travels of Perry Smith and Dick Hickock through Florida and whatnot, which takes up so much of *In Cold Blood*. We were interested in Mexico because there we were recovering some of the evidence that helped us in securing the convictions. As far as them going along picking up pop bottles, hell, I couldn't care less.

MARIE DEWEY He became very fond of Perry. He didn't like Hickock.

ALVIN DEWEY Hickock impressed you as an individual that wanted to be a big shot, wanted to throw his weight around. Smith was more, hell, I don't know how to say it, but he was just more the deadly type. He'd just as soon kill you as look at you.

Truman saw himself in Perry Smith, not in being deadly, of

course, but in their childhood. Their childhood was more or less the same; they were more or less the same height, the same build.

MARIE DEWEY Their mothers and fathers had separated. Truman said to us that it's strange: in life you follow a path, and all of a sudden you come to a fork in the road, and either you take the left or you take the right, and he said in this case he felt he took the right and Perry the left.

CHARLES McATEE (*former Kansas Director of Penal Institutions*) Warden Crouse knew that Truman was homosexual and he thought the last thing in the world that he needed was to put up with a known homosexual visiting two guys on death row. He has enough problems with homosexuality inside the prison.

Truman did not visit them more than a couple of times before their execution. The thing he wanted most was the right to correspond with them and he got that over our objections. He would call. When I was in the governor's office, he would call occasionally. Once I had a new secretary, and Truman called and in his high-pitched voice asked, "Is Mr. McAtee there, please?"

My secretary said, "Yes, ma'am, may I tell him who's calling?"

"This is Truman Capote."

She came to me flabbergasted at her faux pas. She said, "Mr. Capote is on the phone for you. I thought it was a woman." I said, "Don't worry about it, I'm sure it didn't bother Truman."

HARRISON SMITH I don't think Truman had to work real hard to win Perry's and Dick's confidence. You can imagine you're sitting in a li'l ol' cell and can barely see daylight coming in a little window; you got to stand up to see out. And here they get all the magazines, cigarettes, and candy they could use. I would have good feelings toward somebody sending me stuff like that.

CHARLES McATEE I'll tell you one thing going to prison does for most people. If they can write when they go there, it improves their penmanship. They really become quite skilled.

JOE FOX (*editor*) He adored Perry. Perry was a sort of doppelgänger, of course.

CHARLES McATEE Perry was, in his own way, sort of a darkly handsome young man. Short, stocky. Hickock, because of a car accident had, as Truman said, this face that was a bit askew. One eye went off in a misdirection.

ALVIN DEWEY Truman and I had one point we didn't agree on, and that was whether Perry had committed all four murders. Truman felt he had, but I felt Perry committed two and Hickock committed two. After the two defendants were returned to Garden City that night, my partner and I took a detailed statement from Perry Smith before a court reporter. He admitted that he had killed two, Mr. Clutter and his son Kenyon, and then he handed the shotgun to Hickock and said, "I've done all I can do, you take care of the other two." Then, while the statement was being typed up, he sent word to me that he wanted to change the statement. I said, "Well, why do you want to do that?" He said, "Well, I was talking to Hickock and he doesn't want to die with his mother thinking he committed two of those murders. I have no folks, they don't care about me or anything, so why don't we just make it that way." I felt that his first statement, the one that he made under oath, was the correct statement. Truman felt Smith really did kill all four. Smith was more of the killer type. He didn't think Hickock had the intestinal fortitude to do it.

HARRISON SMITH Truman was too smart an individual to say, "I'm going to get you off of this thing." What he could do was give them encouragement, and say maybe the higher courts would overturn the verdict. What he was actually doing was draining their brains: what they did from the time they'd committed the murders, during their flight, and when they got caught. You could have had the best defense attorney in the world defending either one of those guys and it wouldn't have changed anything. What could they do? The only thing that we could have done was to see that they had a fair trial.

They'd confessed. How are you going to beat that down. They weren't crazy. They knew what they were doing.

I don't recall that Truman and I ever had any discussion as to the merits—pro and con—of capital punishment. You could argue till doomsday and you'd never get anyplace. I think that as time went on Truman had a real sympathy for those two guys and he hated to see them done in. As far as the book was concerned, it didn't make any difference if they were going to be hanged or given life sentences. He just needed to know what the final act was going to be. At least that's what he always said.

HAROLD NYE I got into trouble with Truman because he had sent me a couple of galleys from his book about my trip to Las Vegas when I went out to get evidence on the killers, and what he had in the galleys was incorrect. It was a fiction thing, and being a young officer, I took offense at the fact that he didn't tell the truth. So I refused to approve them. Truman and I got into a little bit of a verbal battle and he wound up calling me a tyrant—I was invited to the black-and-white ball until that moment. What he did was to take this lady who ran the little apartment house in Las Vegas where Perry Smith had been, and fictionalize her way out of character. Accuracy was not his point. I took offense that he was changing the facts. He wasn't writing about our investigation. He was writing about these two dudes who traveled around the country, who went out and killed four people on a false lead. What I did in Las Vegas, the people I talked to out there, it just was not written truthfully. It was probably an insignificant thing, except I was under the impression that the book was going to be factual, and it was not; it was a fiction book.

JOHN KNOWLES The theme in all of his books is that there are special, strange gifted people in the world and they have to be treated with understanding. That was the theme of Other Voices, Other Rooms, the theme of The Grass Harp. That was the theme of Breakfast at Tiffany's and even, you might say, of In Cold Blood. These two men committed a monstrous crime, but if you understand their terrible childhood, and so on . . .

The execution of the two murderers in Kansas was a terribly traumatic experience for him. But I don't think there was any one turning point in his life, no moment when Truman's life turned around. If there was, it was the success of *In Cold Blood*. It was such an overwhelming success in every way, critically, financially. I think he lost a grip on himself after that. He had been tremendously disciplined up to that time. One of the most disciplined writers I've ever met. But he couldn't sustain it after that. A lot of his motivation was lost. That's when he began to unravel.

PIEDY LUMET We were going to Eugene, Oregon, or wherever the prison is up there. We stopped to look at the redwood trees. The highway there is quite high above the ocean, seven hundred feet or so, but there's a path that leads down into a state park. Truman stayed in the car and I started walking toward the ocean through the redwoods. This was a year after Perry and Dick had been executed. I heard this piercing call of alarm from Truman: "Come back! Come back! Perry and Dick are down there!" It wasn't a joke. A terrible, poignant intensity. He just got frightened. It didn't make any sense and I never made any reference to it.

April 14, 1965

Richard Hickock (left), tall, well built, fair, had a reasonably stable homelife, which would not have suggested a life of crime. Bouncing checks was his specialty. It landed him in the Kansas State Penitentiary, where he heard from a fellow inmate, Floyd Wells, that a wealthy farmer, Herbert Clutter, in western Kansas, for whom Wells had worked always kept $10,000 in a safe. Hickock pressed him for details, which included a map of the Clutter home. It was Hickock who finally broke under questioning and confessed. Perry Smith (right) was about five feet five, a stocky 160 pounds, with raven-black hair, a swarthy complexion, and a number of tattoos. He had a rough childhood—sisters who committed suicide, a mother who abandoned him, and a father who was always on the move. Smith spent four years in the army, including service in Korea, where he won a Bronze Star with Cluster. After his military discharge, two motorcycle accidents put him in and out of hospitals and on crutches for the better part of two years. Theft convictions landed him in the Kansas State Penitentiary, where Richard Hickock was his cellmate. *(UPI/Corbis-Bettmann)*

CHARLES McATEE There was a light rain. It was a very dark night—just the kind of night a movie director would pick for the setting. A dog was howling in the distance. Dick and Perry were taken by car from the deputy warden's office out through the gate and along the south wall of the penitentiary through these big, double overhead garage doors into the warehouse. The gallows were just inside the door in the southeast corner. Always were there. Of course, when capital punishment was abolished, they were dismantled and given to the Kansas Historical Society, which has them in storage.

Truman said he could not finish the book unless he witnessed the execution; he had to personally feel it, okay? A state statute limits the number of witnesses at an execution, and pretty much identified who they would be: the deputy warden, the clergyman in attendance upon the condemned, the executioner and his assistants, three witnesses designated by the condemned, and others, not more than six, picked by the warden. It limits the number of news media. One of the biggest problems we had was how we were going to divvy up the limited number of news media—the *New York Times* and all of them, all over the country. Every major newspaper in the state and the Midwest wanted to attend. Oh, you ought to see some of those letters. We got a letter from a neurosurgeon who specialized in cervical and spinal cord injuries and who was studying the biomechanics of executions by hanging worldwide. He wanted to attend. Then you had the kooks, the weirdos, the crazies, the nuts that crawl out of the woodwork, who write these, oh, just disgusting, despicable letters, volunteering to come and pull the trapdoor. "Let me do it! I'll be glad to pull the lever to drop them through the gallows floor."

Truman was not eligible under our statutes to attend. But the condemned can select three witnesses. Both Hickock and Smith wanted Truman as one of their witnesses. They also wanted Nelle Harper Lee. I sent a telegram to Truman that said, "H. and S. request Nelle as a witness, please advise." Truman came, of course, and Harper Lee did not. Those two guys wanted to spend the last evening, their last hours until they hanged, with Truman. I think Truman intended that. He told me that he'd be arriving at the Muelenbach Hotel. The Muelenbach used to be *the* hotel in downtown Kansas City. So he said in his telegram: "Arriving at the Muelenbach, such and such a day; assume you will know why." Well, he got to Kansas City, at the Muelenbach. He came fully intending to rent a car and drive out to the institution to spend the afternoon and that final evening with them. He called me about two o'clock or so from the Muelenbach and said, "Chuck, I just can't do it." I said, "What do you mean?"

"I just can't . . . just can't . . . I'm so emotionally distraught and just so strung out, I just can't do it."

I said, "Well, does that mean you're not going to attend the execution?"

"Oh, I'll be at the execution. I have to be there. I'll just have to bring myself to do it. I'll be there but I just can't . . . I can't go see them beforehand. I can't talk to them."

JOE FOX Truman wanted me along. He wanted company. I was going to be the editor of his book. Perry and Dick's demise had held him up. He couldn't publish the book until there was a definite conclusion—either of the two of the sentences: life imprisonment or hanging. He really needed help to get through the hanging. We went to the Muelenbach Hotel, where we had a suite. Immediately we were inundated with phone calls from the prison, from Perry and Dick.

They were always seeking his help in getting another stay of execution. Truman had given them as much help as he could. He had suggested various lawyers and so on. Finally he had no more inventive ideas and he couldn't bear to talk to Perry and Dick on that subject. My job was to field the telephone calls, including theirs. I never spoke to them directly. It was always the assistant warden at the prison who got on the line: "I have Perry and Dick in my office. They want to talk to Truman."

Truman said, "I just can't do it." He was in tears a lot of the time. He never slept. He never left the room. I slept on the bed and he slept on the couch.

CHARLES McATEE Frankly, I had no plans to go over to the penitentiary until about nine o'clock that evening. About four-thirty, the phone rang. It was a minister from Kansas City, Kansas, who said that he was the minister for Dick Hickock's former wife. Hickock had written to his wife several years earlier (she'd divorced him and remarried) and told her that he wanted to leave his share of the royalties of Truman Capote's book in a trust fund for their children's education. She had written him back a very caustic and acerbic letter and told him, in effect, to "go to hell, no way." She didn't want anything for her or for her children to remember him by. Her husband had adopted their children, and they had the adopted name. She wouldn't even tell Hickock what her married name was.

Well, she had come to the minister, these years later, quite distraught, and hadn't changed her mind, didn't want anything, but the thought of Dick being executed without her being able to apologize for her letter and to say goodbye tormented her, and she wanted to know if she could go up to see him before he hanged. I told her minister this; I said, "You know, there's not a ghost of a chance. She's his ex-wife. She's not been on his 'Mailing and Visiting' list. Security's going to be very, very tight up there tonight. We've got all kinds of kooks coming, and I just don't think it's going to happen. But," I said, "if it's at all possible, it will happen earlier rather than later. It's now four-thirty. You're only twenty-five miles away from the institution. I'll be over there by around six o'clock this evening. If there's a chance of her seeing him, it's going to happen at six o'clock and not at ten." He said, "That's fine." I asked, "Just you and the former Mrs. Hickock?" He said, "That's correct."

When I got to the warden's office that evening, Warden Crouse told me that Hickock's former wife and her minister were waiting. He said, "They told me you said that she could see Dick Hickock. Listen, we've got those guys down off death row behind the deputy warden's office. Everybody's antsy and uptight, and we've got all kinds of security problems." So I said, "Now, Warden, let me talk to them first and let's see what we can do."

Mrs. Hickock was a very nice, neat, well-groomed, well-mannered, well-spoken lady—the last person in the world you'd think would be his wife. As I recall, she was a minister's daughter. They'd been going together since he was sixteen. Hickock said that her daddy never did like him, said he was a full-time nobody. Anyway, over the warden's objection, I called up Chaplain Post, the

Protestant chaplain at KSP, and asked him to come to the warden's office. He's a super guy—a solid influence at the penitentiary. When he arrived, I said we ought to find out if Hickock wanted to see his ex-wife. I asked Chaplain Post to go back and ask him, and Hickock said he most certainly did. Hickock and Smith were in separate rooms in a holding area behind the deputy warden's office getting ready to have their final meal. She and Hickock didn't touch. They didn't embrace. The guards were standing around. He was seated in a chair over at a table. It seems to me he had already had some royal shrimp. That was part of his request for his last meal, royal shrimp and strawberry pop. My gosh! How long has it been since you drank a strawberry pop? It's certainly not something I'd want as my last meal.

Hickock did have leg chains on but because he was eating those shrimp and so on, he was not handcuffed. Anyway, she said, "I just want to tell you that the children are fine. About your letter, and your offer a few years ago, I just want you to know that I haven't changed my mind. I really don't want anything from you, nor do the children." She just told him she thought it was a nice gesture. And she wanted him to know she couldn't stand the thought of not being able to say goodbye without having told him that. With that said, and a few more things I don't recall, she and her minister left. They weren't in there five minutes, Hickock turned to me and he said, "You know, Mr. McAtee, I should have had my neck broke over there in that corner"—it was known as "the corner" in the institution—"a long time ago . . . long before we ever pulled that caper out in western Kansas, for what I did to that woman and those kids."

Afterward I sat and talked with Hickock and Smith, although I didn't intend to. They wanted to share their last hours with Truman. I really think they had things in their hearts that they wanted to tell him. When he didn't show up, I believe in retrospect that, unintentionally or not, I was Truman's surrogate that night. Hickock was reminiscing about his childhood and his youth—good times—and Don, a childhood friend of his, a lawyer in Topeka, I happen to know. They went all the way through grade school and high school together—played football, hunted and fished together. Every time I'd see Hickock he'd say, "Gee, be sure to tell Don hello from me."

He focused on Don. That evening he said, "We were in fifth grade. We had played hooky so many times, we were suspended from school for three days. We could not come back to school until we had a note from our parents saying that they had discussed this with us, and got us to promise we were not going to play hooky anymore. If we played hooky one more time, we were going to be expelled for the rest of the year. We hadn't been back in school a week. It was a beautiful spring day, and the sun was shining, the teacher was up at the blackboard, with her back to the class. I looked at Don and nodded. Out the window we went. We beat it down to the local drugstore, back at the pinball machine. I'll bet we hadn't been there five minutes when the phone rang. The pharmacist went to the phone and said, 'Yes, ma'am, they're both here' . . . 'Yes'm, I'll tell them.' He came back to the pinball machine. He said, 'Boys, that was your teacher, and she says that she needs a bottle of black ink and she needs it right now.' Boy, we grabbed that bottle of ink, and we hiked it back up to school, just like we'd been on an errand."

That's a nice story and that's exactly what the kid told me that night. He said, "You know, Don had a Packard that they had painted purple . . . tremendous pickup power. You oughta seen the girls it could pick up. We called it 'the Passionate Purple Packard.' Boy, it was some car. You could get that up to sixty miles an hour out on those country roads, and that old purple paint just started peeling off the doors."

He was just tripping the light fantastic. He would laugh as he told the story. He was trying to ignore the inevitable that was about to befall him.

Perry Smith, on the other hand, was very deep in the meaning of life and death. Chaplain Post had given him a little thin book—Thoreau's *On Man and Nature*. Perry had highlighted it, and underscored it . . . highlighted it in green and yellow, and put dots and circles next to the quotations that meant so much to him. He knew that book backwards and forwards. He had the book that night and read passages from it. "No human being past the thoughtless age of boyhood will wantonly murder any creature that holds its life by the same tenure as he does." Then: "Not until we have lost the will do we understand the true meaning of life." He was just deep in philosophical thought about what was about to happen to him. At about a quarter to twelve they had already shackled both of them up—these leather clamps that come over the back and the arms, and buckled in back, and Perry Smith looked up and said, "I got to go to the bathroom."

I said, "Oh, come on, Perry." He repeated that he "had to go to the bathroom."

We had a deputy warden there, a guy that I never did like much. He heard Perry tell me that he had to go to the bathroom. He was standing on the other side of him. He looked at me, and said, "No way." Perry said, "Mr. McAtee, don't make me go over there and shit in my pants."

I said, "Unbuckle him."

If looks could kill, that deputy warden would've killed me. They unbuckled him. They unlocked one of the handcuffs—the right one—so he could use his right hand. They left the leg chains on and took him into a latrine just off the deputy warden's office. An officer went in with him, of course. There's always that fear that they're gonna beat the hangman's noose by committing suicide, doing themselves in, and that cheats us somehow, of our justice, for crying out loud! Well, he went in and just exploded. I mean, you talk about flatulence. I looked at the deputy, and I said, "I really think he had to go."

JOE FOX About 9 P.M. on April 13 we drove out to the prison. Truman had changed his mind about seeing them. My memory was that we all piled into one big car. Alvin Dewey says it was two cars. With us were three other Kansas Bureau of Investigation agents who had solved the case. It was raining very hard; we had to drive very slowly. When we reached the prison, Truman and the KBI agents went to visit Perry and Dick while I stayed behind in the waiting room. Suddenly, after about twenty minutes, a side door opened and Truman beckoned urgently to me. When I entered the adjoining room he introduced me to Perry and Dick, who were waiting in handcuffs only a few feet away. It seemed to me wildly inappropriate to meet these two men for the first time only a few hours before their deaths. The warden must have thought so too. He descended on me within seconds after we'd been introduced and told me peremptorily to leave. "Get that man *out* of here!" I'll never forget that warden. He was six feet seven, weighed a hundred and twenty pounds. They said he was dying of cancer. He would have retired earlier, but he felt he had to see the case through. He was in a rage. I couldn't think of a single thing to say to either party. I think I was about to say, "Well, what did you have for dinner?" Or something. "Very nice to meet you," I think I said. "I've heard so much about you." It was just awful.

Within minutes they went to the warehouse where they were to be hanged, it was interminable. It was about an hour's interval between Dick's hanging and Perry's. They were hanged in this big warehouse where the scaffolding had been set up, outside the prison walls. It was about 2 A.M. before Truman came out.

CHARLES McATEE Warden Crouse thought these guys went to the gallows showing absolutely no remorse, no regrets, and that they were still animals, and I didn't agree with that. Those two people we executed were not the same people who committed the crime. That's not to be maudlin about it. That's not to say they were entitled to a reprieve or executive clemency. I still believe in capital punishment. I'm just saying that these two people had learned an awful lot about themselves in the five years they spent on death row. And Perry especially. He looked at me, and said, "Mr. McAtee, I'd like to apologize. But to whom? To you? To them? To their relatives? To their friends? . . . And undo what we did with an *apology*?" Then he handed me a poem. I gave a copy to Truman. It's really, in its own way, quite good. It starts off, "Oh would that I might raise my eyes above these walls of grey / To cast my hopes to freedom's skies / And go on my merry way."

We let them say goodbye to one another before we took Hickock over and hanged him. A very simple exchange. Hickock said, "See you 'round." Hickock emphasized that night that what they did was wrong, but he was not personally responsible for killing any of those people. I believe Perry killed them all. I really do. Mostly a feeling, and mostly just putting it all together. I think those two personalities, Herb Clutter and Perry, sort of fed off one another. Perry saw in Herb Clutter everything that he'd ever wanted in a father and didn't have—a home, stability, a family. I think he loved him and hated him. I believe Perry, in effect, killed his father. Perry's quote in *In Cold Blood* is: "I liked the man; I really did. I liked him right up to the minute I cut his throat."

I first saw Truman in the warehouse. I do not recall talking to him that night at all. I do know one thing. Bennett Cerf repeatedly told the story that Truman became nauseous and ill and went behind some stacks of lumber or something and barfed. I don't recall that at all. Although I saw him, I don't believe we shook hands or even spoke that night. But I was aware of his presence. I had the responsibility to assure that only those authorized by statute were present. I was constantly with the warden and the doctor and the KBI agents who were there. I remember Senator Ed Reilly was there—the state senator from the Leavenworth area. Senator Jack Barr, from Leoti, out in western Kansas, who ended up being in the movie *In Cold Blood,* sat at the defense counsel table out there. I would say there was a total of about twenty people in the warehouse.

The warden and the doctor and I had arrived in a car, just ahead of Hickock. There isn't a director in the world that could have staged that execution. I mean, sometimes fact is fiction, fiction is fact, truth is stranger than fiction. A light drizzle started that night, around ten-thirty. They took these two in a car across the ballpark to the southeast corner. That's the first thing that I consciously remember—the rain, not a heavy rain, but just a patter of rain on the roof. It seemed terribly cold. We're talking April. Then a dog began a mournful wail off in the distance. I'm serious. It was eerie. I'll never forget it.

In total, there were about twenty people there. No chairs. Everyone was standing. Not anything like they're doing it today with the electric chair or with lethal injections—a visitor's gallery and seated witnesses. This really was a warehouse where building materials were stored. It didn't even have a concrete floor, as I recall, just a dirt floor. Really sort of dimly lighted. When he did the film *In Cold Blood,* Richard Brooks wanted to film there in the penitentiary and to use the gallows. We didn't want them filming in the penitentiary; it would cause too many problems and too much turmoil. So when he couldn't film there, Brooks wanted to dismantle the gallows and send them out to Hollywood, saying he'd pay for it. We didn't do that, but we did—and in reflection I don't know why— sell him the latrine facilities that were in Hickock and Smith's cells during their five years plus on death row. He bought them, paid for them, and we crated them up and we shipped them off to Hollywood. For the life of me I don't recall ever seeing those in the film. They must have ended up on the cutting-room floor. I think they were $150 a piece or something like that. I know we got the check from Columbia Pictures.

The two men were brought in separately, their first car ride in some five years. It was all strictly business. Each was taken out the back seat. The car did not leave the warehouse. It just stopped there in front of this group of people and then pulled on down further in the warehouse and sat there. Hickock was first. I don't recall how that was decided. It seems there was a coin toss, or maybe it was just alphabetical. Warden Crouse read the death warrant directing that on April the 14th after 12 A.M. they were to be hanged by the neck until dead. Of course, they weren't hooded at the time. The warden asked if they had any last words.

ALVIN DEWEY Hickock said something to the effect that he was "going to a better place." He hoped people would forgive him. They walked him up the thirteen steps, put a hood over his face, and then a noose around his neck. He stood on a little platform released by a lever. The chaplain read the Lord's Prayer, and as he's reading the Lord's Prayer, the hangman pulls the lever and . . . You know, I always thought that a person's neck really stretched when they hang 'em, but they don't because when they hit the end of the rope, it just breaks their neck, and for all practical purposes they're dead.

There was a big pile of lumber there in the warehouse. Truman and I and several others were kind of leaning against that pile. Standing room only. I've seen a lot of people die in my time, but never a *planned* dying. I didn't know exactly how I'd feel about it. So

I thought, well, might just as well lean up against this stack of lumber here, give me a little support.

They just hang there until the doctor pronounces them dead. And then the rope's cut, and they are put in an ambulance and hauled away. And then Smith was brought in and the same thing happened there.

JAMES POST (*prison chaplain*) We went up the steps together, Perry and me following two steps behind. He was chewing gum. I had given him half a stick of Juicy Fruit in the preparation room just a short time before. It's interesting what people will do with only a short time left. Lowell Lee Andrews smoked a half-dozen cigars. He weighed about three hundred pounds. He'd had an enormous meal, two fried chickens, and then he'd asked for these cigars. He was eighteen when he killed his family down there in Wolcott and he'd never smoked one before. He thought he'd find out before he went. Perry chewed gum, never seemed to be without something moving in his mouth. Up on the gallows he stopped chewing and looked around sort of guilty . . . like a boy in church who realizes he shouldn't be chewing gum . . . and he caught my eye, like I was his father sitting next to him, and I stepped over to where he could spit the gum out onto my palm. I still have the other half of that Juicy Fruit package and I've shown it to at least several hundred school kids when I've gone around to high schools lecturing on the *In Cold Blood* case. As for what I had in my hand, I guess I threw it away. Maybe I shouldn't have. It's amazing how valuable things like that get to be.

ALVIN DEWEY People didn't have a hell of a lot to say. Truman was just standing there, looking and listening. He did say in *In Cold Blood* that I closed my eyes, which was not true. I didn't. I'd seen this thing from the start and I would see it to the finish. After seeing the way that little Clutter girl looked, I could have pulled the lever myself.

CHARLES McATEE The one person I do remember that night is the executioner. I'll never forget him. I had a call from a reporter just about six months ago wanting to know if I could give him the name of that executioner. Wanted to get in touch with him and interview him. I told him I didn't know and I didn't think anyone in the state of Kansas other than Warden Sherman Crouse would know. That's the only instance I know of where you don't cut a voucher and get a check. You do not cut a check in the state of Kansas to John Doe, executioner. The executioner is paid in cash so there's no trail to him.

Anyway, the executioner! He wore a black hat with the brim pulled down all the way around. And his collar pulled up around his neck. He had about a four days' growth of beard, and then those eyes—those black eyes! I told Richard Brooks that he could never, ever find anybody to look more like an executioner than that man.

JACK BARR (*state senator*) I never got this officially, but they go to the street and find someone and offer him a hundred dollars in cash to pull the lever. This character had a zoot suit with pants that didn't match the jacket.

CHARLES McATEE He stood up on top of the platform, he and Chaplain Post, just the two of them. There are always thirteen steps and that includes the last one up, the thirteenth step. The steps were very narrow. The guards helped Hickock and Smith up the steps and helped place the black hood over their head, full and long, which came down over their shoulders, far enough so that when the rope went over their head, it went over the hood too and the neck. The knot has to be positioned just precisely behind the ear and right there on the base of the skull bone.

HAROLD NYE When Smith came in, he was the second to go, Truman fell apart. He ran out of the building, out the west door. He stayed and watched Hickock executed, but when they brought Smith in Truman ran out of the building, would not witness it. There was a reason. They had become lovers in the penitentiary. I can't prove it, but they spent a lot of time up there in the cell, he spent a considerable amount of money bribing the guard to go around the corner, and they were both homosexuals and that was what happened. I wasn't there, so . . .

TONY JEWELL *(reporter)* I didn't talk to Capote during this particular time. I was standing close to him. I can remember all the details of the hanging, but nothing to do with Capote except that I was standing close to him. I didn't close my eyes. I would guess that's probably correct, because it's something that you don't want to see but something that you have to see.

JAMES POST When they get upstairs, the chaplain has a chance to read a little Scripture. I usually read the Twenty-third Psalm. When I get through, I stand back, and then the hangman pushes the lever like on a wagon train, about a four-foot handle. The two-foot square trap flops open . . . gravity takes hold and does a pretty good job. They go straight down and they dangle around and twitch.

CHARLES McATEE When they drop they're in full view. There's a strong spring on the trapdoor and there's a loud clang when it snaps open. The body drops straight down. They're trussed up, straight as a board, almost as if you put a two-by-six right up their back. They go up the steps in chains. Sufficient slack to mount the steps, you know? Then those leg irons are taken off and the ankles are strapped together. They are wearing a harness, a leather harness, really just a straitjacket. Their hands are strapped straight down to their sides, against their thighs. The harness keeps their spinal column straight and rigid. Shoulders rigid. The body doesn't swing. It does bounce a bit. Comes straight down and . . . that's it. The head is off over to one side. The neck is broken. I still believe that hanging is one of the most humane methods of execution if it's done properly. The strength of the rope and its length has to be determined and compared to the weight of the individual. We had a captain of the guard there who had been involved in the executions of Nazi war criminals at Nuremburg. He had done the mathematical calculations. So we had a man doing that work for us who did it very well. We had a doctor at the penitentiary—great old guy—but who just absolutely did not believe in capital punishment. We kept getting bad press because the newspaper stories would read: "The trapdoor was sprung at 1:19 A.M. and at 1:41 the doctor pronounced him dead." Well, that conjures up a terrible vision of some poor fellow struggling at the end of a rope for twenty minutes, you know, but that's just not the way it was. They're dead when they hit the end of the rope. The neck, the spinal column is broken, you know, but you'd get muscle reflexes. You know, you cut a chicken's neck off, and it hops around the yard for about five or ten minutes, but it's not alive. It's still on the farm, but it's not alive. Well, the doctor'd go up and open their shirt and listen with his stethoscope. As long as he could hear a muscle spasm or a gurgle, or any kind of residual sound in that stethoscope, he would not pronounce them dead, and he didn't. He did that to me four times. I talked to him about it after Hickock and Smith. I said, "This is bad press, you know."

"As long as I can hear 'em."

So we waited. It seemed like an eternity. I do remember that the executioner did not stay up there between the executions. He came down and disappeared somewhere back in the shadows of the warehouse.

I don't remember anybody saying anything until it was time to bring the ambulance, and then there was just a hushed, whispered conversation when they were taken down. My recollection is that we had two separate ropes. That's another interesting thing. Wonder what happened to them. If we sold 'em, we would have sold 'em to Richard Brooks. I have a feeling that their shelves back in the penitentiary were probably cleaned out that night and that stuff was destroyed.

TONY JEWELL It was not the greatest thing in the world, being there. We filed out very, very quietly. I did a little writing, took a few notes, and did my broadcast on KIUL radio in Garden City. Then I went back to the hotel, where we talked over what had happened since that Sunday morning six years before, and then I went to bed.

JOE FOX I sat next to Truman on the plane ride back to New York. He held my hand and cried most of the way. I remember thinking

how odd it must have seemed to passengers sitting nearby—these
two grown men apparently holding hands and one of them sobbing.
It was a long trip. I couldn't read a copy of *Newsweek* or anything
like that . . . not with Truman holding my hand. I stared straight
ahead.

Interlude

CHAPTER TWENTY *In Which*

Chaplain Post Describes a Portrait in His

Living Room

Perry Smith's charcoal drawing, sketched in
Kansas State Penitentiary during his first
incarceration there. *(Courtesy of Chaplain James E. E. Post)*

JAMES POST I buried them both on Prisoners' Row.
The Row originally was within the prison walls
themselves and visitors, if there were any, had to
walk by the hog pens of the prison farm to see it.
Now the Row is in the local cemetery about four
miles from the federal prison at Leavenworth, and a
row is exactly what it is—about a hundred yards

long, unmarked except for maybe a few crosses. But for Perry and Dick there were two headstones . . . which I believe were paid for by Truman himself. No one came to the burial itself. It's very rare anybody does. Warden Crouse came that time, I recall. Usually, the sexton and I are the only ones and we wait a bit, sitting in the car, for someone to come. Then I walk up and I say a few prayers. We turn away. It's very sad. The casket is on the lowering platform and the gravediggers, off to one side, watch us leave.

I met Perry Smith and Dick Hickock when they came into Kansas State Prison to serve their first sentences. Perry Smith had broken into an automobile store, burglary job, and he got a minor sentence for that, his first offense. The only trouble the other character, Richard Hickock, had was writing checks. I got to know Perry Smith much better than Hickock. He was a cell mate to my main office clerk, John MacRill. I knew Perry as a quiet-mannered, talented fellow who was a fine painter. When he got out and headed with Hickock for this horrible thing out in Holcomb, he gave me two paintings he had done. One was about a three-by-four painting of a frustrated fisherman hightailing it for the shore because the storm is coming. The psychiatrist said that it's probably just a self-portrait . . . a loner, you know, on rough times. But then he gave me this picture of Christ—a charcoal drawing actually. I was amazed at the subject matter. I said, "Well, Perry, I can't thank you enough for giving me these beautiful paintings . . . and especially this one. But you weren't a Christian. You didn't come to church. How come you painted a picture of Christ for me?" He said, "Well, I just thought that you would enjoy the subject matter."

I have it hanging in my living room. I brought it up to our church and I said I'd be happy to let them hang it in the front of the chapel. One of the pastors looked at it, amazed by its beauty, but when I told him where it came from, he said, "You mean Perry Smith, the killer of the Clutters? I'm not going to let something hang in the front of my church that was painted by a murderer." I said, "Well, your timing is wrong. He was not a murderer when he painted that picture." So I gave it to another pastor, and it hung for twenty years in his church. When they sold the church, I brought the painting home, where it will not be separated from me again.

When I heard the news of the Clutter murders, I was more than stunned. I just couldn't believe it. I was subpoenaed out there, as a character witness. I took along a photograph of the picture. I was asked what I knew about them and I said, of course, that I knew Perry better than I did Hickock. I said, "I brought this picture along to show you his gift as an artist. If he could have had a chance to do something about that . . ." And the prosecution lawyer stopped me immediately and said, "We're not here to talk about his art abilities; we're here to punish him for being involved in the worst crime that ever hit Kansas." So my testimony lasted about five minutes. I was there for the whole trial, of course. And then I welcomed them back to prison and I spent time with them on Death Row. It's very restrictive and I would go in there whenever I wanted to.

I was on the gallows with them because that's the position of a chaplain in the case of a hanging. I'd been to others before. I had met them down at the bottom of the gallows with the warden, who reads them the entire prison sentence, which is pretty ridiculous because everyone knows what it is. The dying takes usually about fifteen or twenty minutes. The only one with any official duties is the state doctor, and he comes over and rips their shirt collar open and puts his stethoscope on the chest to check how long the heart's gonna keep on beating. He makes his report about every five minutes: "Not dead yet!"

The waiting ends finally when he says "I officially pronounce him dead" at whatever time it is. The only one with something to do officially is the undertaker in town, and he pulls his hearse in alongside the gallows, reaches up with a very sharp knife, and cuts the rope. The next day I have the job of burying them in Prisoners' Row.

An interesting thing happened. A few years later I got a call from Dick Hickock's wife in a little town down south of Kansas City about fifteen miles. She said that her son was reading *In Cold Blood* as so many high school kids were required to do—a masterpiece of literature—and he had got to putting two and two together. Although his mother had remarried when he was a baby and he had been given his stepfather's name, all of a sudden it came to him with a great shock that Dick Hickock was his father. He threw the book to the floor and ran out to the high school counselor's office and collapsed there. I got a telephone call in about fifteen minutes from his mother, whom I had met, of course, when she came to visit Dick. She said, "I hate to impose upon you, but I'm afraid we've got a problem. Rick has finally found out who his father really was. We're afraid of what he's going to do to himself." She said, "I'm in the counselor's office right now." So I said, "I'll be glad to do whatever you want." She said, "Would you please come out and talk to him, and tell him what you know about his father?"

So I said I'd be glad to do whatever I could, so I drove there to tell him about how I knew his dad. I didn't minimize the horrible thing that he'd done or anything like that. But I said his dad wasn't the sex fiend that Capote tried to make him out . . . like trying to rape the Clutter girl before he killed her . . . it didn't happen. And other things . . . lies, just to make it a better story. The boy was really impressed by my concern in telling him the truth about his dad. He said, "Well, would you do me one more favor, please? Would you take me up and show me my dad's grave?"

So we drove straight up from their home to the Leavenworth Cemetery. I took him down to Prisoners' Row there. The two graves were together. As I came over the hill, I noticed something really strange. The headstones were *missing*. Somebody had stolen the headstones from the graves. I don't know whether they were ever replaced or not. I called the sexton of the cemetery—he was a friend of mine, of course—and I said, "Did you know that you have two very famous headstones missing?" He came down there in a hurry.

The boy was about seventeen then. A senior in high school. He really was a very well-adjusted kid, as it turned out. He called me here a little while ago, just after a remake of the Clutter murder had appeared on television. He remembered me. He was calling to say that he was okay—he must be in his mid-twenties now—and that he wanted to remind me how much he appreciated my interest in him. So that was good news, wasn't it? They were a good family, they really were. Nothing wrong with the family, especially his blessed Christian mother. It broke her heart, of course.

January 16, 1966

CHAPTER TWENTY-ONE   *In Which*

TC Discusses, in a New York Times

Interview, In Cold Blood *and the Form*

He Claims to Have Invented—the

Nonfiction Novel

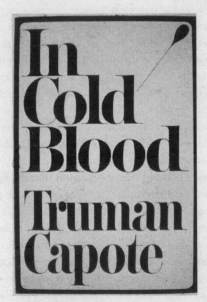

(S. Neil Fujita)

Why did you select the particular subject matter of murder; had you previously been interested in crime?

Not really, no. During the last years I've learned a good deal about crime, and the origins of the homicidal mentality. Still, it is a layman's knowledge and I don't pretend to anything deeper. The motivating factor in my choice of material—that is, choosing to write a true account of an actual murder case—was altogether literary. The decision was based on a theory I've harbored since I first began to write professionally, which is well over twenty years ago. It seemed to me that journalism, reportage, could be forced to yield a serious new art form: the "nonfiction novel," as I thought of it. Several admirable reporters—Rebecca West for one, Joseph Mitchell and Lillian Ross—have shown the possibilities of narrative reportage; and Miss Ross, in her brilliant *Picture,* achieved at least a nonfiction novella. Still, on the whole, journalism is the most underestimated, the least explored of literary mediums.

Why should that be so?

Because few first-class creative writers have ever bothered with journalism, except as a sideline, "hackwork," something to be done when the creative spirit is lacking, or as a means of making money quickly. Such writers say in effect: Why should we trouble with factual writing when we're able to invent our own stories, contrive our own characters and themes?—journalism is only literary photography, and unbecoming to the serious writer's artistic dignity.

Another deterrent—and not the smallest—is that the reporter, unlike the fantasist, has to deal with actual people who have real names. If they feel maligned or just contrary, or greedy, they enrich lawyers (though rarely themselves) by instigating libel actions. This last is certainly a factor to consider, a most oppressive and repressive one. Because it's indeed difficult to portray, in any meaningful depth, another being, his appearance, speech, mentality, without to some degree, and often for quite trifling cause, offending him. The truth seems to be that nobody likes to see himself described as he is, or cares to see exactly set down what he said and did. Well, even I can understand that—because I don't like it myself when I am the sitter and not the portraitist: the frailty of egos—and the more accurate the strokes, the greater the resentment.

When I first formed my theories concerning the nonfiction novel, many people with whom I discussed the matter were unsympathetic. They felt that what I proposed, a narrative form that employed all the techniques of fictional art, but was nevertheless immaculately factual, was little more than a literary solution for fatigued novelists suffering from "failure of the imagination." Personally, I felt that this attitude represented a "failure of the imagination" on their part.

Of course, a properly done piece of narrative reporting requires imagination!—and a good deal of special technical equipment that is usually beyond the resources—and I don't doubt the interests—of most fictional writers: an ability to transcribe verbatim long conversations, and to do so without taking notes or using tape recordings. Also, it is necessary to have a 20/20 eye for visual detail—in this sense, it is quite true that one must be a "literary photographer," though an exceedingly selective one. But above all, the reporter must be able to empathize with personalities outside his usual imaginative range, mentalities unlike his own, kinds of people he would never have written about had he not been forced to by encountering them inside the journalistic situation. This last is what first attracted me to the notion of journalistic reportage.

What is the first step in producing a "nonfiction novel"?
The difficulty was to choose a promising subject. If you intend to spend three or four or five years with a book, as I planned to do, then you want to be reasonably certain that the material will not soon "date." The content of much journalism so swiftly does, which is another of the medium's deterrents. A number of ideas occurred, but one after the other, and for one reason or another, each was eventually discarded, often after I'd done considerable preliminary work. Then one morning in November 1959, while flicking through the *New York Times*, I encountered on a deep inside page, this headline: "Wealthy Farmer, 3 of Family Slain."

The story was brief, just several paragraphs stating the facts: A Mr. Herbert W. Clutter, who had served on the Farm Credit Board during the Eisenhower administration, his wife and two teen-aged children, had been brutally, entirely mysteriously, murdered on a lonely wheat and cattle ranch in a remote part of Kansas. There was nothing really exceptional about it; one reads items concerning multiple murders many times in the course of a year.

Then why did you decide it was the subject you had been looking for?

I didn't. Not immediately. But after reading the story it suddenly struck me that a crime, the study of one such, might provide the broad scope I needed to write the kind of book I wanted to write. Moreover, the human heart being what it is, murder was a theme not likely to darken and yellow with time.

I thought about it all that November day, and part of the next; and then I said to myself: Well, why not this crime? The Clutter case. Why not pack up and go to Kansas and see what happens? Of course, it was a rather frightening thought!—to arrive alone in a small, strange town, a town in the grip of an unsolved mass murder. Still, the circumstances of the place being altogether unfamiliar, geographically and atmospherically, made it that much more tempting. Everything would seem freshly minted—the people, their accents and attitudes, the landscape, its contours, the weather. All this, it seemed to me, could only sharpen my eye and quicken my ear.

In the end, I did not go alone. I went with a lifelong friend, Harper Lee. She is a gifted woman, courageous and with a warmth that instantly kindles most people, however suspicious or dour. She had recently completed a first novel (*To Kill a Mockingbird*), and, feeling at loose ends, she said she would accompany me in the role of assistant researchist.

If I had realized then what the future held, I never would have stopped in Garden City. I would have driven straight on. Like a bat out of hell.

What was Harper Lee's contribution to your work?

She kept me company when I was based out there. I suppose she was with me about two months altogether. She went on a number of interviews; she typed her own notes, and I had these and could refer to them. She was extremely helpful in the beginning, when we weren't making much headway with the townspeople, by making friends with the wives of the people I wanted to meet. She became friendly with all the churchgoers. A Kansas paper said the other day that everybody was so wonderfully cooperative because I was a famous writer. The fact of the matter is that not one single person in the town had ever heard of me.

How long did it take the town to thaw out enough so that you were accepted and you could get to your interviewing?

About a month. I think they finally just realized that we were there to make the best of it. Under the circumstances, they were suspicious. After all, there was an unsolved murder case, and some of the people in the town were tired of the thing, and frightened. But then after it all quieted down—after Perry and Dick were arrested—that was when we did most of the original interviews. Some of them went on for three years—though not on the same subject of course. I suppose if I used just 20 percent of the material I put together over those years of interviewing, I'd still have a book two thousand pages long.

How much research did you do other than through interviews with the principals in the case?

Oh, a great deal. I did months of comparative research on murder, murderers, the criminal mentality, and I interviewed quite a number of murderers—solely to give me a perspective on those two boys. And then crime. I didn't know anything about crime or criminals when I began to do the book. I certainly do now! I'd say 80 percent of the research I did I have never used. But it gave me such a grounding that I never had any hesitation in my consideration of the subject.

What was the most singular interview you conducted?

I suppose the most startled interviewee was Mr. Bell, the meatpacking executive from Omaha. He was the man who picked up Perry and Dick when they were hitchhiking across Nebraska. They planned to murder him and then make off with his car. Quite unaware of this, Bell was saved, as you'll remember, just as Perry was going to smash in his head from the seat behind, because he slowed down to pick up another hitchhiker, a Negro. The boys told me this story, and they had this man's business card. I decided to interview him. I wrote him a letter, but got no answer. Then I wrote a letter to the personnel manager of the meatpacking plant in Omaha, asking if they had a Mr. Bell in their employ. I told them I wanted to talk to him about a pair of hitchhikers he'd picked up four months previously. The manager wrote back and said that they *did* have a Mr. Bell on their staff, but that it was surely the wrong Mr. Bell since it was against company policy for employees to take hitchhikers in their cars. So I telephoned Mr. Bell and when he got on the phone he was very brusque; he said I didn't know what I was talking about.

The only thing for me to do was to go to Omaha personally. I went up there and walked in on Mr. Bell and put two photographs down on his desk. I asked him if he recognized the two men. He said, "Why?" So I told him that the two were the hitchhikers he said he had never given a ride to, that they had planned to kill him and then bury him in the prairie—and how close they'd come to it. Well, he turned every conceivable color. You can imagine. He recognized them all right. He was quite cooperative about telling me about the trip, but he asked me not to use his real name. There are only three people in the book whose names I've changed—his, the convict Perry admired so much (Willie-Jay he's called in the book), and I also changed Perry Smith's sister's name.

How long after you went to Kansas did you sense the form of the book? Were there many false starts?

I worked for a year on the notes before I ever wrote one line. And when I wrote the first word, I had done the entire book in outline, down to the finest detail. Except for the last part, the final dispensation of the case—that was an evolving matter. It began, of course, with interviews—with all the different characters of the book. Let me give you two examples of how I worked from those interviews. In the first part of the book—the part that's called "The Last to See Them Alive"—there's a long narration, word for word, given by the schoolteacher who went with the sheriff to the Clutter house and found the four bodies. Well, I simply set that into the book as a straight, complete interview—though it was, in fact, done several times: each time there'd be some little thing which I would add or change. But I hardly interfered at all. A slight editing job. The schoolteacher tells the whole story himself—exactly what happened from the moment they got to the house and what they found there.

On the other hand, in that same first part, there's a scene between the postmistress and her mother when the mother reports that the ambulances had gone to the Clutter house. That's a straight dramatic scene—with quotes, dialogue, action, everything. But it evolved out of interviews just like the one with the schoolteacher. Except in this case I took what they had told me and transposed it into straight narrative terms. Of course, elsewhere in the book, very often it's direct observation, events I saw myself—the trial, the executions.

You never used a tape recorder?

Twelve years ago I began to train myself for the purpose of this sort of book, to transcribe conversation without using a tape recorder. I did it by having a friend read passages from a book, and then later I'd write them down to see how close I could come to the original. I had a natural facility for it, but after doing these exercises for a year and a half, for a couple of hours a day, I could get within 95 percent of absolute accuracy, which is as close as you need. I felt it was essential. Even note-taking artificializes the atmosphere of an interview, or a scene in progress; it interferes with the communication between author and subject—the latter is usually self-conscious, or an untrusting wariness is induced. Certainly a tape recorder does so. Not long ago a French literary critic turned up with a tape recorder. I don't like them, as I say, but I agreed to its use. In the middle of the interview it broke down. The French literary critic was desperately unhappy. He didn't know what to do. I said, "Well, let's just go on as if nothing had happened." He said, "It's not the same. I'm not accustomed to listening to what you're saying."

*You've kept yourself out of the book entirely. Why was that—
considering your own involvement in the case?*

My feeling is that for the nonfiction-novel form to be entirely
successful, the author should not appear in the work. Ideally. Once
the narrator does appear, he has to appear throughout, all the way
down the line, and the I-I-I intrudes when it really shouldn't. I think
the single most difficult thing in my book, technically, was to write it
without ever appearing myself, and yet, at the same time, create
total credibility.

*Being removed from the book—that is to say, keeping yourself out of
it—do you find it difficult to present your own point of view? For
example, your own view as to why Perry Smith committed the murders.*

Of course it's by selection of what you choose to tell. I believe
that Perry did what he did for the reasons he himself states—that
his life was a constant accumulation of disillusionments and
reverses and he suddenly found himself (in the Clutter house that
night) in this psychological cul-de-sac. The Clutters were such a
perfect set of symbols for every frustration in his life. As Perry
himself said, "I didn't have anything against them, and they never
did anything wrong to me—the way other people have all my life.
Maybe they're just the ones who have to pay for it." Now in that
particular section where Perry talks about the reason for the
murders, I could have included other views. But Perry's happens to
be the one I believe is the right one, and it's the one that Dr. Batten
at the Menninger Clinic arrived at quite independently, never having
done any interviews with Perry.

I could have added a lot of other opinions. But that would have
confused the issue, and indeed the book. I had to make up my
mind, and move toward that one view, always. You can say that the
reportage is incomplete. But then it has to be. It's a question of
selection, you wouldn't get anywhere if it wasn't for that. I've often
thought of the book as being like something reduced to a seed.
Instead of presenting the reader with a full plant, with all the
foliage, a seed is planted in the soil of his mind. I've often thought
of the book in that sense. I make my own comment by what I
choose to tell and how I choose to tell it. It is true that an author is

more in control of fictional characters because he can do anything
he wants with them as long as they stay credible. But in the
nonfiction novel one can also manipulate: if I put something in
which I don't agree about, I can always set it in a context of
qualification without having to step into the story myself to set the
reader straight.

When did you first see the murderers—Perry and Dick?

The first time I ever saw them was the day they were returned to
Garden City. I had been waiting in the crowd in the square for
nearly five hours, frozen to death. That was the first time. I had
tried to interview them the next day—both completely unsuccessful
interviews. I saw Perry first, but he was so cornered and
suspicious—and quite rightly so—and paranoid, that he couldn't
have been any less communicative. It was always easier with Dick.
He was like someone you meet on a train, immensely garrulous, who
starts up a conversation and is only too obliged to tell you *everything*.
Perry became easier after the third or fourth month, but it wasn't
until the last five years of his life that he was totally and absolutely
honest with me, and came to trust me. I came to have great rapport
with him right up through his last day. For the first year and a half,
though, he would come just so close, and then no closer. He'd
retreat into the forest and leave me standing outside. I'd hear him
laugh in the dark. Then gradually he would come back. In the end,
he could not have been more complete and candid.

How did the two accept being used as subjects for a book?

They had no idea what I was going to do. Well, of course, at the
end they did. Perry was always asking me: Why are you writing this
book? What is it supposed to mean? I don't understand why you're
doing it. Tell me in one sentence why you want to do it. So I would
say that it didn't have anything to do with changing the readers'
opinion about anything, nor did I have any moral reasons worthy of
calling them such—it was just that I had a strictly aesthetic theory
about creating a book which could result in a work of art.

"That's really the truth, Perry," I'd tell him, and Perry would say,
"A work of art, a work of art," and then he'd laugh and say, "What an

irony, what an irony." I'd ask what he meant, and he'd tell me that all he'd ever wanted to do in his life was to produce a work of art. "That's all I ever wanted in my whole life," he said. "And now, what has happened? An incredible situation where I kill four people, and *you're* going to produce a work of art." Well, I'd have to agree with him. It was a pretty ironic situation.

Did Dick and Perry see sections of the book?

They saw some sections of it. Perry wanted terribly much to see the book. I had to let him see it because it just would have been too unkind not to. Each only saw the manuscript in little pieces. Everything mailed to the prison went through the censor. I wasn't about to have my manuscript floating around between those censors—not with those Xerox machines going clickety-clack. So when I went to the prison to visit I would bring parts—some little thing for Perry to read. Perry's greatest objection was the title. He didn't like it because he said the crime wasn't committed in cold blood. I told him the title had a double meaning. What was the other meaning? he wanted to know. Well, that wasn't something I was going to tell him. Dick's reaction to the book was to start switching and changing his story . . . saying what I had written wasn't exactly true. He wasn't trying to flatter himself; he tried to change it to serve his purposes legally, to support the various appeals he was sending through the courts. He wanted the book to read as if it was a legal brief for presentation in his behalf before the Supreme Court. But you see, I had a perfect control agent—I could always tell when Dick or Perry wasn't telling the truth. During the first few months or so of interviewing them, they weren't allowed to speak to each other. They were in separate cells. So I would keep crossing their stories, and what correlated, what checked out identically, was the truth.

How did the two compare in their recounting of the events?

Dick had an absolutely fantastic memory—one of the greatest memories I have ever come across. The reason that I know it's great is that I lived the entire trip the boys went on from the time of the murders up to the moment of their arrest in Las Vegas—thousands of miles, what the boys called "the long ride." I went everywhere the boys had gone, all the hotel rooms, every single place in the book, Mexico, Acapulco, all of it. In the hotel in Miami Beach I stayed for three days until the manager realized why I was there and asked me to leave, which I was only too glad to do. Well, Dick could give me the names and addresses of any hotel or place along the route where they'd spent maybe half a night. He told me when I got to Miami to take a taxi to such and such a place and get out on the boardwalk and it would be southwest of there, number 232, and opposite I'd find two umbrellas in the sand which advertised "Tan with Coppertone." That was how exact he was. He was the one who remembered the little card in the Mexico hotel room—in the corner of the mirror—that reads: "Your day ends at 2 P.M." He was extraordinary. Perry on the other hand was very bad at details of that sort, though he was good at remembering conversations and moods. He was concerned altogether with the overtones of things. He was much better at describing a general sort of mood or atmosphere than Dick, who, though very sensitive, was impervious to that sort of thing.

Is it one of the artistic limits of the nonfiction novel that the writer is placed at the whim of chance? Suppose, in the case of In Cold Blood, *clemency had been granted? Or the two boys had been less interesting? Wouldn't the artistry of the book have suffered? Isn't luck involved?*

It is true that I was in the peculiar situation of being involved in a slowly developing situation. I never knew until the events were well along whether a book was going to be possible. There was always the choice, after all, of whether to stop or go on. The book could have ended with the trial, with just a coda at the end explaining what had finally happened. If the principals had been uninteresting or completely uncooperative, I could have stopped and looked elsewhere, perhaps not very far. A nonfiction novel could have been written about any of the other prisoners on death row— York and Latham, or especially Lee Andrews. Andrews was the most *subtly* crazy person you can imagine—I mean there was just one thing wrong with him. He was the most rational, calm, bright young boy you would ever want to meet. I mean *really* bright—which is what made him a truly awesome kind of person. Because his one flaw was that it didn't bother him *at all* to kill. Which is quite a trait. The people who crossed his path, well, to his way of thinking, the best thing to do with them was just to put them in their graves.

What other than murder might be a subject suitable for the nonfiction novel?

The other day someone suggested that the breakup of a marriage would be an interesting topic for a nonfiction novel. I disagreed. First of all, you'd have to find two people who would be willing— who'd sign a release. Second, their respective views on the subject matter would be incoherent. And third, any couple who'd subject themselves to the scrutiny demanded would quite likely be a pair of kooks. But it's amazing how many events *would* work with the theory of the nonfiction novel in mind—the Watts riots, for example. They would provide a subject that satisfied the first essential of the nonfiction novel—that there is a timeless quality about the cause and the events. That's important. If it's going to date, it can't be a work of art. The requisite would also be that you would have had to live through the riots, at least part of them, as a witness, so that a depth of perception could be acquired. That event, just three days, I would take years to do. You'd start with the family that instigated the riots without ever meaning to.

With the nonfiction novel I suppose the temptation to fictionalize events, or a line of dialogue, for example, must be overwhelming. With In Cold Blood *was there any invention of this sort to speak of—I was thinking specifically of the dog you described trotting along the road at the end of a section on Perry and Dick, and then later you introduce the next section on the two with Dick swerving to hit the dog. Was there actually a dog at that exact point, or were you using this habit of Dick's as a fiction device to bridge the two sections?*

No, there was a dog, and it was precisely as described. One doesn't spend almost six years on a book, the point of which is factual accuracy, and then give way to minor distortions. People are so suspicious. They ask, "How can you reconstruct the conversation of a dead girl, Nancy Clutter, without fictionalizing?" If they read the book carefully, they can see readily enough how it's done. It's a silly question. Each time Nancy appears in the narrative, there are witnesses to what she is saying and doing—phone calls, conversations, being overheard. When she walks the horse up from the river in the twilight, the hired man is a witness and talked to her then. The last time we see her, in her bedroom, Perry and Dick themselves were the witnesses, and told me what she had said. What is reported of her, even in the narrative form, is as accurate as many hours of questioning can make it. All of it is reconstructed from the evidence of witnesses—which is implicit in the title of the first section of the book—"The Last to See Them Alive."

After their conviction, you spent years corresponding and visiting with the prisoners. What was the relationship between the two of them?

When they were taken to death row, they were right next door to each other. But they didn't talk much. Perry was intensely secretive and wouldn't ever talk because he didn't want the other prisoners—York, Latham, and particularly Andrews, whom he despised—to hear anything that he had to say. He would write Dick notes on "kites," as he called them. He would reach out his hand and zip the "kite" into Dick's cell. Dick didn't much enjoy receiving these communications because they were always one form or another of recrimination—nothing to do with the Clutter crime, but just general dissatisfaction with things there in prison and . . . the people, very often Dick himself. Perry'd send Dick a note: "If I hear you tell another of those filthy jokes again, I'll kill you when we go to the shower!" He was quite a little moralist, Perry, as I've said.

It was over a moral question that he and I had a tremendous falling-out once. It lasted for about two months. I used to send them things to read—both books and magazines. Dick only wanted girlie magazines—either those or magazines that had to do with cars and motors. I sent them both whatever they wanted. Well, Perry said to me one time: "How could a person like you go on contributing to the degeneracy of Dick's mind by sending him all this 'degenerate filthy' literature?" Weren't they all sick enough without this further contribution toward their total moral decay? He'd got very grand talking in terms that way. I tried to explain to him that I was neither his judge nor Dick's—and that if that was what Dick wanted to read, that was *his* business. Perry felt that was entirely wrong—that people had to fulfill an obligation toward moral leadership. Very grand. Well, I agree with him up to a point, but in the case of Dick's reading matter it was absurd, of course, and so we got into such a really serious argument about it that afterward, for two months, he wouldn't speak or even write to me.

How often did the two correspond with you?

Except for those occasional fallings-out, they'd write twice a week. I wrote them both twice a week all those years. One letter to the both of them didn't work. I had to write them both, and I had to be careful not to be repetitious, because they were very jealous of each other. Or rather, Perry was terribly jealous of Dick, and if Dick got one more letter than he did, that would create a great crisis. I wrote them about what I was doing, and where I was living, describing everything in the most careful detail. Perry was interested in my dog, and I would always write about him, and send along pictures. I often wrote them about their legal problems.

You once said that emotionality made you lose writing control—that you had to exhaust emotion before you could get to work. Was there a problem with In Cold Blood, *considering your involvement with the case and its principals?*

Yes, it was a problem. Nevertheless, I felt in control throughout. However, I had great difficulty writing the last six or seven pages. This even took a physical form: hand paralysis—very awkward, as I always write in longhand.

Your feeling about capital punishment is implicit in the title of the book. How do you feel the lot of Perry and Dick should have been resolved?

I feel that capital crimes should all be handled by federal courts, and that those convicted should be imprisoned in a special federal prison where, conceivably, a life sentence could mean, as it does not in state courts, just that.

Did you see the prisoners on their final day? Perry wrote you a 100-page letter that you received after the execution. Did he mention that he had written it?

Yes, I was with them the last hour before the execution. No, Perry did not mention the letter. He only kissed me on the cheek, and said, "Adios, amigo."

What was the letter about?

It was a rambling letter, often intensely personal, often setting forth his various philosophies. He had been reading Santayana. Somewhere he had read *The Last Puritan,* and had been very impressed by it. What really impressed him about me was that I had once visited Santayana at the Convent of the Blue Nuns in Rome. He always wanted me to go into great detail about that visit, what Santayana had looked like, and the nuns, and all the physical details. Also, he had been reading Thoreau. Narratives didn't interest him at all. So in his letter he would write: "As Santayana says—" and then there'd be five pages of what Santayana *did* say. Or he'd write that he didn't care what I thought, and he'd add five or ten pages of what he agreed with Thoreau about.

The case must have left you with an extraordinary collection of memorabilia.

My files would almost fill a whole small room, right up to the ceiling. All my research. Hundreds of letters. Newspaper clippings. Court records—the court records almost fill two trunks. There were so many federal hearings on the case. One federal hearing was twice as long as the original court trial. A huge assemblage of stuff. I have some of the personal belongings—all of Perry's because he left me everything he owned; it was miserably little, his books, written in and annotated; the letters he received while in prison . . . not very many . . . his paintings and drawings. Rather a heartbreaking assemblage that arrived a month after the execution. I simply couldn't bear to look at it for a long time. I finally sorted everything. Then, also, after the execution, that 100-page letter from Perry got to me. The last line of the letter—it's Thoreau, I think, a paraphrase—goes: "And suddenly I realize life is the father and death is the mother." The last line. Extraordinary.

What has been the response of readers of In Cold Blood *to date?*

I've been staggered by the letters I've received—their quality of sensibility, their articulateness, the compassion of their authors. The letters are not fan letters. They're from people deeply concerned about what it is I've written about. About 70 percent of the letters think of the book as a reflection on American life—this collision between the desperate, ruthless, wandering, savage part of American life, and the other, which is insular and safe, more or less. It has struck them because there is something so awfully inevitable about what is going to happen: the people in the book are completely beyond their own control. For example, Perry wasn't an evil person. If he'd had any chance in life, things would have been different. But every illusion he'd ever had, well, they all evaporated, so that on that night he was so full of self-hatred and self-pity that I think he would have killed *some*body—perhaps not that night, or the next, or the next. You can't go through life without ever getting anything you want, ever.

1966

In Cold Blood missed out on the two main literary prizes of the year—the Pulitzer (won by David B. Davis's *The Problem of Slavery in Western Culture*) and the National Book Award (won by Justin Kaplan's biography of Mark Twain, *Mr. Clemens and Mark Twain*). The word was that one of the National Book Award judges had persuaded his fellow judges that *In Cold Blood* was too commercial—a slight that infuriated Truman. He is shown here standing in the living room of the Clutter home in Holcomb, Kansas. *(AP/Wide World)*

LOEL GUINNESS I've got a copy of *In Cold Blood* somewhere, but I don't particularly like it. It's much too long anyway. I think most books should be treated with ergonomics—a new word, because I can't find it in the dictionary. It's the word for the study that people make of the inside of a motorcar to make it more comfortable for the owner. When you press a button, it's there in the right place. You don't have to look to find something. That's ergonomics. I think the ergonomics of a book should be thought out. A man wants to be able to hold a book to read it. How can you read Henry Kissinger's book except by sitting at a table strong enough to hold the book up, then turning the leaves over? It's the only way you can read. I didn't tell Henry this, but I took his book and foxed it—that is, I broke it into three sections so I could handle it more easily. That's the trouble with *In Cold Blood*—much too big and much too long.

JOHN KNOWLES At dinner at the Bennett Cerfs' I came up to him and said, "Truman, I've read the first installment of *In Cold Blood* in *The New Yorker*. I missed the second, but I can't wait to read the whole book." He said, "That's the most insulting thing that anyone has ever said to me!" I said, "But, Truman, you don't understand, I was in La Camargue in the South of France riding horses; there was no way of getting *The New Yorker*."

"You should have had it *sent!*"

He later forgave me, but he was really pissed off that I had not organized my life around getting the second installment of *In Cold Blood*.

GEORGE CHRISTY (*Hollywood columnist*) Some years ago it was quite the thing for the literary crowd to go to the YMHA at Ninety-second and Lexington to hear Elizabeth Bowen, Mary McCarthy, Dylan Thomas, Auden. Truman brought out a full house for the first reading of *In Cold Blood*. Diana Vreeland, Gloria Vanderbilt, they were all waiting there in the hushed quiet for his first words. He strolled out in a maroon cardigan and gray flannel pants, then paused and let everybody look at him. Turning so that everyone got a good look, he put on his glasses and shrugged, "Well, this is the end of vanity." After a moment, he started to read. And, of course, everybody was mesmerized.

JAMES KIRKWOOD (*writer*) The experience of reading *In Cold Blood* was vivid with me. I was staying with a couple in Connecticut. They had a house up on a hill, way up, off by itself in northern Connecticut. I was up there writing and taking care of their house when *In Cold Blood* came out in *The New Yorker*. It was an eerie-looking farmhouse, an old Victorian thing. There were oak trees and chestnuts—things were hitting the roof in the wind. Every week the magazine came out, I would read it at night when I got in bed. I really got caught up in that. I was in a farmhouse, the kind where the Clutters lived and where Dick and Perry arrived . . . I still remember the experience of reading the sections. When I told Truman about that, he cackled and giggled and thought it was marvelous that he could frighten me like that.

NORMAN MAILER One of the dopiest things Truman ever got into was his outrage at *The Executioner's Song*. He used to go around saying Norman Mailer stole it all from *In Cold Blood* and never gave me credit for it. I thought it was idiotic for a professional to carry on like that. So we were a little chilly toward the end. Of course I had read *In Cold Blood* and had obviously taken it into account. But Truman didn't invent the form. After all, Lillian Ross had written *Picture*. So it wasn't as if he had discovered the "nonfiction novel." It's amazing how there are no good titles for that kind of work: true-life novels? Nonfiction novel sounds like a prescription for some nonspecific disease.

I wasn't an enormous admirer of *In Cold Blood*. It's a hell of a damned good book, beautifully written, but I do think it's limited. I was unsatisfied when I read it. I thought, "Oh, there we are again, that goddamn *New Yorker*, always ready to put a headlock on everything." It was too stripped down. You didn't know enough about those killers finally. It was too behavioristic. What the hell's *In Cold Blood* finally? It's a description of a crime from the outside. I think Truman decided too quickly this is all heredity, that in their genes his killers were doomed and directed to act in this fashion; there was no other outcome possible. All that I thought was too quickly solved by him. Those are the kinds of questions that should keep you up at night—and they were not in that book. Has anyone ever written an interesting critical piece about the work—taken it very seriously, yet also pulled it apart, truly delineated its strengths and weaknesses?

WILLIAM F. BUCKLEY, JR. *(writer)* I was on the Johnny Carson show one night and the subject of capital punishment came up. I said, "Well, we've only had a certain number of executions in the last few years—whatever it was—and two of them were for the personal convenience of Truman Capote." Which was a funny line. I got a call about a week later from Jackie Kennedy's sister Lee. She said that Truman had very hurt feelings about that. I said, "Oh, for Pete's sake." She said, "That's what I told him. 'For Pete's sake.' Bill was just having fun." I was just making a wisecrack. I've never seen any serious allegation that he had it in his power to suspend the execution of that sentence.

NED ROREM In 1963 Glenway Wescott gave a small dinner to which Truman was invited. Truman did most of the talking, describing his adventures in Kansas, and in particular describing the qualities both of mind and body of the two young murderers, one of whom, Perry Smith, he seemed clearly in love with. He told us about the book—a nonfiction novel he called it—and at one point said, "But it can't be published until they're executed, so I can hardly wait."

I never forgot that remark. About a year after the boys were hanged, I sent a letter to the *Saturday Review of Literature,* which printed it. Here it is:

> Capote got two million and his heroes got the rope. This conspicuous irony has not, to my knowledge, been shown in any assessment of *In Cold Blood.* That book, for all practical purposes, was completed before the deaths of Smith and Hickock; yet, had they not died, there would have been no book. The author surely realizes this, although within his pages it is stated that $50,000 might have saved them—that only the poor must hang.

Auden, in his libretto "Elegy for Young Lovers," portrays a poet who, for reasons of "inspiration," allows two people to perish, and from this act a masterpiece is born.

Now I am suggesting no irresponsibility on the part of Capote other than as a writer: I am less concerned with ethics than with art. Certainly his reportage intrigued and frightened me, and certainly he presented as good a case against capital punishment as Camus or Koestler. But something rang false, or rather, didn't ring at all. His claim to an unprecedented art form gives cause to wonder.

An artist must, at any cost, expose himself: be vulnerable. Yet Capote the man, in his recent work, is invisible. Could it be that, like the Ortolan-eaters so admirably depicted in Janet Flanner's recent *Paris Journal,* he is hiding his head in shame?"

The reference to the "Ortolan-eaters," incidentally, is to French gourmets shown in old engravings eating little yellow sparrows, roasted alive, and gobbled bones and all, "with napkins hoisted like tents over the eaters' heads to enclose the perfume, and maybe to hide their shame."

Truman was not amused. He came up to me at an Arts and Letters ceremony. I was getting an award. Perhaps he was getting one too. He looked pretty good with a pink tie and a cobalt-blue shirt. He said, "Of course, I didn't see your letter myself, but people told me"—which I don't believe for a minute, because *of course* he saw it—and he started yelling at me. I didn't say anything; he was hysterical. It was terribly public. I didn't know what I was supposed to do with this harridan who was screeching at me. Then Kenneth Tynan took the same tack.

KATHLEEN TYNAN (*writer*) In the spring of '65 Ken met Truman, I think, at a Jean Stein party. The decision had just been made that the guys would be hanged and Truman, according to Ken, hopped up and down with glee, clapping his hands, saying, "I'm beside myself! Beside myself! Beside myself with joy!" So Ken was pretty shocked. They had an argument; Ken complained that this was really pretty outrageous that he should be celebrating this kind of disposition.

That autumn Truman was in London staying at Claridge's. I think he suspected or had heard that Ken was going to review *In Cold Blood* and he came over. He looked rather like a banker, not looking elf-like at all, a small banker. It was a rather edgy, coy meeting. Truman clearly realized that there was trouble afoot. He sent Ken a plant. Ken must have had one of his colds or something. It was a small, rather miserable little plant with a message—"Something to scent the sickroom . . ."—and then he apologized for the alliteration: "Love, Truman."

Ken wrote his review. All hell broke loose. We had to go to Seville for the Feria. Telephone calls started coming in from Terry Kilmartin at *The Observer*. Ken realized he was in trouble. In the review Ken had suggested that, despite Truman's claim to the contrary, the book might have been difficult to publish had the boys lived. The hangings made it easier for Truman, tied up all the knots. His view was corroborated by a "prominent Manhattan lawyer" who had not read *In Cold Blood* but said as much on the basis of the evidence that Ken presented. "We are talking," Ken went on to write, "about responsibility. For the first time an influential writer in the front rank has been placed in a position of privileged intimacy with criminals about to die and, in my view, done less than he might have to save them . . . Where lives are threatened, observers and recorders who shrink from participation may be said to betray their species. No piece of prose, however deathless, is worth a human life." That is a truncated version of Ken's review.

BODIE NEILSON (*friend*) Tynan's argument was that he let them die because that made the book dramatic. I mean, get a better ending for your book . . . sort of like letting the *Titanic* sink for literature's sake.

KATHLEEN TYNAN Truman delivered a violent rebuttal to *The Observer* and accused Ken of having the "morals of a baboon and the guts of a butterfly." He wrote that no one who worked on the case "ever thought that a successful appeal could be made in a Kansas court which abides by the McNaughton Rule on the basis of insanity or diminished responsibility." He doubted whether "the prominent Manhattan lawyer" existed and he offered to send a check of $500 to Ken's favorite charity should the lawyer produce an affidavit.

Ken won the bet. He got his lawyer not only to prove that he existed but to confirm that he'd said that although he hadn't read the book, he thought it unlikely it would have been published if the murderers had lived.

It wasn't a legal problem. Ken's honor was at stake. First, that Prosch (the lawyer) would step forward and corroborate his opinion—because it would have been terrible if he hadn't; and also, that he was accused of being a vile person and of being unfair.

The next time we met him was sometime in the late sixties walking down one of those huge corridors at the UN Plaza. Coming in the opposite direction toward us was his tiny figure. As he passed us, Ken nodded politely to him and Truman dropped a little curtsy, "Mr. Tynan, I presume," and walked past. That was the first time Ken had seen Truman since the confrontation. It was a wonderful theatrical moment because of the length and the height and width of those corridors and wondering what the heck Capote was going to do. Was he going to hit him? Was he going to spit on him? It was a moment of fun theatrical tension. A long-drawn-out moment too.

DIANA TRILLING I reviewed *In Cold Blood* for the *Partisan Review,* and I liked it very much and reviewed it favorably. The whole story fascinated me. He did a very good job of reporting. Then I read in an issue of *The Observer* in England a piece by Kenneth Tynan which attacked him fiercely for having conspired in the deaths of the murderers by not having fought for their being relieved of the death sentence. He wrote a lot of very nasty things about Truman. He wrote that Truman had set out to eke money out of these poor, poor murderers. I was sickened by that. If Truman Capote happened to write a very successful book and made a lot of money out of that story, I thought that's fine—it's a reward for his skill in being able to do such an excellent job. He had no obligation to the murderers except to tell their stories truthfully. He had the moral obligation to be very accurate in the way he handled that.

I don't happen to believe very fervently in capital punishment. Let's not take the chance of perhaps being wrong; let's not get rid of people quite so easily. But, in this case, if ever, the death sentence was warranted—wanton, brutal killers and I didn't feel any sense of sympathy for them, which was what Truman was calling for. Tynan invoked psychoanalysis, claiming to have a statement about what this all meant from some woman analyst who had never read the book or set eyes on Truman Capote. I thought this was viciously wrong on the part of both Tynan and the woman analyst, if she existed. I was very angry. I immediately went right to my typewriter and wrote a long response and sent it off to *The Observer*. David Avsder did not print any responses. He closed all discussion at once. Maybe it was sensible of him, but it was awfully frustrating. Stuart Hampshire, whom I knew scarcely at all, was in America and came to dinner. Having this English philosopher on hand, I—stupidly, I suppose—asked him what he thought. I should have known that he would always take a radically chic attitude on such issues and that he would have been in agreement with Tynan, which he was indeed. I was disgusted with him and that I had asked him to dinner. I think that grown-ups ought to be able to hide their jealousy a little better than all these people did. Just because Truman made a couple of million dollars? Great, he earned it, he did a good job, he earned the money. But they couldn't control their jealousy. It was disgusting. They had to find a high, philosophical ground on which to defend a nasty personal motive.

GEORGE PLIMPTON Truman was absolutely furious at Tynan. What he'd said stuck in his craw and he simply couldn't clear it out. I remember having lunch with him in an East Side Italian restaurant that he favored less for its food than for its acknowledged Mafia connections. These were the days when the detective pulp magazines lay around his house in Sagaponack in thick heaps. He waved for a drink. He told me the waiter was a Mafia hit man who had killed dozens of people. Then suddenly he began describing a fantasy about Tynan, which, as he described it, I had the feeling he had been fine-tuning, turning it delectably around in his mind for many months, like rolling a candy drop against the back of his teeth. It started with a kidnapping, Tynan picked off a quiet city street and bundled into the back of a Rolls-Royce. Blindfolded and gagged, he

was taken to a very smart clinic somewhere out in the country—
quite a grand place with a gatehouse and a long gravel driveway,
lawns stretching out everywhere—and deposited in a well-appointed
hospital room. I remember Truman was very careful with the details.
He described how pleasant the nurses were, what a nice view there
was out the window, and that the meals were excellent. Then his
voice took on an edge as he described how on occasion Tynan would
be wheeled off somewhere in the clinic into surgery to have a limb
or an organ removed.

Truman announced this last chilling detail quite cheerily,
followed by a burst of laughter. In that oddly deep voice he used for
dramatic effect, he then went on to describe the extensive
postoperative procedure, the careful diets, a complex exercise
program to get Tynan back into good shape . . . at which point he
would be carried off to the operating room yet again to have
something *else* removed, until finally, after months of surgery and
recuperation, everything had been removed except one eye and his
genitalia. Truman cried out, "Everything else goes!"

Then he leaned back in his chair and delivered the denouement.
He said, "What they do then is to wheel into his hospital room a
motion-picture projector, a screen, along with an attendant in a
white smock who sets everything up, and what they do is show
pornographic films, very high-grade, enticing ones, absolutely
nonstop!"

1966

CHAPTER TWENTY-THREE *In Which Folks from Kansas Come to New York and Are Treated by TC to the Lights of Broadway*

It was very much like Truman to impress out-of-town friends with the wide range of his knowledge of New York nightlife. (*UPI/Corbis-Bettmann*)

DUANE WEST I've heard various people say that Truman didn't quote them correctly. I say, "Well, I have to agree with them. I know he mistakenly described my part in the book. The book makes it appear that I really didn't have much to do with the case. In fact, I handled all the investigation, worked with the investigators, prepared the trial brief, handled all the evidence that came and went into the FBI. Mr. Green was hired to assist me, which he did. I made the opening statement to the jury. Truman took part of what I said and attributed it to Mr. Green. I frankly didn't give a damn what Truman said about me in the book. I think the book had no redeeming social value whatsoever. This business of a new art form—"nonfiction novel"—is a bunch of *garbage*. I felt the same way about the movie. I think he was out here simply to make money. I don't think the book was a major contribution to the volume of great American literature.

No, we never had any cross words at all. We were on friendly terms; when he left here he said, "You know, if you ever come to New York, why, be sure to get in touch with me. I can help you get tickets," and this and that. Later, I found out that I'd be going to New York as a delegate to the national Red Cross convention. I'd been chairman of the Red Cross chapter here for seven years. So I told my wife, "My gosh, I think we ought to write to Truman and see if he can get us tickets to *Hello, Dolly!* because it had just opened on Broadway. She said, "Oh, he won't pay any attention to us." So I sat down and wrote. One evening I came home from a Jaycee meeting and my wife, Orvileta, had the funniest look on her face. She said, "Well, you'll never guess who I had a telephone call from tonight. Truman Capote called." I don't think she'd ever even met him. He had been in Spain for the last six months, so that's why the letter hadn't reached him. He apologized for not having answered the letter and he said he was happy to hear we were coming to New York. He hadn't seen *Hello, Dolly!* either, so he had gotten us tickets and he wanted us to go out to dinner with him. He said, "Now, call me when you get to town." So we called him. He said to take a taxi and come up to Sardi's. "We'll meet you at Sardi's, me and Harper Lee." She is a fascinating person and I really enjoyed getting acquainted with her. So anyway, that's where I had my first experience with cold potato soup, which is supposed to be a delicacy. I told my wife, I said, "If you ever brought me a bowl of cold potato soup out of the kitchen, I'd turn around and ask you to heat it up! Vichy-shwash or whatever." I said, "That's gotta be a big-city ploy if ever I heard one."

Anyway, we had a nice dinner. Then we went to see *Hello, Dolly!* and we had third-row aisle seats. I think Henry Cabot Lodge's son was sitting in front of us. I don't know what Truman paid for the seats, but it was a high-priced evening. When the curtain came down at the end of the first act, all of a sudden I felt this big yank on my arm. I look around and there's Truman with my wife in tow and he's about a third of the way up the aisle. No one else in the place is standing up. Everyone's clapping. Harper jumps up and says, "Come on, let's get out of here," and drags me up the aisle. We were mortified. There was this little bar around the corner where all the New York characters have their caricatures painted. Well, Truman's had just gone up. He wanted us to see that he had finally made the bright lights. That's all it was. "Oh, everybody comes here for a drink during intermission." Well, we don't use alcohol, but we said fine, we'll have a Coke. As it was, we were the only two couples who were there. No one else was in the place. He wasn't embarrassed. He was interested in showing us that his picture was finally up there on the wall with all the rest of the famous New Yorkers. But, oh my God, we were so embarrassed rushing up the aisle when everyone else was sitting there clapping.

Hello, Dolly! was great. It was just a tremendous show. Afterward we went backstage and spent twenty-five to thirty minutes talking with Carol Channing. He introduced us to Marge and Gower Champion. Of course, we were embarrassed because these people had really worked hard. Carol Channing was so warm, such a wonderful person. You would have thought we were her long-lost relatives. Then Truman took us out to El Morocco dancing. The dance floor was not very big at El Morocco. It was so crowded they kept bringing chairs and putting them right on the dance floor till finally there wasn't much more room for dancing than the size of this desk. Of course, I was never enthused with Truman being on a real personal basis with my spouse, you know. Anyway, they got up and tried to dance, but of course you couldn't hear because the orchestra was sitting right there making so much noise that you couldn't hear. We were really disappointed, both of us. You couldn't visit in a place like that at all. When somebody's blowing a horn in my ear, I can't enjoy myself or concentrate.

I've not read the book except for little parts and pieces. I've got an autographed copy I'll be glad to sell you. People who've read the book tell me it makes Mr. Dewey out to be the hero, more or less. Dewey wasn't the hero of the piece at all. When the information came out from the penitentiary about Hickock and Smith, Dewey kind of pooh-poohed the idea. Instead of him going and checking that out, he stayed here and we sent Nye and Roy Ben Church to run all that down. It was Rich Rohleder, our assistant chief of police here, who did the basic police work at the time of the crime. Al was a good fellow, a good sheriff, a good law-enforcement man, but it's upsetting, you know, when a guy who really did the real hard work was kind of ignored. That's why I say the whole thing was garbage as far as I'm concerned, especially if there are any parts that portray Hickock and Smith in a sympathetic way. I am sympathetic to them from the standpoint that they were human beings who went astray. But I also look at the damage that was done. Herb Clutter was an outstanding fellow, you know, a man making a tremendous contribution to his community and, of course, the lives of his wife and those two kids that were snuffed out—that's the true tragedy of the circumstance.

You had people who got acquainted with Truman; it was a big deal for him to be going up to them at the country club and kissing their wives hello and all this and that. There are people who thought the movie company coming here was a great big deal too. They took over the courthouse up here, shot the scenes, and never paid the county one dime. I can't imagine how our commissioners at the time could have been so dense. We had a United Fund drive going on that fall. They could have said, "Hey, write us a check for $75,000 to the Finney County United Fund." They never made a dime. I went up there one day while they were shooting the movie. They had a red light, a blinking red light on the landing between the second and third floors with a patrolman standing there. I had a case to file for a client. I started up the stairs. He said, "You can't come up here, they're shooting a movie." And I said, "Get the hell out of my way. I'm coming up to a public office to file a case for a client." I said, "Those people don't have any more right to be shooting in there and to interfere with my access to this floor than the man in the moon."

I said, "Just get the hell out of my way." I don't swear at length, but I was very unhappy. People just fell all over themselves.

I didn't see the movie. I wouldn't walk from here to that doorknob to see the movie. I'll be damned if I'm going to give them some of my money for something like that. They didn't even ask me to portray myself, but I wouldn't have if they'd done it. I was just not in favor of them making the movie here or anyplace else for that matter.

CHARLES McATEE The phone rings and it's Truman. "Oh, Charles, I've just seen the most delightful play. You must come to New York and see it with me. It's just wonderful."

I said, "Tell me, Truman, what is it?"

"Oh, you'll just love it, it's *The Odd Couple*."

I said to myself, "Oh-oh. Truman's asking me to come to New York to see a play about an odd couple."

I felt a little threatened. I didn't know what the play was about. I don't read the *New York Times* every Sunday. We have people in Topeka that *do,* you understand, but I'm busy briefing cases or down at the firm reading law books.

I said, "Who's in it, Truman?"

"Walter Matthau and Art Carney, and they're wonderful!"

I do get to New York now and then, and by that time I had found out what *The Odd Couple* was about—nothing to do with odd couples. So I was not quite as threatened. I decided to call him. We had dinner at the Park Plaza. We went to the theater. It was absolutely delightful. Backstage afterward, he introduced me to Art Carney and Walter Matthau. I shook their hands! This is tall clover for a farm boy from Mahaska! Walter Matthau and his wife had just had a baby three months before and asked us over to have a drink. Truman said, "No, we're going to go to the '21' Club for drinks." I wanted to go see Walter Matthau's new baby!

So we went to the '21' Club just a couple of blocks up the way. William S. Paley and his lovely wife, Babe, joined us. Coming from the sticks in Kansas and sitting at the '21' Club with Truman Capote and being introduced to people like Bill and Babe Paley . . . that's pretty heady stuff.

He introduced me as an acquaintance out in Kansas, the Director of Penal Institutions. He introduced you to whoever descended upon him or his table. You were one of his friends. I sat there that night spellbound. Truman was going to his chalet in Switzerland and he was quite upset because he wanted to take his bulldog, but was concerned about its welfare on the airplane. Mr. Paley said, "Not to worry, Truman. When are you leaving?" He was leaving the following week. It turned out that a week or so later, the Paleys were flying over to Europe in their private jet. They'd be glad to bring Fido over, or whatever his name was. Truman said, "Would you do that? Oh, that would just be lovely." I'm sitting at the '21' Club with Truman Capote, and the chairman of CBS, and his wife, and they're talking about flying a bulldog to Europe in a private jet! I'm impressed.

1964

A portrait of Jack Dunphy in Sagaponack. It was Dunphy who was responsible for the two settling on Long Island. When Truman had considered Mount Kisco, near the Bennett Cerfs, Dunphy had written him, "No, I want to be within bicycling distance of the water. Salt water." Truman bought two small houses, one for each. Eventually he gave Dunphy the deeds to both houses, handing them over in a butterfly box. *(Harry Benson)*

GEORGE PLIMPTON From the Montauk Highway to the sea, Sagg Main runs for about a mile . . . past potato fields, then a hummocky wooded area, the fields again, dunes, and finally the ocean. The older houses are quite close together—so that settlers in the earliest times could warn each other that wolves were about. It's a rather astonishing street for the number of writers who have lived along it or just off it. James Jones lived on Sagg Main (his daughter Kaylie is a novelist) and down the line, at various times, Kurt Vonnegut, Peter Matthiessen (who told me about the wolves), John Irving, Alfred Wright, the poet Fred Seidel, the Walt Whitman biographer David Reynolds, Linda Bird Francke, James Salter, a couple of artists— Bob Dash, and Charles Addams, the *New Yorker* cartoonist—and Caroline Kennedy, who has written a few books on the Constitution. My wife then and I owned a house (next to the Vonneguts) which had formerly been lived in by Betty Vreeland, an accomplished poet, and the writer she lived with, Peter Tompkins, who wrote *The Secret Life of Plants*. We even had a literary agent, Maxine Groffsky. Quite a crop! Truman lived on Daniel's Lane with Jack Dunphy, also a novelist, of course, a few hundred yards off Sagg Main, with a dirt road entry shrouded by trees—two small houses, one for Jack Dunphy, and the other, Truman's.

JOE FOX A very simple two-story house about thirty feet wide and fifty feet long. Downstairs it's all one big room except for a small bedroom in back and the kitchenette. A lot of detective magazines. I think they were from Perry and Dick. They sent them on to Truman because he once said he loved pulp magazines. He never seemed to throw anything away.

FRANK PERRY *(film producer)* In the house in Sagaponack, very early on, maybe a year after the winter of the ball, I went upstairs to a kind of sleeping loft. All the walls—it had three whole walls—were covered with press clippings about Truman. A lot of them from really unimportant, obscure gossip columns . . . a reflection of an obsession about being in print. I always felt that if you're really famous you don't collect your own notices. It didn't seem as if Capote would do that, so I was really shocked that he would stoop to collecting and mounting and sticking such things up on a wall . . . not even pasted on, like movie stars in a schoolgirl's bedroom, like Rock Hudson. These three walls were just covered with his own clippings. From really small papers, the *National Enquirer,* not *"Life Magazine Goes to Truman Capote's Party,"* but really junky little newspapers.

PIEDY LUMET His house was painted a very strange blue. It looked like a house that no one lived in. It had a double-storied living room with a flat roof. There was a carved lion, big, wooden, perhaps a cat. A pillow that he said Cocteau gave him, needlepointed. A unicorn. The porch had a little border of ivy which was quite springy and prosperous. I remember when Maggie, his bulldog, was a puppy she went off the porch and vanished because the ivy was high enough so that she vanished in it. Truman went berserk. Charlie was the first dog, an English bulldog, the second was Maggie, and then a perfectly elegant cat called Diotima. Bob Keen had a picture I always wanted in the back hall of the Southampton bookshop of Truman with a crow on his shoulder, which was evidently a pet when he and Jack were in Sicily.

His bedroom was bleak. A tiny affair. A square room with a narrow bed and a floor completely covered with detective magazines. A single bed, a little pallet. He had two-story-high bookshelves and a ladder that moved along on a track. You didn't feel that there was any special focus in that house. I think he was much happier in Jack Dunphy's house next door. The temperature is much warmer there because Jack really lives there. A little spare, but in a wonderful way.

LEE RADZIWILL The Sagaponack house epitomized Truman to me— the way I like to think of him. It was very simple; it had one room with this little cubicle office in which I slept on two precious November nights annually. He painted the floor a shiny darkish blue. It had a big fireplace with white brick painted over it. He loved butterflies; there were quite a few frames with butterflies. The room had a very high ceiling. It had a few things in it—only the things that really meant something to him. Some photographs of a few people who meant the most to him at that time. It really represented Truman much more than his apartment in New York, where his precious Tiffany paperweight collection was. This little house in Sagaponack was Truman, in his simplicity and his purity.

I often came down in November, when I'd come back to New York from England. I loved it. I'd sleep in the most miserable bed, next to a steaming radiator that banged all night that we couldn't ever turn off. That was when I saw him at his best. He'd know where you'd get the most delicious vichyssoise in Bridgehampton and the best this or that. He loved to cruise around; he loved stopping to buy things. It was so beautiful in the fall, you'd want it never to pass. We'd talk very late. That part of knowing Truman was really touching because he bared his soul. Then later on he started to lose his soul. But that wasn't his fault . . . perhaps he was treated like a toy.

DOTSON RADER (*writer*) I was at Easthampton for Christmas. I knew Truman had no place to go. Truman was like about two-thirds of the famous people I know—nobody invites them anywhere on holidays. They sit at home on Thanksgiving with the TV turkey dinner watching the parade. So I called him up and invited him to join us on Christmas Eve. My father's a preacher. You know, "Be healed!" He's an evangelist like Jimmy Swaggart. My mother plays a really great piano. So Truman rolls by and has Christmas dinner with us. After dinner, my mother sat down at the piano and we all had a carol sing-along. Then my father read the Christmas story in the Book of Matthew—"There came a decree from Caesar Augustus . . ." Truman was very moved by it. He was in his cups, but in the best form I've ever seen. He started telling stories. It went on for about three or four hours. Our eyes were tearing from laughter. One of the stories he told was about his Moscow days. He was living in some dumpy hotel with these huge windows. The heat was so ghastly that you had to keep the window open when it was forty degrees below outside or you ended up roast pig in the morning. One morning he woke up. "I think, my God, it's cold in here and it's so dark!" He moves his arm and he's under a snowdrift! He started yelling in there, "Help me!"

WILLIE MORRIS *(writer)* One afternoon in the middle of the fall, my dog Pete, a big black Lab, and I were walking up the sidewalk right in downtown Bridgehampton. This big car pulled up to the side of the curb. "Willie, Pete, hop in! Let's ride around and gossip!" So Pete would get in the back seat and I'd get in the front. He'd just ride around and around the block. He'd tell me about a luncheon he'd had the day before, or last week, Côte Basque, or something, with Jackie and the Princess. He'd go through the menus. I remember asking him once, "Truman, how old were you when you wrote *Other Voices, Other Rooms*?" He said, "I was only nineteen and I was so brilliant, *so* brilliant in those days!"

JOHN KNOWLES I never called Truman, he always called me. He usually wouldn't answer the phone, it was usually off the hook. So at quarter of eleven many mornings the phone would ring and this voice would say, "Beauty? Gorgeous? Adorable One? This is Truman, do you want to have lunch?" So we would have lunch at McCarthy's restaurant, or later at Bobby Van's. He always came rehearsed. He would never just have lunch with you, he'd lined up things to tell you. He came loaded for bear. Always. Always had stories about who had had the latest shots at that clinic in Switzerland, or some scandalous gossip about some cardinal of the Catholic Church. He came bearing news. He was an entertainer, he rehearsed. He had it ready. He had me all sized up and what would entertain me, what would interest me. He never came—I'm talking about Truman before he really deteriorated—when he wasn't prepared. I could see that mind ticking. He'd get this story out and he'd get that story out and then he'd get the other story out. There was never a dull moment or silence on anything. He was also a very good listener. We had a terrific rapport and we had a hell of a lot of fun. I didn't dare prepare. He was too complicated. I couldn't read him the way he could me. I just had to wing it with Truman. I simply couldn't prefigure him enough to prepare stories. Plus, I didn't have access to the things he had access to. I didn't have his fund of stories.

The lunches would be very long. We'd have two vodkas or something. Maybe Truman had four, I'd have two. Then we had to go shopping. We'd go to that shop on Job's Lane which has bric-abrac and lamps and things. Buy a lamp or something. Then usually he'd follow me to my house—the Tree House—and he would lie on the long white sofa over by the fireplace and have his orange drink, and his orange drink, and his orange drink, and we would talk about everything under the sun. Finally, God knows how, he would drive himself home. And make it. That was a wonder!

He'd lose his license and keep on driving. He got into terrific problems with the law. He appeared in court in shorts. The judge was absolutely outraged, furious that Truman'd dare to affront the court in these little shorts. Truman thought he looked rather fetching, I'm sure. The judge was not amused at all. Truman was a terrible driver. He couldn't see over the wheel. He didn't have good vision anyway. He'd go over curbs. Once we drove up to Gore Vidal's house, Edgewater, years after Gore had ceased to live there. Near Rhinebeck. I had rented it one summer. Truman insisted on driving up the Taconic Parkway. I almost died. He changed lanes, he couldn't see. Cold sober, he was a menace. Drunk, he was the end.

WILLIE MORRIS He asked me to drive him home—either to drive him or to follow him home. I think to follow him home. His car was weaving back and forth on those back roads between Bridgehampton and Wainscott. At his house, he poured us a vodka. We had a long talk about literature. He had his paperweights out. I was admiring a particular paperweight which had a butterfly inside the glass. He said, "Well, take it, it's yours. Isak Dinesen gave me this. It's yours."

I said, "Truman, I can't take this. This must be worth a thousand dollars."

"No, I want you to have it." So he gave me the Isak Dinesen paperweight with a butterfly. I've still got it—it's in a box somewhere in the basement. I tell people that, even if it's not. But he knew Isak Dinesen and she collected paperweights.

WINSTON GROOM (*writer*) Truman was wearing a black Vietnam guerrilla pajama suit and a white hat. He was sitting on the sofa. Gloria Jones asked him, "Truman, why were you thrown in jail?"

"Well, I was thrown in for driving drunk. The sheriff's wife came in and she said, 'Oooh! Look who we have here! Can I get my friends to bring in their books to be autographed?' " This was at some unearthly hour of the morning. He agreed, yes, certainly. So the wife came in with all these people and these books and he sat there in the jug and autographed them.

JOHN KNOWLES We would drop him off at the foot of the driveway. That was good because your car would be scratched to bits from the overgrown shrubbery. Yes, he always wanted to do that little walk. He liked to exercise, however minimally. I think he told himself that was his constitutional.

JUDY GREEN I never went to his house in Sagaponack. The strangest thing in the world was that even when he lost his license and I would drive him home, I left him at the end of the driveway.

JAN CUSHING If you walked down the driveway, the house was empty and suddenly there was a voice: "I'm in the kitchen, I'm marinating a cucumber."

PIEDY LUMET He'd say, "I've got the dynamite soup of all time. This is one secret I'll tell you but no one else." It turned out to be chicken broth and asparagus, which he'd mixed in the blender. He'd say. "Mmmmm . . . isn't that wonderful?"

I remember him coming to our house in a very, very ancient Harris tweed coat that had no more fight in it . . . it was completely relaxed. It had an ancient hat to match. That's the first image I have of him. He looked like a little coat with feet. He was very fetching.

Finally, though, I felt slightly oppressed by him. I felt I was being crowded. He'd come around and shout my name underneath the windows. Just very cheerfully, very optimistically, very buoyant, saying, "I know you're there!" Around the little house, he used to go right around saying my name over and over again. "I know you're up there!" After a while it was easier not to come down, because it meant a long time with him. I think he had a lot of free time.

He did sort of perk up the day. Animate your life and yet sometimes you'd have to bolt the doors and hide. He had a very funny take on things, very concentrated, just hilarious. He could imagine anything for you . . . how he was going to start his "Just Ducky" restaurant and serve duckburgers. Duck soup and duck dessert. He said that I could be the go-go girl in the Tar-Baby bar at the Just Ducky restaurant. After he heard how it sounded, he'd like it. Just something that threaded through the days.

KURT VONNEGUT (*writer*) Truman would come over afternoon after afternoon to talk and drink. His story was that he was treating his bursitis, so he would swim very slowly up and down the pool. He was very lonesome, and also nobody else in his community would give him a drink. A mutual neighbor chewed me out one time for giving Truman a drink, but in my whole life, I've never shut a drinker off. It's probably time I did.

Anyway, Truman would help himself. He knew where it all was—vodka and orange juice. Then we would chat. The subjects were all the same ones he dealt with on talk-show programs. Bob Dash, the painter, who still lives on the other side of the hedge, kept trying to figure out what the hell was going on over here. His first impression, listening to our voices, was that I had a maiden aunt visiting me.

We just sat out here in the yard, and Truman would ramble on about this and that. He spoke badly of other writers, and I assume he must have done the same about me. We never had a conversation that gave me any indication that Truman had read anything I had written. My work was never discussed. But he was pleasant enough. Across the hedge he always had Bob Dash distracted.

Then he'd swim. That was his sport—swimming. That's what he thought he did very well. I saw scant evidence of any skill. He did the sort of breaststroke my mother used to do to keep her hair perfectly dry although she wore a bathing cap. This frog kick, that's the way Truman swam.

I'd sometimes have to take him home. I would ask if I could. He would never let me drive in his driveway. No matter how shaky he was, I had to leave him at the entrance. That long hooded road. I've never been to the end of it.

Interlude

CHAPTER TWENTY-FIVE   *In Which*
TC and His Contemporaries Have a Word
to Say About Each Other

Three of the most important writers of their generation—Gore Vidal, Truman Capote, and Tennessee Williams—in an early photograph suggesting amity, though in fact each could rarely find a kind word to say about the other. (*Photo by Jo Healy, courtesy of Erin Clermont*)

DOTSON RADER I think the author he admired most was Willa Cather. He was very proud of the fact that he had met her. He told me once about when he was working as a mail boy at *The New Yorker*. Truman didn't have much money and he used to spend a lot of time at the Society Library on Seventy-ninth Street. She lived right around the corner. One day he saw her and he got up enough courage to follow her to a bus stop on Seventy-ninth Street and said, "Aren't you Miss Cather?" He told her how much he admired her and knew all her books and about when he was a boy in the South and used to read them and how lonely they would make him feel, how he could feel her loneliness. She invited him up to tea and they went up to her flat. He stayed there about thirty minutes talking to her, and though it was the only time he was ever with her, that was one of the great moments of his life.

DORIS LILLY Truman worked very slow, and his handwriting! My original manuscript with his corrections and suggestions (*How to Marry a Millionaire*) is at Boston University, where they have a Doris Lilly archive. They have that manuscript with his teeny-weeny spidery handwriting. Truman had said, "Why don't you write a book?" I said, "I can't write." "Of course you can write. You wrote to me when I was at Yaddo, very funny letters, Doris. Really funny, I enjoyed them. I let everybody read them. You can write." I said, "I can't write." He said, "Write. I'll help you." I said, "What will I write about?" "Write about what you know about," he said. "Always write about what you know about. Don't write a book on how to care for your poodle. You don't have a poodle. Write about what you know about." I said, "I don't know about anything." He said, "Yes, you do. Every time I look at the newspaper, I see Doris Lilly is with a Whitney, an Astor, a Vanderbilt . . . write about a rich man. Write about how to marry a millionaire. Every woman will want to read it." I said, "Do you think I dare?"

He gave the book to Bennett Cerf, who turned it down. After it became a success, Bennett Cerf said, "I'm the man who turned down *How to Marry a Millionaire*."

PAUL BOWLES I first met Truman at a cocktail party on Tenth Street. He was sitting in the middle of the room on a circular love seat with two or three other people, all facing in different directions and talking. Jane and I opened the door and Truman was very quick. He looked up and said to the person sitting beside him, "Yes, Paul Bowles is a very *good* writer." They weren't talking about me at all, but he said it in such a way that I would hear it as I came in. So that gave me my first impression of Truman and it was totally accurate: he was a consummate actor. He wrote all his roles and acted them out.

WILLIAM STYRON When *Set This House on Fire* came out, I was in Rome again by sheer chance, and out of the blue—this must have been 1969—I got a very lively letter from Truman saying how much he liked the book, and so on, which cheered me greatly. It was not getting a terribly good reception. It helped endear him to me. Because he was so rough on so many fellow writers, I always felt that I was not in that category—I'm sure he was bitchy behind my back with someone else, but maybe not.

JOHN KNOWLES Oh yes, he was competitive. When *A Separate Peace* was about to be published in this country in 1960, Truman was asked for a blurb to put on the jacket. There had been a lot of problems with the book: it had been turned down by every publisher in America of consequence, even though it came from one of the leading literary agencies and thus was read by important editors. Finally it was published in London by Secker and Warburg. It had these wonderful reviews there; E. M. Forster wrote me a letter comparing it to Sophocles and saying that the book had set him thinking of *Philoctetes* because both deal with physical prowess and pain and with betrayal. Well, I took one look at this and I told Macmillan, which had finally decided to publish the book in the United States, to stop the presses and put that on the cover.

They wanted Truman's quote. He had written, "John Knowles is a promising American writer. There are carloads of those, but only one as promising as the author of *A Separate Peace*." Or something similar to that. Well, I already had E. M. Forster comparing me to

Sophocles and I didn't really need Truman Capote calling me "promising," because I knew I had left "promising" in the dust years before. But my publishers insisted on putting it on the jacket because Truman, they felt, would sell copies. They weren't sure anyone would know who E. M. Forster was. Or Sophocles.

Oh yes. Truman was terribly competitive. He was a dear friend of mine and a great admirer of my work; but he wasn't in any hurry to help anybody: I might just possibly develop into competition.

JOE PETROCIK (*friend*) He despised Lillian Hellman. He called her "George Washington in drag."

CAROL MARCUS MATTHAU Bill Saroyan and Truman got along very well. They were funny about human situations. Writers. They both hated Hemingway. They talked about the fake hair on his chest and all that. They talked about André Gide's diaries. Family things, human things. On a superficial, social level—there was no one more charming than Bill. He was fun to be with. But it exhausted him. I mean, if he had dinner with someone like Truman, he had to go to bed for three days afterward. It exhausted him to be that nice for so long.

NORMAN MAILER What I said about him all those years ago was that he wrote the best sentences of anyone in our generation. He had a lovely poetic ear. He did not have a good mind. I don't know if there was ever a large idea that bothered him for one minute. While he wrote poetically, he didn't think like a poet. He didn't have that concentrated sense of metaphor that a poet works toward. But he had a sense of time and place. *Breakfast at Tiffany's,* for example, is on the one hand a slight book. Looking at it with a hard Marxist eye, it's a charlotte russe. On the other hand, if you want to capture a period in New York, no other book has done it so well. So in that sense he's a bit like Fitzgerald. If I were to mount them all up on a wall, I'd put Truman somewhat below Fitzgerald, but of that ilk. He could capture period and place like few others.

I had a lot of respect for him as a writer and I was very competitive with him. I was competitive with all of them. The question "Are they better than me?" was all I ever lived with in those days. But with Truman I had a different feeling—mainly because I felt that what we were interested in and the way we wrote were so different. We really weren't ever going to compete one on one.

We met in a limousine. We were going on the David Susskind television show. My wife Adele was looking pretty sexy that night and she sat between us and practically engulfed him. It was as if a small monkey had been suddenly sat down next to Carmen. So I was enjoying that. It was going for me.

At the beginning of the show Truman was tight and Dorothy Parker was in a total state of nerves. I did all the talking. I thought that I was being absolutely extraordinary. The more I talked, the stronger I felt. Susskind was irritated. He wanted to get Truman talking and there I'm going rapatarapatarap. I thought, "This dumb son of a bitch Susskind, if he doesn't stop looking at his watch, I'm going to stop speaking." So I did. I clammed up. Dumbest thing I've ever done. Truman was off to the races then and he never stopped. It never had occurred to me that he was equal in any way. He was so small physically that I felt so much larger. Of course, on TV what they were doing was getting long shots of me and closing in on him, head and shoulders. So he looked pretty dynamic on TV. But he didn't know that at the time, and he was so depressed when the show was over that he insisted on taking us out to El Morocco. He kept saying, "I knew I shouldn't go on the show. I told Bennett Cerf I didn't want to. Bennett said I'd do very well, but I told him no. TV is for *you*, not for me." It was very late at night by the time the show was over—midnight on a Sunday. No one was at El Morocco. We sat in one of those striped booths and the waiters took care of him. Fawned over him. Slowly, he led into this: "Well, this has been quite an evening for me. The only consolation I have is that I have these two wonderful new friends, Adele and Norman Mailer."

The next day I woke up to gather my accolades. The phone rang and the first friend of the morning said, "Oh, man, did Truman murder you!" So I started calling people to find out. Even people who were totally on my side would say, "Well . . . I thought you did well . . ." That's what my sister said. And she added, "But that Truman's fascinating." He won New York that night. More damn people said, "Did you see that show?" What did it in part was his remark about Jack Kerouac . . . "It is not writing. It is only typing." That one remark! Truman was so much what he was. No one had ever seen anyone like him before . . . never had known there was anyone like that alive. There he was! So alive, so sure of himself, so much what he was. There I was floundering all over the place with these huge philosophical concepts and long speeches I couldn't quite put together.

WILLIAM STYRON Truman and I were roughly the same age. I remember when I was an editor at McGraw-Hill around 1947, *Life* magazine came out with one of those . . . in those days when *Life* was such a big deal, everyone read it . . . they had a spread on "The Younger American Writers," and there was a picture of Truman looking very decadent and cute. Plainly freakish, but rather delicate and pretty in this earlier incarnation. I remember wondering who he was. Then I read some of those stories. I was knocked out by them. Absolutely devastated because they were just so brilliant. Here was a guy my age who had published these stories . . . they were so good and more than precocious, really quite mature. I think at that time I had just barely started working on *Lie Down in Darkness.* I remember being so impressed and feeling that here was a guy who was my exact contemporary, who (though I was properly envious) was a kind of inspiration to me. If he could do it, maybe I could do it too. I remember being bowled over by his talent. I didn't much care about his outer nature. Everyone knew by that time . . . he'd already established his legendary posture. It didn't matter to me that he was gay and a freak. I was very much in awe of his talent.

GORE VIDAL I don't find many of my contemporaries very interesting, which is a bum rap because some of them must indeed be. I'd like to read more Heller, Vonnegut. I read anything new by Paul Bowles; I read anything by Anthony Burgess, William Golding. I'm apt not to finish anything by Bellow or begin anything by Capote. No. It's not a question of competitiveness as journalists like to think. First of all, my interests are not their interests. I write about the fifth century B.C. and comparative religion and Confucius and the Buddha and Zoroaster and Socrates, and, of course, American history. Subjects of no interest to my contemporaries. I don't approach their territory. Nor they mine. I don't want to know about marriage. Suburban adultery. And who gets custody of the children. I'm not even interested in the awakening of the young homosexual in the South and whether or not to wear crêpe de chine before sundown. Important though these things are to the sensitive author, they do not tug at my heartstrings. So if you're that different from the others, how can you feel competitive about them?

Once, Capote said to me, "Thank heavens, Gore, we're not intellectuals." I said, "Speak for your fucking self!" "Intellectual" was the worst word in his vocabulary.

PAUL BOWLES Gore could imitate Truman on the phone. It was perfect, he could fool anyone. He would call up Tennessee and say, "Hullo." Tennessee would say, "Yes, who is this?"

"This is Troo-man!"

"How are you, Truman?"

Then Gore would go into a long diatribe: "I thought you'd like to hear this; there may not be anything in it, but . . ."

Tennessee would get rather upset.

DIANA TRILLING It's interesting to compare Gore Vidal and Truman Capote. In some ways I prefer the Truman Capote way of doing things. I was thinking of Gore because recently I saw a movie on television about West Point called *Dress Gray.* It was very good. Gore wrote the teleplay from a successful novel about a West Point murder. And did very well indeed. He's skillful. It was well acted and well directed. But it was full of Gore's anti-establishment politics—his left-wing anti-Vietnam War, his anti-establishment, anti-military-industrial complex, and anti-religious wrath of oblivious fathers. The works, he gave us the works! Now, no matter what you say about Truman, he did not go sliding along the greased path of political, liberal, enlightened—supposedly enlightened ideas. Truman's chic was what you might call designer chic—it was the chic of the homosexual smart world and he did not take on the cultural and political views of people who secretly think of themselves as so much better—like the way Gore or Kenneth Tynan or *The New York Review of Books* do. In some sense Truman was pure and braver, in my view. He didn't just "dress up" his books with a lot of political, unexamined, regurgitated folderol from the left.

DOTSON RADER Truman hated academic writers. Hated them. People like Barth, the schoolteachers. Even Bellow. He thought they were playing on a field that wasn't level. He thought it was stupid that schoolteachers were writing books for other schoolteachers to teach. Nobody would read Barth if he wasn't taught. Nobody rushes to the bookstore and says, "Give me the new Barth!" They're not lining up outside of Doubleday's. If you want to find Barth, you've got to go to the Harvard Coop. Again, it was the pretense. They weren't taking any risks. They got their schoolteacher salary whether their book worked or didn't work. I think he thought of writers in the cocoon of academia as artistically cowardly and, in a way, that they'd sold out. His animus toward schoolteachers was so great because I think secretly he wanted their approval. When he couldn't finish *Answered Prayers* after all the hullabaloo, he knew he'd failed in their eyes.

He liked Faulkner. He felt sorry for him. He was jealous of those who knew him. He'd pick up the newspaper and read some column and there'd be an item about Ruth Ford having a party and he'd read that Faulkner was there.

I said to him, "Well, you know, Ruth was such a great friend of Faulkner's and he wrote a play for her, *Requiem for a Nun*. She's got all these Faulkner letters and stuff. She's got letters from everybody, you wouldn't believe . . ." She's sitting on twenty million dollars' worth of letters and photographs. She's like a pack squirrel. If you want to be immortal, send her a letter. Anyway, I said, "She's a great friend of Faulkner's."

He said, "Oh yes? Bill never mentioned her to me."

I asked, "How did you know Faulkner?" He told me that at Random House Bennett Cerf would give his very special writers keys. Particularly out-of-town writers because they'd have no place to work when they visited New York. Truman said he saw Faulkner in there a lot at night. Finally, Bennett complained to Bill about the

Truman and Katharine Graham, the guest of honor at his black-and-white ball. *(Henry Grossman)*

The Grand Ballroom of the Plaza. *(Elliott Erwitt/Magnum)*

Marella Agnelli. *(Henry Grossman)*

Tallulah Bankhead. *(Henry Grossman)*

Penelope Tree. *(Henry Grossman)*

Cecil Beaton. *(Henry Grossman)*

Marianne Moore. *(Henry Grossman)*

Candice Bergen. *(Henry Grossman)*

Mr. and Mrs. William F. Buckley, Jr.
(Henry Grossman)

Frank Sinatra and
Mia Farrow.
(Elliott Erwitt/Magnum)

Mr. and Mrs. Norman Mailer. *(Henry Grossman)*

Mrs. Henry Ford. *(Henry Grossman)*

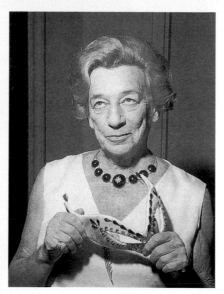

Lillian Hellman. *(Henry Grossman)*

Susan Burden and escort. *(Henry Grossman)*

Marisa Berenson
and escort.
(Henry Grossman)

Princess Peggy D'Arenberg
and Prince Serge Oblensky.
(Henry Grossman)

Mr. and Mrs.
Irving Lazar.
(Henry Grossman)

Henry Geldzahler. *(Henry Grossman)*

Charles Addams about to identify himself.
(Henry Grossman)

Mr. and Mrs. Oscar de la Renta. *(Henry Grossman)*

Lee Radziwill. *(Henry Grossman)*

Jean Stein. *(Henry Grossman)*

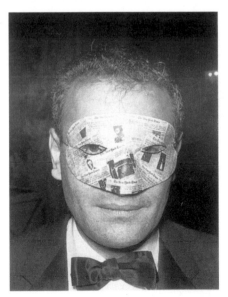

Arthur Sulzberger. *(Henry Grossman)*

drinking because it was making the offices smell like a brewery. They'd come in in the morning and find him passed out on Cerf's sofa. It was bad for business. People would see an old drunk and they didn't realize this guy was going to win a Nobel Prize.

Anyway, Truman liked Faulkner a lot. Faulkner had this thing— he pretended to be a hick, used "ain't" a lot and that sort of thing. Good old boy. Truman said that Faulkner got drunk at some party of his and asked if he could take a bath. He was in the tub for forty or fifty minutes and Truman got worried about him, so he went into the bathroom and found Faulkner in the bathtub crying. Truman sat on the toilet and he said they didn't say a word, but it was a great comfort to Faulkner that he was there.

KURT VONNEGUT You could touch Truman off by asking, "How come Harper Lee never wrote anything else?" That would go on for a while. He spoke badly of other writers; I assume he must have done the same about me. Almost any name I brought up he would dismiss. He dismissed James Jones. I think he dismissed Updike. He blew Vidal away, just kind of farting around with him.

JOHN KNOWLES I liked her [Harper Lee] very much. I met her only once. The Cerfs gave a dinner party at their house in New York after the publication of *In Cold Blood*. The Deweys were there from Kansas. I sat next to Harper Lee, very nice, charming, down-to-earth, masculine sort of woman. Very nice. You can see how they would have gravitated toward each other as children. She was a real tomboy and he was this strange little elfin person. They were both very talented and special. They adored each other, were very close.

PEARL KAZIN BELL He implied, and I have a feeling it may be true, that he wrote a good part of *To Kill a Mockingbird*. She never wrote another thing after that, which may or may not be explained by the fact that he helped her enormously. It's not a book that I particularly like—a little too obvious in some ways, too predictable. I remember when my son was in the seventh grade that was one of the books being assigned to the class as an example of great literature. So I went dancing around to the teacher and said, "Look, there is one book that should be read at that age (they were all around twelve at that point)—it's a perfect book for young people growing up, and that book is called *Great Expectations.*" She said, "I would love to have the kids read *Great Expectations,* but the parents, the nice liberal parents in Cambridge, Massachusetts, would come around and say, 'You're putting too much pressure on my child. That book is too long.'" So it had to be *To Kill a Mockingbird,* which was really rather a pity. If he did write some of it, it was certainly not his own voice, but in a voice that he assumed would be taken for hers. He was clever at that sort of thing. He would have made sure that it fit in with the rest of it, that it wasn't just a sudden spurt of Capote-like lyricism coming in the midst of this rather pedestrian prose.

DAVID JACKSON We rarely talked about writing. I can only remember once having lunch in a little café on the coast of Greece. "Now, David, you have got to write. It's hard, but you've got to sit at that typewriter and write." I said, "Well, T, if you haven't got anything to write about, I just don't want to gas on." He said, "You know what I've discovered is that if I can gas on and on, then I just cut it to shreds and out of that comes meat."

It wasn't bad advice, you know. I never followed it. He was always trying to urge Jimmy [Merrill] to do that. Jimmy is meticulous. Oh, my God—*months* on one ten-line poem. Truman just thought it was maddeningly wasteful. "Jimmy, just let it out. Let it out!"

WINSTON GROOM I said, "Truman, I'm thinking about going back to Washington." At that point I'd been living out on Long Island for a long time—two winters. Truman said, "Go to New York, live hard, high . . . don't pull any punches . . . don't write down anything you see . . . live in New York and write about what you think! And trust your instincts! That's important!" So I tried to do that and it was a disaster. Mailer and all those people, they'd been living in New York all their lives, and writing about it and I'm a Southerner! Well, I took his advice as best I could and for ten years all I wrote in New York was checks. There were some spectacular checks. Ten years and all I wrote was checks!

DOMINICK DUNNE *(writer)* I went through a terrible period in my life. I'd become a drunk and I went broke and lost my family and all these awful things happened. I went off to Oregon and lived in a little one-room cabin in the Cascade Mountains. I lived there for six months; I just dropped out of my life and actually thought of staying there forever. The only people who knew how to get hold of me were my kids—there was a way to phone me through the person from whom I'd rented the cabin—and that is when, by the way, I started to write. I was fifty years old. I had never written before. I had been a movie and television producer. Anyway, one day, out of the blue, I got a letter from Truman Capote. I couldn't get over it. I couldn't figure out how he knew where I was or why he would write. Although we had always liked each other, we were not letter-writing friends . . . I mean, I don't want to exaggerate my friendship with him. So it was quite a unique experience that he wrote. It was a letter of admiration and encouragement for what I had done: it was one of the kindest letters possible and he ended it by saying this: "But remember this, that is not where you belong and when you get out of it what you went there to get, you have to come back to your own life." Eventually, I left Oregon, closed up my Hollywood life totally, and moved to New York. I kept thinking of that letter. We were not that good friends that I deserved that kind of letter. So what I had done is obviously what he knew that he should have done. I quit drinking during that period up there. I kept thinking to myself, he'd be alive if he did what I did. I had to weep at the memorial service. After he died, you know it got very fashionable to kick him. Not me. I've never forgotten the letter he wrote me. I never will.

NORMAN MAILER Something very nice happened to him while he was writing *In Cold Blood*, which was that he was getting more masculine—which was terribly important to him. It was much more important to him than to any other homosexual I've known. He really wanted to be a most fearsome little man. He did not want to be received as a homosexual. Getting to know all those people out in Kansas—the KBI men, people like that—had given him fiber. He was toughening up, and now you could see what a strong man was there along with everything else. Then of course he got fat. Then he got impossible. He turned dictatorial and boring. By the time he knew Jan, what I couldn't bear about him was he was boring. Truman had become boring. Terribly opinionated. He used to remind me of J. Edgar Hoover toward the end. Looked like him.

CAROL MARCUS MATTHAU The last time I saw Truman was on the Dick Cavett show. Dick was getting ready to come in on a slant, as he does in his dry, wry way. Truman stopped him and said, "Dick, I came on the show tonight . . ." (and it wasn't the caricature of Truman at all. It was the real Truman. I recognized it immediately by the pitch of his voice). "There's something I have to say," he told Dick Cavett. "I hope you don't feel I'm using you, because I didn't come on the show to try to be witty or funny."

Cavett was very gracious and sat back. Then Truman began to talk straight about Tennessee Williams's death and what it really meant . . . that one of the foremost artists we have had died. The last twenty years of his life had been hell because he went into a room every day and he wrote for many hours. But he knew that no matter what he wrote, even if it far surpassed *Glass Menagerie, Streetcar,* all of them, that they would still throw cabbages at him because he had gone out of fashion. But because he was an artist he still did his work everyday. It takes a lot of bravery and strength to do it under those circumstances. America is very, very cruel to its artists. It doesn't give them a chance for growth. It doesn't give them elbow room for change. There's no room at all for failure.

1966

CHAPTER TWENTY-SIX *In Which TC Decides to Give His Black-and-White Ball*

MR. TRUMAN CAPOTE

Requests The Pleasure of your Company at

A Black and White Dance

On November Twenty-eighth

at Ten o'clock

New York, N.Y.

in The Grand Ballroom of The Hotel Plaza

R.S.V.P.

name etc.

Telephone number

Dress Black tie.

Gentlemen: Black tie.

Ladies. Black or white dress. white masks. Fans. Jewelry— only diamonds and pearls and Jet

(Truman Capote Papers, The New York Public Library)

JOHN KNOWLES Don't you think Truman sat there in Monroeville, Alabama, when he was about ten, deeply rejected and out of it, strange little outcast, even in his own house, and said that someday he would hire the most beautiful ballroom in New York City and he would have the most elegant and famous people in the world there?

KATHARINE GRAHAM (*publisher*) Truman called me up that summer and said, "I think you need cheering up. And I'm going to give you a ball." Well, I said, "I don't need cheering up and what are you talking about?" I was totally baffled. He said, "Yes, yes, I've always had this idea for a black-and-white ball." He told me that he'd always loved the black-and-white scene at the racetrack in *My Fair Lady*. Also, he said that he loved the ballroom in the Plaza and always wanted to have a party there.

I was still sort of baffled. But then he got rolling with it and the publicity got started. I felt a little bit that Truman was going to give the ball anyway and that I was part of the props. Perhaps a "prop" is unfair, but I felt that he needed a guest of honor and with a lot of imagination he figured out me.

PHYLLIS CERF WAGNER I first learned he was going to do it sitting around the pool. He'd been dreaming about it for a long time. The Plaza was his place, as you know, his security blanket. Before his books came out, he and I had become really instant friends, and we would go to the Plaza to have lunch there. In the beginning the only place that he felt secure enough to go to. Eventually he spread out to Voisin, La Côte Basque, and so forth, but earlier the Plaza was the place that was elegant and classy enough for him. It represented something to him. I would guess that was why he decided to have the ball there.

ASHTON HAWKINS (*museum executive*) Truman recognized that she was a powerful woman who didn't really know anything about the big world outside of Washington in those days. She hadn't pursued it or expected to. He chose her as his guest of honor and got all these people together. She was kind of shy about it, unused to the attention and not that comfortable with it. She didn't seek it out; she was quite pleased that somebody would do it for her.

ELEANOR FRIEDE At the beginning of that summer in Bridgehampton I was a kind of zombie. My husband, Donald, had died suddenly on Memorial Day. That summer, 1965, Truman would come every day and sit by the pool. This may be a fantasy, because I was in a very strange state, but I thought he was *inventing* the ball to keep *me* going! He came every single day to the pool with a guest list he was working on. For a time I just couldn't believe it. "I'm not going to invite the Lyndon Johnsons . . . those Secret Service men are so boring! Maybe just Lynda Bird." Even when I realized it wasn't a fantasy, it was all quite magical. I don't think I could have gotten through the summer without him.

LEO LERMAN The ball was one of his major works. As much a major work as some of his short stories. He sat there planning it all summer long. I came back from somewhere to find him surrounded by these notebooks. I wondered what work is he writing? It turned out to be this ball. One of the things he adored saying was "Well, maybe you'll be invited and maybe you won't." He'd say things like "Well, are we going to have so-and-so?" Then he'd make little notes. He had the most marvelous time doing it. It was his reward for all those years he kept to himself. It was ostensibly for Kay Graham. It was for Truman.

DOMINICK DUNNE Two years before Truman's ball, on my tenth wedding anniversary, my wife, Lenny, and I gave a black-and-white ball where the ladies were asked to dress in black and white. We had a policy that no one could bring houseguests or anything because there was just limited space. At the last minute Truman called and said, "Yes, yes, I'm coming, I'm going to be there, but I'm bringing three guests." Well, we didn't have the nerve to say to him, "Well, you can't bring them." They turned out to be Alvin Dewey, the FBI agent, his wife, and a third person involved in the *In Cold Blood* case. It was a very glamorous affair, filled with film stars. These people from that little town in Kansas were absolutely awed by it. I mean David Niven, Gina Lollobrigida, Natalie Wood, Loretta Young, Jennifer Jones, I mean it went on and on. That was 1964, the days when Hollywood was still the kind of Hollywood that we fantasize about.

We had our house totally cleared of furniture and off the library in the back there was this tent so huge that friends who had been coming to our house for years were disoriented, they didn't know where they were. We had two bands. It was very beautiful, an extravagant waste of money. I mean, later in life I went broke, and that was a perfect example of why. Truman loved it. I have these incredible photographs of him dancing with Tuesday Weld, talking to Jennifer Jones. He was one of the last ones to leave. Then two years later he gave his great ball, the black-and-white ball, did the same thing, but he didn't invite us!

GEORGE PLIMPTON Truman must have kept at his guest list all that summer, pruning, adding, mostly pruning, I suspect. I remember one summer day at the Bennett Cerfs' in Mount Kisco—the estate they called the Columns because the money to build it had come from the proceeds Bennett got for his syndicated columns— "Tradewinds," "Cerfboard" among them. It was a hot day and I remember the luncheon guests gathered around the swimming pool that afternoon—Frank Sinatra, Mia, his young wife then, and Truman of course. Mia in a black bathing suit, as I remember, was lying on her back in the sun by the edge of the pool—just enchanting, and not really part of the conversation or anything, when suddenly a butterfly landed on the exposed part of her breast, just above the line of the bathing suit. It was one of the large swallowtail variety, the kind that fans its wings absolutely straight up and holds them there motionless, a sail for an instant, and then fans them again. Absolutely beautiful, of course, obviously because it had picked Mia to land on, faunlike, childlike, and we all stared spellbound. Then Truman broke it, quite abruptly. "What about the Goetzes?" he called out quite loudly, or some such name. "Should I invite them, or consign them . . ."

SHANA ALEXANDER (*writer*) I had just got divorced in California, and was in New York having dinner at the Lafayette restaurant with David Merrick. David said, "I'm going to a party called a black-and-white ball and you're not invited, so you can't come. Truman is giving it. He's hired squads of security men to keep out crashers." David didn't know that Truman and I were old friends, or that I happened to notice that at the next table a piece of paper was curled in the glass that read "Capote." By chance, Truman's table was reserved, right at the next banquette. So I thought I would be clever. I went into the ladies' room and wrote on my card, "Have black-and-white dress in suitcase, just hit town." Because I lived in California, I thought if I stuck it in Truman's pocket unobtrusively, if he didn't invite me, if Merrick was right, it wouldn't be embarrassing. He would simply find this card in his pocket from an old friend.

He came and sat down. To make himself look slim he had on one of those Morty Sills suits with no pockets. But I didn't know that. I kept trying to find a pocket to slip my card into. He finally asked, "What the hell are you doing to me?" "I was trying to put this card in your pocket," I said. He looked at it and said, "Of course you can come to my party, I'd love to have you come to my party." Merrick, well—his balloon was punctured but mine was blown up.

TOMMY PHIPPS (*writer*) He'd call us up and talk about it. I distinctly remember him talking about the people who thought they were being terribly cunning by saying, "What are you doing on Monday the twenty-eighth?" knowing full well that he was knee deep in the Plaza. That old trick. It's worked many, many times. But not with Truman.

R. COURI HAY (*reporter*) Truman always claimed he invited 500 of his friends and made 15,000 enemies.

PETER DUCHIN (*orchestra leader*) We had been asked by Truman to play at his ball, obviously a private affair. He'd said to me, "Please don't tell anybody." Of course, everybody knew instantly, because there was an awful lot of talk about the ball before it was given. One day I got a call in my office from Earl Wilson, the columnist. Earl said to me, "Gee, Peter, I hear you're playing Truman Capote's black-and-white ball." I said, "Yes." He said, "Well, you know, they're not allowing the press in at all." I said, "Earl, that is unfortunate and what a shame." "Well," he said, "you know there's this wonderful thing I once did"—I can't remember if he'd done it or someone else, which was that he had snuck into the White House during Roosevelt's administration as a fiddle player. He said, "I wonder if you'd consider letting me sneak into the party as one of your trombonists." I said, "Let me think about it, Earl." So I thought about it, and thought it wouldn't be a terribly good idea. I do remember the way Earl Wilson looked, short and bulbous, and that a trombone would have been a suitable instrument.

ELEANOR FRIEDE Truman was absolutely terrible about his guest list. If he liked the husband and didn't like the wife he'd invite the husband. He wanted lots of single men. Ken McCormick was dating Ann Hutchens, whom he later married, but Truman was insistent. "Absolutely not!" He was ruthless.

JAMES MERRILL I hadn't been asked, which was perfectly all right with me. It's not my idea of the best way to spend an evening. But whom it mattered to tremendously was Grace Stone, the novelist. She and her daughter, Eleanor Perényi, were Truman's great friends in Stonington, though Truman had mixed feelings about Grace. We went out to Brooklyn one night for dinner after he'd had his Stonington summer. He'd hoped just David and I would come, but we said, "Oh, Grace is in town. Wouldn't you like her to come along?" So he said sure. Truman's apartment had this room that had been multifariously reupholstered: he brought back all these swatches of silk from the Orient and every cushion was done in a different one. He'd taken the bolts of cloth to an upholsterer and said do what you can. There were too many cushions for a *van* to carry out to Brooklyn. There were a couple of rather nice armchairs upholstered in yellow brocade. Anyhow, we went in the kitchen for dinner and somebody smelled something burning; Grace's cigarette had landed in an armchair. Truman was very gentlemanly about it:

"Oh, it doesn't matter. Don't be silly." But after dinner, he put on records and wanted to dance. I was dancing with Truman: "That old bitch, I didn't want her here anyway!" Very cross about his armchair.

So she wasn't on the party list. I think she ought to have been. I think he thought she ought to have been too, because people he had met through her, like the Lionel Trillings, were invited. She was an old friend and had known him from the days of his first success. So when she wasn't on the invitation list, she could not resist writing him a note: "Truman, I didn't think that you were the kind of person who climbed atop corpses of your former friends. As it happens, I shall not be in this country when you give your affair. I'm flying to Rome the day before, and I won't have been there, but I do think you might have invited me."

Well, I saw the letter that she got back. It was on a loose-leaf lined pad with his little handwriting: "Gee, I wish you had spared yourself writing me this cruel letter. Of course an invitation was sent to you to East Seventy-ninth Street. Of course I expect you. Please let me know whether you will come and the name of your escort." Handling it very nicely.

But Grace had already cut off her nose, as it were, and couldn't have gone to the party without the stitches showing! She left for Europe that day or the day before. She might have changed her plans. We talked about it. I said, "Grace, you can't, not now."

BOB COLACELLO (writer) Truman did invite Andy Warhol to the black-and-white ball, but he couldn't bring anyone, which for Andy in the sixties was a major agony.

JANE HOWARD (writer) It was much more fun to get ready for the black-and-white ball than it was to go. It was actually kind of a letdown. I remember being annoyed because he gave me to understand that I should not bring somebody. I was kind of miffed.

This guy I was seeing then took pictures of me getting ready and then I was off and I thought, "Gee, without him. Why can't he come too?"

MARISA BERENSON (*model, actress*) Halston was a close friend at that time. He did my mask and my dress—a whole outfit where I was supposed to come as a rabbit: I had a long black velvet dress, ears and a rabbit face. Then I missed a fitting and he thought I wasn't going to go. So he gave the dress to Amanda Burden. I was absolutely devastated. At the last minute he had to make me something completely new. I wore a turban. I turned from a rabbit into an Indian princess—extremely exotic. Halston always did wonderful things.

DENISE BOUCHÉ (*friend*) I looked pretty silly. At Kenneth's I had my hair dyed black on one side and powdered white on the other. Talk about a skunk! I wore it sort of like Madame Pompadour. Then I had a mask left over from the masked ball for Sheila Rochambeau that her stepfather, the Duc de Talleyrand, gave for her just outside Paris, where we all wore opera capes. Saint Laurent did it for me— little black sparkles in it, cat's eyes with a little red in the corners. For Truman's it went perfectly with a black-and-white crepe evening dress I already had from Simonetta or Princess Marietta or Galici, I forget which. So I didn't have to do much except for my hair, which was my idea. At Kenneth's they're never surprised by what I ask for. I was rather embarrassed to find myself sitting next to Kay Graham—with my hair going black and white while she seemed to be having a fairly simple hairdo!

KATHARINE GRAHAM I'd been over there the week before and I had my hair done on the second floor. This woman Murray was at the top of the stairs. She said, "We're all so busy preparing for the ball." It was sort of like Cinderella. I said, "Well, the ball's being thrown for me." She said, "It's being thrown for *you*?" She said, "Well, who's doing your hair?" And I said, "I don't know, Jonathan somebody," and she said, "Well, Kenneth has to do your hair." Which he did after he put thousands of ringlets in Marisa Berenson's hair.

ADOLFO (*designer*) Some of the orders for masks came in many weeks before the ball. I would be shown the design of the dress and then suggest what the mask would look like to go well with the

dress, or with jewelry . . . a blue sapphire. Oh, we did many, many—
for Drue Heinz, Adele Astaire, Merle Oberon, Amanda Burden,
Betsy Bloomingdale. Hers I remember best—a very delicate one,
made in the shape of a butterfly and held up on a stick. All of them
had sticks, sometimes in the middle, sometimes on the side. A mask
that fits the face disturbs the makeup and so on when you take it
off, so they all had little sticks to hold. We were very busy. I was
invited to the ball, but I don't do very well at such things. So
Truman came in later and told me all about it.

PETER MATTHIESSEN (*writer*) Truman was kind of upset when I told
him my book was going well and I didn't want to break off to go to
the black-and-white party. I explained that I would only get drunk
and lose the drift of things for two or three days, but he was utterly
unmollified. He was even more annoyed when Bill Styron stayed
home, too, for the same reason. Bill had rung up to ask if I was
going to Truman's party, and when I said, "No," he said, "Great! I'm
not going, either!" As it turned out, we missed something wonderful,
and Bill upbraids me every few years—"You talked us out of the best
party in history!" Next time I saw Truman, he was still a little sulky.
When I asked if I was forgiven, he burst out, "Cecil Beaton came all
the way from London for my party, and you wouldn't even come in
from Sagaponack!"

GEORGE PAGE (*television executive*) While I was in Vietnam I began
to get calls from Truman, who had figured out how to call me there,
a rather amazing feat in and of itself, and he told me about this
party that from the outset he began to talk about as "the party of the
century," how I absolutely must come. I would say, "Truman, you
know there is no way I can come all the way from Saigon to New
York." Having since learned that people were absolutely fighting and
would kill for invitations to that party, I've concluded I must be just
about the only one who declined Truman's kind invitation.

MARIA THERESA CAEN (*literary agent*) I flew from San Francisco to
New York, carrying my mask. Literally everyone, porters at the
airport, cabdrivers, strangers, it seemed like all of New York knew

about the party. I couldn't put my mask in my bag, it would have been all squashed and ruined. It was on a stick, covered in cellophane, and everyone knew I was going to Truman's ball. They'd say, "Oh! You're going to Truman's party!" Not to "Capote's party" but to *"Truman's* party." It was so intimate. For a while it looked like I was going to Truman's ball with a bath towel and the mask because the airline lost my bag with my dress. It finally arrived at the hotel two hours before the ball. In the meantime, Geraldine Stutz sent over something I could wear from Bendel's in case my dress didn't arrive. There was great excitement in the hotel. The maids would come running in and say, "Oh, your dress is here, your dress is here!"

HERB CAEN It was the talk of New York. The elevator operators, the taxicab drivers, the doormen, as soon as they saw you with a mask or headdress, they said, "Going to Truman's ball, huh?" New York had that funny small-town feel to it; they were all excited that you were going to the ball. That part was fun. It was like the Super Bowl. There was such a buildup that by the time the game was played, it didn't amount to much.

PHYLLIS CERF WAGNER I guess we all were glad to be there, that's the name of the game. If you hadn't been invited, you would have been terribly hurt. It was a good party as parties go. I mean, certainly the world was there, and you wouldn't have wanted to be left out of the world. So there we were.

November 28, 1966

CHAPTER TWENTY-SEVEN   *In Which*

the Band Strikes Up

Peter Duchin's was the orchestra of Truman's choice for the black-and-white ball. Peter was asked to feature Cole Porter's music in particular—the rest of the repertoire mostly Gershwin, Rodgers, Kern. (Henry Grossman)

JOEL SCHUMACHER (*film director*) There were dinner parties before the ball. Afterward, buses with manned bars and champagne took everyone to the Plaza. So who was invited to whose party was very important. It was not enough to go to the ball; you also had to go to one of these five or six major parties that took place *before* the ball. Hosts and hostesses, as I remember, were extremely nervous. They had given their word to Truman that they would be on time for the ball. They had to make sure that their parties didn't last too long. There was a wonderful man who worked at *Vogue*, the Baron Nicholas de Gunzburg, one of the taste arbiters. The hostess of the dinner he was going to was so nervous about being late that she kept calling him, saying, "Now, we've promised Truman we won't be late . . ." He was very droll. He had this little cigarette he was smoking. This was about two days before the party. He said, "Well, why don't we just all get dressed and go *now*. We won't be late."

PIEDY LUMET We gave one of the dinners before the ball. We had the writers. Norman Mailer sat next to me; he said, "You ought to be an elevator operator. You just go up and down." I don't even want to think about what he meant by that.

NORMAN MAILER I met Pat Lawford at dinner before the ball. Piedy Lumet gave the dinner. Lawford and I were seated next to each other. We got along like a house afire because we did nothing but insult each other all night. It was wonderful. She said, "I don't know why I'm sitting next to you. I've heard you're awful." Or some extraordinary thing. I said, "Well, that just shows how dumb the people are that you know." We've gotten along ever since.

JOHN KENNETH GALBRAITH (*economist*) Kitty and I went down to New York and went to Jean Stein's dinner beforehand where I sat next to Alice Longworth. A few days before, Jonathan Daniels's memoir about Franklin Roosevelt had just been published, which for the first time gave wide recognition to the existence of Lucy Mercer. So I immediately asked her about that, and got a marvelous Longworth response which I don't think has ever been repeated:

"Absolutely nothing to it—everybody knows that Franklin was paralyzed from the waist down."

MARY LAZAR *(friend)* Donald Brooks had designed me an enormous and very funny headpiece. Enormous! It looked like something Josephine would have worn if Irving had gone as Napoleon. Black velvet, net, and things. It was so large I couldn't get in the car after the dinner with it because it was too high. We had the Rolls-Royce in New York at that time. We took Lauren Bacall and other people to the Plaza. The car had a nervous breakdown that night. The weather was cold and damp, a slight rain. It broke down in front of the Plaza, so that was lucky. It wasn't used to the weather. It froze.

MIA FARROW *(actress)* I remember the great excitement, the throng of press at the door of the Plaza, and all the beautiful gowns, but I didn't know who Katharine Graham was, and in fact I didn't know who anybody was.

KATHARINE GRAHAM Truman and I had drinks with the Paleys, and then we went off to a room upstairs in the Plaza and had a box dinner which I'd ordered from "21." Then about ten we went down to stand in the receiving line.

JOHN KNOWLES I thought the masked ball was a hoot. I felt as though we were in Versailles in 1788. People were applauding us in the street as we walked in. We had our masks on. I thought next year it'll be the tumbrels taking us to Herald Square, but at the moment we were the last of the aristocrats. I remember arriving at the side entrance of the Plaza. There was a solid phalanx of news media. I forget exactly what group I was with but no stars were with us. We arrived and the klieg lights went on because we were masked. They turned on the lights and looked at us. Nobody. The lights went off again.

AILEEN MEHLE *(society columnist)* With most parties you can tell when you walk in the door, *this is going to go.* I mean everything from a little dinner party of sixteen people to a huge ball for a thousand people. You go in and you *know this is going to go.* Or you go in and you say to yourself, *uh-uh, no, no, no.*

When I came in at the start of the party Truman said, —"Darling"—the way he always said "Darling"—"stay close by us and that way you can see everybody as they come in." He thought that would be an excellent vantage point for me. And he wanted me to see the guests, of course, because he knew I was going to write about it all. It was the most dazzling party that I had ever been to . . . so *far,* of course. If anyone else had given it, it really wouldn't have been that dazzling. But it was Truman, who meant so much then, it was Kay, a powerful woman, and it was the guest list. Also, it was the costumes. Everyone went all out. It was the first time I'd ever seen Penelope Tree. She looked like a forest creature, these great eyes staring out and her hair hanging straight and I remember she was dressed as a wood nymph. Most of the costumes were superb. Oscar and Françoise de la Renta came with big furry cat heads on, one black and the other white, and they were marvelous.

The mask thing was very clever of Truman. If people had come in dinner jackets and evening dresses, well, it still would have been a glamorous party, but it never would have had that extra cachet that Truman created by (a) the guest list and then (b) asking them to dress like that, masked and marvelous.

JACK DUNPHY I had a mask, a little thing. As soon as I came into the room, Truman was so disgusted with the way I looked he pulled it right off and said, "Kay, here's Jack." That mask business was very funny. A member in my party said, "I've lost it." I said, "You haven't lost it at all, you've just lost your identity. You're so confused at the idea of covering those lovely orbs of yours." He did, he just threw it away.

BEN BRADLEE *(editor)* There was Truman sort of beaming and next to him Katharine with a wonderful mixture of being proud and yet wondering whether or not this was the path down which she wished to travel. But for a moment there she was—the belle of the ball and she wore it so nicely. I was quite moved. But then when you walked in . . . well, I had never quite endorsed the Beautiful People because there were so many weirdos. Still, there were a lot of people in the ballroom who don't ordinarily go to such events, and therefore it had a sort of unjaded quality.

JOHN KENNETH GALBRAITH I didn't buy a mask. My professional dignity overwhelmed me, and also the fact that since I'm six feet eight and a half inches tall, the likelihood that I would be concealed by a mask was minimal. We made our way up the stairs to the ballroom just behind Bill Buckley and his wife, Pat, who turned and said to me, "I'm going to choke you before the evening is over for what you said about Bill." I'd forgotten what the hell it was I said about him. I do remember going up the stairs, facing the wrath of my tall fellow Canadian, and to be greeted at the top of the stairs by, of all people, Truman Capote and Kay Graham.

WILLIAM F. BUCKLEY, JR. I recall meeting Ken Galbraith for the first time. It was rather extraordinary in that he took the occasion to apologize for an indiscretion he felt badly about. What had happened was that he had upbraided a distinguished economist for having written for the *National Review* at the time Kennedy was killed. It was an entirely emotional decision, the idea nobody that high up in academe ought to be associated with any magazine that opposed Jack Kennedy so strongly. Well, he took that occasion to apologize for having done that.

GEORGE PLIMPTON I had a mask which was glued together about one day before and I could barely . . . I went staggering past Truman and Kay Graham in the receiving line. I spent most of the evening quite sick with this mask. I had gotten rather *précieux* and had this thing made. It hadn't been stitched together; it had been glued. When you put the thing on it was like being in a glue factory. They always say sniffing glue gives you a high but this didn't. It made me quite nauseated. I reeled around. I took it off after a while.

JILL FOX (*friend*) I was wearing a great boa of white ostrich feathers. I was trying to be chic, and every time I breathed a feather would shoot up my nostrils. A photograph appeared somewhere of me being greeted by Truman. It was of a strange person I don't think I ever knew in my life, and it was myself . . . very thin, strange little person, smiling brightly, and Truman was looking over my shoulder . . .

JOHN BARRY RYAN I wore a very simple mask. I believe I'm the only man whose feet only have ever appeared in *Women's Wear Daily*. According to *WWD*, I was the only person at the ball who wore classic dancing pumps. That's my claim to fame.

HAROLD PRINCE It was the last time we ever went to anything remotely like that. We were back out on the street within half an hour of arrival. Donald Brooks whipped up a feathered mask for my wife, Judy. I remember we were both rather uncomfortable about the whole thing. At the Plaza Hotel I got a lot more uncomfortable because of the people on the street. The French Revolution came to mind and our place in the tumbrels. Of course, the receiving line was enormously cordial. Truman was enormously nice. But we sat down, we took one look around us, and we quietly left, out of discomfort. I would lie if I didn't say out of disapproval too. But we went, didn't we?

POLLY KRAFT (*artist*) All of us from Washington were rather terrified, titillated, thrilled to be invited. Those swan-necked Italians were just ravishing . . . Marella Agnelli just like Richard Avedon's portrait of her . . . so beautiful one gasped. Babe Paley. Gloria Guinness. One was almost numb with the glamour and excitement of it all. Of course, we were all younger then. None of us had become blasé or jaded . . .

LOEL GUINNESS Gloria went. I did not. I do not like that sort of thing. Wearing a mask . . . absolutely childish. I probably went to bed that night.

JACK DUNPHY I had a good time. But I don't know that anyone else did. I've never seen such ghettoizing in all my life. No group mixed with another group. They were scared shitless of one another! When I asked Babe Paley to dance, this old Jew who sat next to her said, "Don't go away now . . ." and started clawing her all over. When I asked Gloria Guinness to . . . well, they were the kind of people who would be with gentlemen who would say. "Well, you know, I can't, you know, should I wear iron pants?" She was clawed too. Not by their husbands. I don't remember seeing Bill Paley there at all. They had to return to their little table where they were surrounded by old tycoons. It was a riot. There was no mingling there . . . I'd just dance, that's all. I think it was the last time I ever danced. Gloria Guinness, whom I liked, said, "You certainly cut a mean rug. Do you practice by yourself? I do."

GORDON PARKS (*photographer*) Everyone was looking at each other. I got the feeling that half the people there didn't know the other half—at least as friends. Quite a lot of nervous bowing and greeting. I went with my second wife, Elizabeth. She spent a fortune getting a rhinestone mask made. We didn't eat for two weeks. I didn't wear a mask. With a mask people wouldn't know that I was black. After all, I was there to make it a real black-and-white ball.

LEONORA HORNBLOW (*novelist*) I went to the great ball with Arthur Hornblow, Jr., the Cerfs and the Leland Haywards and Frank Sinatra, then married to Mia. The Backers were there. George. Evie, who did Truman's apartment for him in the UN Plaza. Everything was so beautiful, all that black and white. I had my hair painted white. I couldn't believe it. I had a mask made with beautiful white feathers to go with my white hair. Sinatra wore one of those little five-and-ten masks. I was so entertained by myself that I really had very little time for anyone else. I was very busy being photographed. Truman was very pleased with me, really pleased because I'd gone to some trouble. I couldn't wait for the next day to come so I could have this terrible liquid flour washed out of my hair.

DENISE BOUCHÉ We seemed to sit around a lot in chairs in corners and watch everyone. Ronnie Tree was at our table. Diana Vreeland had just made his daughter, Penelope, famous in the pages of *Vogue* and she was sitting at the table, very, very thin, with her big saucer eyes and her straight hair, so devoted to her father, sitting there rather like a little calf.

MONROE WHEELER (*curator*) I remember Ronnie Tree's daughter Penelope was so beautiful. Cecil Beaton took one look at her and spent the rest of the evening dancing with her.

LEE RADZIWILL Everyone stood back when Jerry Robbins danced with Betty Bacall. When they started out in a corner, people were dancing everywhere, but the two of them were so superb the dance floor just cleared.

ARTHUR SCHLESINGER, JR (*historian*) I saw Betty Bacall dancing out on the floor. I've known her for years. So I went and started to cut in. She looked at me with considerable scorn and said, "Don't you see whom I'm dancing with?" And I looked, and it turned out to be Jerry Robbins, whom I had never met. So I retired crestfallen.

JOAN AXELROD I remember watching Jerome Robbins and Lauren Bacall doing a fantastic jitterbug together. I remember Truman coming up and whispering that so-and-so was at the ball because his wife had threatened suicide unless they were invited . . . running around filling your ear with nonsense like that. I had a whopping good time. Beautiful. Full of real gaiety. Marvelous cast of characters.

DR. RUSSELL MAXFIELD (*friend*) I asked Lauren Bacall to dance. Oh boy! She'd just been dancing with Jerry Robbins, a fantastic dancer, and I was kind of embarrassed. But I wanted to dance with her and talk with her a bit. I went up to her table and asked her. That was the reason for the mask. You were supposed to be able to ask anyone and they would have to dance with you. She was a perfect lady. She'd just sat down. I didn't realize she was so exhausted. On the dance floor she talked about how hot it was and how she was perspiring. We did just a little two-step with the music and then I took her over and sat her down. We barely got up and down.

CHRISTOPHER CERF *(television producer)* I was just out of college. I remember dancing with Mia Farrow a lot. That was pretty exciting. It was like, "Hey, this is me and look what I'm doing!" She seemed to be my age when everybody else was a lot older.

SUSAN PAYSON BURKE *(crasher)* I was just out of college working in New York. I had gone with a date to some black-tie party, and we were having a drink at Trader Vic's at the Plaza. We saw all these lights and cameras. My date and I looked at each other. I said, "What a challenge!" In those days, everybody went to everybody's parties. My date was a guy from Texas named Jerry Jones. He took my arm and we walked into the Plaza ballroom with a bunch of people, and they never checked us. It was fabulous. The first person I saw was Mia Farrow . . . and Frank Sinatra and every other person in the world whose faces I'd seen in papers. Truman came up and he was very jovial—couldn't have been more friendly. He said, "I'm so glad you're here" . . . clearly not knowing who I was.

I said, "Yes, it's awfully nice of you. I'm Susan Payson."

He said, "Oh yes, of course."

My date said, "I'm Jerry Jones."

"Oh yes," Truman said, "what are you doing in New York?"

Jerry said, "Well, I just finished business school and I'm working at McKinsey."

Truman said, "I don't remember where you're sitting, but why don't you come to this table." He introduced us. "These are my friends from Kansas." At first it didn't dawn on me who those people were.

"Kansas?"

"Yes."

"And what do you do?"

One guy said, "I'm with the police. I'm a detective."

Then all of a sudden the light dawned on the two of us. Here we were smack in the center of Truman's cast of characters from *In Cold Blood!* It was divine. We stayed until the end, we danced, and had the most marvelous time. Didn't know a soul. It was perfect. I danced with the detectives. I can remember saying, "You don't seem to have a gun."

The next time I saw Truman was a few years later. I had married. Phyllis and Bennett Cerf were great friends of ours. They had a house nearby, the Columns, in Mount Kisco. One Sunday lunch I was reunited with Truman. He kind of looked at me for a couple of hours and I smiled. Phyllis and Bennett had no idea I'd ever met him before. Finally at a quiet point—we were all sitting down by the pool—I said, "Truman, you looked like you might remember me, but I don't think you really know from where."

He said, "No."

I went on. "Actually, I was the only person with my date who managed to crash your party, the famous black-and-white ball in New York."

He said, *"No!"* in that high little voice. I told him this with quite a bit of trepidation. But he thought it was the most wonderful thing. From then on, he would take my hand and say, "This is the person who crashed my party." He was darling. He would do this at parties in New York. Even toward the end when he wasn't, sadly, in very great shape, he would always remember me. "This is the girl . . ."

KENNETH JAY LANE *(jewelry designer)* I remember meeting Tallulah Bankhead for the first and last time at his dance. She looked exactly like Tallulah Bankhead. I was very flattered to have been invited. I had just sort of arrived at the star scene, having made my first bits of jewelry which all the ladies loved desperately. So I got into Noah's Ark that way.

GEORGE PLIMPTON Tallulah Bankhead wore an extraordinary mask made up to look like a great bird of prey. Brendan Gill, who wrote a biography of her, said that she was frightened about going, fearful that no one would talk to her. Instead, she had been startled and very pleased by the number of people who stopped by her table to chat. One of them was a man named Jesse Levy, who curiously was not on the guest list but was there in the Plaza ballroom nevertheless. After the party he and a few other guests went back to

Tallulah Bankhead's apartment. He must have made quite an impression. According to Brendan Gill, he afterward became her paid steward-secretary-escort, whatever . . . played the piano for her, cooked her meals, got her in and out of bed, and so forth . . . so seeing to her needs that when she died he was left the piano and a quarter of her estate. So at least as far as Tallulah Bankhead was concerned, and indeed Jesse Levy, they must have been very grateful to Truman. On the other hand, perhaps that can't be said of Alice Roosevelt Longworth, Teddy Roosevelt's daughter. She had her town house in Washington burgled while she was in the Plaza. She was quite funny about it. Her house was famous for being in disorder. I went there once and remember a tattered lion skin hanging askew on a wall. The only perfectly ordered thing was a huge dollhouse, everything in it just so. Not at all like the rest of the place. When the police told her her house had been ransacked, she asked, "How do they know? It always looked ransacked."

ALFRED KAZIN The last time I was famous was when I was a guest at Truman Capote's black-and-white ball. When someone asked him who I was, Truman kindly said that I had written a book called *A Walker in the City*, and he said, "I think Alfred's an artist." Ah, artist or no artist, there I was . . . looking at Mrs. Joseph P. Kennedy constantly replacing her makeup, John O'Hara joining in with his friends naming racehorses, and I thought, "Oh boy, I'm a celebrity."

CANDICE BERGEN (*actress*) I remember faces: Frank Sinatra and Mia Farrow, Norman Mailer, Douglas Fairbanks, Jr., wearing a black executioner's hood, Henry Ford, Christina, all in these extraordinary carnival-like headdresses, some of them birds of prey. I was a new girl in town and wasn't really sure why I'd been invited. I was dressed in a white mink rabbit mask made by Halston . . . quite enough to live down for the next twenty-five years. Of course, at the time I thought I looked sensational. We had dinner at Carter Burden's under a Francis Bacon painting, one of his screaming cardinals very likely. I remember the ball being a lot of work. I was quite relieved to get home. I've never been very good at party chatter. The ball was so charged; there was so much freight it carried that it was not a relaxing evening. I never really shared that exalted sense of entitlement that these people enjoyed. You know how those things are. Just a few weeks ago I was at a ball outside Paris and I felt the same way. It was paralyzingly intimidating to me, and yet everyone else was just gliding through. It was so civilized that a man near me leaned forward to a woman standing too close to a candelabra and quite quietly said, "I think your hair is on fire." She said, "Oh . . ." She moved away; it was put out, tufts of hair on the floor, but she had never even raised her voice. Or anyone else around. In America, we would have screamed, "Oh my God!!!" Nothing was said. It was all in slow motion.

The other thing to remember about Truman's ball was that it was during Vietnam. I remember the guilt I felt, or actually the guilt the other people thought I should feel. I was nineteen, I think, when I went to the ball and I hadn't yet sprouted that kind of consciousness. Reporters, going in and out, accosted me. Wasn't it "inappropriate" to have a ball for four hundred people when a war was going on . . . the homeless, starving? What did I say? "Oh, honestly!" Those rabbit ears bobbing. Somebody said—could it have been Douglas Fairbanks in his executioner's hood?—"The question's inappropriate." Somebody else said, "The war's inappropriate," somebody who was wearing a mouse mask with little ears. It was a question of deflecting guilt. Nowadays I don't see how anyone can rationalize a gesture like a ball at any point in these times. I only went to that ball outside Paris because they were friends of my husband's family. A bizarre, probably obscene choice. There's something especially decadent about a ball.

NORMAN PODHORETZ (*editor*) There was a small episode, almost a fight between Norman Mailer and McGeorge Bundy. I may have introduced them, I'm not sure. Anyway I was talking to either Bundy or Mailer and the other came over. Bundy was then at the White House and there were ugly words. I remember Mailer saying to Bundy, "I paid you too much respect." He actually, I think, invited Bundy outside. Bundy said something very haughty. He said, "Mr.

Mailer, I think this is silly, you're childish," or words to that effect. But for the rest, it was great fun and very glamorous—especially if you weren't used to that kind of glamour.

NORMAN MAILER That night I had an altercation with McGeorge Bundy and invited him outside. We had an argument about Vietnam and at one point he put his hand on my arm very kindly and said, "Well, of course, you really don't know much about it." I said, "Let's go downstairs." I was very brave, because he was obviously in better condition than I was. I was dissolute and full of drink. But I'd have killed him that night, I was so angry: one night every three years you can win if you're gonna have it. That was one of those nights. I had a terrible argument with Lillian Hellman as a result. Because she overheard it, she stopped it. She was always such a celebrity fucker. It must be said of Lillian that when the chips were down she'd always go for the guy who had the most clout. And there was no doubt in her mind that McGeorge Bundy had a good deal more than I did. So she turned on me right in front of him and said, "How *dare* you, Norman!" I said, "You get lost!" We had this huge fight . . . like an older sister and her kid brother. Then we didn't speak for a year or two. I wasn't going to speak to her ever again. Right in front of McGeorge Bundy. Anyway, Truman's responsible for all of this. Now, multiply this by—there are only three of us—one hundred and thirty-three and the scenes you got . . . !

WILLIAM F. BUCKLEY, JR. He was challenging everybody to fight. A lot of people were pretty lubricated that night, including Norman. In the semi-affectionate way in which we have always contended, he did seem that way with me. "Put up your dukes." But there was nothing serious about it.

JOHN KENNETH GALBRAITH It was one of those rare occasions when you knew by sight or by fame or infamy everybody there. What I particularly remember was organizing a musical football game with George Plimpton. It was a sort of mellow dance to the music in which he picked up the ball, passed it to me, I reversed it to him, and he ran with it, keeping time to the music. Somebody had come, as I recall, in a mask and a top hat, which he had left on a table, and we were using the top hat as a football. A grand evening. There's no question about that. Of all the evenings that have disappeared from my memory, this one is distinctive in the way it remains.

JILL FOX I remember being pushed around in a chair over the ballroom floor by Ken Galbraith or was it George Plimpton? There was a top hat involved. Was I in a football game? Was I in the backfield? Certainly it was the gayest moment of the evening.

VIRGIL THOMSON I understand Truman told the Plaza people he would be sending his own whiskey and brandy for the party. They said, no, you pay the hotel by the drink. Cost him a great deal of money, that party, but it was a good party. They can give a good party at the Plaza. He was a good host; he went around from table to table and would sit with everybody. People had bits of costume on. It was full of celebrities. Not many people give a celebrity party like that privately. That kind of party is usually paid for by some movie company.

AILEEN MEHLE There was a wonderful, hectic gaiety about the whole party. Truman was the ringmaster. Kay was having a wonderful time, but I think it was all rather overwhelming for her. It was Truman who was really going all out. He would hop, skip, and jump from table to table and say, "Aren't we having a wonderful time? Aren't we having the most wonderful time? I love this party."

ALAN PRYCE-JONES (writer) I thought it was one of the more terrible parties I'd ever seen. Everybody tremendously got up in mundane masks, and television cameras flashing. You couldn't get into the Plaza. The whole of New York was concerned with who was asked and who wasn't. And why weren't certain people . . . When you actually got there, there really wasn't a party. It never got off the ground at all. I left with Marianne Moore around midnight. We wondered what we were doing standing in this enormous crowd with nothing to eat, nothing to drink, no way of getting on the floor, and everybody, by then, rather tired of their masks.

HERB CAEN About midnight, Sinatra was having a bad time. He was with Mia. He said, "Hey, let's get out of here." So we were sneaking out the door to go to one of his joints—Jilly's, that awful bar he used to hang out in. Truman caught us at the door and tried to put a body block on us. I said, "No, we're leaving, but we'll come back." He said, "No, you won't. You won't come back, I know you won't come back."

Well, we didn't. I think he was hurt. It was one of those great parties that never got off the ground. People did what they always do—getting up and going into their little cliques and corners. If you're not a part of the group—we being from the West Coast—we got that "who's that?" look most of the time. Sinatra just hated the whole thing.

MIA FARROW We went somewhere else afterward. Jilly's for some chow mein.

KENNETH JAY LANE There are very few parties here with a late supper, breakfast really. It's not an American policy; it's more like a European ball. It's a nice break; it keeps people on, greedy for that sausage. Anyway, Benedetta Barzini and I were having breakfast together. She was a model then, very, very beautiful. She was wearing a necklace of mine as a mask and looking through the holes. Sam Spiegel came up, seeing this ravishing creature, and asked to be introduced. I said, "Sam, do you know Benedetta?" She just got up and turned on her heel to walk away. He watched after her and asked, "What's the matter with that girl, what's wrong with her?" I had no idea, but later I asked her, "Why were you so awful to Sam Spiegel?" She said, "When I first came to America my father gave me two letters to old friends. The first person I went to see was Mr. Spiegel. When I went to see him, he tried to seduce me. I was seventeen. He doesn't remember." So that was it. Sam had tried to pounce. The next day he called me and asked, "Did you ever find out?" I said, "Well, er-um, you know who she is, Sam. Her name is Benedetta Barzini and her father is Luigi. I think you've met her before." Sam said, "Well, er-um, I'll talk to you soon."

LEWIS LAPHAM *(editor)* I passed through the police barricades in front of the Plaza and listened to Pete Hamill, among others, shouting at me that this is the beginning of the end, that the tumbrels will be soon rolling. He was then a *New York Post* reporter and he was speaking for the sansculottes, that this was all too brash and arrogant a display of wealth and celebrity and it was being thrown in the teeth of the democrats in the streets, and so forth.

I remember the evening being extraordinary for one reason. At most New York parties there's always a degree of anxiety, it was good to be there, but was one at the *right* table, or was one being seen at the *right* end of the room or with the *right* people? But on this occasion, *every* table was the right table. Simply to be present was to be, for the time being, safe . . . on the high and sunny plateau. So all the tables were equally fine and everybody was just pleased to be present. Then I noticed this extraordinarily beautiful woman, whom I later found out was Luciana Pinatelli. She had some sort of a career as an Italian model, or was somehow associated with the Italian *haut monde*. Clearly she had that manner. I remember that she was wearing an immense jewel—an emerald or a ruby, possibly a diamond—in the middle of her head! She wore a kind of head ribbon, and in the center of it was this great stone. I don't know whether it had come from India or had once been worn by an elephant or the Tsarina of Russia. But it was clearly a stone that had a history. Empires had perished, many had died in order to provide this brilliance for the head of Luciana Pinatelli. I noticed that every time she moved or danced or glittered in the light, about three guys were standing around whose eyes never left her forehead. She had more security than any of the Kennedys present. Apparently, she had borrowed this jewel from Harry Winston, and Winston had let it out of his sight only on the condition that it was followed by three heavies with guns!

At the end of the party, Gianni Agnelli wanted to go someplace and play poker. It was two in the morning. One of the places to play poker at that hour was Elaine's. Among the cognoscenti, or the "Friends of Gianni," as they were known, someone had suggested, "Why don't we all go to Elaine's and play cards?" Somehow I ended up in the same limousine with Luciana, who was part of this entourage. She was not wearing the jewel, the guards had removed this thing from her forehead. I may be exaggerating. Maybe she went tastefully into a ladies' room, put it into a portable safe, and presented it to the guards that way . . . a lead-lined casket. In any case, the jewel did not get into the car; it didn't get out of the hotel, and it never graced Elaine's.

PETER DUCHIN The remarkable thing to me was seeing these legendary people you just didn't see out in public much, dancing at four o'clock in the morning. The Jock Whitneys, the Paleys, people like that you just never expected to see dancing late at night. And they did have a heck of a good time.

DENISE BOUCHÉ I liked the way he stood with Kay at the end of the evening to say good night to his guests . . . "Good evening," he said to everyone.

DR. RUSSELL MAXFIELD Those of us from Kansas were the first to arrive at the ball and the last to leave. In fact, there was hardly anyone left in the ballroom but us. Just then, a large number of people came back and started wandering around, peering down at the floor. It turned out this lady had lost a huge pearl that had fallen off one of her dancing pumps. We all got out there and looked for it—the last people there in a big search party! We finally found it— this immense pearl. When we went back up to our rooms in the Plaza, Truman joined us. He was just so excited. He wanted to talk to us all night.

JOAN AXELROD There had been a late supper and then there was breakfast. I had stayed for the lot. Scrambled eggs with caviar and smoked salmon. In retrospect, I would feel very superstitious about giving myself a party like that. It's like putting a period on the sentence. It is spooky to say, "Here I am in all my splendor."

Lauren Bacall dancing with the famous choreographer Jerome Robbins. When they
stepped on the dance floor, Peter Duchin's band was playing Irving Berlin's "Top Hat."
(Henry Grossman)

1966

JOHN SARGENT *(publisher)* In my diary I have this
curious poem. I have no idea whose it is. It just sits
there:

> *Truman Ca-potty*
> *Is not nearly as dotty*
> *As some of the people*
> *Who went to his party.*

JOEL SCHUMACHER The ball reminds me of those
incredible drawings from Thackeray's *Vanity Fair*,
illustrations of rich, unconscious people getting
dressed up and dancing on the edge of the abyss
with skeletons. It was like the barbecue at the
Wilkeses' at the beginning of *Gone With the Wind*,
all those people playing out this thing while the Civil
War was happening under their noses. That's the sort
of thing Truman's ball really represents. It has no
other significance. Nothing happened at this party at
all except people who knew each other pretended to
kiss each other on both cheeks because they didn't
want to smear their makeup or have to readjust their
masks.

NORMAN PODHORETZ I was not just astonished but flabbergasted by the way the world responded to that party. It was the first such party, at least to my knowledge, publicized that intensely. The guest list was published in the *New York Times*. I don't remember any party before or since treated that way by the *Times* . . . except possibly for state dinners at the White House. I discovered afterward that virtually everywhere I went people knew that I had been at that party and were either envious or affected to be contemptuous—and I stress the word "affected." I was at Yaddo not long after the party and that's all anybody would talk about in my presence. Whoever decided to give it that kind of coverage—the *Times* society editor, I just don't know—but whoever did sensed, and maybe quite accurately, that this party represented some turning point in the cultural history, the social history of New York, even the United States in the sense that the confluence of the fashionable social world, and the literary world and the world of political power was embodied in that guest list. Those are the worlds that in this country, say, in contrast with England or France, have always been separate and have rarely even intersected. One reason for that is that the United States, as others have observed, is unusual in having its political capital in a different city from its cultural capital. London, Paris, or pre-World War II Berlin or Vienna—all great European countries had the cultural center and the political capital in the same place. Here in America, starting with the Kennedy years, the split was being bridged. I think Truman had a very shrewd sense of this kind of process and was himself very much in the center of it. In effect, he dramatized the change by making that party's guest of honor a Washington figure, Kay Graham.

LOUIS AUCHINCLOSS (*lawyer, novelist*) I had a client, now long deceased, who was going to another law firm; when she read that I was at the party she decided to stay with me a little longer.

NORMAN MAILER *Women's Wear Daily* gave me the award for the worst-dressed man at Truman's ball. I was wearing a dirty gabardine raincoat with my black tie.

But I have good memories of the ball. It was one of the best

parties I ever went to. So much action . . . so many people of a sort
you'd never met before. For example, there was Tallulah Bankhead!
For twenty years she'd been enjoying the coup her public relations
man had given her when as the legend had it, she said to me, "Oh,
you're the young man who doesn't know how to spell 'fuck.'" For
those who are too young to know, it was because I had used "fug" in
The Naked and the Dead. Of course we had never met. For me it
was like a burr under a saddle. Of course I blew the opportunity to
tell her off. She looked too attractive and, big surprise, too
vulnerable.

It's probably hyperbole to say that everything there felt anointed
that night. Truman had certainly brought it off. It certainly was his
greatest coup. For some, and I might be one of them, that party was
even greater than any particular one of his books.

PETER DUCHIN The Venice balls, extremely beautiful—the Save
Venice Ball, all candlelit, and you came off the water in gondolas
and walked into the large room where the band was playing. The
Paleys gave a party for their daughter Kate where the dance floor
was painted aubergine. Extraordinary. But Truman's really ranks way
up there, no question.

JOAN AXELROD It's hard to compare. My idea of a great party is
having entertainment, people sitting down at the piano. We had a
great old time at the Gershwins'. Oscar Levant. Judy Garland. She
used to tell stories. Wonderful raconteur . . . endless old vaudeville
jokes that took forever to get off the ground and put everyone on the
floor. Harold Arlen at the piano playing a new score. Or Julie Styne.
The Cerfs gave wonderful parties. So did Frank Sinatra. There was
always a lot of entertaining going on. What does every old lady in
the world say? They don't make 'em like they used to? Those parties
don't exist now. People just go in and snort their coke or sit and look
at the movies.

JOEL SCHUMACHER There are a lot of people who can get by in life
by having the talent to amuse. I certainly can't criticize that. If you
can better your lifestyle, your position, by being somebody whom

people like to have around because you amuse them, and you can live with it on your own terms—then fine. But we're talking about a great American writer . . . all those years to have gone by and for so little to have emerged. A lot of that has to do with the experience he was having . . . being treated like a Pekinese, sitting on needlepoint pillows for everybody to say how darling, how bitchy. It's hard for any artist of integrity to have self-respect. I think the ball, in many ways, was the beginning of the end. The celebrity ball took precedence over his own craft.

JOE PETROCIK The year before he died he began talking about doing another ball. It was just one of his little pipe dreams but he talked about it frequently. He was going to give it in Asunción, Paraguay. He was absolutely convinced that everybody he'd want to invite had never been to that place, and that they'd come. The invitation read something like this: *Don Señor Truman Capote requests the pleasure of your company for a masked ball. Place: A palace in Asunción, Paraguay. Dress: A Paraguayan aristocrat circa 1860. Masks until midnight.* He went on and on about it.

JASON EPSTEIN *(editor, writer)* I had fun at it. I wouldn't mind going again, if only somebody would ask me.

Interlude

CHAPTER TWENTY-NINE *In Which*

TC Steps into Bullrings and onto Yachts

Truman ventured into a bullring in Spain, but the photographs above to the contrary, he rarely went ashore or into the water off his friends' yachts. *(Photos by William S. Paley, collection of Kate C. Paley)*

PETER VIERTEL *(writer)* He came to Madrid with Slim Keith and Leland Hayward. There he was, this strange little blond creature, and whenever he was introduced to a Spaniard—Capote means a "fighting cape"—they'd say, "Señor Capote, olé!" He always took that kind of remark very gracefully and laughed.

During that trip we went out to one of the ranches near the Escorial for a *tientas*—which is when amateurs can get into the ring with year-old calves. I've got pictures of Truman fighting in a *tientas* with Luis Miguel Dominguín. A bullfighter takes one end of the cape and they hold it up together. Truman didn't move.

Six or seven years ago, one of these cows killed Antonio Bienvenidas. He had retired and was contemplating a comeback. Antonio turned his back and the cow went across the ring and hit him. Broke his spine. They took him to the hospital in Madrid. He was lying there. Luis Miguel Domínguín went to see him. He spoke to Miguel, turned his head, and like that, he was gone. There's a big monument to him in Madrid. So it was a tragic thing—somehow ironic . . . this man who had so many *cornadas,* I think he'd fought over thirty years—to be killed by a small cow. His brother went back to the ranch and found this cow and killed it. Very strange story, but as I say, a little cow like that can break your arm. Didn't get Truman, though. It took nerve for him to go out there. Here was this little effeminate guy in this macho environment where everybody was laughing at him when he walked out in his little light beige linen suit. He had a lot of guts.

HERB CAEN When he was in San Francisco, he always said, "I've got this *finca* in Spain and you must drop in and spend a few days." Much to his amazement, I did. I dropped in on him on the Costa Brava. He wasn't really ready for me. Gore Vidal's the same as Truman; he invited me and Maria Theresa to go to Ravello when he lived in Italy. We built our whole trip around going there. We got to Switzerland and then we were going to go to Ravello. So I called Gore from Switzerland and he feigned surprise, "What are you doing here? Oh, my heaven! I'm not expecting you until August!"

I said, "Oh, the hell with it. See you around."

Anyway, Truman was more hospitable. He had Gloria Vanderbilt and that lantern-jawed lady who was in *The Unsinkable Molly Brown,* Tammy Grimes, there. She was a big musical star during the sixties. She was sore as hell being in Palamós. She said, "I was having such a great time in Rome, having a wonderful affair, and here we are like we're in a monastery. You can't even get a drink around here!" She was merciless, she would barely talk to Truman she was so mad. Truman and Gloria would have these long conversations, whispering. He was trying to talk Gloria into divorcing Sidney Lumet. He kept saying, "You don't *look* right together. He's too short and you're too tall. He's too Jewish and you're too WASP. It's just a horrible mistake." Truman was very possessive while we were there. We wanted to go into the town to some nightclub. He didn't. So we sat there in the *finca,* which was a monastery-like place, outside of Palamós.

Fortunately, Bob Ruark was there. He had a huge house across the road. Truman and Ruark got along very well, even though they were opposites, Ruark being hairy-chested and the poor man's Hemingway. Both were working on their books. Ruark prided himself on writing thousands of words a day. He really pounded it out on the typewriter. He had sort of an assembly line. A secretary retyped it as soon as he got through with one page, somebody was there for the research . . . he had three or four people in the same room. The house was a kind of factory where he wrote.

Ruark was a great admirer of Franco; he had a decoration from Franco. All we heard was how wonderful Franco was. And Ruark. He showed me his Rolls-Royce, which had license plates R2R, English plates, and he said, "I've got R2R, guess who has R1R?" I said, "Harold Robbins?" I thought he was going to swing on me. "The *Queen* has R1R," he said. Ruark loved little symbols like that.

So, anyway, we got together one night. Truman had been sitting at his writing desk, writing in longhand as he always did. And Ruark said, "I wrote five thousand words today, Truman, and I bet you sat there at that desk with your quill pen and wrote one word." Truman said, "Yes, Robert, but it was the *right* word," which was the best line I ever heard Truman get off. I printed it in my column and it's been picked up a lot, but it really happened. I can't think of any other great one-liners of Truman. He sort of embroidered stories and used wonderful words and was fascinating to listen to. A monolinguist. He talked and you listened, but it was worth it.

Denmark

SLIM KEITH He took me to see Isak Dinesen. We went out to the country. She looked like a cadaver. Wonderful. I thought there was a great beauty to the kohl around her eyes, and this tiny little frame, the very prominent bones. Thin, thin, thin. The tea was served at four o'clock and it was the most elaborate thing I've ever seen. Pâté, and toast and crêpes suzette, a lot of desserts and cakes. She said about a book Truman had asked about, "Did you like that book?" She said, "Yes. But there wasn't enough air or water or sky in that book." You knew exactly what she meant. There just wasn't enough space.

She said to me, "Is there anything I could do for you?"

I said, "My favorite book, almost, in the English language, is *Out of Africa*. I would love to have a copy with your name in it for me."

She said, "Well, I'll send it to you tomorrow." Indeed, the next day there arrived a copy of the book. It was signed: "To Nancy Hawks, in remembrance of a lovely day . . . Karen Blixen." Then she must have discovered I was no longer married to Howard Hawks, but at that time to Leland Hayward. The following day I got another book. It said: "To Nancy Hayward. He who makes no mistakes seldom makes anything. Karen Blixen."

Italy

MARELLA AGNELLI He came with lots of trunks. He never knew exactly how long he was staying, where he was going. So he would come with his Vuitton trunks, full of disorder.

Very often he would call and say, "I'm in Verbier and I'm dying of boredom. Can I come and visit with you in Turin?" There was a big blue room—one of the guestrooms—in Turin. There were three or four, but the one he liked was the blue room. So when he called, he would ask, "Is the blue room empty?"

"No, there's somebody in it."
"Check them out!"

Yachting

LOEL GUINNESS He came yachting with us in the *Seraphina* with people like Ros and Freddy Brisson, Bill and Babe, Carter Burden. I took them to the Dalmatian coast. Truman was not a great sightseer. Nor am I. Quite frankly, if you see a Greek theater and you see another Greek theater, unless you have an eye like a hawk, you don't know the difference between one and another. It's like a cathedral— it can be better decorated than another, but I must say, I'm not all that mad about going to look at them.

ELEANOR PERÉNYI He was exactly like Warhol in that he knew *nothing*. Absolutely nothing. He had no form of culture. He didn't know anything about European literature. The *idea* that he was going to be Proust—I mean, this is again part of the pitifulness of his claim. He never looked at a piece of architecture; he never looked at a painting; he never went to an art gallery. Mother dragged him to the Vatican in Rome. He was so bored, he was hysterical. When the Agnellis or whoever it was took him to the Greek islands: "I don't want to see those old ruins." Nothing of that sort interested him. Europe to him was restaurants and couture, and of course grand parties. Warhol was exactly the same. Never been inside the Louvre. I don't think he'd ever seen a painting done by anyone earlier than his own contemporaries. He went to city after city with these fantastic art collections. He never looked at them. Truman was the same. I think that's a reason that his writing collapsed. He really had nothing to build on in the end. He was just an empty, silly little man sitting around in Mona Williams's villa on Capri—that kind of thing.

MARELLA AGNELLI He adored yachting. Truman was lazy. He didn't participate much in the life on the boat because he read, he stayed in his cabin, he couldn't stay too much in the sun. We went sightseeing madly. I remember saying once, "Truman, you must come with us at least once." And he said, "Oh, forget it. One old stone is like another old stone." He was not interested in sightseeing whatsoever. He would swim in the sea . . . everything with great calm . . . but no rushing around. Didn't like Chris-Crafts and speedboats at all.

ELEANOR FRIEDE He would be gone for the month of August on the Agnellis' yacht, and then he'd come back and he'd say, "I'll never do that again. They're so boring." He used to tell that story about sitting on the yacht, and someone said, "Oh, those melons are so good, where do they come from?" This girl studying the millionaires—the Mellons among them—said, "Pittsburgh!" He always came back with a batch of new stories, but he'd say, "Oh God, I ate so much, I was so bored." And I'd always say, "Truman, you don't have to go, you know." But every year he went, so the answer, of course, was that he loved Mrs. Paley and Amanda and Drue Heinz. A big part of him would have loved to just be swooping around the Hamptons, but he thought he might miss something, I guess, one good story.

DORIS BRYNNER (*friend*) It was a quiet sea off Yugoslavia, some island, and Truman told us this horrendous murder story involving a lily pond. We sat there transfixed, and Truman, with his high-pitched voice, went on and on and on . . .

Interlude

CHAPTER THIRTY   *In Which TC Is Observed as Jester, as Little Brother to the Rich, and as Celebrity*

Truman dressed to the nines. *(Jill Krementz)*

JUDY GREEN One of the wonderful things about Truman was he
always had the element of little-boy wonder in him. That's a
delightful characteristic in someone. As jaded as his appetites were,
his surprise and wonderment never ceased. If someone paid him a
compliment, he was thrilled. It was as if it were the first time. Of
course, other times he'd say, "I started this new kind of journalism
and I'm the greatest that ever was." But still the little-boy wonder
was there. Imagine someone who was brought up in very shabby
circumstances suddenly coming into the rolling lawns of Long
Island and being accepted where Gatsby never was. Truman didn't
have the yachts or the house across the sound or the looks, or the
money. Yet people were crazy about him. To reach the apogee of
acceptance with his black-and-white ball . . . he was more than just
a darling, he was a social lion. An arbiter. If you weren't invited to
Truman's ball and he didn't accept you, that was a black mark in
society. To reach that level? I mean, it's almost an insanity, it's a
fluke, it's weird. Was he a product of the times? Would it have
happened in Edwardian England? God, no. Who could ever dictate
like that? He was foppier than any of them. I mean, Noël Coward
couldn't have done it. Oscar Wilde, if he'd stayed out of trouble,
couldn't have done it. There were writers who wanted it—Fitzgerald
wanted it at one time; O'Hara was desperate. Truman used all of his
physical disabilities as attributes—the voice, the body, the hand
movements, the tongue. Then the metamorphosis took place . . .
from prince to frog. The swollenness that took over his whole body,
that was grotesque—a still boyish face with that swollen, strange
body. But I never knew him when he wasn't sweet to me. Odd. He
said to me, "You know, people have a look and they have to keep it.
When you keep a look, you never grow old."

I said, "What do you mean?"

He said, "Claudette Colbert. Her bangs, her hair. The way she
looked in It Happened One Night. She stayed with it." He told C.Z.
Guest, "Always keep your hair the same way. Always that sweater
tied around your shoulders and you will always look young." She
does. "Let fashion—the Mainbochers—come and go. You stay the
way you are." He said to me, "I see you in skin shoes. Always in

glasses. Classic, sporty, sports clothes." I said, "Really?" And he said, "Yes, always wear glasses." It's funny, I have them on now. It was fascinating. He said, "Women age so poorly compared to men. If they keep an image, they'll age less." Not that he wasn't a believer in cosmetic surgery! Truman could talk forever about anything to do with women. He knew about skin oils. Mesmerizing! He would go on endlessly about hands and veins and spots. You'd listen to him and you'd sit on your hands.

JOAN AXELROD Truman invented being a snob. Let's not forget that. I think it's the reason he and Cecil Beaton became such great friends. I guess he learned snobbism at Cecil's knee. He took lessons. A lot of people felt they had been had by his snobbism—that it was not beyond the pale to break a dinner date with somebody if C. Z. Guest or Babe Paley summoned him.

CAROL MARCUS MATTHAU One night in the Gold Key Club he described the whole New York social structure. The ladies, the men. I could have drawn it, it was so graphic and so exact. How the hierarchy was set up in terms of power, money, and fame. The Paleys, the Cerfs, Gloria, Slim—he knew it all.

JOHN BARRY RYAN Court jester is such a bad way to put it. He was so much more. He was a catalyst in their lives. He made their lives entertaining. It made *them* more entertaining. Leland Hayward could be one of the most dour people in the world. Fascinating, but dour. When he was around Truman, he was a totally different person.

GEORGE PAGE I couldn't pass up the opportunity to have lunch with Truman and the Paleys in Capri. I arrived for an alfresco luncheon, beautiful little restaurant, and it was just Truman and Bill Paley. Both of them were dressed for the beach, I remember. I thought Truman was a bit more discreetly dressed than Paley, who was actually wearing a bikini, his shirt wide open and all sorts of gold chains—he looked very Aristotle Onassis . . . Greek on that particular day. It was a typically fun lunch with Truman no matter who was along, and they sort of pummeled me for stories of the Vietnam War and I was happy to talk about something I could talk about. But mainly it was the image of the two of them sitting there at the table with the umbrella and the beautiful Italian sun beaming down, both of them looking very famous and very rich. I couldn't help but think of all the power that Bill Paley represented, and how apparently fond he was of Truman.

LOUISE GRUNWALD (*friend*) He wouldn't have been visiting them in Capri, Nassau, all over the world if Mr. Paley didn't like him. Mr. Paley called the shots, and so did Mr. Guinness. The wives couldn't have had him unless they got the okay.

SLIM KEITH When he first met Kenneth, who was a sort of musical-comedy Englishman I was married to, Kenneth walked into my bedroom where Truman was sitting at the foot of my bed. Kenneth's jaw dropped four feet. I said, "This is Truman Capote."

My husband said, "How do you do?" And Truman said something like, "Hello, Big Daddy . . ." Afterward—he was staying for dinner—Truman was out of the room washing his hands or something, and Kenneth said, "Let's keep him. We can put him on the mantel." He did enjoy him. He didn't quite get the point, but Truman was so bright and entertaining . . .

KAY MEEHAN We were in St. Moritz at the Palace Hotel. My husband, Joe, was out skiing. The Agnellis had a helicopter which flew them up into the snowfields. When Joe got back to the hotel, he told me that a little man in a business suit had come up to him in the lobby and punched him in the stomach. "He said he was taking you out. Who the hell is that?"

And I said, "Oh, Truman's here!"

"Well, you can keep him the hell away from me!"

Well, all I can tell you is that I would go to bed at night and leave the two of them talking. Joe would start worrying about Truman's income tax . . .

LEONORA HORNBLOW Arthur felt Truman was untrustworthy. He
always grumbled when Truman was to come to the house and then
he would be unable to separate himself from him! Truman was a
marvelous, wonderful storyteller. A lot of writers are not talkers,
they're writers.

Once, when we were living in London, he turned up and invited
himself to dinner the next night. I said, "Well, Arthur's working, we
have to get up very early."

"Well, I have to get up even earlier, honey," he said. "I've got to
take the earliest train back to Switzerland and to Jack." So the next
night he came about seven o'clock and we had dinner and I think he
left at three! With Arthur begging him not to go! When he was good,
he was very, very good.

KENNETH JAY LANE It's almost as if he had no shadow. I mean, I
really kind of racked my brain. I could give you a thousand Diana
Vreeland quotes; I could give you a hundred of John Richardson. I
could give you ten amusing things that Lee Radziwill said. I cannot
think of one funny thing that Truman has ever said.

He was good at one-liners. After someone might have discussed
somebody at lunch, he would say, "Oh *really?*" Everybody would
think he was rather funny. Somebody would be discussed at lunch
. . . he killed three wives and his dick is artificial . . . he's really Adolf
Hitler in disguise   that sort of thing for twenty minutes, and
Truman would say, "*Really?*"

It was actually the sound of Truman's voice that made one laugh.
Actually he was quite serious. All of his writings were quite serious.
They had a tinge more irony than real down-and-out humor. Can
you think of anything he ever said that was hilarious? That made
you giggle, I mean that made you snigger? Of course, his names for
people were wonderful . . . "Tiny Malice." Do you know who I mean
. . . Edie Backer? That was after Edward Albee's play.

DOTSON RADER He was a great raconteur. Probably the greatest
of this century. He was a great after-dinner companion. He would
tell stories on himself and you'd hear the stories and you'd get

comfortable and say, "Oh my God, I can't believe he would tell me that." And then to keep his interest, you'd tell him something awful about somebody you knew. Or about yourself. Only, what you didn't know was that he'd remember it and you'd have a hangover the next morning. Sometimes you'd go to a dinner party with him and he'd see how much he'd get away with. How shocking he could be. He'd use street language. He'd tell filthy stories and they'd sit there and laugh because they were afraid of offending him.

LOEL GUINNESS Truman wasn't too hesitant about telling dirty stories. He was a nice little man, until he . . . I can't bear dirty conversations in front of women. I don't know why, I've never been able to, and if anything ever began to get a little murky in his conversation, I'd always stop it at once. "Forget it." I'm built like that. I don't give a damn, I can talk fuck and bugger and everything with another man. I don't care a row of pins, but when it comes to women, I don't like it.

JOHN KNOWLES I sat and listened to Truman talking about himself for about forty-five minutes and then I found myself telling Truman every intimate fact about myself that existed. He had set me up for this. Three days later I realized what had hit me. I called him up and said, "Truman, you little son of a bitch, you told me all about your life because you knew two things would happen which would make me tell you everything. First, I would say to myself, 'Well, I've got so much on him it doesn't matter what I tell him about myself.' And second, 'After all, I've lived too. Things have happened to me. I've lived and suffered.' "

He said, "You're very intelligent."

I said, "Now I've figured out how you got that interview with Marlon Brando." This was the famous "Duke in His Domain" interview, in which Brando spilled his guts about his alcoholic mother in the hotel room in Japan while filming *Sayonara*. Poor Brando was victimized by Truman as so many people were. He didn't take notes while he did this sort of thing. He didn't record either. He just memorized it. He'd sit there with those tiny hands folded and tell you this terrible story and you found yourself telling him everything.

JOHN RICHARDSON I think it was making the best of a bad job. He had this campy high-pitched Southern whine, but, like a singer, he knew how to make it very expressive; he could change the color of his voice—that's why he was such a wonderful storyteller. He also had marvelous timing with it, used it like an actor's . . . The rise and fall of his voice and the sort of hush, the shrieks of laughter and giggles and chuckles and so on. He used his voice marvelously. His voice never changed. It just got slower and slower, like a gramophone that needs rewinding.

STEVEN M. L. ARONSON (writer) One night back in the fifties he paid a call on a well-known writer whose husband at the time told me— decades later—how her young son, who was trying to sleep in the next room, became very unsettled by Truman's voice, so strange and nasal and androgynous. He started crying, "Mummy, Mummy, what is that *thing* out there with you?" That boy is now a middle-aged tenured college professor, so, I mean, we can't exactly say that it scarred him for life, but it *was* one of the nighttime terrors of childhood.

JOHN KNOWLES While he didn't bemoan anything about his stature, his voice, he was always trying to improve things—always having little tucks taken in his face which made him look different, but, I must confess, not necessarily better. He had $32,000 worth of work on his teeth. He had hair transplants. He didn't have a very clear self-image. He didn't think his voice was strange and he didn't think he lisped. Very vain. He didn't see himself as others saw him. Some people thought he was very cute, particularly when he was young with these very silken, blond bangs and this cute sort of face. I suppose some people found him attractive. He went to great trouble with his clothes. Dunhill's, I think, was one of the stores he went to. He had London tailors. He'd always wear pink and beige and yellow sweaters. But I don't think he was quite aware how singular-looking and sounding he was.

MARIA THERESA CAEN We took him to the first topless bar in San Francisco. It was called The Condor. The first topless dancer in San Francisco went by the name of Carol Doda. We watched her dancing for a while and Truman turned to me and said, "How can she be dancing up there when my breasts are bigger than hers?" So he had a few more drinks and he jumped on top of the table and decided that he was going to dance. There was a lot of whoop and hollering and dancing and what have you. The word spread about who he was. He had taken off his coat and tie and was unbuttoning his shirt, beginning to scare the patrons, when we stopped him. After Herb wrote about it in the column, Carol Doda, who's a very sweet woman, was so hurt that she went out and had silicone implants. Maybe we should credit Truman with starting the entire craze!

BOB COLACELLO When Truman was in a good mood, he would wear bright colors. He would really put an effort into his outfit. When he was not in such a good mood, he would turn up in his sweatshirt, his jeans. He was always into everything matching, everything having a certain flair. When he was drinking, he lost that flair. Even in the way he dressed. Truman considered himself a sartorial expert in the same way that he considered himself an expert on food. A great gourmet. I don't think he was really either. It was a bit too much. It was too contrived. There was a lot of commedia dell'arte in Truman, a bit of a court jester in him. He wore any color. Most men tend to wear black, brown, blue, and gray. Truman wore any color. Even pink. On one of his reading tours everything was pink and black. It was part of a whole shtick. But shtick just sounds like such a wrong word for Truman. As much as he was a New Yorker, he was never really from New York. He was so much the South. That's why shtick just doesn't seem right for him. So whatever the Southern word for it is, his public apparition, his affect was very Tennessee Williams. Andy used to have that great line, which you probably have heard—that Truman, Tennessee, and Gore should hire out Madison Square Garden and do imitations of each other and have fights. Gore had suggested that they have Norman Mailer as the token heterosexual referee.

STEVEN M. L. ARONSON He was a strange-looking creature. People speak of his beauty when he was young. But I look at those pictures and to me he was misshapen . . . a huge-headed dwarf. He was grotesque. Imagine what he had to suffer; imagine what it took to create himself. I mean the genius aside. You can be a genius with the shades pulled down and the doors shut. But this is somebody who made it fashionable and indispensable for society to know him. It's an age-old process, isn't it? He flattered, he charmed, he cajoled, a little civility of attention. The little notes sent, the little books dedicated to.

DANIEL AARON Truman would tell preposterous stories about himself. Inventions. One of them I remember was about a train ride that he took from Italy to France and an old woman with a large parrot in a cage and how the train was stopped and policemen came in and snagged the old lady. They unhooked the cage and found drugs. He described this as vividly as if he had been on the train. I am convinced this was just something he was inventing on the spot. He was a wonderful storyteller and he was also very good about the South and reminiscing in that kind of high-pitched Southern voice. There was something very brave about him.

NORMAN MAILER To the degree he loved me, he loved me for having said he was a ballsy little guy. He repeated that a great deal and kept improving on it until at one point years later we had a run-in. I read somewhere in print that "Norman Mailer says I'm the bravest man in New York." I was offended. He had no right to go that far with a simple remark. So I wrote a letter and said, in effect, "Come on, Truman, get off it. You may be a ballsy little guy but you're not the bravest man in New York. There are guys waiting in line in New York to be the bravest."

JERRE MANGIONE I do remember his bragging that he could be bisexual by demonstrating the depth of his voice. It would suddenly become very masculine and deep. He loved to show off his dancing. He was terrific on his feet. Going down the street, he would suddenly burst into a kind of dance of his own.

JANE GUNTHER In the beginning he wanted terribly to be in the world of money and power. His way to get in was to charm those women. I do not think he wanted to be in that world to write about it. It was some terrible lack in himself.

KAY MEEHAN He loved the big time. He loved power and clout. There's no question about that. He was able, too, to communicate with powerful people. He loved the backgrounds of the glamorous . . . a house that was attractive. I remember he talked about how only the rich have very small vegetables. He came to dinner one night in New York. He was the only one who noticed that in the winter I had lilies of the valley on the mantelpiece . . . because they were small flowers and I could get more of them. He noticed all that.

CAROL MARCUS MATTHAU He was interested in the rich. He said that there was a certain kind of money that gets in people's bone marrow. They are different.

I said, "In what way?"

"Well, they might give you a Rembrandt for Christmas, but if you need to borrow five dollars . . . well, you'd better not borrow that from anyone you know who's rich."

WILLIAM F. BUCKLEY, JR. Truman had a sharp eye for upward mobility and he liked to know everybody who was heading upstairs. I've never found rich people particularly attractive. I mean, they might be attractive for other reasons. But I've never found somebody whose attractiveness traces to his or her being rich. The most boring man I ever met was H. L. Hunt, who was also the richest man I ever met. As often as not, there's an inverse ratio.

JANE GUNTHER The vegetables are better. The flowers too. More champagne. Even the down in the pillows.

KENNETH JAY LANE Potatoes the size of peas. Absolutely. "Baby, baby, baby, baby . . ." as he would say. "Oh Betsy," he would say, "they're almost as small as Babe's were last week."

GORE VIDAL I'll tell you when Jackie first met Truman. It was in the summer of 1960. All these stories about "We had a tête-à-tête . . . she was asleep on my shoulder at the movies while Jack was away philandering during his campaigns . . ." Nonsense! She didn't meet him until a few months before the election. She rang me up—this was July or August 1960—and said, "Well, I finally met him."

I said, "Who?"

"Capote, at lunch, at C. Z. Guest's. After the lunch, he said, 'Do you have a car? Can you drop me off?' "

She said, "Yes, I do." So he got in the car.

I asked her, "Did he rivet everybody's attention with the most terrible, scandalous gossip about everybody not present?"

"Yes, he did." Jackie said that once in the car, Truman gave a great Pagliacci sigh and said, "Well, you heard me singing for my supper."

ALAN PRYCE-JONES I remember one curious luncheon I had with him. Jean Vanderbilt had a little luncheon party which consisted of Truman, Alan Lerner, me, Mrs. Lyndon Johnson, and a Johnson daughter. Just five people. It was fascinating because Truman was liable to needle anyone. He was a natural needler. Suddenly he did this to Mrs. Johnson: "Oh, come on, Mrs. Johnson, I'm sure you wouldn't understand what we're talking about . . ." That sort of thing. She was absolutely sublime. She squelched Truman so gently that he never came back to the surface again. She did it with extreme kindness but great force. I was impressed, because if you're the First Lady, which she was then, it's quite difficult in a little room where you're being needled by Truman. She wasn't the least bit rude. She just said, "Now, just stop your nonsense."

JOHN BARRY RYAN If you were doing a book on celebrity and you really wondered how did society turn into the jet set and how did the jet set turn into whatever god-awful mishmash we presently have that passes for the front page of *People* magazine fodder, Truman played a role in that. Society had reached a moment when the mixture of old-line society and the corporate jet-setter, the show-business figure had just started to mix. Old-line society was intolerably inbred and boring. Most people in the theater and in movies, unless talking about their own business or industry, were boring. Truman was not boring. Truman was articulate, entertaining, observant, wry, incredibly gregarious. Because he was all those things, the people whom he chose to be his king and queen, the court that he formed around them, was made a much more enjoyable place because of his presence.

I think this all began with *Beat the Devil*. Truman had just written the picture for David Selznick, starring Jennifer Jones and Humphrey Bogart. At that point Truman may have been familiar, and a legend, in the world of homosexual artists—I'm talking about his social visibility—but suddenly what went on in that little Machiavellian mind was: "Gee, the way David Selznick lives is really kind of neat, but Jennifer obviously has nobody to talk with. She can't gossip because David doesn't like gossip. She can't take him dress shopping or whatever, yet David wants somebody around who's going to be good company for Jennifer, and who is also capable of being entertaining at dinner and with pretty much anybody in the movie industry." After *Beat the Devil*, Truman said that he could get away with going anywhere, being around anybody, and manipulating anybody he chose. *House of Flowers* tremendously broadened Truman's social world: he picked up Oliver Messel, who nicely tied in the London scene; Harold Arlen, that was a good entree to the music world; he picked up Peter Brook and so on. *House of Flowers* became sort of a social cause célèbre. It was so elegant, elegant people went to see it, fascinated. This extraordinary little creature had written this amazing story about a whorehouse in the islands. He was off and running. He never really looked back . . . or wondered whether he needed a visa to get into any particular court that he chose . . . he had a royal pass in his pocket.

ANDREAS BROWN Capote learned a lot from Cecil Beaton. Many of his techniques and gimmicks and important associations are patterned after Cecil. He simply grabbed hold of the coattails of Cecil Beaton. At first, Cecil was saying, "Who is this nuisance from America who's written this one book and is so persistent in being my friend?" But, of course, Capote was so captivating, charming, witty, clever that Cecil was immediately impressed. Cecil Beaton was a blatant snob. You either had to be titled or immensely wealthy, powerful, or an absolute genius at some form of art, or absolutely wonderful company, or Cecil wouldn't have anything to do with you at all. He was very interested in power. Obsessed with power. He would sell his soul if he could get invited to tea with the Queen. He would have done it in a minute.

Capote not only used Cecil to meet people, but observed him at close hand, his style, the methods he used to reach people. He became a very important friend of Cecil's and Cecil included him in much of his social activity. A little later in life, when Capote began to make public statements about Cecil and began some of his heavy manipulations, Cecil became a little wary of Truman, and Truman began to frighten him a little bit. Cecil was beginning to realize the power Capote was accumulating. Just sheer, raw international power. Clout. When somebody gets that powerful, you begin to fear them a little. Truman was said to be famous for calling up Johnny Carson when he had a real vendetta. He claims he could call up Johnny Carson and say, "I want to come on tonight. I want to be on this evening," because he had somebody he wanted to go after. Capote could get on. Pronto. Now that's clout. And if you wanted to say something nasty about somebody, what more effective way than to go on television and tell the millions of people who watched Johnny Carson. People feared Capote. No doubt about it. Perhaps everybody except Gore Vidal. He was perhaps the only person who did not fear Capote and in fact relished doing public battle with him. They were real enemies. Vidal eventually sued Capote for libel. Capote suffered a humiliating defeat and the public feud ended.

DOTSON RADER The moneyed classes are most tolerant of gay people. If you're gay, you get in the most trouble if you decide to live in Princeton or out in the suburbs with the middle class. That's where the real bigotry is. Among the poor there's very little bigotry. But the great bourgeoisie—those are the people who'll cut your balls off. Social prestige in New York, and I suppose to a lesser degree in London and Paris and other world capitals, rests to a very large degree on the cultivation of artists. Once you get a lot of money, you've got to buy social prestige. The only way to do that is to buy taste. You've got to prove that you're worthy of the money by buying tasteful things with it. So you spend fifty, one hundred million dollars on art so that every square inch of wall is crammed with old masters. It's vulgar. But that's what gives you the in. Then there is the question of parties. To make your parties, you can't just have people with money; they're all boring. Rich people in this country are useless, they're nonproductive and they're boring. So, if Kay Meehan's going to give a party, unless she spikes everybody's drink with amphetamines, she's got to have Truman or Tennessee or Albee or Rauschenberg or a filmmaker or someone who can talk about something other than the servant problem and the price of property. So artists are cultivated that way. Since American art is to such a large degree a product of homosexuals and Jews, regardless of how anti-Semitic you are and how anti-gay you are, you've got to hide it at least until they leave the room. You're dead socially without them. Artists give the imprimatur, the validation of your taste. So, even though Truman was a flamboyant queen, he was such a great artist they had to suck in their breath and kiss his ass. He had too much clout in terms of validation. In fact, after the black-and-white party, he was a social arbiter as much in this country as whatever the guy was who worked for Mrs. Astor, Ward McAllister. I remember going to parties with Truman where it was embarrassing, the kind of ass-kissing that went on. You'd wonder how these people could look in the mirror the next morning. "Oh, there's dear little Truman . . . just give me five minutes . . ." Truman was no dummy. Very quickly he caught on to this and used it. But he believed certain people—C. Z. Guest and Winston, Babe Paley, premier of all, Lee Radziwill—were class acts.

NORMAN PODHORETZ Although it was more extreme than some other cases I knew, it was not all that unusual among literary people.

Many people I knew, to my astonishment really, were hung up on the rich and the titled. I said in *Making It* that I had weaknesses, but this was not one of them: I never could understand the attraction for people like that. Mary McCarthy had this hang-up, was such a person. Lillian Hellman, radical that she was. Many of

Lillian's closest friends were very rich people who had no particular qualities that I could see other than being rich. These literary people, including Truman, seemed not to care whether anybody was nice or interesting so long as there was money there and preferably family lineage, in addition. In Truman's case, it was more extreme, as I say, but not particularly unusual. That high-society hang-up was also, in my experience, quite common among homosexuals. There, too, not at all unusual. Truman clearly meant to make something of it as a writer. But I don't think it was very deep or serious. It was, for him and the others, a kind of small-scale snobbery that infected people who, coming from either small towns or backgrounds they weren't very happy about—Jewish or provincial—simply couldn't get over the idea that the best people meant the rich, the fashionable, and the titled. I once knew these two Sicilian princesses. Their mother was American, their father a Sicilian prince. I liked them very much. I remember being told by one of them in very amusing detail the way they were treated, as a result of their title, in *this* country. They themselves were contemptuous of the people who were sucking up to them all the time—although they were perfectly happy to be treated that way—and it never ceased to amaze them how many Americans, particularly American artists, writers, intellectuals, and so forth, were suckers for a title.

STEVEN M. L. ARONSON These people were powerful, many of them were beautiful, they had marvelous houses, they set marvelous tables, they had wonderful yachts. Society as it was when he set out to achieve and then conquer it was a very aggressive place to be. Now it's anything. It's of really no interest. But Society with a capital "S" was it then, and he was there to penetrate it against the highest possible odds.

ROBERT FIZDALE Peggy Bernier was visiting us and asked, "Would you like to see Truman?" She was a very good friend of his. By that time he was very famous and he had become what I would call a "professional adorable man." He came to dinner. He spoke only of himself, full of himself. We were all rather disappointed because we expected to have a nice old-fashioned chum meeting, and instead he dwelt on himself, his life, his adventures and misadventures, which we all could have done but chose not to. We realized he had now become Act Two, which was the famous Truman Capote.

JOHN KNOWLES He was very nice. He was always oblique. They'd take pictures. He'd get a little tired of having to pose for photographs. I got a little pissed off if they didn't ask for my autograph. He never told them who I was. Never!

Celebrity was absolutely essential to him. I do not think he would have survived as long as he did without it. So extraordinary and so easily mocked, he became so famous—I walked hundreds of times with Truman on the street or in restaurants or at Gurney's Inn, Palm Springs, you name it—everyone recognized him, always. Only Ernest Hemingway was more recognizable. There are only two American writers who are recognized by the man in the street in this century: Truman and Ernest Hemingway.

KENNETH JAY LANE He probably was the most lionized writer since Voltaire, socially. To have Truman around was a social plum, a decoration.

STEVEN M. L ARONSON I walked down the street with him several times, took some long walks. It was amazing. I've walked down the street with lots of people, including Jackie Kennedy and Pearl Bailey—people who've had incredible face recognition, but never anything like this. Traffic practically stopped.

DAVID JACKSON We saw him in Greece. Jimmy Merrill had a house there. Truman came over for a two-week stay with these very rich people in Aegina. This massive, huge house. Extraordinary woman who had a total body lift. I've never seen anything like it. She's seventy and looks ten. Incredible. She was in that international set Truman knew. So she asked him to come and stay and she gave party after party. Endless. She had about eighteen houseguests, Truman among them. We spent four days with him in Athens and everywhere there were always people swarming up to him, all these tourists wanting his autograph—because by then he'd been on so many talk shows. Gore Vidal arrived with Claire Bloom, the actress. We told him about these people, these groupies . . . Gore was quite angry about it all. Then we told him that one night Truman and his rather dull friend, John, and Jimmy and I went to the only good restaurant in town—a last meal before he went off to the islands with his millionairess. About two tables away from us was this really good-looking couple, very handsome Americans, obviously American, staring at our table riveted. T's eyes would shift over there, wondering when they were going to approach for an autograph. Finally, the man got up and came to our table. Truman had his writing hand flexed. The man leaned over and said, "Mr. Merrill, could I have your autograph?" It turned out he was a poet. Truman had the most peculiar look on his face as if it was inconceivable that the great man had been passed up for the minor one. It thrilled Gore to hear that.

JAMES KIRKWOOD I had a little house down there in Key West. I was there when they had the wrap party for *92 in the Shade* at a place called Louie's Backyard. Very nice, open restaurant right on the water. A great place for a party. Tennessee Williams was there and Truman and James Leo Herlihy and Tom McGuane. There are more writers down there than you could shake a stick at. It was Truman's first trip. Tennessee had always been the king of Key West. Hemingway was long since gone. Tennessee was the reigning king and it was almost like a marauding king was coming down to unseat him in the person of Truman. Where everybody always used to yell, "Tenn, hey, Tenn!" Truman was so new he got all the attention. He kind of preened. People would bypass Tennessee because they were all used to seeing him. But this little Truman Capote, that was something different.

RICHARD BROOKS (*film director*) When we arrived at Lawrence, where the university is, I met Truman and asked him what he was doing there. He said, "They've put a stand out on the football field, the students are going to come, and I'm going to talk to them."

"About what?"

"I'm going to read some poetry and my 'Christmas Story.' "

Truman Capote

"You're going out to a *football* field and you're going to read poetry? To these people at night? Outside?"

"Yes, why not?"

I turned to Tom Shaw, my assistant director, and I said, "See if you can get a couple of police, because I think they're going to lynch him."

We went out there that night and there were about fifteen goddamn thousand people! To see this guy who wrote the book . . . who's four foot one, with blond hair, and he's gonna read poetry! They couldn't get any police. I said to Tom, "Why don't you get on one side of the stand and I'll stand on the other. If they start coming for him, we can get him the hell out of here." Tom's a pretty rough-looking guy. Between the two of us we were going to take care of Capote. So, he starts to read this stuff and what happens . . . not only do they not walk out of the stadium onto the football field, but by the time he's finished, fifteen thousand people are cheering and roaring like he's a football player! Goddamn, that was the most amazing experience. I realized then that this guy was a superstar. I really thought there was going to be violence. Not a chance, they loved him! They were going to carry him on their shoulders like a winning football coach.

Interlude

CHAPTER THIRTY-ONE *In Which the*
Reader Is Treated to a Brief Disquisition
on Fibbing

A pose suggestive of Truman's attitude about telling the truth. *(Harry Benson)*

PETER BEARD *(photographer)* He swore that True
cigarettes were named after him.

GEORGE PAGE I remember sitting in Truman's
apartment at the UN Plaza late one afternoon having
a drink. He was sitting on the little banquette
looking out over the East River. There was a sort of

lull in the conversation and he pointed to those huge Con Ed smokestacks over in Queens. He said, "You see those smokestacks, George?"

"Yes, Truman."

"Well, they used to be an absolutely horrible gray. One day Mort Zuckerman was up here and I told him to paint those smokestacks because I was tired of looking at that drab gray, and that's how they got to be red, white, and blue."

"Oh, come on, Truman," I said. He just laughed.

JOANNE CARSON Let me explain about Truman's embroidering the truth. Truman and I were in Palm Springs at a dinner party, the most boring dinner party I'd ever been to in my life. We came away saying, "My God, those people are so boring, can't stand it, falling asleep." The next night we went to another party and Truman was telling about the night before, how much fun it was, and this and that, making it sound fabulous. It certainly didn't sound like the party he and I had gone to. So as we were driving away I said, "Truman, I was at that party with you last night. That's not the way it happened." And he said, "If that's not the way it happened, it's the way it should have happened." So in Truman's mind, he doesn't lie, he makes things the way they *should* have been.

LEONORA HORNBLOW He said he'd seduced Norman Mailer. My husband got up and went out of the room. Truman said there was nobody that he couldn't seduce. Norman Mailer? I wouldn't believe that if I saw it on this carpet!

GEORGE CHRISTY Somehow one's antenna would go up and you'd think, "Did this *really* happen?" He mentioned a bunch of powerful names, and I wondered, "Did he have a bim-bam with them?" Fantasy time. Boozy dreams.

ROBERT FIZDALE In Ischia he told us about his love affair with Garbo. After this rather dazzling bit of information, Arthur [Gold] said, "I notice something about Truman. Whenever he begins to fantasize or tell lies, he looks up. His eyes go heavenward and he

doesn't look at you. Just watch, whenever his eyes go up, whatever
he is telling you is not the truth."

ARTHUR GOLD A sort of a seventeenth-century Madonna look.
"Around then . . ."

ROBERT FIZDALE His lies were better than other people's truths.
Much more interesting.

JANE GUNTHER He had a lot of imagination. It sounded like the
truth, but it wasn't. For instance, I know he never went to Greta
Garbo's apartment. But that's the kind of thing he did to amuse
people. He did it well enough so that it usually sounded like the
truth. He dined out on descriptions of her apartment over and over
again. I think it probably had been described to him by Cecil Beaton.

R. COURI HAY He told me he and Garbo were holed up alone in her
apartment for days at a time. Greta Garbo had a very big art
collection and he would always tell her that of the four or five
Picassos in her living room, half of them were hanging upside down.
I remember he said if anyone ever made his life story, he wanted
Greta Garbo to play him.

SAM GREEN (*gallery owner*) Truman claimed that the Picasso's were
hung upside down in Greta Garbo's apartment and there were no
mirrors. Garbo said to me once in that apartment, "that little man
has never been here. Why do people say they have been places
when they haven't or they know people when they don't?"

GORE VIDAL There are different sorts of liars. For instance, Lillian
Hellman lied in order to make herself appear a noble, good, and
admirable person, if not indeed a genius. Someone unique among
us, someone we are undeserving of. Her lies were lies of self-
aggrandizement. But Capote's lies had a double purpose: one was to
attract attention to himself and to distract attention from what he
looked and sounded like. Second, ultimately they were calculated to
destroy other people—these lies were usually sexual anecdotes

about famous people that he would improvise as he went along. You could not mention anyone famous to him—"Oh, I know him so well"—and he'd start in. If you knew anything about the case, you'd know he was just making it up as he went along. Joyce Susskind once said he was responsible for more New York divorces than the most busy of correspondents.

I'm often the victim of what I call the total reversal. Example: I was on the morning show that Tom Brokaw did on NBC. Jimmy Carter was president. We watched a film clip of him in Brazil. Then Brokaw said, "You've written a lot about bisexuality." I said, "Tom, let me tell you something about these morning shows. It's too early to talk about sex. Nobody wants to hear about it at this hour, or if they do, they are doing it. Don't bring it up."

"Yeah, uh, but Gore, uh, you have written a lot about bisex—"

I said, "My new book has nothing to do with bisexuality so—" He started in a third time and I said, "Now let's talk about Carter . . . What is he doing with these Brazilian dictators pretending they are freedom-loving, democratic leaders." I talked about Carter till our time was up. Two or three years later, *Time* magazine ran a cover story on anchorpersons. Brokaw was quoted: "Yes, I've had some difficult interviews. For instance, I had Gore Vidal on the morning show and I wanted to talk politics and he wanted to talk about bisexuality." Total reversal. To make me the villain of the story. It's almost as if there's a law.

KARL BISSINGER George Davis, who was important to a lot of us as an editor in those days, had asked Truman to go to Haiti and do a sketch for *Harper's Bazaar*. Truman asked me to go and take photographs. I met up with Truman in Port-au-Prince. During the day I wandered around taking photographs. Truman became ill—Montezuma's Revenge. It strikes most people in the tropics sooner or later, and you simply go to bed for a couple of days. But he was pretty sick, so he called a doctor. He was staying at the Olaffson Hotel. This middle-class black doctor arrived in a white linen suit. He gave Truman a charcoal pill, which everyone knows is the cure for diarrhea. I was visiting him when the doctor came in. When the piece came out in *Bazaar*, I was astonished to read that Truman had

visited a *witch doctor* who performed all kinds of voodoo to cure
him. An out-and-out lie! I was stunned. Truman was being his own
kind of journalist . . . with fiction and fact all mixed together. With
the later things like *The Muses Are Heard* you wondered just how
much of it was *arranged* by Truman. It's too bad you can't trust
everything he says. On the other hand, there was a certain amount
of romanticism to it. The concept of a witch doctor coming through
the Olaffson Hotel, cock feathers and painted up and all.

NANCY RYAN *(reporter) The Muses Are Heard*, his book about the
Porgy and Bess tour in Russia, however entertaining and however full
of pieces of fact, is a very stage-managed and rerigged version. I
gather that he's talked about having the world's best memory.
Perhaps he did have a good memory, but he also had a very vivid
imagination. He tried, for my own amusement, to make situations
happen that he thought would be amusing. You couldn't possibly
have had a more entertaining traveling companion than Truman, but
he was very manipulative about people's relationships with one
another. Mainly because he was going to write it down, you see. So
he stage-managed all sorts of things. When he wanted to make a
funny remark or crack, he had to find a mouth to put it in, and it
was usually my mouth.

He started writing *The Muses Are Heard* while we were in
Leningrad. He worked quite hard on it. I'd come back late at night.
He'd sit at the end of the bed and say, "Now, listen, I'm going to
read you some more." He'd start reading the latest paragraph he'd
written, and if there was some sort of an interruption—if I
interrupted, or he interrupted or laughed, or I said it didn't happen
that way, or something occurred to me—he would always insist on
going right back to the top of the paragraph. The meticulousness of
that was astounding. He'd do it over and over again. He didn't just
want you to hear the narrative flow, he wanted the effect of the
whole passage without any interruption. He didn't mind the
interruptions—they'd often take a long time—but then he went
right back to the top.

At one point Truman discovered that I was keeping a diary during
the trip and he asked, "Can I use some of it?" Then he went around

to find other people who were keeping diaries. Some of them he instructed to start keeping diaries if they weren't already. I can't remember how much he adjusted other people's diaries, but he put a whole lot of stuff into my account. Not only did he put various things into my diary but also my mouth—all the way through. When the book came out, I thought, "Oh my God, I come off as this terrible, loud teenager always saying 'For God's sake . . . For God's sake' all the way through."

JOHN RICHARDSON Truman had absolutely no respect for the truth. He felt that as a fiction writer he had license to say whatever came into his head as long as it had a surprising point or shape to it, or an unexpected twist to its tail.

PAUL RANDOLPH (friend) He became, I thought, awfully boring when he'd come over here. He spent all his time telling me about his conquests. Doctors and respectable bankers. The most unlikely people. I remember he told me about the very respectable doctor who came to see him and he seduced him. Well, this is fairly boring stuff unless you're another queer. You can only hear those stories so many times. I suppose it does tickle you a bit if you're another queer.

He was probably one of those people who were good company because you keep expecting them to be so. I expected Dorothy Parker to be good company. You kept waiting for these pearls . . . which never arrived. It seems ridiculous to say it about Truman—it's like calling Oscar Wilde a bore—but I really didn't look forward to seeing him very much.

I would say, "Oh, well, I don't believe it, Truman."

He would say, "The doctor came in with his little medical bag and the next thing he knew I had him in the sheets!" It was in Doctors Hospital. He was very proud of that. It was a real coup. I was a real coup for him. I'm a boy from the country and at first I was a little riveted . . . fairly saucy stuff. I think he wanted something in return. Douglas Fairbanks told me about a lady in Cincinnati in a wheelchair! I said, "Now you're showing off." He qualified it. "Well, she was on crutches!" That was his worst. I came up with a couple of bad ones myself. I have to think that there would be no point in Truman telling me unless it was to get something in return.

HORST P. HORST *(photographer)* He did have some story about a cardinal he had seduced on board a ship.

VALENTINE LAWFORD Every day at four o'clock. An archbishop or a cardinal.

PETER BEARD He told me this story about a great friend of his who was a friend of Errol Flynn's. This guy and Errol Flynn were drinking in a bar and Errol Flynn passed out early, and the guy brought him back and threw him on the bed—completely nude on the bed. He went back to the bar and realized he could make some cash off this. He said, "Anybody who wants to see Errol Flynn in the nude for ten dollars, come see me." He gathered quite an entourage and escorted them all up—maybe fifty or sixty people—and brought them through the room where Flynn was passed out.

GERALD CLARKE Lots of people thought Truman was a pathological liar, but many of the things he told me I found out to be absolutely true—things I hadn't really thought about very closely. But with me he was different. As time went on, he began to be more truthful . . . I think because I made it clear I didn't always believe him. I didn't believe him, for instance, when he told me that he and Errol Flynn had had a one-night stand in California. This would have been in 1947, when Errol Flynn was in his forties and Truman was twenty-three. As Truman described it, it didn't sound very romantic, and he didn't make it into a big deal: they just had a one-night stand, both very drunk. In any event, I didn't believe him. Errol Flynn was a macho idol, very handsome, with everybody falling at his feet. Later on, a biography of Errol Flynn said he was bisexual; biographies also came out about Tyrone Power, which said that Tyrone Power and Errol Flynn had had a big fling. And I myself have talked to men, men of reliable word, who said that they had gone to bed with one or the other. That doesn't necessarily mean that Truman and Errol

Flynn had a thing, but it makes the notion much more believable, especially if you remember that at the time Truman, who was almost a sylph, was very attractive to a certain kind of person. There were others. Camus, for instance. I mentioned this to Jenny Bradlee. She was French, married to an American and the agent for most of the important American writers. She was a very old lady in her nineties when I talked to her, and she knew Camus very well. She hooted at the suggestion that Camus was attracted to Truman. I don't know, I wouldn't say no, and I wouldn't say yes. Generally, however, I found that most of the things Truman said turned out to be true or true enough for me to learn the truth. One of the big exceptions was *Answered Prayers*. Truman gave a wonderfully convincing portrayal of a man being very upset about the missing chapters John O'Shea had supposedly stolen. Why might O'Shea have done it? To get money out of Truman, possibly, or he might have done it just to get back at Truman—for spite.

WILLIAM F. BUCKLEY, JR. There's so much invention with Truman. One time he told me that he was in Paris. Somebody had said to him, "Oh, would you mind taking this package to Bill Paley? It's a present he's bought for Babe." And he said sure. When he got to his New York apartment, he called up Bill and said, "I've got your package and I want to give it to you." Paley said, "Don't move! Don't answer the phone! Don't answer the door unless it's knocked on four times!" Truman asked why and was told never mind. Whereupon a vice president of CBS came and knocked on the door four times, took the package from him, flew to Paris, turned around, flew back to New York, and declared the $100,000 bracelet, or whatever bauble it was that Bill had bought for his wife. Truman had inadvertently acted as a courier, a felon, not declaring it. Terribly amusing. But again, he told a lot of very funny stories. Some people are that way: they began improvising and it becomes part of their repertoire; they don't bother to rearrange it or reconcile it with documentable facts. I'm awfully glad those people exist; they make life a lot more fun. Of course, there is a point at which I think one feels, "Well, this is about enough of Truman for one evening." I don't think I would have accepted an invitation to go to the Himalayas with him.

1968

Photo of the living room in Truman's Palm Springs home taken by
the Alvin Deweys, who were there for Christmas. Note stockings.
(Truman Capote Papers, The New York Public Library)

GEORGE CHRISTY I'd visit Truman in Palm Springs when he had his house on Paseo el Mirador, where he'd invite houseguests the likes of Lee Radziwill and John Knowles. He would occasionally host lunches and dinners for them. And, of course, there were all these mysterious cousins coming and going. I don't know who they were—mysterious cousins coming in from San Diego or somewhere.

Truman loved to entertain. He'd have Mabel, his cook, fix us simple foods—hamburgers and apple pies. He, of course, enjoyed his booze. How vividly I remember that . . . I gave a luncheon for him at my hideaway in Palm Springs, and he arrived at twelve-thirty or one o'clock. I don't know how many martinis he'd had before he came—he stayed until ten that night. It was one of his nonstop drinking days. "Well, what shall I have next? Shall it be champagne? Do you have any cream sherry? A little port?" That little house was cleaned out. His capacity was enormous. He loved Palm Springs at that time. Then he was burglarized and began to get upset about that. Burglarized several times.

HERB CAEN He bought a red Jaguar, a 3.8 sedan from me in 1963 or '64. He was on his way to Palm Springs, where he had a house. He said, "I love that car; I have to have that car. I want to drive it down to Palm Springs."

I said, "Truman, it's a wreck." You know what Jaguars were in those days, falling apart. I said, "You'll never get to Palm Springs."

He said, "I'll get to Palm Springs. I can drive." Cocky. He paid me some ridiculous small amount like $3,000. Sure enough, he got about as far as Fresno and the car broke down. He called up and said, "You sold me a lemon, you sold me a lemon!" I said, "I told you it was no good, Truman."

He had it towed to Palm Springs, where it sat in his garage and finally just collapsed. It was a beautiful car. He never should have had a car like that. Such a pretty car. I still have pictures of him getting into the car waving bye-bye. I could see his blanched bones in the desert near Palm Springs. He made it, but not in that car.

LEE RADZIWILL The house in Palm Springs was very nice—the usual bar with red leather barstools. I remember Richard Brooks came quite often with Jean Simmons when Richard was making *In Cold Blood*. Yet I thought it was the most unreal place I had ever been in my life. It gave me the creeps, Palm Springs. Nobody had any idea about the desperate things that were happening in Vietnam. It was amazing to find a world that was so out of touch with what was happening. I guess you could slip into it very easily. Truman had very busy afternoons in the spa clubs there. He would go for massages and water treatment. His days were well worked out.

That dreadful dog, Maggie, always went slobbering around. I came to stay with him right after New Year's in Palm Springs. My husband, Stas, had given me this beautiful sable coat for Christmas. Truman told me it was very cold there late at night, so I thought this was the perfect place for me and my sable coat. But it didn't get that cold and I left it in the closet. I left the door open and Maggie leapt up and got it off the hanger and chewed it to pieces. Truman thought it was hilarious, the funniest thing imaginable and laughed for days.

JOHN KNOWLES It's charming. It was all on one floor. Open. The living room was almost square. There were glass doors that slid open and the patio had a canvas awning. Beyond that the heated pool and a very large walled lawn and garden. A high wall. Big. With real privacy. He had Mabel, a former Cotton Club dancer, who was the housekeeper and cook there.

She was down-to-earth, tough . . . good for him. She was not going to let any of these guys take her Truman. She told me, "I got connections in this town. Any of these guys start threatening my Truman, one phone call, they're rubbed out. I can take care of anybody." I don't think she told him this. She told me. Every word of it I believed too.

His pool in Palm Springs was always about ninety degrees; Truman would dog-paddle back and forth. He always had this urge to exercise, but he couldn't follow through on it. He came to see me once in a health spa in Pompano Beach—Palm Aire Spa. I was exercising like hell and doing all kinds of things to try to get into shape . . . and succeeding, I think. Truman would do everything passive. He'd have all the massage and all the steam and all the mud, but we couldn't get him to *do* anything.

MIA FARROW When I would go and see Truman in Palm Springs, Frank would rarely come along. They would have fun bantering, you know, in the evening, but in the daytime Frank didn't seem to know what to do with Truman, so I would go over there alone. It was never boring with Truman, still some of the naughty little kid in him, and that's what made him so easy to spend time with because I was, you know, with one foot in childhood at that time. One afternoon, as we sat sipping our drinks, Truman had the idea that I should play the boy in *Death in Venice*. Well, I rushed out and read *Death in Venice* and that got me started on Thomas Mann.

MARY LAZAR Nice house. Just a little Palm Springs house, but they'd done the insides very well—a very grand house in a tiny fashion. Small bedrooms. Small, like Truman. He had all his little things around—his paperweights, little Mexican things, odd paintings that weren't important. He always made a nest for himself. That began a terrible period in Truman's life because that's when he met that awful guy Danny,* who was filling gas tanks at the airport. Kitty Miller said to him, "And what do you do, young man?" All decked out in his leather jacket, Danny said, "I gas 'em up at the airport. I filled Sinatra's tank today."

SLIM KEITH His means of supporting himself was topping-up airplanes, which meant he would go and fill them up with gas at night, and in the day he repaired air conditioners. He was married, had two children, a wife who lived in Chicago.

JOAN AXELROD "The air-conditioning man," as he was known. Everybody used to blame the air-conditioning man on me because I had found Truman his house. The local air-conditioning man came into the house one day to fix the air conditioner. It's as simple as that. He had a wife and a couple of children. I think he was baffled. I think this was his first homosexual experience, and he really picked one, didn't he?

*Danny is not his real name.

LEONORA HORNBLOW The air-conditioning man was in the pool. As he came out of the pool, Truman, who had been making us Bloody Marys, leapt to his feet, grabbed a bath towel, ran over, and wrapped him up in the most tender and loving way.

IRVING LAZAR (*literary agent*) This fellow had never worn a white shirt or a tie in his life. He was a hustler. He'd perform or allow himself to be performed on—he didn't care. But he didn't want to stay home. The day I met him he looked like a laborer. Then Truman took him over to an Italian shop in Palm Springs, Battaglia, and bought him a blazer with brass buttons and had him fitted for trousers. He was taught to wear a tie and shirt, had his fingernails cleaned. Truman cleaned him up. Then this fellow wanted to go everywhere Truman went. And Truman took him.

SLIM KEITH Truman was crazy in love with him. I've never seen a man or a woman more in love. He wanted to give the world to Danny. He had his teeth fixed; he gave him a Mercedes; he took him to the tailor—everything. He got him all spiffed up and took him to Europe. The last thing Danny wanted to do was spend four sunlit days on the Agnelli yacht. He didn't know the Agnellis; he didn't understand Italian; he didn't like the food; he got sunburned. He hated it!

MARIA THERESA CAEN Danny was so visibly out of place and so uncomfortable that I wondered why Truman insisted on bringing him. After he took him on the Agnelli yacht and it didn't go over very well, I asked him why he had brought him. He said, "Well, they get to bring whoever they want, why can't I?" He was extremely loyal.

JOHN RICHARDSON Truman brought him to Europe for one of those very smart Truman summers which involved staying with the Brandolinis in Venice, going on the Agnellis' yacht for a bit, or the Loel Guinnesses', or whatever. This dimwitted working-class young man hated every minute. There was nobody he could talk to; he felt lost. He had a certain dignity, which is what, I think, endeared him to Truman. Truman kept trying to sell him on this grand life and impress him with these fine people he was meeting and the fancy experiences he was having. But the boy wouldn't have any of it. He was utterly, utterly miserable. Since the Brandolinis were away and there was nobody else in their palazzo, Truman felt lost and lonely and would bring the friend over every day to lunch at Cipriani's, where Virginia Chambers, an old friend of Truman's, and I were staying. The boy would say, "All I want is a baked potato. I haven't had a baked potato since I left America. Where can I get a baked potato?"

So we asked Cipriani's chef to cook him a baked potato, but he said he didn't have the right potatoes. One day I went to the market and found some big potatoes. So I took them to the chef and explained that they were to be cooked in their jackets. We sat down to lunch in a state of great excitement. With a huge flourish, the silver dishes arrived and there were the inevitable sautéed potatoes! The chef just couldn't believe that you cooked potatoes in their jackets. The boy was so crestfallen, so dismayed about this that he sort of lapsed back into total gloom. If he had got his baked potatoes, I think he might have hated Venice a bit less.

MARELLA AGNELLI The last summer Truman and I saw each other we were staying in a beautiful house in Spain that belonged to the Fierros . . . remote, on this sort of fjord. Lee [Radziwill] was there. We had about eight or ten or twelve friends. Lots of children. Truman called me. "Can I bring a friend?" I didn't like the idea because, in a way, I was jealous of his friendship and didn't want to share it with anybody. So I said, "Well, Truman, let's see, I'm afraid I don't have two rooms." He said in his tiny voice, "It doesn't matter, we can sleep in the same room." So I had no choice. He came with Danny. The following winter I remember walking with him in this beautiful pine forest and asking, "Tell me, Truman, what is the point of Danny?" He said, "You know, it happened so suddenly." In Palm Springs something went wrong with his air conditioner, so he had called somebody to repair it. He told me, "I heard this Southern

voice that suddenly brought me back to my childhood. I ran into the
room and I saw Danny."

I never understood it. He was not even very good-looking.
Certainly not very interesting. Everybody tried to do their best with
him, but nothing moved. Danny probably was bored to tears too. He
found himself out of his world completely. He stayed a long time,
about ten days.

JOHN RICHARDSON He was obsessed with this boy, telling us all the
time that the boy was heterosexual. Truman said that all the loves of
his life had basically been heterosexual. I didn't like to say that the
mere fact of the boy going to bed with him made him no longer
heterosexual. I mean, there had to be a sort of flaw in their
heterosexuality. Vanity prevented Truman from understanding my
point. It was very important for this little dwarf monster to feel
capable of seducing straight men away from women. It was a feather
in his cap. In this particular case, anybody could have seduced this
poor boy. He was so will-less, getting him into bed didn't prove
anything. Not that I think there was a great deal of sex. Truman was
more obsessed with having this wretched boy as a trophy—a *straight*
trophy. He was Truman's prey, his victim. They went off, to
Denmark or somewhere. On the plane from wherever it was to
London to stay with Lee Radziwill, the boy broke the news to
Truman that he just couldn't stand it anymore and he was leaving
him. And that triggered, I think, one of Truman's big collapses.

SLIM KEITH He was devastated. I have never seen anyone in such a
condition. You'd *look* at him and he'd cry. You'd say, "Tru, it's going to
be all right. Believe me, I've been to this fire. I know it's going to be
all right."

"But I love him so much . . ."

1972–1973

CHAPTER THIRTY-THREE   *In Which a Banker Comes to Call on TC at the UN Plaza*

In 1966 Truman moved from Brooklyn into a two-bedroom apartment on the twenty-second floor of the United Nations Plaza at First Avenue and Forty-ninth Street, with a sweeping view down the length of Manhattan. For it he paid $62,000, considered high at the time. *(Truman Capote Papers, The New York Public Library)*

LEONORA HORNBLOW Curiously enough, Truman's apartment at the
UN Plaza was a very Southern apartment. I don't know why. It had
Tiffany lamps and a wonderful feeling of age and time, which is
difficult to do in the UN Plaza, that disaster of a building, that air-
conditioned nightmare. I'm very grateful to Henry Miller for that
title. He didn't mean it for a building, but it fits.

LENORE HERSHEY (*editor*) He collected paperweights, but mostly
portraits of himself—large ones, little ones, photographs, paintings,
they were all over the place, including the famous one of him on the
sofa. The Cecil Beaton one. And the painting by Réné Bouché,
which he didn't like. He collected Victorian things, Tiffany glass.
Babe Paley had given him a lot of things. The apartment had a lot of
reds. A lot of dark colors. A lot of books.

JAN CUSHING Very eccentric, very depressing. I mean, it was run-
down. It had a beautiful view. But just messy. He didn't look like he
was happy in the apartment. I think he was happier at Peartree's
across the street.

WILLIAM STYRON We were both houseguests at Kay Graham's house
in Washington. Everyone else had gone to bed. He got very
confidential and frank with me and he just spilled out so many
things. I remember him telling me about his first encounter with his
lover—John O'Shea. He said that O'Shea had come to his
apartment in the United Nations Plaza to talk over finance. They
were sitting there talking and this sexual excitement passed between
them. He hadn't expected this, because he was getting all the loving
he needed in terms of being just carnal, getting laid, or whatever,
Truman being Truman. O'Shea said, "Can you tell me where the
bathroom is?" Truman said, "Well, yes, it's right over there." Truman
said that as O'Shea passed him, he leaned down and kissed him, not
on the mouth, but on the cheek or the brow or something, and
Truman said, "My heart was racing like a maniac. I said, 'Would you
please stop that . . . in about fifteen years?' "
    That was it, they just fell into each other's arms and that was the
beginning of this wild romance.

LESTER PERSKY (*film producer*) Truman brought this man around to whom he introduced me, a middle-aged, dark-haired man who looked a little like W. C. Fields—it was John O'Shea. When I was with him, he was absolutely well behaved, polite and kind of formal; Truman told me that this man had a wife and a family of four children.

I'm sure Truman did something very evil without intending it, because he disrupted this man's life. Now, O'Shea was obviously waiting to have his life disrupted, waiting to be pulled out from that existence with his family, but if it hadn't been for Truman he might have gone on and in ignorance . . . in the bliss of that ignorance of what his dissatisfaction was.

At first I actually thought he was a good influence on Truman, because here's a man who is as straight-arrow as anybody. He was too square. He was presentable. He came on like you could run him for sheriff of San Diego. You couldn't envision the two of them in any embarrassing situation, I mean you couldn't. He seemed perfectly proper. So I thought that he might be a stabilizing influence. I later found out, from Truman mostly and from my own experiences, that, of course, he was not a stabilizing influence at all.

CAROL MARCUS MATTHAU Unrequited love. They say that if you take away someone's first love, it can kill a person. Loss changes your body chemistry. The big love was Jack Dunphy. Jack always loved and protected him.

But O'Shea was different. I thought he *was* a killer. I think he hastened Truman's death. Truman went into total pain about him. Truman never wrote me about O'Shea, but he talked about him. I thought I was going to meet God. When I met him, I saw this bank teller in a dark gray suit and puce-colored hair—that dirty blond, college-boy color. He looked like any other bank teller who doesn't really have much to say. Some people are very charming in their inability to say things. He was so ordinary that it was breathtaking. I said to Truman, "You have this weird fascination for the ordinary."

JOHN KNOWLES I said, "Truman, you're heading for the white water with this one."

MARIA THERESA CAEN Truman and Johnny O'Shea rented a house in Mendocino. I remember their drinking a lot of vodka. I've never been a heavy drinker, so I would drink maybe one glass of wine for every three or four they were drinking. O'Shea was really a drunk, so it quickly became uncomfortable to be around him. But Truman was crazy about him. Their relationship was totally puzzling to me. Here was Johnny O'Shea, who had been ostensibly happily married as a heterosexual for twenty years when Truman came into the picture. He had four children. I didn't ever understand Truman's friendship with Peg, O'Shea's wife. One day he called to say he wanted to bring "Peg" to San Francisco. I asked who she was and he said, "Well, she's Johnny O'Shea's wife." I thought, "This is a bizarre play; now he's bringing the *wife* here." And he did. She'd never been to California, so he brought her out here to show her around. Don't you find that bizarre? And she was so fond of him. He showed her all around San Francisco, took her shopping on Union Square, took her to Gump's. Truman loved the blinis and caviar at Alexis's restaurant, which used to be across from the Fairmont Hotel. He took us there. She was very sweet to him, Truman was very sweet to her and everyone was very sweet to everyone else, even though he had run off with her husband. No discussion at all. He had a separate friendship with her entirely.

HERB CAEN I recall being shocked. I guess I led a more sheltered existence than I realized. Truman alluded to his romance with O'Shea. He'd say, "Well, he has the most perfect penis."

They invited us to come up there. It wasn't the invitation I was really looking for, but I drove up to Mendocino and there they were in this falling-down, dirty, frontierlike mountain cabin. It was awful. O'Shea was sitting there with his vest on, but the tie off, still looking Boston, drinking beer and watching some sporting event on the tube that Truman couldn't have cared less about. We spent the night there! Truman had said, "Bring your sleeping bags!" So we did. It was a strange experience. O'Shea was a hard guy to figure. Very sad man. Obviously going through some terrible torment. He talked about his wife and the kids quite often, after the third or fourth Irish whiskey. I remember he said the words "unnatural relationship." If there were two people who didn't belong together, it was Truman and this jock-banker.

CAROL MARCUS MATTHAU O'Shea and Truman and I went out to lunch at the Bistro one day. Toward the end of the lunch I wanted to be dead because O'Shea began to speak to Truman in this humiliating fashion, humiliating him in front of me. I stopped him. I said, "John, I have a gun in my purse. I'm a perfect shot and I'm old and I can sit in jail and reread Proust. I'm going to shoot you." They all started laughing and it was over. But the whole thing was very painful to me.

ALAN SCHWARTZ This relationship with O'Shea became very violent—guns being pointed and talk about guns and so on. Truman had a .38 caliber detective revolver. He was telling me about how O'Shea pulled the gun, or he pulled the gun on O'Shea, and all this and all that. I took the gun away from him. I dumped half of it in the East River and half in the Hudson River. I remember telling one of my law partners, "I can't figure out where to throw this." He said, "What the hell is that?" I said, "This is half of Truman Capote's gun."

About a month later Truman asked for his gun. "Where is it?" I said, "I dumped it." He said, "What!" I said, "I threw it away, and you're not going to get another one." That's the way I used to talk to him.

This sense of violence was not only at the UN Plaza but also in California, in Malibu, where they took a house for a while. O'Shea had FUCK YOU on his California license plates. Since they were always drunk, you can imagine how the police loved that, right?

LESTER PERSKY Once Jack was with Truman, these O'Shea kids were sort of abandoned. The funny thing is that the children came to hate the father and love Truman. He played an avuncular, almost fatherly role. When they had a problem or needed money or something, Truman would take care of them. He was very proud of them. His relationship with O'Shea, however, was very stormy. After an initial three months, things were cooling between them. O'Shea had fallen in love with a girlfriend who was an actress. Things were reaching a critical point. Truman flew out to Los Angeles because he couldn't reach O'Shea on the phone. The house was empty, all the furniture was gone. O'Shea, according to Truman, had cleaned out his bank account and disappeared. The *Answered Prayers* manuscript was gone. Truman, because of the publicity, was afraid to go to the police. They hired a private detective to try to find O'Shea, mostly concerned to get his manuscript back. Truman was very distraught, crying to me over the phone about all the years down the drain; all he had were notes; it would take him twelve more years to redo the book . . . This was his main shot, his *Streetcar,* and the one he'd been babbling on about for so many years. His whole career rested on this one book and Jack O'Shea had it. At least that's what Truman thought. Truman told me a story about having lunch with Jan Cushing at Quo Vadis with some guy who apparently had connections, owned hotels in Las Vegas and knew everybody out there. Jan said, "Why don't you talk to him about it?" So Truman told him and this man said, "I'm going to make a phone call to Las Vegas." He came back and said, "We've got someone going out to LA on the next flight. That manuscript will be on the red-eye to New York tonight. When we find them, do you want to leave them a message?" he added with a chuckle.

Truman asked, "Well, what do you mean a message?"

The man gestured like an arm was going to be chopped. Truman said, "You can break a few bones, but don't hurt his pelvis!"

The next day Truman called me, absolutely tubular. This courier had come in from LA with the manuscript. He gave Truman the license number of O'Shea's car, the license number of the girlfriend's car, where the girlfriend worked, their address, their phone number . . . whether that's the truth I don't know.

JAN CUSHING When the relationship with John broke up, Truman called up Mrs. O'Shea and said, "I've done a terrible thing. I will support you the rest of my life. I'm terribly sorry and I want to help in any way I can. I would like to get your daughter the best modeling job." It was part guilt, and he also loved the children. He went on Mother's Day with Mrs. O'Shea to the school. And that's very sweet, because, let's face it, he had screwed up a family—four children.

Interlude

CHAPTER THIRTY-FOUR   *In Which*

Kate Harrington, John O'Shea's Daughter,

Tells Her Story

Kate Harrington (left), Truman's protégée, at Studio 54 with Truman and Gloria
Swanson. *(Ron Galella)*

KATE HARRINGTON (*friend*) Truman was my father's lover. I met him in my mother's living room. I was raised out on Long Island and came from a very ordinary, Irish, middle-class family. We lived this very conventional life: my mother and father had four children. My father was forty-two years old in 1972 when somehow or other, and I'm still not sure how, he and Truman connected. I've heard many different stories. Very funny, they make me laugh now. My father's version was that he was always a frustrated writer. A banker at Marine Midland, he used to come home at night and go down to the library to write. We never knew what he was writing—just a typical frustrated writer. He was a very smart, self-taught man. He read a lot. Supposedly what he did was send Truman a bunch of letters and things that he'd written, which even Truman confirmed. But it's hard to believe that Truman answered, because when I lived with Truman we used to get his mail and throw it in the incinerator. So I doubt that he read my father's things. That was my father's story—that he called him and asked to come see him. It doesn't seem likely. It seemed like my father must have led a bit of a double life. Truman used to say, "Oh no, he did write me (as it were) but he met me at some men's gay bathhouse on the Upper East Side."

That probably is more true. My parents had a hard marriage. Anyway, my dad came home one day and sat us all down as a family and said, "I'm going to leave the bank and go work as a business manager for Truman Capote." The rest of the kids didn't say anything, and I said, "Who's Truman Capote?" You know, excuse me! I was eleven at the time. My father, who was sort of a teacher for all of us, was furious that I didn't know who Truman Capote was. "He's a well-known writer," blah, blah, blah.

For about a year my dad supposedly worked for Truman and traveled around the world with him. My parents stayed married. Because he had been sort of unhappily married to my mother, everyone was very happy about this, because my father was finally happy. He would come home and Truman would come to our house for dinner on Sundays, all very kind of jolly. My mother loved Truman; he was pretty irresistible. That's how I got to know him, sort of suspiciously, because I was very close to my father and I thought, "Who is this guy?" Anyway we came to know him in that way, the whole family. He was an uncle figure.

I remember the first gift he ever brought when he came to Wantagh. He gave us gifts that I understand completely now—what people didn't need. I was from a "you'll get a new pair of shoes at Christmas" kind of family, a middle-class family. The whole concept of giving gifts as a gesture, or because they are just beautiful, was something new to me. He bought me this big rock of amethyst. I thought it was the Hope diamond. I would carry it around, this big sparkly thing. I thought, "How amazing. There's a whole other world out there where people think of things like this. You give a gift just because it's pretty to look at!" It was really a big change. He gave my mother that *Observations* book by Richard Avedon.

No one spoke of his homosexuality in my family and, to be honest, at that point in my life I don't think I even knew what a homosexual was. I didn't know what was going on. I was a young eleven. I was happy that my mother was happy and my dad was happy and we liked Truman; he was funny and all that. But he changed our lives without a doubt, but in a nice way.

My dad sent these postcards from all over the world—being with the Agnellis and visiting the Chaplins. It was like my father was living a kind of *My Fair Lady*-esque life. I think my mom was in denial that they were lovers. Finally one day my mother heard something about my father . . . that he had started to get into drugs. Living in Key West for the winter (Truman, Dad, and Jack Dunphy), he had gotten involved in cocaine. Truman told my mother about it because my father had become really violent and loud. My mother was very innocent and really believed being involved with drugs was the worst thing in the world; she was so terrified she decided to leave my dad. They got separated. Everything got pretty bleak for my poor mother. She began to work. She'd been a housewife. She got a job at a law book publishing firm out in Long Island but she didn't make much money. The two eldest children sort of fled, so it was the little brother, Christopher, I, and my mom. It was a very dark period. My mother was very Miss Haversham about things. Things got terrible with money, really terrible. No money, no heat, and just dreadful. My mother essentially had a breakdown and she began to drink. I had turned twelve. When you come from a hard family you're very grown-up at twelve, so I rang Truman—his number was always up on the wall above the phone in the kitchen. "Hi, it's Kerry and I wondered if I could talk to you about something."

He did this adorable thing. He acted as if he was making an appointment with an adult. He said, "Okay, why don't you come in on the train." I'd never come into New York on my own, ever. He told me how to do it and to give the cabdriver a note that read 870 UN Plaza.

So I snuck out, didn't tell my mom, and went to New York and we had this lunch at Antolotti's on Forty-ninth Street. Just the two of us. I said, "Look, I know you know a lot of important people and I really need a good job because my mom needs money."

I explained the whole situation to him. I said I wasn't asking him for money, but from all the stories he told us I figured someone could use a helper.

Truman said, "Well, let me think about it. Are you willing to quit school?" I was in the seventh grade. He said that smart people don't need to go to school, which was obviously his own situation. I said, "No, no, no."

"Let me think about it for a week," he said, "and you come back, this time next week."

So I did that. Cut school and did it again. Truman said, "The only thing someone who's this young can do is to be a model."

I came from a family which exalted reading and writing, very first-generation. Study, study, study. A real Irish household in the sense that they don't overflatter you, so I was stunned because I wasn't very secure about modeling. After he convinced me that was a possibility he helped me. He invited me to come and see his friend Wilhemina, who ran the modeling agency. At the first meeting she said, "I have a Terry O'Neal. Kerry O'Shea's too similar. Any other name?"

I remember looking at Truman and thinking, "What do you mean, any other name?" I had never heard of anyone changing their name. I grew up in a dumb little town where no one changed their name unless they got married.

He said, "Well, her mother's name is Harrington." Anyway, before you knew it, by the time we walked out my name had been changed from Kerry O'Shea to Kate Harrington and it's never come back.

To be honest, it did bother me, though I'm very proud of my mother's side of the family, where I'm not of my dad's. The Harringtons are a very nice, big family, very smart. People to be proud of. The O'Sheas are a small family whom I never knew, and my dad had a very dicey reputation all around. So I think it was kind of great for me to detach, though it got me into a lot of trouble with the people in my town and my brothers, thinking I was acting puffed up and all that.

"Well, let's just shoot an amazing portfolio for you," Truman said. I wasn't the prettiest girl on the block, but I was thin. Richard Avedon photographed me in my school uniform. I couldn't imagine anyone wanting me to be a model, but I just believed Truman. All these famous photographer friends of his shot this portfolio—Avedon, Victor Skrebneski, Scuvullo. They were doing him a favor. When I would go out on go-sees people used to say, "Who *are* you? How'd you get all these pictures?" Truman always said that I should refer to him as "an old friend of the family." An old friend of what family? "My family from the Bronx."

More and more, I would stay at Truman's. He was often gone. He'd be with my dad, who was never in New York when I was there—I think he was afraid my mother would serve him with divorce papers—and he stayed in Palm Springs.

I'm grateful now, but then it was very confusing because I didn't belong anywhere. I have all this in my journals. The day I went to stay with Truman he handed me a black-and-white composition book, and he said, "This is what kept me alive during my adolescence. Keep writing in a journal. You can't stay with me unless you keep one."

So I did. It is very funny to read. Full of spelling mistakes. The day I went to see Avedon I would misspell his name. "I went to see a photographer today who Truman says is very famous." I would describe the whole thing in the journal. "There was a big umbrella with a lightbulb in it." Very naïve and funny. Or I'd go see really famous people with Truman, wonderful people, and I'd say, "They're

some of the most unhappy people I've ever met." Isn't that
something?

I went back to Long Island every Friday to take my tests at school
and then I'd spend the weekend there. We're not talking the
Hamptons. We're talking "gateway to Jones Beach"—Wantagh,
which Truman used to laughingly refer to as "wonderful Wantagh."
He'd say, "And how was wonderful Wantagh this weekend." And
he'd just howl with laughter. It was so surreal because one day you'd
be having lunch with the Kissingers and they'd be asking you, "Oh,
do you have a beau?" And da, da, da, da, da, and then I'd go home to
this . . . uck! Just a nightmare. But I loved my mother very, very
much. As time went on, it was very *My Fair Lady*, where you didn't
fit in either place fully. But, so it is.

The first time I walked into that apartment with this beautiful
view of the East River, right next to the UN on the twenty-second
floor, for someone like me it was a real gasper. That feeling didn't go
away for a long time. The whole apartment had that kind of view.
His room was at the very end of a little hallway and mine was right
next to it—a little peach-colored room, a beautiful little daybed right
by the window, very simple and plain, with pillows. He also had a
desk in there where he used to write and talk to people on the
phone. It had beautiful taffeta curtains that were lavender; it was
very peaceful and simple. Lots and lots of books sent to him to
review, tons of picture books. The paperweights were in the living
room, millions of beautiful paperweights with all these bursts of
colors. I never got tired of looking at those. The whole idea of
collecting things was so wonderful. It's funny how you go through a
period where something startles you for a long time and you think
it's so interesting and precious and finally it makes sense and then
you're looking for paperweights. He had three stuffed snakes—
which were so icky, but you got used to them. He had this thing
about reptiles. He had those needlepoint pillows with sayings on
them and he had "H. Golightly" on the door of my room. I had never
seen *Breakfast at Tiffany's*. I watched the movie recently and it made
me laugh, because a lot of the things Truman taught me are strictly
from that character. The whole idea of diamonds are tacky before
you're forty and all that stuff.

Truman didn't have a television set. I remember when I first came in the apartment at 870 UN Plaza, I said, "Well, what are you supposed to do here?" He had this big, vast apartment. I used to walk around and look at all the paintings all day and the knickknacks. I said, "There's not even a television." He brought me to this little red room with all these books and he said, "There's your television. Read those." All those picture books he had. I really believe that's how I ended up being interested in pictures, because I just used to sit, out of boredom, and look endlessly at these pictures. And read and read.

He changed my entire life, because he had me read everything. I came home one day in the seventh grade and I said, "I have to write a book report and I don't know what book to read," He said, "Read *Out of Africa*." So I did a book report on *Out of Africa* and my provincial seventh-grade teacher . . . nobody had heard of it. In the eighth grade, I had a clever teacher. Truman said, "Let's do a book report on *In Cold Blood*." He brought out the old real pictures of the real murderers. His little Pandora's box of Dick and Perry. How hilarious to be out in Wantagh saying, "And here are the murderers." My teacher couldn't believe it. He grabbed me at the end of class and said, "Where'd you get all that stuff?" It was so funny, really too much. I was like, "Oh, I'm friends with the man who wrote that book." All the way through high school, that teacher was always asking, "How are you?"

What amazes me now is that I convinced the school board, a Catholic school out on Long Island, that it was a great opportunity for me to have a career, that going to school was nonsense, and they said *yeah*.

I did pass my courses at school. I ended up studying at night and then I would take the quizzes on Friday. I passed. It was easy. I think what was uncomfortable was not being a part of school and always being an adult. I would go through these little rebellions where I really hated modeling and I would tell Truman, "I don't want to do this anymore." I joined the boys' high school track team and ran on the team. I was quick. I was good. In fact, it was my whole life when I was young. I used to run every single day and night. I ran the 1,500 meters. Crazy.

Truman was such a multifaceted person and, all his self-destructiveness aside, he had one of the biggest insights of anybody I'd ever met. He was a very complex person who could be a million things. There was a decided part of him that was like a child who had never grown up, so that was the friendship that he gave me.

He taught me in a very gentle, understated way. He would never embarrass me. There was a part of him that was incredibly sensitive. He must have watched a lot of behavior or read a lot of things from books himself. If you think about where he's from, down in rural Alabama, people down there weren't really hanging around with Babe Paley. As I look back, and it's been many years, I'm sure that he identified with me more than I realized. I didn't understand that before, because he was so exalted and everything.

My parents were really strict, so I think manners went a long way; I don't think he would have had me around if I didn't have decent manners and was clunking around, bumping into things. The sad thing is, I always felt the first few years that I was walking around on eggshells, not because he demanded that, but if I put one foot wrong, staying in his apartment, I wouldn't have my job and then I'd have to go back, doomed to a life sentence in wonderful Wantagh.

He absolutely taught me everything about dress. He was great friends with Halston and those people. His idea that fascinated me was that dresses should be very plain and always the same for a woman. He would say, "Always keep your hairstyle the same and never change it," and all that. Then I would visit those women with him, Babe Paley or Mary Lazar in California or whatever. I mean, I can just *imagine* the whispers at dinner that I never heard: *"Oh, it's that mean boyfriend's daughter."* I'm sure they felt: "poor thing." But it could have been worse. He was a lovely person and he couldn't have been sweeter, no matter what his motivation was. Truman never forced me to do anything. I just think he was trying to help me be *something* and he couldn't think of anything besides what he did for me. It's extraordinary that we ended up staying so close all the way to the very end of his life, because I don't think he expected that either.

I never thought of him as my dad at all. He was very much a

friend on one hand. I was used to having alcoholic parents. There's a thing that happens—role reversal where you're their friend and their comrade. They're not looking after you. It's more equal or you become the parent. That happened very much at the end with Truman, where I got to pay him back for looking after me because he had no friends. It wasn't awkward for me.

We sat in on rainy days. He'd have these long legal yellow pads and he'd say, "All right you write a story and then I'll write a story." Then we'd switch and read them. I was so naïve and not really that well-read. I didn't even know that he was such a great writer. I figured that was his job. He wrote books for Random House. He'd say, "Okay, you say a sentence and I'll say a sentence and then we'll have to write the stories." That's how it went. He'd say, "There was a woman who lived in Shanghai and her name was Beatrice Bald and da, da, da," and I had to make a story out of that. Then I'd say one to him. We'd switch and read. When I think of having the nerve to give him one of *my* stories—how embarrassing! Mostly it was humorous, though, so much laughter and cynicism.

He had a side to him, which was probably his downfall, as is the case with most alcoholics, and that is that he had a thread of sensitivity that was maybe just *too* sensitive. Truman once said to me when he was at the hospital, for the millionth time drying out . . . something about the glare of life being too much for some of us. I always remember that. His struggle with all of that was very sad and hard to deal with. He would try so hard and get all cleaned up, really healthy, drinking cases and cases of Tab, and he'd want to be fabulous and all that and I understand that so much now. Then he'd start slipping and he'd say, "Don't let me have any more of these," and he'd hand me the pills. I'd have them under my pillow when I went to bed—my room was next to his—and then he'd come in at two or three in the morning and he'd say, "You have to give them to me." We'd have this argument and I'd say no and he was just so sad.

Looking back on it, I see how strange it was, that he never found dates for me. That's a typical kind of gay thing. He would talk about people who theoretically would be good for me. He set his sights a little high for me. He wanted me to be with the sons of the women he knew, really powerful women, who had married very powerful men or men who were very rich—the sons of the really elegant wives of these kinds of men. Until I was about seventeen he would act like I was too young to date. I went out with a boy from my hometown who had moved up to Connecticut. I went out with him for about five years. Truman didn't disapprove but he didn't approve either. One time he wanted me to go out to the Winston Guests' for the weekend where Diana Vreeland was supposed to be. He said, "This is a really good opportunity and you should go." I don't know what possessed me but obviously I was feeling pushed around. I opted for a boring weekend in Westport, Connecticut, with my boyfriend and his family instead of going out to the Guests' to see Mrs. Vreeland. I just couldn't bear another weekend with all the adults yakking away. I remember fighting with him. The only thing that ever made him upset was when I missed opportunities that he deemed to be opportunities.

I was like a sponge for about fifteen years. But I didn't know where I fit in comfortably because I'm a fairly honest person and I don't do well masquerading. I have too much of this Irish grit in me to really do that for too long.

I remember he brought me to Richard Avedon's opening at MOMA, his retrospective. He said to me on the way over, "Now don't tell anyone where you're from. Don't tell anyone ever that you're from Wantagh." I felt this was a huge betrayal because I started to think there was something wrong with my beginnings. I thought, "Gee, he's really ashamed of where I'm from." I can see that what he was trying to do was mastermind some plan. The *My Fair Lady* thing. "Just say I'm an old friend of the family's," he said, and I said okay. But that's pretty sad. My mother wouldn't like that. As I got older, I began to see that the people at parties like Mr. Avedon's openings were an insular little group who liked to believe that everybody was someone they sort of understood. I resigned myself to the fact that it was just easier. But that was a very difficult thing for me to undo after he was gone—to see that it's much more important for peace of mind to authentically be yourself.

We went to California a couple of times. I'd never been on a plane and I'd certainly never been to California. We stayed at the Beverly Wilshire. We'd get to the hotel and he'd say, "Let's have a nap in the afternoon." I didn't want to have a nap, I had all the energy I needed. So I would just walk around or go to bookstores. Then we'd get ready for the evenings. We went to these dinner parties every night in Bel Air until I thought all they did in California was to go to each other's living rooms and have lunch and dinner.

Truman decided I was going to be an actress. Truman had this whole Hollywood connection—Swifty Lazar, Carol Matthau. He sent me to Halston, who was nice enough to give me all of these beautiful little frocks that were too sophisticated for me. My mom was all excited. Butterflies in the stomach. She packed me away. Truman was going to introduce me to Sue Mengers, the biggest agent on the coast. I mean, the whole idea was so silly. When a camera gets on me, forget it! I'm not supposed to be on that end of the camera. I was crippled by self-doubt, completely a wreck. Besides, I wasn't ambitious in that way. I had a certain amount of star quality, Truman always used to say, but I think a lot of people have that little spark inside them, enthusiasm and who knows where the heck it came from, you're sort of born with it. But he interpreted it as true star quality. For me it was more like a love of life. He didn't understand the essential little Irish girl/humble Catholic that I couldn't outgrow. You can't live on someone else's fuel.

So he took me out there. They had a series of dinner parties in my honor. I remember saying to him on the plane out, "Why do all your friends always have dinners for someone? Can't they just have dinner? Why would they have a dinner for *me*? They don't even know me." At the first party all these people were there. I was so crippled. I was dressed in this flowy chiffon thing, two pieces of chiffon, a navy and white thing that Halston had made, and these little slippers. I came floating in with Truman, into one of those sunken LA living rooms and there was Sammy Davis, Jr., and Ryan O'Neal and all these people and I was like, "Oh my God."

Back in New York, Henry Kissinger, Norman Mailer, and all those people were real. I could deal with that. I got very comfortable with all the Park Avenue ladies. But this was just too much. I walked in and I thought, "Oh, dear God in heaven"—saying hello to all these faces that in my hometown the people used to stay glued to *People* magazine to look at. Everybody paired off and went into the living room. Everybody had to be walked in by someone else, which now I understand, but back then I was thinking, "Don't worry, I can get in there by myself." They said I should walk in with Ryan O'Neal. I had seen *Love Story* with my sister in the local theater and I remember we went into the bathroom and cried and cried over Ali MacGraw dying. It was a little much for me—being escorted by Ryan O'Neal into the dining room!

Someone had made a mistake about Sammy Davis, Jr., being there. He didn't get along at all. He had probably said some mean things about Truman or something. They shouldn't have invited him. It was a nightmare because even as far away as they put him from Truman, Truman got plastered and started saying things down the table.

Then Ryan O'Neal decided he had a crush on me. I was fifteen or sixteen and he was thirty-six or something. He said, "Can I drop Kate off, Truman? I want her to meet Tatum." Truman was like, "Well, it's entirely up to her." But then he stepped back from Ryan and waved no, no.

I remember Mary Lazar taking me into the loo with her—all this is in my journal, where I wrote, "They call the bathroom the loo"—and she was very sweet. She said, "Remember one thing. No matter what Truman tells you about who you should be with, the only thing that matters when you're with a man is that they have a good sense of humor and that they have a good heart. I've had lots of men like me all my life and the happiest I've ever been is with Swifty and look at him." She was quite pretty and it struck me immediately, "What's she doing with this little bald man with the big glasses and everything?"

Every night there was a different party. Jan Cushing. Mary and Swifty Lazar. I remember Swifty asking me, "Can ya sing? Can ya dance? Well, what can you do?" I said, "I don't know." Thank God I never did a screen test. I never wanted to be an actress. I had no interest, none. I like going to movies, that's it.

Modeling was fine because I loved being in *Mademoiselle* and *Seventeen*. But it was really because I was proud of myself to be the breadwinner. I was proud for my mom and my best girlfriend to see my picture. But I also was not stupid; I knew I wasn't six feet tall. I didn't care about being a star model. It was just a means to an end. But with the acting, I put my foot down because I knew it would embarrass me. I was very strong-willed. I would never let someone push me into something. Also Truman was becoming less of an authority figure, because his life was slipping down. I was starting to take care of him. So I wasn't taking every stitch of advice anymore. I said, "Truman, you don't understand. I don't want to do this. I have no desire to do it. None. And I have no talent. I'm not going to make a fool of myself. What are you going to do? Give me singing lessons? I don't want to sing."

He was like, "All right. I was just trying to help."

So he let it go.

1975

CHAPTER THIRTY-FIVE *In Which*
Society Recoils from TC's Bombshell

(*Truman Capote Papers, The New York Public Library*)

KATE HARRINGTON I remember when he decided to put the excerpt from *Answered Prayers* in *Esquire*. I was talking on the telephone to my dad and I remember him saying, "That's social suicide." That was the end for Truman, let's face it. He showed me the little excerpts—the little stories that he was going to lace together. Some of them were really little and he didn't even print them.

I read it as a story and I thought it was very intriguing, though I didn't recognize the thinly veiled identities. Now Dominick Dunne's doing it all the time, but those people felt betrayed. Of course, Truman had a side to him that was really wicked. Naughty. I don't know what that stems from—if he actually resented the people he was so close to; or that some part of him thought it would be the epitome of what he wanted at that level of society, but when he got up there perhaps it wasn't as satisfying as he thought, or perhaps he was unhappy inside anyway.

It was a sort of desperate move. The book wasn't done and he wanted to give them a taste to keep people interested. I remember him being very excited by the prospect of it actually coming out—making funny jokes with that big hearty laugh, saying "Ah, wait till you see when this hits the stands. People are going to be . . ." He thought it was going to be a sensation.

MARELLA AGNELLI My breakup with him came before the *Answered Prayers* pieces appeared in *Esquire*. He told me one or two things to hurt me. I never understood why. There was something so vicious, so nasty that I got frightened of Truman. My husband, Gianni, was very much amused by Truman, very much. He thought he was the best company. So did Bill Paley. Loel Guinness thought he was the best company. But Truman didn't really like them. You could tell. He would say so. He would tell you about their little *défauts*, their *faiblesse*, trying to woo you away from them in a funny way. I know he was doing the same thing with Babe Paley. And then finally he went too far. With Babe, he went much too far.

GERALD CLARKE One day Truman appeared and took me swimming at Gloria Vanderbilt's. He spent his summers in his friends' pools. Gloria Vanderbilt and her husband, Wyatt Cooper, were in Europe.

So we had her pool to ourselves. They kept it heated to something like ninety degrees for the entire time they were gone—this during an energy crisis! I sat in a lounge reading the "Côte Basque" excerpt from *Answered Prayers* while Truman was in the water floating on an air mattress. I recognized the real people behind most of the characters. But not all. When I finished—and he explained who everybody was—I told him that people weren't going to be happy with this. He said, "Naaaah, they're too dumb. They won't know who they are."

LOUISE GRUNWALD He was a pot-stirrer. He had this great quality of getting things out of people. He was a good listener and he was sympathetic and cozy. Also these women had a need to talk. Why Truman? Because he wasn't threatening. If they told another woman, it would have been losing face. They felt that Truman was unshockable. So there wasn't that to worry about. He had all the time in the world to listen and sympathize. So they told him things they should have been telling their shrinks . . . only. He was so cozy, such a good friend that it was hard to think of him *first* as a novelist, then as a friend—which was probably stupid of everybody.

MARELLA AGNELLI He gave me a little bit of it on the boat. I don't read in English, only very slowly, so it was better when I would hear him reading. On the boat we had lots of time, and he read me some bits and pieces. What he was writing was very shallow, it was like gossip columns, and I remember him getting quite cross one day. I had said, "Oh, Truman, this is gossip column, what are you going into?"

DOTSON RADER Truman's having a bullshot. He's on the phone from LA to *Esquire* in New York, talking to Don Erickson, who was the editor. They're negotiating the sale of the stories from *Answered Prayers*. He hangs up and he tells me what *Esquire*'s offered— $16,000. Earlier *The New Yorker* had offered him $18,000. He wanted to know which offer to take. I asked, "Well, what audience do you want to reach?" Truman at that point was very worried about the aging of his audience and he wanted to be in a magazine that had a younger readership. I said, "Do you know demographically the occupation of the greatest number of *New Yorker* subscribers?" He said, "No," and I said, "Well, if you break their audience down by occupation, the leading subscribers are dentists. That's your audience—people with toothaches waiting for the drill."

So he called *Esquire* back. He made certain demands. Cover approval. There couldn't be any changes in the text. The third thing was that the editor of *Esquire* had to fly to Key West to pick up the manuscript, which made no sense to me at all. He was going to the Yucatán, where he was going to see Lee Radziwill. From there he was going up to Key West. I remember this limousine picked us up to take us to the airport. Truman had the manuscript of *Answered Prayers*—about 800 pages wrapped in brown paper and tied with a string. He had it on the seat of the limousine next to us.

He also had a packet of about an inch of yellow legal pads in his tiny little handwriting. That was in his luggage, but the manuscript itself he had on the seat of the car. We got to the LA airport, the car left, and we went up to the Aeroméxico desk to get Truman's ticket. Suddenly he realized he didn't have the manuscript. He was absolutely horrified. I mean, Truman went into total panic! "Oh my God, my God . . . Did I leave it at the hotel? . . . My God, my God, I can't believe it . . . Twelve years of my life . . . My God, I can't . . . I'll never be able to duplicate . . . Where . . . ?" So I said, "Let me call the hotel." I got through to the hotel housekeeping: there was nothing in the room. He then said to me that he'd probably left it in the limousine. So I called the limousine company and they radioed the car and indeed the manuscript was in the car and they brought it back to the airport. Truman grabbed it and held it to his breast; he never let go of the thing until he got on the plane.

GEORGE PAGE He was staying at that motel in Key West in a trailer out back, parked close to the water's edge. He told me Don Erickson of *Esquire* was coming down to bring the galleys or the proofs or the dummies, whatever they were, and he wanted me to read them. "Oh God, let this cup pass," I said. "I don't want that responsibility. What do you care anyway? I mean, you wrote the stuff."

He said, "I don't know, I might want to change it."

So anyway Erickson came. He was just gleeful he was going to publish these excerpts from *Answered Prayers* because he knew how explosive they were. I remember saying to Truman, "I think they are fascinating. But do you *really* want to do this?"

"Well, I'm not using real names."

I said, "Truman, it's so totally transparent." I remember saying, "Are you really prepared for the consequences of what you're saying about the Paleys and these other figures of New York society you have skewered in that piece?" I don't remember his exact words, but Truman in effect said he wasn't worried about it; he thought his friendships with them were stronger than that and that they would see it as the work of art that it was.

I remember that evening he was very drunk. He was having a fight with O'Shea. It dawned on me that his publishing those excerpts was a very self-destructive act and that I think he knew it. When he was sober he took a sort of impish glee in what was about to happen; I really believe that he knew he had thrown a bombshell that was going to change his life. And it did, you know . . . it knocked him for the most part right off his extraordinary social pedestal. I don't think he wanted that to happen, but there was something about Truman that made him want to shock. My theory is that he must have been thinking that he couldn't write anymore, that he would never be able to write as well as he did earlier. He never wanted to repeat himself. He would not have done another nonfiction novel. I wonder if he wasn't saying to himself, "I have to do something dramatic or the world is going to get tired of me . . ."

JOHN RICHARDSON It was offensive—café society gossip of the trashiest kind—but it was rather brilliantly done. Shit served up on a gold dish. Extremely disconcerting, I felt. He'd obviously gone through a lot of pain to make it crisp, sharp, and pointed. But I couldn't understand why he was wasting his time writing blind items about his best friends.

KURT VONNEGUT It's fun, but it's amazing that he would claw these people the way he did.

DIANA TRILLING That was very nasty, wasn't it? It wasn't a nice thing to do. But in a different sense the ones he skewered had used him as a kind of entertainer, a court jester; he had used them as a kind of social prop. It was pretty even, don't you think?

JOHN BARRY RYAN How could Truman turn on these people who "befriended" him? That is sheer unadulterated bullshit. The people who had Truman around (when they were not 100 percent manipulated by Truman into *having* him around) had him because he was entertaining, great company, loved the life that they lived, and brought fresh zest to it that they had long since lost by virtue of overindulgence, or the fact that they were so accustomed to it that they just didn't see why it was fun anymore. They didn't befriend him. He didn't need them. That people who entertained Truman, who shared their innermost secrets with him, who used him as their therapist, their court jester . . . that those people should have been surprised that Truman's indiscretion might extend to publicly revealing *their* indiscretions (as opposed to privately—as though that made a difference in that world) I have always found astonishing.

The people who after "befriending" Truman, accepting this asp onto their bosoms, were surprised that the snake bit! Snakes bite. Truman certainly signed no Official Secrets Act. Everybody who was exposed to him in the period I'm familiar with knew that if you told Truman something, it was the equivalent of telling forty other people. You would no more ask Truman to treat something as if for his ears only than you would throw bread upon the water and expect it to come back! That's what made him so enjoyable . . . that when you had Truman to dinner, he would tell the most outrageous stories about everybody else. You *knew* that the people he told stories about would have him to dinner the following night and then he would tell outrageous stories about you! The level of his indiscretion, in many ways, depended on the level of your indiscretion.

He repeated incidents. He created gossip. For his own amusement. He then took that material which originally had been created for his own amusement and said, "I now choose to make this material available to a broader public. In exchange for these entertaining stories I expect to be flown in for dinner." A masterful gossip. Probably the preeminent purveyor of gossip as entertainment of our time. Certainly if a Suzy or any other gossip columnist had chosen to be as indiscreet as Truman, they would not have a newspaper column for long. Somebody would have had them shot. Or fired. Or somebody would have bought the newspaper and shut it down.

CAROL MARCUS MATTHAU Once he said to me, "Honey, I want to read you what I've written about you." He began: "Carol has gardenia skin . . ." I said, "I don't even want to talk about it. It's fine. I don't care what you say about me." Writers write. Anyone who doesn't know that is silly. You can't take that away from them. It's like women who take alimony. I don't believe in that either. There are very few things that are beneath me, but those are two.

The "Côte Basque" story didn't destroy him. In fact, it could have been the beginning of his life as one of the greatest writers ever. For him to be the court jester to the people of the moment, or those who are rich or have enough heritage or background so they don't need to be rich, well, that's a joke. He knew better than that. A writer is another person behind the typewriter. Babe Paley's not Babe when Truman's behind the typewriter. He would have written the pieces even if he'd known what the repercussions would be. He had more balls than anyone.

WILLIAM STYRON The pieces couldn't have bothered me less, especially the people they were written about, largely because it's hard to have a great deal of respect for café society trash. But when I got a glimmer that they were about real people, I said to myself, "I wonder how on earth he expects to get by with this." These people were going to learn that they'd been written about, and they were certainly going to react negatively. It was disastrous. And to me, inexplicable. Writers don't have to destroy their friendships with people in order to write. It seemed to me an act of willful destruction. If those real people are our friends and we write about them in such a way to expose them, as Truman did, as bizarre and misbehaving and creepy and loony, then we can only expect to get some sort of retaliation. And he got it.

LEE EISENBERG (*editor*) I don't know that he fully anticipated how inflammatory it would be. Truman was a very shrewd person, but he was also very innocent. I'm not certain he foresaw the controversy, the losing of friends, the animosity and the scandal that "La Côte Basque" would bring. If he was concerned with any of that, he didn't share it with us at *Esquire*. We were, frankly, not prepared for it. It really wasn't until Liz Smith wrote the piece that we fully appreciated what we had. We just thought we had a most engaging novel in progress. We were not at all aware that it was going to be what it was.

GEORGE PLIMPTON It was Liz Smith, then freelancing, who brought to public attention what was going on. She wrote a long piece for *New York* magazine about high society's reaction to "La Côte Basque 1965," Truman's roman à clef story about lunchtime goings-on at Henri Soulé's fancy restaurant opposite the Hotel St. Regis, which had appeared in *Esquire*. The story was called "Truman Capote in Hot Water," and the subhead, a quote from her story, read: ". . . Society's Sacred Monsters Are in a State of Shock. Never have you heard such cries of betrayal, such screams of outrage . . ."

For those who hadn't read the story in *Esquire,* Liz Smith described some of the indiscretions. Most of them were from the mouth of one "Lady Ina Coolbirth" (purportedly Slim Keith). Some of these ("splashed across the pages," in Liz Smith's felicitous words, "like hollandaise that has missed the asparagus") were rather mild— the Duchess of Windsor never picking up a check, Gloria Vanderbilt's failure to recognize her first husband as he came in the restaurant, so-and-so with bad breath . . . but others were not, especially the devastating retelling of Ann Woodward's (she was "Ann Hopkins" in the story) rags-to-riches career, ending in the shotgun shooting of her husband, William Woodward, Jr., mistaking him in a darkened hallway for a cat burglar. "Thinly disguised" is hardly the way to put it in her case. In fact, Woodward committed suicide a few days before *Esquire* appeared on the newsstands, and there were many who spread the word she had jumped from the window because she had seen an advance copy. I remember a story about that, which was that Truman had it in for her because in Italy he had overheard her saying, "Yes, that's that faggot Truman Capote." And he did this: he pointed a finger at her like a pistol and went, "Bang, bang, bang."

Less tragic but no less shocking was Ina Coolbirth's story about the liaison in the Hotel Pierre between "Sidney Dillon" (undoubtedly Bill Paley, the head at the time of CBS) and the "governor's wife" (Marie Harriman, according to Liz, but more likely Mary Rockefeller, Nelson's wife). The scene ends with the Paley character trying to scrub menstrual blood from the sheets before his wife (Babe Paley), expected any minute, returns from a European trip. Rough stuff! As Smith wrote: "It is one thing to tell the nastiest story to all your fifty best friends; it's another to set it down in cold Century Expanded type."

LIZ SMITH (*columnist*) Truman's "Côte Basque" was all anybody was talking about. So Clay Felker, the editor of *New York*, asked me if I would write about the furor surrounding it. Truman was thrilled that I was going to do it. I went to Hollywood to interview him. I'll never forget how distraught he was because the pressure was building. In the Padrino bar in the Beverly Wilshire he said, "I'm going to call Mrs. Vreeland and you'll see that she's really on my side." He caused a big ruckus and they brought a phone. He called her. He said "I'm sitting here with Liz Smith and she tells me that everyone is against me, but I know you're not." He went on and on, holding the phone out for me to hear. She was just saying these things—like she always said—that meant everything and nothing! Such as, "Your description of the vegetables of the rich—ravishing!" But I'll never forget how worried I was about Truman because it seemed as if he was going to go all to pieces.

NORMAN MAILER I would never have thought that he'd be so incautious—not even bold, but rash. I'd seen him being bold—he'd been bold all his life, but not *rash*. I thought the Paley piece was bad, finally. I mean, who gives a damn? For Truman, that would be the true nightmare—go to bed with a woman and she's bleeding all over the place—but for the average heterosexual that's not that big a deal. It's happened, it'll happen again. It's not agreeable but you don't hit bottom. The fact that it was Bill Paley involved was what was wrong with it. It was an in-house joke. You have to know it's *Bill Paley* on his knees scrubbing out the sheet in his bathtub in this hotel, and if you don't, it's much smaller. Jean Malaquais once said to me, "Don't ever put anything in a book because it's lively now. Always think, 'Will this be alive fifty years from now when people don't know who you're talking about?' " The Côte Basque story depends on knowing who all the players are.

JOHN KNOWLES Truman had ridden out there on a very long motor trip with Johnny O'Shea, up through Canada and down the West Coast—a ten-thousand-mile odyssey by car. He was completely out of touch with the social world and how it reacted to those pieces in *Esquire*, particularly "La Côte Basque." I could tell he was very upset and shocked. I commented, "You didn't expect anything of the sort, did you?"

He said briefly no, he hadn't foreseen this at all.

MARIA THERESA CAEN I don't think he ever suspected that would be the reaction. I think he really felt they would say, "Oh, Truman, you've been a naughty, naughty boy." I think he was very surprised at the reaction. He sent me a copy of *Esquire* magazine before it hit the stands. I remember reading it . . . I remember exactly where I was . . . I was in the garden. It was a very warm day, but I was all bundled up because I was recovering from a kidney infection. I read it and I just got colder and colder. I thought, "Oh, Truman, what have you done?" He had asked me to call him the minute I finished reading it and I couldn't do it. I had to wait three or four days to call. In fact, he called me because he was so anxious to know what I thought. He didn't understand that their devastation would be to the degree that it was. People are generally much more hurt by what they read than what they hear.

JOHN KNOWLES He imagined that these ladies were going to sit around and say, "Oh, that little rascal, look what he's done *this* time!

Isn't he too much!" Then they'd invite him to the yacht. Well, it's all right what you do, but you don't do it in the street and frighten the horses. But he did—he went public, using, in some cases, the names of real people, and in other cases, it was incredibly transparent—obvious, dirty linen being washed in public.

So they dropped him like a hot potato, which he never, ever expected.

He was completely unstrung. He had built up this incredible edifice of social connections and great success and it crumbled overnight literally. The problem was that he had no stature socially speaking. He had no family. He was only an ornament. There was nothing for him to fall back on. You could drop Truman Capote overnight because you weren't going to alienate anybody. Truman was just all by himself out there.

SLIM KEITH Barbara Paley called me up on the phone and said, "Have you seen *Esquire?*" I said no, and she said, "Well, go get it."

I was living in the Pierre Hotel. I sent the maid down: "Bring me back this magazine . . ."

I read it and I was absolutely horrified, because there I was. My character is simply the person he's lunching with. All of the stuff— the story about the sheets, the story about Ann Woodward . . . was told by *me,* a person called Lady Coolbirth. There was no question in anybody's mind who it was. He described how I look and how I speak. It was like looking in a mirror. Very odd experience.

Babe had said, "Call me as soon as you're finished." So I called her. She asked, "Well, well . . . ?"

I said, "I feel absolutely . . . as though I've been *hit.* All the breath is out of me."

"So who do you think it is?"

I said, "Who do I think *who* is?"

"Well, that story of Truman's."

"I don't know."

"Have you any idea?"

"No idea in the world who it is. It could be anybody." She was sick with her cancer then; it was the last thing I was ever going to tell her.

She said, "I can't figure out who the woman is, but I think maybe I know who the man is."

It was very tricky ground.

It couldn't have taken Bill Paley long to figure out who the man was. I'll tell you something amazing. Sister Parrish, who is not the dumbest lady we've ever met, was talking about it last summer. And she allowed, "Well, Truman was a dreadful man, wasn't he?" And I said, "Well he wasn't a nice man, that's for sure."

"That awful piece he wrote about Douglas Dillon in the bathtub scrubbing away . . ."

"Douglas Dillon! That wasn't Douglas Dillon."

"Yes, it was. He's Jewish, you know."

Well, I really didn't know that, but I know it's not Douglas Dillon! Bill was very smart about it. He was called by the press and asked what he thought about it. He said, "I haven't read it. I probably never will. I don't know what you're talking about."

MARY LAZAR I remember we were in Sydney, Australia, at Christmas time with the Erteguns and Slim Keith—right after the *Esquire* article had come out—and Truman sent a wire to Slim that said, "I forgive you, Big Mama." A joke. But she never forgave him.

SLIM KEITH I really felt bereft. I grieved, having lost a very nice, good part of my life. I enjoyed him and I knew an element that had given me pleasure was gone. I knew I never would take it back under any circumstances. What I didn't understand, to this day, is what sort of thinking brings a person to that point and to do something like that. It can't be because he wants to sell books. None of those things that Truman had written had I ever said or ever thought. It was unjust and dreadful to put those words in my mouth. I'll never forgive him, never.

I never spoke to him after that. He called often and I wouldn't take the call. He'd have John [O'Shea] call, who'd say, "Truman's upset that you're very upset."

I said, "Well, he's quite right, I am. He understands correctly."

So John would say, "Well, don't you think it was well written?"

I could hear Truman breathing on another extension.

"No," I said, "I didn't think it was well written. It's too easy. I just thought it was terrible."

"Well, he thought it would make you laugh a lot because it really isn't you at all. You don't think that person is you, do you?"

"Oh, John, come on," I said. "I've got two big blue eyes. I can read."

He said, "No, it's Pamela Harriman."

"Pam doesn't bring to mind the picture of a cowgirl. Besides, she doesn't deserve the piece either. I never want to see, speak to, or hear from Truman again. I've lost my friend, and I'm sorry."

And that was that.

THOMAS QUINN CURTISS Theodore Dreiser published a beautiful book about his youth called *Dawn.* He had made a lot of money selling *An American Tragedy* to the movies, so he had a big estate somewhere up on the Hudson—Sneden's Landing, I think it was. His brother and sister lived up there too. They'd just finished reading *Dawn* when he arrived. He got out of the car and they started to beat him half to death because he'd told the truth about them! They were absolutely incensed. I think the Truman café society crowd was more civilized than the Dreiser family. They gave him the cold treatment, which is much more devastating.

JUDY GREEN It's much more virulent and it's much more an attack on the men than it is on the women. Any attack on the women, the women who took it so personally, was all because of the men. He really loathed the men and adored the women. Yet women were the ones who retaliated and thought it so horrible. But I think, in his warped way, he was trying to say, "I understand how awful it's been for you. I'm your only friend, I'm your savior. The world thinks Averell Harriman was this, or Bill Paley was that—immortalized by their big businesses and their great deeds—but I'll show them: you will be the true heroines." That's basically what he wanted to convey—almost an offering, an obeisance to them—something that people could read and say, "Oh God. These fantastic women and these despotic men." Of course, the men he'd decried were all macho, the complete opposite of Truman.

JOHN BARRY RYAN It all started to bubble to the top. They would say, "Are you seeing Truman or are you not? Are you talking to Truman or are you not?" I was never a part of either the ayes or the nays.

SLIM KEITH Sometimes I used to see him in Quo Vadis when that was the place to have dinner or lunch. As he'd come in, I would be very busily eating my spinach while he passed the table. Never looked up. Never looked up at his face again. He would go back and forth and make phone calls. Back and forth . . . back and forth, and I never . . . One day Babe walked in. She was going to have lunch with somebody. Her lunch date wasn't there yet. Sitting at a table were Phyllis Cerf and Truman. Truman looked up and said, "Hello, Babaling . . ." And she said, "Hello, Truman."

Afterward I told her, "You're a traitor. We've sworn with our blood that we'd never speak to this man."

"Well, I didn't know what to do. I mean, that's such bad manners."

Bad manners . . . sweet woman!

JOHN RICHARDSON Virginia Chambers was one of the closest friends of Babe Paley and her two sisters. Virginia was almost blind. She could just see her way around, but could barely distinguish people. One day Babe Paley and I were lunching at Quo Vadis waiting for Virginia. We were sitting on this little banquette in the corner of the bar when to our horror we saw that Truman had come in and was sitting bang on the way to our table. When he spotted Virginia blundering toward us, he waylaid her and pulled her down. At first she didn't realize what was happening, but when Truman opened his mouth—"I have to talk to you. Just sit here for a minute"--she panicked. After the "Côte Basque" piece, there was no way she would talk to him. She struggled and got away. She arrived at our table outraged but also thrilled.

KENNETH JAY LANE Jimmy Fosburgh, who was Babe's brother-in-law, had lunch with Truman at Quo Vadis. Everybody was up in arms. He was called on the carpet: "Jimmy, what are you doing, having lunch with Truman!" He said, "Well, I felt sorry for him. I hadn't seen him in so long. It couldn't do any harm."

No, they just refused to see him. I was having lunch with Betsy Whitney and Irene Selznick and Truman's name came up. Irene brought it up, I think. Betsy simply said something like . . . almost with tears in her eyes because she's a very nice woman and I think she was fond of him . . . she said something like "I simply can't discuss him." It was just cut off.

DIANA VREELAND He said, "Are you going to stick by me, Diana?"
I said, "No, I'm not . . . if by that you mean believing you're the purest of the pure. No, Truman, I am not taking any sides whatsoever, but I'm definitely not on your side: you have offended your friends. That is something you have no excuse for whatsoever." That was the end of it. But it wasn't the end of it. Whenever we were in public—if he was standing across a room in the Waldorf Hotel—I'd walk over and say, "How do you do." This is when no one spoke to him. I always went out of my way to stick with Truman in public. But I never saw him in private.

DOTSON RADER I was at a party at Josh Logan's. I remember showing up and Nedda Logan coming at me like a water buffalo, snorting and just furious. I'd done a radio talk show the night before. I talked about Truman as a writer . . . what a great writer he was and that I was astonished people would be so upset. She came barreling over to me. "How dare you, you've been a friend of ours, you've been a guest in my house. How dare you go on television and defend this filth that little toad Truman Capote has written."

"Well, Netta, it wasn't television, it was a radio interview, and I never even talked about what he had written. I haven't read it myself."

"I heard you, I heard you, I was watching television last night."
I said, "I wasn't even *on* television last night."

I told Truman about it. He said, "Oh my God, I'm collecting enemies among people I never even met!"

The only one that hurt him was Babe. Truman was the kind of

snob that is peculiar to gay people. Gays that become snobs are in a funny way more obsequious and more desperate than just simple social climbers.

BODIE NEILSON He would list the people who weren't talking to him. James Jones and Irwin Shaw weren't particularly sympathetic. Truman couldn't understand why they weren't sympathetic. He felt it was a "writer's problem" rather than *his* problem. He felt he could enlist their aid socially or as colleagues.

LEONORA HORNBLOW I saw him only once afterward, which was at Phyllis Cerf's one night. It was a last-minute dinner that Phyllis put together. I walked into the library—she was not yet downstairs—and there was Truman. He said in that special little voice, "Hello, honey! Are you speaking to me?"
  I said, "In this house, I am."
  And he said, "In other houses?"
  I said, "No."
  "Did you really think it was Babe? Did you really think it was Slim?"
  I said, "Truman, come on, of course I did." And I quoted Garson Kanin's line to him, which is immortal or should be, from *Born Yesterday:* "Never crap a crapper." And he laughed. That was another charm. He was a lovely laugher.

MARELLA AGNELLI I got calls from friends saying that Truman was heartbroken, but at that point I was petrified of him. Petrified because I had liked him too much; we'd had a deep relationship and I was frightened that he might hurt me again. I never replied. One of the excuses I gave him was that I don't know how to write in English. That was reason enough.

WINSTON GROOM Truman called me up one day when I was living on Seventy-ninth Street and he said, "Wouldn't you like to come to dinner?" If you waffled, that was the end of it. It was cold, March. I said, "Sure that'd be fine." He said, "Would you do me a favor and bring Hilary Byers?" Hilary was Bill Paley's daughter. She and I had had a couple of late nights in various saloons—with other people—there was no romance or anything. So I picked her up in a taxi. We went to Truman's place at the UN Plaza. I'd never been to Truman's apartment. When we knocked on the door, this Chinaman answered. I walked in and there was this goddamn stuffed rattlesnake, this son of a bitch coiled up and as high as a cobra, ready to get you. In the apartment he had all these bizarre things, at least I thought so. Truman was a wonderful host. Just the three of us. My feeling was that I was basically what they used to call "the beard." Truman had some problems with the Paleys and that whole crowd. I think it was his way—and this is just a guess—of trying through Hilary to make peace with that whole group and especially the Paleys, because he had offended them more than he had offended anybody else. He was lonesome.

LESTER PERSKY He was ostracized by many of his friends. Yet some who had impeccable credentials in society were more loyal to him than ever. It was as if they wanted to prove to him that they were passionate in their loyalty and friendship. C. Z. Guest never for one moment turned her back on him. Kay Meehan, Carol Matthau, Felicia Lemmon, Audrey Wilder, they've always been steadfast.

JOHN KNOWLES There's a wonderful story about C. Z. Guest. When Truman got out of Silver Hill, he came to her house for lunch. Diana Vreeland was there. We had a wonderful lunch next to the rose garden. We went back to the guesthouse where the notorious nude painting of C.Z. by Diego Rivera was hanging on the wall. C.Z. walked in and said, "Well, there it is. That's the only way to deal with it: take the bull by its horns. What did all those silly women expect a writer was going to do? Of *course* he was going to use the material sooner or later." Then she said, "But then I never told Truman anything of any importance."

KAY MEEHAN He asked me to have lunch with him. I remember thinking, "He's testing me," and that I would be crazy to get involved with him, but I didn't want to be a phony, so I said sure. He told me we'd meet in the Oak Room of the Plaza. It was teeming rain. I went in dripping wet. My God, he had Richard Burton with him on one of those banquettes. This man got up with that *voice:* I nearly collapsed. I looked like a drowned rat. Burton was getting ready to play the psychiatrist in *Equus*, and he wanted to put his own imprint on the role. He had a tape recorder and he and Truman were going over the lines. He was picking Truman's brains. He wanted his interpretation to be different than his predecessors'. They would play the lines and then talk back and forth. What I remember so well was the difference between their voices. It was the most fabulous lunch. I think Truman was rewarding me for not turning my back on him, but I think he was also testing me. After all, he didn't say he had Burton with him. It could have been just lunch in the Oak Room with him and everybody was going to say, "What are you doing with *him?*" He wanted to see if I'd turn up.

Truman used to come to Southampton, a little out of heart or sad, or boozed up or whatever. He was always gentle with me, and that wasn't necessarily the way he was with other people. My own feeling was that Babe was really the main thing in his life. Sitting around the pool when Babe was still alive and very sick, he was terribly upset. He said, "It kills me that she won't talk to me. Do you think if I wrote her a letter . . . ?" I remember saying to him, "Truman, if you did to my husband, Joe Meehan, what you did to Babe, I wouldn't just not talk to you, I'd kill you!" I don't think he ever really understood.

You couldn't really be as faithful as you'd like to be to Truman because you couldn't handle it. One day he was here and I was going to East Hampton that evening to see a play at Guild Hall which starred Dina Merrill. What was I going to do? I couldn't bring him with me. Not that he was that drunk or anything. He knew I was going. Finally around six o'clock he got up from where he was sitting by the pool and went up onto the porch, where there was a bar. I could see him make a drink and slug it down. He came back and said, "Well, you're all too much for me." He got in his car. The car was so big that it looked as though the car was driving him. And he left.

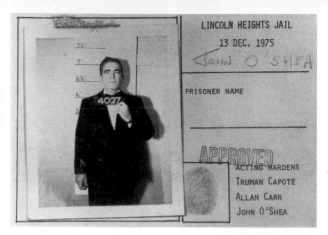

LINCOLN HEIGHTS JAIL
13 DEC. 1975

JOHN O'SHEA

PRISONER NAME

APPROVED
ACTING WARDENS
TRUMAN CAPOTE
ALLAN CARR
JOHN O'SHEA

John O'Shea, who is hardly seven feet two. A picture taken in a penny arcade on December 13, 1975. Truman is listed as "Acting Warden." (*Truman Capote Papers, The New York Public Library*)

Truman photographed in his UN Plaza apartment in New York. (*Jill Krementz*)

Truman with three fellow writers from the Bridgehampton area—John Knowles, Willie Morris, and James Jones. (*Jill Krementz*)

Slim Keith, one of Truman's "swans."
(William S. Paley, collection of Kate C. Paley)

Babe Paley and Gloria Guinness. *(William S. Paley, collection of Kate C. Paley)*

Bill and Babe Paley. *(Collection of Kate C. Paley)*

Truman and Babe on a Mediterranean cruise. *(William S. Paley, collection of Kate C. Paley)*

Carter Burden, Loel Guinness, Truman, Babe Paley, Bill Paley. *(Collection of Kate C. Paley)*

Truman and Babe Paley mixing drinks aboard ship. *(William S. Paley, collection of Kate C. Paley)*

Truman with Bill and Babe Paley at their estate in Round Hill, Jamaica. *(John Rawlings, courtesy of the Museum at F.I.T., New York)*

Truman and Lee Radziwill in the driveway at Kiluna, the Paleys' estate in Manhasset, Long Island. *(William S. Paley, collection of Kate C. Paley)*

Gloria Guinness on the stern of *Seraphina*, the Guinnesses' yacht. *(William S. Paley, collection of Kate C. Paley)*

Truman with Gloria Guinness in the Flower Room at Gemini, the Guinnesses' estate in Manalapan, Florida. *(Truman Capote Papers, The New York Public Library)*

Truman relaxing with Lady Orr-Lewis, Gloria Guinness, and the Countess Derby at the Lyford Country Club in Nassau. *(Truman Capote Papers, The New York Public Library)*

The Clutter house in Holcomb, Kansas. *(UPI/Corbis-Bettmann)*

The Clutter family: Herb; his wife, Bonnie; and their children, Nancy and Kenyon. *(UPI/Corbis-Bettmann)*

Alvin Dewey of the Kansas Bureau of Investigation— the field agent in charge of investigating the Clutter murders— informs the press of the criminals' confession. *(UPI/Corbis-Bettmann)*

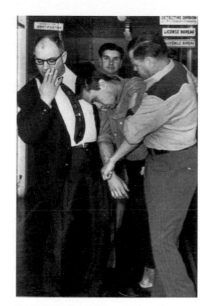

Dick Hickock collapsing after confessing to the murders of the Clutter family. *(UPI/Corbis-Bettmann)*

Truman and Al Dewey during the filming of the movie *In Cold Blood.* *(Truman Capote Papers, The New York Public Library)*

Nelle Harper Lee on Main Street of Garden City, Kansas. *(Truman Capote Papers, The New York Public Library)*

Joe Fox, Truman's editor at Random House during the research and publication of *In Cold Blood.* *(Photo by Joe Petrocik, private collection)*

In his later years Truman was a constant contributor to Andy Warhol's *Interview*. (Interview *magazine*)

Truman and C. Z. Guest at the reopening of Studio 54 in 1978. (*Ron Galella*)

Cornelia Guest, Truman, and Andy Warhol at Xenon in Manhattan in 1982. (*AP/Wide World*)

Truman with Steve Rubell, co-owner of Studio 54, in a Polaroid taken by Andy Warhol. (*Truman Capote Papers, The New York Public Library*)

Truman with two of his great friends of his later years, Joe Petrocik and Myron Clement. *(Private collection)*

Joanne Carson, Jack Dunphy, and Myron Clement at the funeral service for Truman in Los Angeles, August 28, 1984. *(AP/Wide World)*

Joanne Carson speaking at the service in Los Angeles *(AP/Wide World)*

Mourners at the service for Truman and Jack at Crooked Pond in Bridgehampton, New York.
(Joe Petrocik, private collection)

William Daley (Jack Dunphy's nephew) and Gerald Clarke (Truman's biographer) pour Truman's ashes into Crooked Pond.
(Joe Petrocik, private collection)

KATE HARRINGTON It was tragic. It was so sad. I remember thinking, "Oh no, another tragedy. Another house was crumbling. When is this going to end?" He went into a colossal depression. It was as if there had been a death in the family. I walked around quietly at the UN Plaza and didn't play the record player. I'd answer the phone for him. Slowly the phone stopped ringing and there weren't so many calls. I remember being so defensively bitter about it myself, and thinking, "Well, that shows how shallow those people always were because they drop you like that." We sat for many, many weeks just hibernating. I did my work and stuff. I was seventeen or eighteen. I used to sit on the edge of his bed and he wouldn't get out of bed and the days would turn into nights; he never opened the blinds and I'd sit and we'd talk. He was so upset he'd cry, and he'd go in and out of that thing that someone does when they've done something tragic, where they have remorse.

I thought that people would be mad for a while, but then I thought they'd come back, and they didn't. He was staggered by that. He never truly picked up again—a few blips of pulling himself together; for two years he sort of went on, but it was never the same. He went heavily into the drinking and drugging. There were some loyal folks, but they weren't the main people. Joe Petrocik and Myron Clement were sweet friends who loved him and Lester Persky. C Z Guest was great. She was a love. She's a lady. And Joanne Carson.

Truman and Joanne Carson. (Palm Springs Life, *courtesy of Joanne Carson*)

Truman and Lee Radziwill. *(UPI/Corbis-Bettmann)*

Interlude

CHAPTER THIRTY-SIX   *In Which the*
Reader Meets Two of TC's Kindred Spirits

JOANNE CARSON I met Truman in the mid-sixties.
Johnny and I were going to Barbados for a week—a
honeymoon. Bennett Cerf was a very close friend of
mine, always supplying me with must-read books. He
sent over *In Cold Blood* the day we were leaving for
Barbados. I got on the plane and started reading it. I
read all the way, all the way through customs, all the
way to Frenchman's Cove, all the way through the
drive to our cottage, and when we got there Johnny
said, "I'll just take a shower and we'll eat dinner." I
sat down and continued reading. He came out of the
shower; I was still reading. We had dinner; I was still
reading. He went to bed; I was still reading—this, in
essence, was our honeymoon—and I put the book
down, I think, about five o'clock in the morning. It
was the first book I ever read where I felt I was being
told a story; I wasn't conscious of reading it. I called
Bennett in New York and I said, "I must meet him.
He has got to be the most fabulous person."

I finally met him at the Cerfs'. Their dining room
was quite large. I was sitting at Truman's table, but

opposite him. He was very animated with his hands; there was a tremendous amount of energy coming from him that absolutely fascinated me. After dinner he came by my table and said, "Bennett tells me you're quite an extraordinary lady. Come, let's chat." He took me into a library alcove, sat me down on a couch, patted me on the hand, and said, "Now, my dear, tell me all about yourself." With me, that's a very dangerous thing to do, because I literally *will tell* somebody all about myself. So I launched into the story of my life.

Basically, what intrigued Truman most was that I had been raised in a convent or by aunts and grandparents, and not by my parents. He drew similarities to his own childhood, which I didn't know at the time because I hadn't read *A Christmas Memory*. Truman said to me, "My dear, we are going to be great friends."

At the end of the evening, people were leaving, going home. He took out his little appointment book and said, "I will meet you tomorrow at twelve o'clock in the lobby of the UN Plaza and we will have lunch." He was very precise. "Twelve o'clock *sharp.*" So the next day at twelve I was in the lobby. He nodded and said, "I like that." He liked promptness. If Truman was coming to our apartment at the UN Plaza for dinner at eight, Johnny and I would sit in the kitchen and watch the IBM digital clock on the building across the way. The minute it went to 8:00, Truman would ring the doorbell. It was kind of a joke about the digital clock. We always claimed that Truman stood outside the door and waited to make sure he rang the doorbell exactly at eight o'clock.

From the UN Plaza we walked to his favorite lunch restaurant, an Italian restaurant. I noticed he had a book under his arm. I thought, "How nice, it's a present for me." But when we got to the restaurant and sat down, he put the book next to him, so I thought, "Well, it's not for me." He ordered my lunch. He didn't ask what I wanted, he didn't ask what I wanted for dessert. At dessert, the waiter came up with an empty silver platter and handed it to Truman. He took it with one hand and with the other he put the book on it and put it in front of my place. That was my dessert—his copy of *A Christmas Memory*. It was inscribed: "To the real Holly Golightly." Truman took over my life from that moment. He choreographed our entire relationship.

Johnny loved Truman. Because Truman took to me so instantly, Johnny used to say, "Well, he was *my* friend first." Which he was, absolutely Johnny's friend first. But from the day that I met him, Truman and I were joined at the hips.

JOHN KNOWLES He had Joanne Carson as a friend after the "Côte Basque" mess but God knows, Lee Radziwill and Truman were also close at one time. She was as close to him as anybody. He adored her for a long time. He thought she could do nothing wrong. Essence of elegance.

PETER BEARD There was no way he was in love with Lee. I'd say he was in love with her as far as he could manipulate her success in competition with Jackie. He was like an artist in life, exhilarated by what he could do.

LEE RADZIWILL We had so many differences that I didn't really think that he could go on imagining that he was in love with me. He envisaged me as he wished to. We had cozy times that were brotherly and sisterly. The whole point of our relationship was that Truman had a great passion for me. Babe was this exquisite object to him, and I was more tangible. There was something about me that got him. I knew he loved me, adored me, as I did him, there was no question about that.

He came to stay with us in Portugal. The children were about six and seven. It was a very isolated, lonely place opposite Lisbon; there was no high life and we had no jet-setters staying with us. We had a boat we went off on every day. It couldn't have been quieter. He was at his very best, because he didn't have to perform. Except he liked to try to for the children. He was very good with children, because that was the best side of his mind, the pure side. The children both had birthdays during that time, and I have photographs of Truman and my husband, Stas, dancing around the table, doing the polka. He was delightful then. I thought he might be easily bored, but I don't think he was easily bored as long as he had good things to read.

STEVEN M. L. ARONSON He wrote *Laura* for Lee Radziwill, adapting
it from the Vera Caspary novel that Otto Preminger made into that
wonderful 1944 film with Gene Tierney. He adapted it as a
television movie as a vehicle for Lee; he had in mind that she would
soar and take off—a private jet. Such a fiasco that vehicle turned
out to be—like an unmechanized wheelchair . . . tethered to the
ground.

LEE RADZIWILL It had nothing to do with practical matters; I never
went to Truman and said, "Listen, Truman, I long to be an actress.
How do you go about it?" It took a great deal of time to talk me into
it, because I thought it was stunningly presumptuous, not to
mention scary. Then he convinced me, and I thought, "Well, I don't
mind sticking my neck out. I think I know what's going to happen,
but I'm game." The whole idea was conceived by him, and it was out
of love. It was a driving force of his to create this career for me! I
never regretted it. I regretted having gone that far, having got
through all that criticism and not continuing. I regretted not going
on to do a George Kelly play with Maureen Stapleton, a film with
Sean Connery, both of which I was offered, and a few things like
that. I certainly didn't want to stop, but my husband wouldn't let my
children leave London to be with me and I felt they were my first
obligation.

TOMMY PHIPPS *Laura* came up. I guess Lee Radziwill must have said
to Truman something like "You know, I want to be an actress." He
hadn't the slightest idea how to do it—to write dialogue or how to
construct a television play or anything. He asked me if I would do it
with him and I said I would. He went off to Verbier. I adapted the
movie for Lee. I sent him the script and he wrote back glowing
letters that it was just wonderful. It didn't have one change. So he
had nothing to do with it at all. Nothing! Terrible reviews, unfair,
because it was perfectly respectable.

GEORGE PLIMPTON I remember Truman persuaded Johnny Carson
(they were neighbors in the UN Plaza building) to give a party on
the night of the broadcast. Television sets, a remarkable number of

them, were set around the apartment so that no matter where you were, sitting or standing, there was Lee playing Laura. It didn't work, which was sad, and of course that was emphasized by people eventually getting up and moving away from the TV sets to smoke and talk. It must have been harrowing for Truman, much less Lee.

LEE RADZIWILL He dedicated *Thanksgiving Visitor* to me. He wanted me to come down to Alabama to see it being filmed by Frank Perry. It was a fleeting visit—quite a different cup of tea from what I had been led to believe about his relatives and his aunt. I met certain relatives . . . an aunt who said, "I just can't believe what Truman has made us out to be and the way he's talked about his childhood. We were a very decent, well-off family, and he's made it to be quite another story." She was hurt by it and couldn't understand why he had found it necessary to invent this woeful childhood.

FRANK PERRY He came down to Alabama and brought Lee Radziwill. The people in the motel were all atwitter because a princess was coming—Princess Radziwill?—and what do you say to a princess? Do you say "Your Highness"? Really, in the coffee shop . . .

LEE RADZIWILL He didn't understand that he was being treated like a toy. That was part of what destroyed him. The rest was his consuming fear that he wasn't going to be able to live up to his own artistic expectations, as well as to everyone else's.

What started his decline, I believe, was his fear that he'd lost his self-discipline, and there was no way he could get it back. He'd tell me what agony—and this was years before he was writing *Answered Prayers*—it was to confront the long legal pad every morning. He said he went through that every day of his life. He'd think of every excuse possible to avoid it: get up, sharpen fifty pencils, go back to his pad, make a telephone call. Writing never came to him easily; he was such a perfectionist: every preposition was of the utmost importance. He was a purist. Every word was written in his miniscule handwriting.

All the time I was with Truman, all during those years, he never worked when we were together. He'd always go to his room; he'd always take the afternoon off, and perhaps he wrote a bit. But it was never more than "I'll see you at lunch because I have to write a bit." He had to be prepared to write. He had to make sure nothing was going to disturb him and that the phones were off, that no car was going to come down the driveway, no interferences. He never carried his manuscripts around. In fact, I never saw him working.

We went through New Orleans together, to Morocco, we took some sailing trips. Once we were with the Agnellis crossing from the Yugoslavian coast back to Italy. All the furniture, and the people, were roped down because it was so rough. Truman screamed for three days. It was scary. Actually he never had any curiosity to see much of a city or absorb any foreign atmosphere. New Orleans was perhaps the most at home I ever saw him. But in Morocco, he might as well have been in a hotel room at any Hilton. He loved Paul Bowles's *The Sheltering Sky*, so I thought going there would intrigue him—the sensuality of the people and the country.

I went with him to that terrible place—Cozumel. The beginning of the end. It's hard to say when the beginning of the end did start, because it would start and then it would stop, which would make you very hopeful. But he was terribly depressed there, and that was frightening. He was immobilized. Anyway, we got out of Cozumel. I chartered a small plane and got him to the Paleys in Nassau. I knew there was a hospital there if necessary. We went on to Miami, and he was okay for a while.

One wasn't worried in New Orleans, which I longed to go to since I'd never been and I couldn't think of anybody more marvelous to go with than Truman. The heat was overwhelming, nevertheless, in the evening he'd sit around with his scotches and talk late into the evening. He carried this little black doctor's bag like an ancient country doctor's—I'd never seen those except in old movies. It was stuffed with pills. He had a barrel of stuff in there to choose from. Something for everything from your big toe to your tummy, your ear. He'd want to crunch it all up for you. I'll never forget when he opened that bag at our hotel, the Maison d'Orléans! I was astonished at the number of things in there, wondering what he'd do if by chance somebody swiped it or he lost it. "This is gonna make you feel fantastic, hon. Take it with a little scotch and you'll feel great in the morning." So he was always very busy with his doctor's bag. They were all prescriptions, because he was an extremely nervous person. He had a lot of stomach and digestive troubles. He needed to take tranquilizers, or he felt he needed to. He was much more tense than people realized, or than he appeared to be when he was trying to amuse everyone. I think his life was a strain every day, no matter if it was trying to write or be with people.

You can't imagine how much I tried. It was despairing. He stayed with us at our house for weeks. It didn't get better; it just got worse. I wanted him to know how much I loved him by letting him come with his friends and stay indefinitely. But, then, it would become too much for anyone to deal with, especially when my children were around. He was no longer the Truman I knew. So of course he could stay at my house for as long as he wanted. You're not going to reject the person you loved a great deal and had so many memorable times with. It's impossible to say you can't come and you can't bring so-and-so. It was very depressing, and I didn't want my children to see that day after day. The greatest way you can save somebody is by showing great love and support. I tried to do that, but maybe it was too late.

1971–1979

Truman on the set of Neil Simon's farce *Murder by Death*. The cast was star-studded:
Alec Guinness, Peter Sellers, David Niven, Maggie Smith, Elsa Lanchester, Peter Falk,
James Coco, and Nancy Walker. Truman, who had always dreamed of being an actor,
was confident of success. He told a reporter: "What Billie Holiday is to jazz, what Mae
West is to tits...what Seconal is to sleeping pills, what King Kong is to penises, Truman
Capote is to the great god Thespis." (*Photofest*)

The Great Gatsby, 1971–1972

MARY LAZAR Truman began to spend more time in California, perhaps as much as anything to get away from his social problems in the East. I think he looked at this world of motion pictures as a place to take the money and run. He wanted very much to do *Gatsby*. Jack Clayton, the director, who had been the production manager for *Beat the Devil*, behaved horribly toward Truman. Truman talked Bobby Evans, who was the head of Paramount, into believing that Clayton, a Cockney Englishman, would be the only one who could do F. Scott Fitzgerald, which was just insane. They went to London to work and Truman was in his bad period then, taking lots of Valium and drinking. I don't know how he functioned. Clayton called Bobby Evans early in the morning to tell him that Truman had tried to commit suicide at the Connaught Hotel. He said he wanted him off the picture. He couldn't write anything; he was no good.

JACK CLAYTON The story about *The Great Gatsby* is very sad. I think I was the only director around who would accept Bob's wife, Ali MacGraw, in the role of Daisy. My own thought was that Truman should never have taken the job because he was ill, which became apparent after about six weeks. He started off beautifully and then it all sort of tailed off. A week passed, then another week. As you know, major studios always press to see every page, particularly somebody like Bob Evans. I tried a brief rearguard action, trying to stop their seeing even one page, which I was able to do. Truman sent me everything on tapes. You could tell his condition, but the strange thing was that there were flashes of his normal brilliance. Just occasionally. Then it would go extremely soft.

We were in California, prepared to shoot. I drove down to his place in Palm Springs. He'd written about a third of the script and obviously was not going to do any more. I stalled as long as I could. His contract was for twelve weeks and it was impossible to stall any longer. So I had to turn it over to Paramount. I made all the obvious excuses—that he was ill. I was always blamed by Swifty Lazar for having betrayed Truman. I suppose I did, but I didn't have any option. If I'd been prepared to shoot the script, that's one thing, but I only had a third of it. Of course, the studio didn't want to pay him. I remember in New York three of the lawyers came up to take what they considered the facts from me. I told them the truth. Then I said, "Oh, and incidentally, gentlemen, this is just between us. But if you call me onto the stand, I will deny every bit of it."

"You mean you'll *perjure* yourself?"

I said, "Listen, I'm talking about a friend. I'm telling you because I owe it to Paramount to tell the truth, but I'm not going to stand up in court and talk about Truman." After about three months, they paid.

After this debacle with Truman, Francis Ford Coppola was engaged to do the screenplay. He wrote an absolutely appalling script—nothing to do with the book.

It was about the time of *The Godfather,* when Coppola was a golden boy, and he was paid an outrageous amount. He did it in six weeks, and what came out I couldn't recognize as the book. It wasn't the film I wanted to make. *Gatsby*'d been made twice before and never with the same story as the book. I just wanted to make the book.

In the meantime, just before we were about to shoot, Ali MacGraw, Bob Evans's wife, started having an affair with Steve McQueen. Bob Evans finally found out. We wondered if McQueen was going to get his knees broken. Finally Ali MacGraw was dropped and I chose Mia Farrow. There was a wonderful scene in this big garden in California. We were sitting at a table—David Merrick, who was the producer, myself, and Bob Evans, who was saying to me, "Now listen, Jack, I think you really must consider Steve for the part of Gatsby."

"Steve who?"

"Steve McQueen." I looked at him. I thought he was joking, because everybody knew that Steve McQueen was having an affair with his wife. Even in my old age, I blushed and I said, "Well, let me think about it." Outside, I said to David, "Do you realize that Steve's having it off with Ali?"

He gave a perfect David Merrick answer. "So what."

Murder by Death, 1975

NEIL SIMON *(playwright)* I wrote the original screenplay. In it this amateur criminologist, who turned out to be acted by Truman, invites the five greatest detectives in the world—Nick and Nora Charles, Sam Spade, Charlie Chan, Agatha Christie, and Monsieur Poirot—to whom he will present a murder mystery so intricate that they can't solve it. He lives in this kind of castle. Where he got his money from I haven't the foggiest, and there was a lot of fog in the picture. I had an ending in which Sherlock Holmes comes in to help out, but the Sherlock Holmes estate wouldn't let us use him. So the plot got very convoluted. In fact, over the years I've gotten letters asking, "Who really did it?" and I would write back, "I haven't got the slightest idea." I was certainly provided with the greatest cast of actors I've ever had. I came in on the first day of reading and there were Alec Guinness and Maggie Smith, and David Niven, and the others—they were wonderful, no complaining about their words or anything; just a lot of laughing at each other. And Truman. Truman was the last person I would have thought of for the part of the mystery aficionado. On the other hand, Ray Stark, the producer, was always looking for publicity, perfectly willing to sacrifice the part and hire someone like Truman. For Truman it was a lark. I had no problem with him. He didn't ask for rewrites or anything. But he was very ill at ease with the dialogue. He was a great raconteur; we all know how funny he could be on his own, but he got stuck when he had lines to say. The big problem was that he just didn't know how to move. He kept looking for his marks, the little strips of masking tape put on the floor where you're supposed to stand. They kept saying, "No, no, Truman, you can't look down!" There was a moment when a door opens and Truman, dead, with a knife in his back, is supposed to fall flat, face forward. But as he was falling you could see his eyes looking back and forth for his marks to spot where he was supposed to fall . . .

GEORGE CHRISTY I was on the set one morning when a chandelier fell and crashed a foot away from Truman. He chuckled. He said, "I guess Gore Vidal is in the wings!"

DOTSON RADER Truman kept up his interest in the gay life when he was in LA making these films. LA is always about fifteen years behind New York in terms of sex. In New York you got used to the back-room bars with a separate room or two, very dark, where men had sex. Everything was wide open. In LA it wasn't—still a risky place for gay people, because Davis, who was chief of police, was very anti-homosexual and they still raided bars. So you had to be careful. The gay porn theaters—there were two or three of them in LA—weren't any fun because you'd sit there and they kept the lights on. Ushers would walk up and down. You never knew if the guy next to you was a plainclothes cop. Back-room bars were just coming in then. In LA there weren't any back-room bars that I knew of, but I heard of one they opened up, I think on Santa Monica. So we went there. Three of us. Truman was in his hat, his usual costume, and we came up to the cashier's window. To keep the police out, you had to join the club in order to get into the bar; the legal pretense was that it was a private club. Five bucks. Truman was handed a membership card to fill out and he said, "What if it gets raided and they find out I'm a member? It'll get into the newspaper." The cashier said, "Well, we can't do anything about that, Truman." He'd recognized him. So he said, "Just put down any name." So Truman put down Gore Vidal and gave his Los Angeles address. Truman debated the next day whether he should secretly call the police and initiate a raid.

The Cheap Show, 1978

CHRIS BEARDE (*producer*) On *The Sonny and Cher Comedy Hour*, Lorne Greene got sick. At the production meeting, I said, "Whose is the most opposite voice in the history of time to Lorne Greene's?" And, of course, it would have to be Truman Capote. I called him up directly. He said, "Hell*oooo.*" I said, "This is Chris Bearde, producer of a variety show called *The Sonny and Cher Comedy Hour.*" He said, "I l*ooo*ve that show! We watch that show every week." "Truman, I don't know how to say this, but I would like you to come and do the show." He said, "I only do interviews. What do you want me to do?" I said, "I want you to play Captain Bligh." I started sounding very ridiculous to myself. He said, "Do you really want me to do it?" When I said yes, he said, "Okay, I'll do it, but can I bring my friend?" "Yes, you can bring your friend and I'll meet you at the airport." So Truman Capote agreed to do *The Sonny and Cher Comedy Hour.* I bought him red high-heeled sneakers with three inches of foam on the bottom. He immediately put them on and became three inches taller. He started looking hip. It was a great experience with him. I got to bond with this little guy very seriously. He played great and he played exactly against type.

He came and did other shows for me. Always, when I called him, he would get on the plane and come out here straightway. He did a show for me that was called *The Cheap Show.* It was on for only one season. It was a classic takeoff of game shows. We did five shows in one day. It was on CBS, a syndicated show. Rather than have three celebrity guests, we only had two and we had an empty chair at the end with names like the Pope or Teddy Kennedy on the last chair and then we made up excuses about why they weren't there. The host was Dick Martin of the Rowan and Martin comedy team. It was a very hip show and it didn't do very well in the ratings, but Truman, Bob Newhart, Jill St. John, and a lot of other very well-known people did the show because they were my friends.

Truman came on the show with a plastic milk container filled with vodka and orange juice. The last two shows of the day, he was asleep in his chair and we just left him there asleep because that was Truman Capote. People got angry at me for letting him go to sleep and not waking him up. But I said, "Hey, I just like the energy of this. He's Truman. What can you do? Do you think he'll be brilliantly funny if I wake him up? He'll probably tell us to all go and fuck ourselves. I'd rather have him stay asleep."

Handcarved Coffins, 1979

GEORGE CHRISTY One Saturday morning he called and said, "Are you free tomorrow for lunch? I really need you to read something I'm working on." I said, "Sure." So we met at Peartree's. He had corned beef hash. And martinis. We went over to his apartment, where he asked me to read the manuscript of *Handcarved Coffins*, which was about a murderer loose in a small Nebraska town. He wanted to know what I thought of it. It was a stunning piece of work.

So he wondered, "What can we do about it?" I'd heard from friends of his how brilliant he was promoting his works. I answered, "Well, I'd love to write that it would make a great movie."

He said, "Please, would you?" I said yes, I would. So I wrote quite a long column about *Handcarved Coffins* and affirmed that it would make an extraordinary movie. We had something like thirty calls from producers the day the column appeared, all asking for Truman's telephone number. He sold it to Lester Persky for the highest price per word any manuscript had been sold for. I think it was nearly $500,000. Unfortunately, it has yet to be made, for reasons, well, only Hollywood reasons. Studio heads change and scripts go into other hands. This is one of those frustrating situations, because in fact it would make a marvelous movie.

LESTER PERSKY I fell in love with *Handcarved Coffins*. I started to negotiate with his representative, Alan Schwartz, his attorney, and I paid a great deal of money for it—something astronomical—$350,000, plus a piece of this and a piece of that, an expensive package. I persuaded United Artists to become my partner in it. I thought that Truman would be available to help in research because he indicated he had a great deal of additional material. Of course, I never got that additional material about the murders, but he would give me clues. He was as elusive as the master killer.

GEORGE PLIMPTON I remember Truman telling some of the stories
that would eventually end up in *Handcarved Coffins*. It always
seemed to me that Truman tried them out on other people before
committing them to paper. Some writers don't, or can't, do this.
Hemingway certainly couldn't. I remember E. L. Doctorow telling
me that as soon as he told a story at a dinner table, that story was
gone. He could no longer use it, at least in his written work.

But that wasn't the case with Truman. His stories often changed
as he perfected them. The story he tried out on me from
Handcarved Coffins was the one in which the murderer booby-traps
a car with rattlesnakes, putting them in the front seat, which set
upon a couple and kill them as they step into the car. Highly
dramatic stuff, especially as Truman was telling it. It was all
supposed to be true, supposed to have happened in Nebraska
somewhere. I pointed out, somewhat nervously, that the whole thing
was highly improbable. Rattlesnakes are fairly lethargic to begin
with. Their poison is hemotoxic, which means it moves through the
bloodstream and is thus relatively slow-acting; and wouldn't the
rattlesnakes rattle if anyone opened up the car door with them
inside?

So the next time I heard him tell the story, the rattles had been
removed, the couple was much older—just teetering on the edge of
life, both with bad heart conditions—and the lethargy problem had
been solved by the murderer's lacing the rattlesnakes with
amphetamines. Even then, it didn't sound terribly plausible. I
remember Truman appearing on the Carson show and telling that
story, and everyone in the audience gave that terrible sound of
"awwww!" you know, that awful derisive sound of complete disbelief.

LESTER PERSKY You're asking me if I thought the story of
Handcarved Coffins was true. Well, I spoke at a memorial luncheon
that C. Z. Guest had arranged after Truman's death. I was sitting
opposite Alvin Dewey, the detective from *In Cold Blood*. I pressed
him. He wasn't too helpful, but he did say that another detective
came to Truman at the time of *In Cold Blood* and said to him, "You
think that's a great story, I've got a better story."

It does check out that it occurred in western Nebraska. I had a great deal of trouble with the studio. They said, "What if? What if this murderer is a real person, we could be sued!" I said, "Listen, I'll personally underwrite the lawsuit if the person wants to come up and say he's the killer and has been defamed. I will guarantee that with a five-million-dollar bond from my insurance company." They accepted that.

Interlude

CHAPTER THIRTY-EIGHT *In Which*

TC Meets an Idol

Peggy Lee was a household name as a singer in the 1940s, '50s, and '60s—with over five hundred records to her credit. A perennial performer in fancy nightclubs, she was once described by the jazz critic Leonard Feather as "Miss Standing Ovation."
(UPI/Corbis-Bettmann)

DOTSON RADER Truman was a great jazz buff. Peggy Lee was one of his favorite singers. So I called up Peggy, who was a friend of mine, and I said, "I'm here with Truman and we'd love to take you to dinner. Are you free tomorrow?"

She said, "Yes, why don't you come for a drink around six?" Typical LA, they eat like farmers. She sends her car for us. The house is in Bel Air and it's got an enormous front door—one of these modern houses with a lot of glass and stone. There's some trouble getting the door unlocked, so we stand there for a while. Then we walked in and there's the biggest living room I ever saw in my life and the longest sofa. Typical Hollywood—two-floor ceilings. Peggy Lee can press a button on a console by her and the screen comes down, the projector turns on, that sort of thing. It's an enormous, dramatic, theatrical Hollywood kind of place. At one end is a solid line of glass sliding doors overlooking her gardens. Peggy is dressed in a very thin white chiffon gown. Peggy hadn't been too well; she moved slow because she had her oxygen tent with her. Truman takes one look at her and goes, "Oh, my God. I'm in the presence of an angel." He goes over to her. She doesn't move. He takes her hand, kisses one finger. She says, "Can I get you something to drink?" Truman says he wants a vodka, and I say I'll have the same. She buzzes for a man to come to get us drinks. He looks sort of bewildered because she doesn't keep any liquor in the house. He brings us Perrier water. Now that irritates Truman. He wants a drink. Peggy says to him, "Well, Truman, can I show you the gardens?" So he says, "Well, all right. Show me the gardens, but then we've got to go." He really wants a drink. She goes over to the sliding glass doors and she can't get them open. So Truman says, "Let me help." So the two of them, Peggy, who isn't very steady, and this little guy, are tugging and kicking and pulling, trying to get these doors open. And we never did get them open.

So we go to Le Restaurant, which is one of the most pretentious restaurants in America, so it's very popular in LA. It had started to pour. It came down cats and dogs. Once at Le Restaurant, Truman and I order drinks and Peggy orders a bottle of Evian water, for which I paid fifty dollars a bottle. It came in a silver champagne holder, right? We are trying to hold a conversation in a room which has a tin roof, so you feel like you're on the Western Front in World War I and the Germans are machine-gunning your lines. We can barely hear a thing. Truman and Peggy and I are shouting back and forth at each other, trying to make conversation. Suddenly Peggy says to Truman, "Do you believe in reincarnation?"

Truman says, "Well, I don't know. Do you?"

She says, "Oh, yes. I've been reincarnated many times. In my other lives I've been a prostitute, a princess, an Abyssinian queen . . ."

Truman sort of looks at her and says, "Well, how do you know all this?"

She says, "I can prove it. I remember being a prostitute in Jerusalem when Jesus was alive."

Truman says, "Oh, really? What else do you remember?"

"Oh," she said, "I remember the crucifixion very well."

He says, "Oh?"

She says, "Yes, I'll never forget picking up the *Jerusalem Times* and seeing the headline 'Jesus Christ Crucified.'"

At that point, she gets up to go to the bathroom and Truman looks at me and says, "She's totally bonkers . . ." You've got to remember all this is shouted over the machine-gunning going on.

She comes back and they start talking about singers. Truman asks her when she got started. Then something happened that I noticed a lot with Truman. He would meet someone, make fun of them, although they weren't aware of it, and then they would say something that would reveal a vulnerability, some heartache or pain, and suddenly Truman's attitude would change. One of the reasons he got along with a lot of people was that they were open with him rather than being combative. I think that's one of the reasons he hated the rich, because—with the exception of a few of his closest friends like Babe—they were never open with him, they were never vulnerable around him. Unless he knew a vulnerability of yours, he never felt safe around you.

Anyway, they were talking about singers in the forties and she started talking about her mother, who weighed 360 pounds and used to beat up her father all the time, and her as well. When she was eleven, her mother took a butcher knife and stabbed her in the stomach. She said she still had the scar. She started singing when she was fourteen or fifteen at this radio station in Fargo, North Dakota, and I forgot who heard her, one of the bandleaders, Jimmy or Tommy Dorsey, and brought her to Chicago to perform at the Pump Room at the Ambassador East. She arrived a couple of days early with a girlfriend. They had very little money; she was scared of the town. They checked into a motel. She was so naïve she didn't realize that the fleabag they had checked into was a whorehouse. She said, "All these painted girls going up and down all the time and it never dawned on me that people did that sort of thing."

When they showed up at the Ambassador East, Mr. Dorsey put them into a hotel room. For a week, until she got her first paycheck, she and her girlfriend would stay up late so that around eleven or twelve o'clock at night, when people had put their room service trays outside in the hall, they could go down the hall and collect buns and butter. They didn't know they could use room service.

This story touched Truman. He suddenly became very protective of her. His whole attitude changed and he asked if she could sing something. Here we are in the restaurant where the bill ended up being three hundred dollars. Truman and Peggy Lee sat there another thirty or forty minutes totally oblivious to everyone around them, including me, singing songs. "Bye-Bye Blackbird," "I'll Be Seeing You," and all these old standards. All the way back in the car, they talked about music and every once in a while the two of them would start singing. It was a lovely evening.

1975—1979

CHAPTER THIRTY-NINE

*In Which
the Reader Learns of TC's Entanglement
with Gore*

Gore Vidal, with whom a smoldering feud had been going on for
over thirty years. *(UPI/Corbis-Bettmann)*

GEORGE PLIMPTON The whole episode goes back to a dinner dance at the White House in the Kennedy administration. If memory serves, it was at that occasion that Franklin Roosevelt, Jr., rose from his table in the East Room to toast Stas Radziwill, Lee's husband at the time. The problem was that Stas at the moment of Roosevelt's toast was in a plane landing at what was then New York's Idlewild Airport. His flight had been delayed by storms. The man Roosevelt was toasting, the man Roosevelt thought was Stas Radziwill, was in fact Oleg Cassini, the dress designer. President Kennedy was highly amused, doubled over in his seat and trying not to let on so that Roosevelt would go on and on with his encomiums.

In any case, the dancing went on after dinner and it was then that I saw the confrontation between Gore and Bobby Kennedy. Gore was standing next to Jackie and in a gesture that one might consider quite proper since they were old friends and related by marriage, he had his arm lightly around her waist, at the small of the back. Bobby saw this, and quite rudely removed Gore's arm, saying to the effect that "that sort of thing doesn't go around here," whereupon there was a sharp exchange of words. My memory is that they involved the power of the word—Gore stressing that no one should treat a writer that way unless he expected retaliation in words and Bobby doubting Gore's ability to do any such thing with his pen, typewriter, whatever.

GORE VIDAL There were no witnesses to what happened. Nobody saw anything. I was squatting down beside Jackie in the north curve of the Blue Room. She was in an armless chaise. As I rose, for support, I needed her knee or shoulder. I picked shoulder. As I did, Bobby came up behind her and took my hand off—she sees nothing. I then went over (and there are *no* witnesses to any of this either) and said to Bobby, "Don't ever do that again."

"What do you mean, buddy boy? You're nobody," something like that. I said, "Never say that; writers have so many words, we usually have the last one." Not bad for my state of rage, which escalated very quickly to "Fuck you!" "Fuck you too!" and that was the end of it. Recently I showed Hillary Clinton the spot where it took place— Blue Room door into Red Room. Should there be a plaque?

GEORGE PLIMPTON Jackie told me many years later that the real
reason for Gore's "expulsion" from the White House circle was that
he had cornered Lem Billings, a former roommate of the President
and practically a family member, and had verbally humiliated him in
a hallway.

Gore, whom I have known and admired since we were
schoolmates years back, has since written me a letter in which he
says that he never saw Lem Billings before or after that evening,
although he did know that he was "Jack's fag friend from Choate."
He went on to write: "As I was passing by, he [Lem] asked, 'Why
don't you come to the meetings of the Council on the Arts?' I
replied, demurely, that I didn't think government should meddle in
the arts. He, drunk or in a choleric seizure, denounced me, ending,
'Well then, why did you go on the Council?' I said J. [President
Kennedy] had appointed me without asking. I graciously said
nothing and never attended a meeting. End of story."

Well, there we are. I should mention that the drinks served at
those White House affairs, those private parties, were tankard size,
and that because of nerves or whatever, everyone tended to
overimbibe. I remember Vice President Lyndon Johnson in a pale
blue dinner jacket taking a header onto the dance floor, falling in a
heap on top of a great beauty, Helen Tchatchavadse, and leaping off
her like a jackrabbit, and hauling her up, all this so quickly that it
was hard to tell what had happened unless you had your eye on
them.

At any rate, what happened then was that Truman gave an
interview to a rather second-rate skin magazine called *Playgirl* (it
had a male Playmate for the centerfold) in which Truman reported
to the interviewer that Gore had been thrown bodily out of the
White House. Lee Radziwill had told him about the incident, and in
a sense it was true, because Gore was never invited back, but it was
that word "bodily" that initiated Vidal's lawsuit. I never could quite
imagine how this could happen in the rather decorous setting of the
White House. In fact, I wrote a parody in which the scene was
described: ". . . *Arthur Schlesinger, Jr., had thrown Gore Vidal out of
the White House onto Pennsylvania Avenue, which was the length of
two football fields away from the front steps, a long toss for anyone, but*

which was logical enough if you knew what a great arm Schlesinger
had and how he had gripped Vidal by the laces and spiraled him." But
Gore didn't accept it that way.

GORE VIDAL I'll tell you what pissed me off. Every time somebody
was doing a piece about me they would go to Capote because he
knows everybody famous in the world and has the lowdown.
Actually, Truman had no information about me. He didn't see me
and he didn't know many of the people I knew. So, each time, he'd
just invent more and more stuff. And I would get more and more
annoyed at this character he was creating. It finally culminated in
my suing him, and I sued him really, I thought, *pro bono publico.* I
wanted to show that lying is not cute; it's dangerous, it's vicious, it's
highly harmful to others. It might have had a salutary value—at least
a shovelful out of the Augean stables. I won the suit. But to no end.
He admitted to untruth. No one stopped a single press.

LIZ SMITH When Truman got involved in this lawsuit with Gore
Vidal, Truman said to me, "Gore really likes you. You're one of the
only people in the world who he thinks is really fair-minded."
    "How do you know that?"
    "Well, I know because people have told me. Now, Liz, if you
went to him . . ."
    I said, "Look, I've already talked to him. I've tried but he won't
drop the suit."
    So then Truman mourns a little more and goes on that he's going
to have to pay a million dollars and he says, "You know, this story
about his being thrown out of the White House is true. This really
happened."
    Well, I didn't know whether it was or not, but I'd been hearing it
for years. Truman certainly wasn't the only person who ever told the
story about Gore and Jackie Kennedy and how incensed Bobby
Kennedy was with Gore.
    So then Truman said, "You know, Lee likes you, and if you go to
her and ask her please to testify on my behalf that this all actually
happened, then Gore won't stand a chance."
    I said, "Well, she's your good friend."

"Well, I've asked her and she says no, but I feel if you ask her, she might do it."

I said, "You have this unrealistic faith in my powers. I don't have any powers to influence these people."

"Yes. Please, please ask her for me. She won't even return my phone calls."

I thought, some friendship!

So I called Lee and I said, "Look, Truman is in really bad shape. He loves you so much, and he really needs you to come forward in this situation and at least say if it did happen, yes, this incident did happen and Mr. Capote didn't make this up. Otherwise, Gore is going to win this lawsuit and it's just going to crush Truman."

She said to me, "Oh, Liz, what does it matter? They're just a couple of fags."

I almost fainted. I just couldn't believe that she had said that. I don't know why I was surprised. Most people are intensely homophobic down deep and these things spring out of them when they're not thinking. I called Truman back. I said to Truman, "She won't do it."

"Well, what did you say? What did she say?"

He went on and on; he was tormented. My common sense held me back from telling him what she had said, but finally in the end I did tell him because he absolutely wouldn't take no for an answer; he had this uncanny thing of knowing you were lying. He started really pushing me around verbally, saying, "Oh, you're such a sissy, and you're so softhearted, and you're never going to get anywhere in life because you can't tell the truth, and this is really important, and I need to know exactly what she said, didn't she ask anything about me," and blah, blah, blah. Finally I became exasperated, I guess, I don't know. I shouldn't have done it. But I told him what she said.

Well, he went totally berserk! He went on the Stanley Siegel show. The next thing Truman was telling on the air was this perfectly awful story about Bill Buckley and Lee. He dredged up the worst thing he knew about Lee. It has the ring of truth, but how do I know? He said that Lee had conceived this great passion for Bill Buckley. She wanted to have an affair with him. But he was so straitlaced and such a good Catholic that she devised a story that she was thinking of converting and she wanted him to give her advice and instruction. Well, I imagine Bill Buckley has been asked a lot of things! I have no idea how far it went or if it happened and I'm sure he's too much of a gentleman to admit that it happened. I said to Truman later, "How could you have told that story? You always said that Lee was the greatest person in the world."

"Well, I'll show her," he said.

I said, "This is not good, and believe me, I don't want to be old-fashioned but no man ever gets anywhere by cackling publicly. It won't go down to your credit."

He said, "I guess you think I give a shit," and things like that. He went crazy, just disintegrated. The situation went from one bad thing to another. So in a funny way he *became* the horrible toad that all of these people had felt he was . . . for betraying their confidences.

JUDY GREEN When he talked to me about the people who had turned on him, it was with the greatest bitterness I'd ever heard. He would talk with tears in his eyes about the people he believed betrayed him. He felt that his strong suit was his loyalty. A terrific betrayal was Lee Radziwill. She was the worst of all, because she wasn't in "La Côte Basque." He had this relentless despair at what had happened to what he thought was one of his best friendships. He didn't feel he'd ever done anything to her. In fact, quite the opposite: He felt he had saved her life. What he did for Babe was to be her confidant, make her laugh. But with Lee he was life-saving, life-giving—whether it was *Laura,* pulling her out of a depression, getting her over the Onassis debacle, or being Jackie's sister. He had a wellspring of Southern compassion that many call "syrup"—but with Truman it was genuine.

GEORGE PLIMPTON The libel suit dragged on for about seven years. It wasn't until 1983 that the case was finally settled out of court when Truman wrote a letter of apology: "Dear Gore: I apologize for any distress, inconvenience or expense which may have been caused you as a result of the interview with me published in the September 1975 issue of *Playgirl.* As you know, I was not present at the event about which I am quoted in the interview, and I understand from your representatives that what I am reported as saying does not accurately set forth what occurred. I can assure you that the article was not an accurate transcription of what I said, especially with regard to any remarks about your character or behavior, and that I will avoid discussing the matter in the future. Best, Truman Capote."

ALAN SCHWARTZ It was a very strange case. The story that came out in *Playgirl* was different from what Truman had said over the tape . . . more sensationalized, though the basic facts in the story were the same as Truman had related them. The appeal we finally made to Gore himself. I got permission from his lawyer. I said, "Look, this guy's in very bad shape. You may feel that you've been libeled and so forth, but I don't think you want to watch the destruction of a writer of this talent, finally, and have anything to do with it."

Anyway, Gore finally settled for a half-assed apology and a quarter of his legal fees, a very minor thing.

GORE VIDAL The last time I saw him was in '68. That was when I sat on him at Drue Heinz's party. There was a very funny exchange in the deposition for our legal case. "But what was *he* sitting on?" his lawyer asked, fiercely. "Obviously," I said, "something smaller." Anyway, he was sufficiently squashy to sit upon and I was much thinner in those days. But I leapt like a gazelle . . . off this pouf, as it were.

1977

CHAPTER FORTY *In Which TC Takes Up the Nightlife*

Truman at Studio 54. *(UPI/Corbis-Bettmann)*

BOB COLACELLO Studio 54 opened in April 1977, the first big party was May, but it didn't really get clicking with everybody until the fall because they didn't have a liquor license that first summer. Then Truman went quite a lot. He used to call it Cinquanta-quatto—in Italian. He liked to go up to the disco booth. I think Steve Rubell, the co-owner, showed him how to work the lights. He loved being up there.

ANTHONY HADEN-GUEST (*writer*) Studio 54 only had eighteen months, basically, of white intensity. Nobody expected anything like it. The *Daily News* on the morning of the opening of the club had a derisive little item captioned "Studio 54, Where Are You?"—poking fun at it because there were too many bad discos then. It is quite wrong to think of Studio 54 as a place where people went to look at celebrities, it was in a way where celebrities went to look at people, crazy people.

Ian Schrager, the co-owner with Rubell, told their publicist, a nice New Yorker type, when they were really riding high, "Ed, put up a chart with a thousand days, and cross off a day every day; that's all anything lasts in New York, a thousand days." It's not always true, but Studio 54 wasn't meant to last. Nonetheless, it had an enormous effect. When I first came to New York, in my mind the social order here was still ruled by people with names like Auchincloss and Winthrop. Studio 54 changed all that, just as London in the early sixties changed with clubs like the Adlib. Suddenly David Bailey and Mick Jagger were at least as chic as the Duke of Devonshire. That's what happened with Studio 54. Suddenly Calvin Klein was a major social force.

KATE HARRINGTON We went to Studio 54 about ten times. It was really exciting. I never drank or anything back then, so I was probably the only person there sober. I remember it vividly, crystal clear. It was very glamorous to me at the time. It was like going to another planet, another world, because it was so dark and strange. When Truman would come, it was like Moses: the seas would part and they'd wave him in. He'd come in that hallway that was black with the spotlighted calla lilies and then all the fans, "Hi, Truman!" The men running around in diapers, the cocktail waiters.

WILLIAM AVERY *(publicist)* Many of the bartenders and busboys were half gay. If they weren't, they were receptive to advances. It was like a maze, like an English garden—well, more like a rabbit warren. I was always invited to the back of the scrim up on the stage. When the scrim dropped, that was the VIP section, where everybody came through the back door on Fifty-third Street. The back-of-the-scrim people kept their clothes on. Downstairs in the basement people took their clothes off. Balcony people certainly took their clothes off too. Dangerous place. At the second-floor bar I knew the bartender, so he gave me free drinks. Someone offered me a cigarette once which was laced with PCP. I was up and down the stairs for about four hours . . . just racing . . . looking at people, talking to people—I'm sure not making much sense—being very convivial and chatting. One night I fell asleep in my tuxedo. I had a gold watch on and a ring. At seven o'clock in the morning somebody was vacuuming the floor. I got up and I left. Nobody had taken my wallet or anything. I was just lying there like a mummy.

ANTHONY HADEN-GUEST The original VIP room at Studio 54 was off the co-owner Steve Rubell's office upstairs, first floor, but that simply became too obvious, going in and out up there, so people went down to the basement. Dingy, like all basements, hideous, lots of little cubicles, diseased-looking banquettes, a lot of disused props, all these odd children's toys. I remember mattresses everywhere where people like Truman would go.

BOB COLACELLO It was like any big basement. It had oil burners and lots of pipes and all these storerooms, which basically were cyclone-fenced cages. It had a bathroom somewhere. There would be puddles from where pipes were leaking. It had cement floors. It was not at all attractive. Steve would set up one cyclone-fenced cage as the room where he'd throw some cushions on the floor, and the next week it would be at the other end of the basement . . . you always had to figure out where it was. You'd go down in through the staircase behind the kitchen. It was mostly the Halston and Andy Warhol group. Mainly we'd go down there and sit around and a busboy would bring us a bottle of vodka. People would take coke there if they didn't want to do it in front of people upstairs, where the bathrooms were always too crowded. You'd sit there under the dance floor, so there would be this bump, bump, bump of people dancing and the music right overhead.

One of the great nights I remember in the basement was when Yves Saint Laurent launched his Opium perfume with a big party downtown in South Street Seaport. Then we all went up to Studio 54. I remember sitting in the basement with Truman and Katherine Guinness's cousin, Hugo Guinness, who had just come in from London. He was very young, eighteen years old, and we were using him as our waiter. He would go back and forth and get Truman and me more vodkas. Barbara Allen was sitting with us. Halston was there. Marina Schiano arrived with Yves Saint Laurent. We all stood up to greet them and Halston and Yves kissed each other—like this big moment. They were big rivals: one was the king of American fashion; the other was the king of French couture. Truman said, "You have just witnessed one of the greatest moments in the history of fashion—if you care about the history of fashion, that is."

ANTHONY HADEN-GUEST Jack Martin told me he was having a drink with Steve Rubell. They went down to the basement. Steve suddenly said, "That's the princess, the princess." Some Eurotrash princess had been taken down to the basement by her own request, handcuffed to a water pipe, and fucked by one of the barmen, who then thought, "My God, I've got to get back to the bar," and forgot about the handcuffs. And had left her down there.

BARBARA ALLEN It was so ugly, that room, the VIP room at Studio 54. The basement . . . a cage in the basement where you'd put your storage. There were all sorts of people from Halston, Yves Saint Laurent, to Sao Schlumberger, and all the film and rock stars. I know people who used to fall asleep and wake up the next morning and think, "Where am I?" There were always jokes about that. You'd just walk over them. Really strange. I'll never forget this cage, just sitting around there on boxes. It was interesting to be somewhere that was secret. Because of the dancing and the music, all you heard was *dun-dun-dun,* you know, that horrible beat of the songs, just *bang-bang-bang.* If you had a headache you couldn't possibly be down there. Just this vibration you'd get. There was one long corridor you went through—I can hardly remember—and there was another office down at the end—they called it an office. It *was* an office, actually, they had a telephone. In this labyrinth if you walked around, you'd run into friends. It wasn't exactly the cleanest place in the world. Yes, there were drugs, but you didn't always see them. Everyone that experienced that time has a sort of secret. We knew we were having the time of our lives; we were loving it; we knew it was an extraordinary time, and we knew it wouldn't last.

Once I saw Truman when he came in pajamas. What do you call . . . those muumuu things? It was a black caftan. You could get away with that there. Those times were kind of a blur for everybody. But everyone looked beautiful, if a little debauched.

NAN KEMPNER I used to love Studio 54. I adored it. Because it took you right out of yourself. Fantasyland. I always went with friends. I never went all by myself. We'd go in a gang, and they were very nice to us; we'd get helped into that roped-in part. You felt very special when you went there. I loved the dancing. I used to dance with all sizes, shapes, forms, colors . . . and I'd come home absolutely limp. It was divine. I'll never forget the night I was standing at the bar, and Halston was handed a pill, sort of a triangular-shaped pill. I said, "What's the matter, do you have a headache?" He looked at me as if I was crazy and he said, "It's a quaalude." I had to ask three people what a quaalude was. I'm rather moronic. I went downstairs to where everybody was either shooting, poking, pushing, or snorting. It was fabulous. I just loved watching all this stuff go on. It was a whole way of life, and it was very interesting. There was a place called the Tunnel. I went down there one night, and some friend of mine who was a designer said to me, "You're not going up there." Up some circular stairs or something. Apparently it was a gang bang going on, at all times, and he said, "No way are you going up there." They turned me around and walked me out the door. I felt I was missing something. A happening. It's always been the story of my life, as you know. I don't want to miss anything. Nowadays the big change has been age, as far as I'm concerned. Now I can't wait to slide into the sheets. Isn't it awful? Isn't it embarrassing? I'm sure that if somebody were to take me to a wonderful place like Studio 54, I'd be all hell-bent to go, but the places don't exist anymore. Those that are still around are very boring. And I'm too old to sit and talk about nothing in the wee hours of the morning over loud music.

LIZ SMITH I always say to people, "I'm sure glad I wasn't hip enough or attractive enough or young enough to be invited to the downstairs room at Studio 54, because everybody who ever went there is dead." Lots of drugs and needles. Truman was really in the thick of it. One night John Berendt, later to write the bestseller *Midnight in the Garden of Good and Evil,* and I went out with Truman and met first at his apartment in the UN Plaza. Truman said, "I'm going to show you something so great that you won't even believe it." He went out of the room and came in with a big glass of cocaine. Our mouths kind of flapped open, because I had never seen so much cocaine. I mean, it had to be $10,000 worth. It was actually more than a big glass, it was in a *bowl.* We weren't going to partake, because even if I had wanted to, I wouldn't have done that with Truman. I didn't trust him. I knew it would become an amusing story. Then he said suddenly, "No. No. I'm not going to give you any. You're not good enough. Neither one of you is good enough." With that he went out of the room with the bowl, and John called after him jokingly, "Well, do you suppose we can have a marijuana cigarette?"

JANN WENNER *(publisher)* If they didn't know Truman by sight, they'd know him as soon as he opened his mouth and uttered a word. All the doors opened for him. People coming up for autographs . . . kind of strange fan club he had. But the funniest was seeing him in the gay discos. In the gay world he was a kind of hero because he was one of the first public homosexuals. So they just loved and adored him. You'd go into a gay disco with Truman and you got seated at the number one table, right on the dance floor, everybody coming over asking Truman to dance. Can you imagine those guys asking Truman to dance?

BOB COLACELLO When Studio 54 opened, Truman decided that I was the only person he liked to dance with; he would insist on dancing with me. He didn't want to disco dance, he wanted to do the jitterbug and it was always a struggle to see who would lead and who would follow. I remember his saying to me once, "You're such a good dancer because you can lead *and* follow." What was funny about Truman was he would always whistle while he danced but it was never the song you were dancing to. He'd be whistling songs like "Whistle While You Work" . . . Walt Disney sound-track songs. He'd be whistling these while we would be dancing to Donna Summer's "Enough is Enough." It would throw me off. Truman liked to dance a jitterbug that was sort of a lindy hop.

JOHN RICHARDSON He loved taking people to offbeat bars. I thought I'd been to most of New York's weird places. But one night I went out with Truman and Patrick O'Higgins and Truman said, "I'm going to take you to a dyke leather bar." He had unearthed this amazing place which was filled with the toughest women you ever saw: all in leather, with huge motorcycles parked outside—like Hell's Angels in drag. Some of them even had whiskers. Truman would scamper around and make friends with them. We had a very comic evening. He was going to take Elsa Maxwell there, he said, and see if she made out. It was typical of Truman—taking the people to some bizarre place and seeing how they react. He liked playing tricks on people, catching them out.

JAN CUSHING He took me one night to a very funny place called P. T. Barnum's. I was jumping on the dance floor to some disco music. This girl came over, very pretty, trying to copy what I was dancing, and I said, "Look, TC, that beautiful girl, she's trying to copy me." Truman said, "I got news for you, honey. You're the only girl in the place." I had no idea it was all transvestites. People were swinging from trapezes.

WILLIAM F. BUCKLEY, JR. One night he invited me and Joe Fox of Random House and Lally Weymouth to dinner. Then we went to some crazy place called the Limelight. Half-homosexual, half-heterosexual dancing joint. It was a long evening. It went from about ten o'clock till about two. It was sort of a go-go place, sort of like Studio 54 five or six years before. But there was a lot of overt homosexuality. Men dancing with men and a lot of people, everybody smoking pot, and this tremendous noise and dazzling lights. It was sort of an interesting place to have seen—once.

GEORGE PLIMPTON He took me once to a bar on Forty-fifth Street that he told me was frequented by a gay crowd largely made up of transvestites. He did this perhaps because he thought it was something that I, as a reporter, should see. He was quite excited about it—as if he were taking me to a wondrous art exhibit that only he knew about . . . a sort of "You won't believe what you're going to see."

Physically, the place turned out to be like any other in that part of town—a long bar reaching back toward an area in the rear which had tables set about. As we walked in, a man hopped off his barstool and touched my arm. "Hey!" he said, very cheerfully, like a long-lost friend. It turned out that he recognized me from a book I'd written about professional football, *Paper Lion.* He wanted to talk football. There wasn't anything about his manner that suggested he was the kind of person Truman had led me to believe we were going to find in there—just a good solid guy from Hackensack or some such place who'd wandered in, obviously quite unaware of the bar's reputation as a hangout for transvestites, in the hopes of finding someone to talk football with. He picked a good place, because some of the other people along the bar joined in the conversation—about Y. A. Tittle's retirement as the Giant quarterback or whatever. We could have been standing along the bar in Toots Shor's sports hangout. This, of course, was not of the slightest interest to Truman. Rather morosely, it seemed to me, he went back to the rear area, where he sat with a couple of people he apparently knew. I never went back there to check on the transvestite business. As I recall, Truman said afterward that it had been an "off night."

MICHAEL FEZNICK (*nightclub owner*) On Saturday nights, they would come into the Flamingo after Studio 54 closed. The Flamingo was a very large gay nightclub-discotheque which opened in 1974. On the corner of Houston and Broadway on the second floor, vast, two hundred feet long, fifty across, column-free. Writers wrote about the Flamingo, so we became the "in" place. It was a private club. A membership cost thirty-five dollars. Truman was very much a fixture on Saturday nights. They would come down, the big entourage, three or four limousines out front, and there'd be upward of twelve people in the group. Liza Minnelli, Cher, Steve Rubell, Truman. They sailed in free, like they owned the place, all of them, of course, semi-famous. Truman was really a voyeur. He loved to hide in the dark corners. It would be very crowded, wall-to-wall people, a heavy dance crowd. The Flamingo was where a lot of the new music would be introduced—Donna Summer's, the master copy. The DJ would play the piece, and if the crowd liked it, then the next thing you knew it was being pressed. Donna Summer, and Band of Gold, the group from Sweden.

MILAN (*designer*) These places opened up because people can't go to sleep in New York. Just like the speakeasies. People can't go home and watch cable TV all night. As long as there's a clientele, these places will stay open. I'll tell you what brought Truman there. At these places, he knew everyone. In the bathrooms in these places were bathtubs, and someone would sit in the bathtub for hours. They would have fights because the people would get jealous and say, "That guy's been in the bathtub too long getting pissed on." But Truman would know that guy sitting in the bathtub; he would know them all. We were doing a lot of dust at that time, smoking dust. Truman liked Special K, Keratin.

DOTSON RADER You went down the stairs [at the Mineshaft]. The police have since closed it. There was a bar. There were different dark rooms. You'd see naked guys lying in slings. There were chains and handcuffs on the walls. It didn't start hopping until about two or three in the morning. Maybe half the guys would be naked. They'd have leather pants with no butt and stuff like that. People would

light up when they saw Truman. He was like a walking television
camera, because he'd come in and people would perform for him.
There'd be a lot more sex when Truman was there than when I'd be
there alone. Because he was a very appreciative audience and he'd
carry on with this running commentary: "Why are you doing that?"
And "Oh my God, that's amazing! Oh my God, that must be twelve
inches!" And they'd get more energetic.

MILAN Some of the clubs were different because you could buy
someone there. You could go in and talk to the doorman and say
what it is you want to do, and he'll give you a prostitute. The basis
of these clubs was pain. The most important aspect was the S&M
pain and having your fate in somebody else's hands.

The Anvil was a truck stop, and upstairs there was a dance floor
where there was a drag act. There were fire-breathers; there was the
boy who put the snake in his ass. The big gay communities had
these transvestites there to represent Miss San Francisco, Miss
Boston, Miss Washington, and they did their act starting at about
four o'clock in the morning. There was a film room downstairs. And
below that was the grossest thing I've ever seen: it was a cellar, all
the runoff from the street coming down the walls; it was a black
orgy room. Every fifteen minutes a guy would walk through saying,
"Gentlemen, watch your wallets." You couldn't see anything. The
booze there was watered down, which got Truman very upset. So we
went to the Mineshaft. I remember they wouldn't let us in because I
had on a fur coat, and you could only wear white T-shirts, blue
jeans, sneakers, and bomber jackets.

The Belle du Jour was a straight place on Twenty-third Street,
and there were women tied up all over the place. It was all velvet. It
was beautiful. That's the reason I always said, "Let's go there,
because if I have to go to a sex club, at least let me sit on something
that's not covered in blood, sperm, and sweat. At least I can sit on a
lovely chair and talk to one of the mavs." It was very clean. The first
time I walked in there, there was this woman in black leather and
high heels, and there was this incredibly beautiful man with his
hands and ankles tied, on his knees licking her boots, and she was
calling him obscenities. Truman was too egotistical to be degraded

in public, but I think that's where his turn-on came from, because he could not believe anyone would find him attractive, because of the voice, the body. He could not believe anyone could love him for his art. Even those people who did didn't matter to him.

NED ROREM I have a feeling about Truman's sex life—that there was probably very, very little. People that public, and that clinically interested in other people's mechanics, aren't usually so interested in sexual contact themselves. They're interested in what makes people tick sexually, but only vicariously. Truman told these lies about going to bed with Errol Flynn and John Garfield and all those famous movie stars because they were fantasy figures. If he had actually done it, he wouldn't have talked about it. A person who is very sexually satisfied doesn't have to write books, much less invent stories about his own sex life . . .

JOHN KNOWLES I went with Truman [to gay bars] a few times. He was instantly recognized by everybody. He was always gregarious. Talked to everybody and he was the center of attention. I don't remember him bringing home people from places like that. That doesn't mean he didn't. But I think he was really a romantic; he wanted a relationship with a father figure, a sexual and affectionate love relationship. He never found that, really. Well, Jack Dunphy . . . But I don't think he was as promiscuous as he liked to make out. He told me he'd go to these truck stops on the Long Island Expressway. These places where you pull over, and people would go into the woods. He'd go in there . . . so he said. Sometimes he said he would pick up one after another. I can't vouch for that. Truman had a way of exaggerating.

JACK DUNPHY Long ago I decided that kind of pickup stuff was very wretched and I stopped. It was based on a certain vanity, because I thought a person of a certain age shouldn't play around like that because you look ridiculous. Nothing worse than an old queen standing at the bar with a bitchy face and refusing everything because he's going to be refused. Snarling and snaky about beauties.

I don't think sex has ever been really that important in my life, a driving kind of thing. A lot of other people—they make it, they pretend, they carry on, these old men with the itch. Forget it! It's all in your head, just calm yourself.

1978

CHAPTER FORTY-ONE   *In Which TC*

Begins to Work for a Longtime Admirer

ANDREAS BROWN When Andy Warhol first came to
New York in the summer of '49, he was extremely
ambitious. He really wanted to make it. And what
better teacher than Capote, who was beginning to
blossom as a power broker, as a person who knew
how to manipulate the New York scene. Andy was
smart enough to see that and concluded, "Gee, if I
could just follow this guy's footsteps. If I could sit at
his feet and learn, I'll save myself years getting to the
top." So Andy began to ingratiate himself. He wrote
him almost every day, called him on the phone, stood
outside his apartment—evidently to the point where
Truman's mother finally said, "Please, stop calling
here and stop pestering my son." At first Capote
thought Andy was just another wacko, and really
tried to avoid him. Eventually they met, and as Andy
steadily gained fame and notoriety, Capote took him
right in as another up-and-coming member of jet-set
society. Certainly they eventually ended up helping
each other play their games. Both were consummate
geniuses at manipulating society. Brilliant at it,
absolutely brilliant.

Truman with Andy Warhol at Studio 54. *(UPI/Corbis-Bettmann)*

BOB COLACELLO Andy Warhol wanted to be Truman. Truman was freaked out by this fanatic fan writing him notes covered in little watercolors of butterflies and angels. "Happy Monday," "Happy Tuesday," "Happy Wednesday," "Happy Thursday," "Happy Friday." Andy would drop them off at Truman's mother's and wait outside the building, hoping to meet Truman. So you could understand how Truman would be freaked out by this. If Andy hadn't become famous, I could imagine him as an autograph seeker on Broadway.

Andy and Truman had a lot in common. Both were geniuses in my opinion. People who are that sensitive, that bright, tend to have this childishness. They tend to retain, to a large degree, childlike qualities. They walk into a room and notice the one thing you're not supposed to notice and that's why they get into trouble. Geniuses are like spoiled brats. They are holy terrors. They are very selfish. They both could be very cold. Like children can be. One minute they love you and the next they don't. Truman liked getting his way. He liked being treated like a star and so did Andy. The two of them (when they were getting along) really fed off each other's stardom. Each made the other feel like a bigger star. If you had both walking down the street, you double the chance of being recognized. They loved that. Someone once came up to the two of them and said, "Wow, *two* living legends! Isn't that great?" Another time, it was raining as they were passing a shop. A man ran out and said, "Truman Capote and Andy Warhol! I have to give you umbrellas!" Andy just loved that. Those cheap umbrellas.

The interesting thing is that Truman wasn't really that interested in Andy Warhol until after "La Côte Basque," until he was forced into exile from high society. I think he saw Warhol and the Factory as an alternative and a way back in, because we did see some of those people of that world, though not Babe Paley and Slim Keith.

Truman's work for *Interview* started off with Andy following him around everywhere—to Dr. Orentreich's, the dermatologist, to his psychiatrist, to the barber, for a massage—and constantly taping him. Truman hated Andy's interviewing because Andy was the sort of person who didn't say much and then all of a sudden, like a child, he'd say something really stupid and throw the whole interview off. It worked well for Andy's own interviews, but it didn't work for

Truman, who had a mind to do a much deeper, more literary kind of thing. So finally Andy said to Truman, "Well, then you should write for us. I'll do your portrait for free if you do a year's worth of interviews."

Well, a portrait, one forty-by-forty-inch silk screen, was worth $25,000. I think Andy agreed to do two. They're quite good. In one Truman had on a yellow fedora and for the other a red one. The backgrounds were white, which Andy rarely did. Truman loved them. We also put Truman on the cover of *Interview*. He liked that one so much that he asked for five hundred copies and wallpapered his extra room at the UN Plaza apartment with them.

When he first said that he'd write for *Interview*, he set all these conditions. The first condition was that nothing could be changed without his permission, not so much as a semicolon or a comma. The feature was to be called "Conversations with Capote." It had to be the first feature in every issue. "Conversations" had to be in black ink and "Capote" had to be in red ink. There could be no advertising whatsoever opposite any of his pages. He was very precise.

We agreed to this. Brigid Berlin would go up to his place and they would sit either in that extra room surrounded by these *Interview* covers of Truman or at the dining-room table, and he would read her what he had written. She would generally tell him how great it was. Sometimes he would give her a choice of words, and she'd say, "Well, that word's better than that word," and he'd make these little fixes.

Actually, there was nothing you ever would want to change about any of them, except toward the last we had a problem—I think it was called "Siamese Twins"—in which Truman interviewed himself. In several instances he puts down "Princess Lee," meaning Lee Radziwill, saying that she was a filly he'd bet on in the fifth, but she'd turned out to be the biggest disappointment of his life. Well, Andy and Fred Hughes said that he couldn't put down Lee in *Interview* since they were rather close to her—we all were. So I had to call him up and say, "Truman, we have one little problem." He said, "I know what it is and I'm not changing a word. That's our agreement; there's no way we're changing anything," and he hung up on me. So I called him back and this went on for a matter of days.

He would scream at me and tell me I was a coward for not standing up to Andy. Finally he gave in and said that we could change it to "Princess Pee." Andy and Fred said no. In the end it became "Princess Zee."

We never knew if Truman actually used a tape recorder. The Marilyn Monroe story he did obviously wasn't tape-recorded. He took it out of his old notebooks or his memory, which was so phenomenal. In my opinion, the Marilyn piece is one of the great masterpieces of journalism. Not to criticize Norman Mailer, but I do think that little Marilyn piece of Truman's created a much more vivid and believable portrait of Marilyn Monroe than his. Truman's piece was much better than *anything* written about Marilyn Monroe—the quintessential actress: someone who is totally insecure, constantly needs the approval of others . . . Do I look good? What should I wear? Every bit of it, every actress I've ever met, spent time offstage with, she's just that to the nth degree. The other great piece is the one about going around with the cleaning lady: "A Day's Work" . . . about those cleaning ladies going from apartment to apartment who know so much about you. They're dusting, they open a drawer. You're not usually there because you don't want to be in their way. It's such a great story and so funny—smoking pot, the people coming home, eating all the chocolate. It's so touching, especially the end, when the cleaning lady is crying about her life, how hard it has been, and her man who'd left her or doesn't work or whatever; he drinks. I was really sorry to see Truman stop doing those pieces. That year he was really productive. He had stayed away from too much drinking, too much cocaine, though he was smoking pot a lot. I remember he told me once that somebody had given him a lot of pot but he didn't know how to roll it. He said, "Can't you send somebody over?" So I asked this friend of mine if he would mind going over to roll some joints for Truman. This friend went over to the UN Plaza. Truman greeted him and set him up in the dining room with all this pot. He rolled a hundred joints and then he thought he'd had it. Truman gave him a one-joint tip and also gave him a pair of evening slippers which he said were his, "especially made for me at Lobb's of London." Except when this friend of mine showed them to me they were very worn-out and you could see the words "Brooks Brothers" coming through on the inside.

Then, within three days, Truman called me again to say, "Could you send this friend of yours back to roll some more joints?" I said, "Truman, he told me he rolled a hundred joints. How could you smoke a hundred joints in three days?" He said, "Well, I shared."

He was very insecure because he hadn't really written much. He needed to have his hand held a lot. He was telling people he'd been writing *Answered Prayers,* but we had the impression that he really wasn't, or hadn't since "La Côte Basque" came out in 1975 and made the big scandal. Most of 1976–78, Truman was bombed and on pills, and in and out of rehab. But in 1979 he turned out ten pieces which were rather good, including *Handcarved Coffins,* which was really of novella length. I think about ten of the fourteen pieces in *Music for Chameleons* are from *Interview.* The funny thing is that once he got it made up into a book and Random House gave him some more money, he went on this big tour and sort of forgot that they were ever done for *Interview.* The year he worked for us he was constantly promoting *Interview.* In every interview he gave, he'd mention the magazine—he'd mention Andy and he'd insist on having copies of *Interview* shipped wherever he was going and he'd give them out. He was the greatest promoter; he really knew how to promote, very much like Andy, of course. But once they were turned into a book, it was like we no longer existed and we hardly saw Truman anymore.

LEE EISENBERG We did have one more professional dealing with him, in 1983, when we were putting together a fiftieth-anniversary issue of *Esquire*—"Fifty Who Made a Difference." The idea was that we would get America's best writers to write about a man or a woman whose work or life or both had had a dramatic impact on America's history from 1933 to 1983. Just about everybody who was anybody in journalism or the literary world agreed to write a piece for that issue. Capote was not well by that time, but said he would write for us. His subject was to be Cole Porter. As the deadline approached, it began to look like a classic Capote publishing adventure: a "you have it, you don't have it; it exists, it doesn't exist;

I've written it, I haven't written it; I haven't written it, you'll love it nonetheless" kind of experience. We were getting very nervous about closing the magazine. So I asked Rust Hills to meet with him on Long Island. He reported that Truman's piece on Cole Porter—were he ever to turn it in—would be very, very scandalous, having to do with frequent visits Porter made to Harlem to indulge in any number of alleged vices. Capote had direct evidence of it, so he said. All this concerned me because, while we weren't trying to write whitewashed biographies of the people we selected, it seemed that we were going to get a piece strictly about deeds that were something less than savory, with little mention of his music. Our problem was solved because Capote decided he wasn't going to write or finish the Cole Porter piece after all. By this point we had another problem. The piece we were expecting on Katharine Hepburn didn't come in. As a last-ditch effort to include Hepburn in the issue, as well as get Capote in it, which was very important to us, we prevailed on him to write about Katharine Hepburn. Which he actually did. He turned in a handwritten manuscript about her, but it was also no less about Dorothy Parker and Tallulah Bankhead. The Bankhead part of it was pretty hair-raising, having to do with an explicit sexual dysfunction that Tallulah suffered from, and supposedly told Capote in a midnight phone call. The Parker vignette was not unkind, but quite frank in terms of Capote's physical assessment of the poor woman. He found her an uninteresting and mournful character. The part on Hepburn was fortunately a wonderful vignette having to do with Truman's casual brushes with her around the East Side. The principal scene was when he ran into her one day as she was raking leaves. It was a literary jewel. That was the last time we published him.

1971—1983

CHAPTER FORTY-TWO   *In Which TC*

Falls on Bad Times .

Truman in Martinique during Carnival, February 1978. *(Joe Petrocik, private collection)*

PEARL KAZIN BELL I believe the slide began because when he finished *In Cold Blood* he didn't feel he could ever match it. It was Eileen Simpson who made this remark to me on Martha's Vineyard one summer. It suddenly struck me that it was very true.

Writers do have a way of realizing when they will not go on, when they will not do the things for which they have become either famous or admired. Dylan Thomas knew when he was in his mid-thirties that he was never going to write the kind of poetry he had written during the war, that it would just be a bad imitation of things he had done before. I think that's one of the reasons he went on drinking—to be done with it.

BOB COLACELLO I'd been told that I was on my way to getting cirrhosis from drinking so much at Studio 54 and doing cocaine—so I was trying not to drink and Brigid Berlin was trying not to drink and Truman was trying not to drink. That kind of brought us closer together. Truman said, "Bob, what we've gotta do is every day you've gotta meet me at the UN Plaza hotel pool and we're going to do a hundred laps." So the first day I got there, Truman was already there and he said, "Where have you been? You're so late—I've already done a hundred laps." I was on time. Obviously he hadn't done anything. So he said, "Okay, I'll do a couple of more laps with you just to keep you company." So we get in the pool and Truman would do this doggy paddle. The whole time saying, "That bitch Liz Smith, did you see what she wrote today?" Everything echoed in the UN Plaza hotel pool, everybody could hear what he's saying. That was the last time we ever did the swimming thing.

BRIGID BERLIN (editor) At the time I tried to get him to AA and he'd go a few times. But he didn't like to do that because so many people stared at him. When Truman would get roaring drunk down at Warhol's Factory in his Mao suit, Andy would egg him on, because he thought he was getting a good tape . . . another tape, and more pages. We'd tape the trip to Dr. Orentreich's, the trip to the gym, the masseuse giving his massage, his masseuse talking to him, that's all on tape, and so are the lunches, the tea parties, and Truman hanging around Andy. It was amusing to see how Andy really felt about tapes. He had taped Liza Minnelli doing her act. Jackie Onassis was in the audience. Now, Jackie doesn't say a word on the tape but Andy lists it as "Liza the Act: Jackie." That's how Andy was. He was so thrilled that she was there in the audience that he lists her actually being on the tape. "Oh, I got Jackie O. today on tape!"

DON BACHARDY *(artist)* When I first heard that Truman was an alcoholic I said it was absolutely impossible. He was so disciplined, so tough by nature, that he would never ever let a habit get the better of him. I couldn't believe it. I just kept hearing more and more and then finally Truman himself told us.

GEORGE CHRISTY We would have lunch occasionally at the Beverly Wilshire Hotel. He would tell me that he was drinking grapefruit juice when it was grapefruit and vodka. He'd sort of fall apart at the seams at the end of lunch. It didn't matter because he was so wonderful. Even when he was stewed, he was still fascinating. He was a very comfortable drunk.

BABS SIMPSON Alcoholics are almost always charming. They have to be, because they have to keep making new friends. They use up the old ones . . . The booze and all that started long before . . . in the very beginning when I first knew him. Everybody drank an awful lot, so nobody thought anything about it. And then when other people began to peter off and get serious, he didn't . . . as far as drinking went.

JAN CUSHING He wore a pith helmet to this rather fancy dinner I gave. He said there were a lot of burglaries going on in Southampton at the time, and there were, and he thought he might scare the burglars off because if they happened to look in, scouting the place, he might look like a policeman at dinner. A sort of built-in guest protection, you know. Then he stood up on his chair and he toasted me. He said something like "Well, to all you superficial jerks who don't appreciate the only nonsuperficial person in the place." He was quite drunk.

ARTHUR GOLD Bobby [Fizdale] and I were in Southampton. Bobby is a marvelous driver, but he just barely scraped the car next to us as we were parking. I looked up and there was Truman sitting in the car, reading a newspaper. I said, "Truman, did you just notice? We grazed a little paint off your car."

"No," said Truman, "I didn't notice, but I'm reading the most *divine* scandal."

Well, he was drunk. He didn't care whether we scratched his car or not. He did say, "I'm going to send you this wonderful African pornography." But he didn't. He was at that point, as they say, "out to lunch."

LESTER PERSKY Right before he got to his house in Sagaponack he was stopped by a police car and arrested for drunk driving. He showed up in court in elegant, bizarre shorts. When he told me what he was going to wear, I said, "How could you possibly do that? Don't do it." He said, "Oh, leave it to me, I know what I'm doing, don't worry, sweetie, don't worry, the judge will love it," or something like that, and of course they hated it. They *hated* it. It was a wonderful attitude, this fairy-tale land his mind inhabited. He accused Jack Knowles of setting up the police, and they stopped talking. They wouldn't talk for a year or two. I said that's absurd, and I spent all this time imploring him, begging, I even have at home a little note that he wrote: "If you can prove that John Knowles did not have me arrested I will give you the rights to *Answered Prayers* free of charge." So they took the car away from him, which was probably the best thing that ever happened, not to him, but to Bridgehampton. Then he couldn't drive for a period of time; he could drink, but not drive. He would have to have people take him everywhere.

WILLIE MORRIS He had on one of those wide-brimmed hats. Jim Jones and I were there sitting at Bobby Van's. He wanted us to come over and talk to him. He talked . . . more or less carried on a monologue for about an hour . . . about his upbringing in the South, about his cousins in Alabama. His mother, who was Miss Alabama. Didn't she commit suicide? Then he started talking about this cousin of his from Alabama, a professional parachutist who was always jumping out of planes. It had the ring of truth. He might have been pulling our leg. The image of the busted-down macho sergeant James Jones and the little fellow with the funny accent from the South. Old macho Jim Jones, who really wasn't macho at all, but looked like it. Jim and I sat there enthralled as Truman unraveled these Balzacian episodes from his upbringing in Alabama. Jim kind of liked him. He was certainly intrigued by him. I'm sure Jim must have admired his prose style, because he was the consummate prose stylist.

BODIE NEILSON Truman made Irwin Shaw rather nervous. I mean, he would always say, "Join us," when Truman appeared at Bobby Van's. But Truman, for one thing, was always rather disheveled. At that point he wandered around in the most unbecoming pajama top. I mean, Jim Jones wore a greasy green jockstrap, a tight-fitting see-through shirt, a pith helmet, plastic sandals, and a cigar. But for some reason it was all right for Jim to dress that way. We all kind of admired Jim's tenacity about the way he undressed. But Truman was out of sync. He would invite himself—suddenly appear—and he'd say, "Oh, you're all here." I mean, as if we had all been waiting for him. I could always see Irwin stiffen. We were all so blatantly, happily heterosexual, but we were also talking about people he wasn't quite sure he knew. He wanted to tell us about Babe or Lee or Jackie or whoever. Irwin didn't like nasty gossip, for openers. Jim Jones would be sort of interested . . . you know, that phrase Philip Rahv used in a movie review: "the fascination of a candied tarantula." Truman did have tarantula quality.

JUDY GREEN It was midsummer. He wore a seersucker suit with nothing underneath, and boots over naked feet, a hat, and sunglasses. I think a lot of the sloppiness in dress was that he was always in a hurry to get where he wanted to be.

ROBERT FIZDALE Rosamond and John Russell were staying with us one weekend and we were invited to Kurt Vonnegut's and Jill Krementz's for lunch. I hadn't seen Truman for a long time, so it was rather a shock to see him. His tongue was like a very old man's, lolling out of his mouth. He seemed very far gone. He wanted to know about everything and tell wicked stories, but there was something Proustianly sad about him, having changed so much.

KURT VONNEGUT Truman suddenly fainted as we went outside for a lunch spread out on this table. All of a sudden his legs gave out and he just happened to be between Michael [Frayn] and me and we caught him. He came around. He was quite used to it. We were not to worry; we were to lay him out. So we did. He started talking about Tic Dolorosa. He said that was an episode. Afterward, we all wondered if he really had had it or not. Tic Dolorosa gives you a very sad countenance, which is why it's called that. Again, I took him home on that occasion. Even though he had fainted, he was adamant that I not drive in the driveway.

JOHN KNOWLES He lost four thousand dollars' worth of cocaine somewhere in the front driveway of my house, we never found it. He got into the house and I said, "Do you want a drink?" Truman took a drink and he began looking around the room, rolling his eyes. I knew that he didn't know where he was—he'd only been in the living room a thousand times—and he looked at me. Either he didn't know who I was, or I was suddenly a very menacing version of myself. A really menacing person. Somehow I got him into bed downstairs in the guestroom. I went upstairs to my room. He fell out of bed a good fifteen times that night. He was very heavy at this time, so I'd hear this crash, usually in the kitchen. I'd come down and get him back to bed. He almost died that night. His breathing became terribly thin, long gasps in his breathing. That was the last time he was ever in my house. I was afraid to have him at home after that. There are spiral staircases and decks. It was physically dangerous for anyone out of control. He was doing ghastly mixings of things.

I began to see less of Truman. I gave a dinner party. Kay Meehan, Truman, couple of other people. Truman began talking in that strange voice uninterruptedly for an hour and a half and no one knew what he was talking about. You couldn't change the subject, you couldn't break in. He would just go on and on and no one knew what he was saying. Well, you begin to see less of someone like that. "We-e . . . ll, nyah . . . Palm Springs . . . we ummm . . . nyah, nyah ridge . . . we tried . . . and then the car . . . nyah . . . nyah . . . mmmnh . . . mmmnh . . ."

He was tormented. He had these depressions and hallucinations. He would see things—robbers—in the apartment, taking the jewels, all the cash he kept around.

He'd go right out of his mind. He induced epilepsy himself. I thought you were born with epilepsy, but you can induce it by abusing your central nervous system with drugs and booze. Truman was an epileptic. Passed out in the lobby of the UN Plaza. Passed out on the road out here in Sagaponack. He was found lying in the road.

When he came back from the clinics he'd be fine, but each time he came back the time period would get shorter. After one of the earliest ones, Silver Hill in Connecticut, he stayed off drinking for months. He was much better, but he was very subdued and kind of depressed. He'd tell me, "I'm going to have dinner with Jack Dunphy. He has his martinis before dinner; he gets more and more brilliant and high-spirited and I'm just sitting there with my iced tea." He just couldn't take that during the day. If he wasn't so high, he bored himself. He saw through people; he would get disillusioned and bored by most of them. So I think he just decided to hell with this, I'm going to be stoned all the time. And die.

GEORGE CHRISTY In New York he often went to Peartree's, which was around the corner from where he lived at 870 UN Plaza. He'd always say, "Let's have lunch"—at eleven. I soon began to realize that the reason he wanted lunch at eleven was to begin drinking. I would say, "I'll get there at twelve." I mean, who can have lunch at eleven? Truman was already there having a drink and enjoying it. Then several more drinks. Martinis.

THOMAS QUINN CURTISS He insulted people, got kicked out of bars, made scandals all over the world.

BOBBY SHORT (*pianist*) I gave up on Truman. He was just another drunk person sitting in my saloon, at the Carlyle Hotel, and I've seen lots of those.

KENNETH JAY LANE He lost the kind of adorableness that he had. One thing was age and the other was fat. He was really getting to look like Peter Lorre. He was becoming quite unattractive, and he didn't seem to like himself. He didn't really want to talk about the people he didn't see any longer. He'd run out of gossip. I mean, if you are a gossip and you're ostracized, what do you gossip about? Very difficult.

JOAN AXELROD It's what is known as compulsive behavior. He was boozing, he was drugging, he was totally out of control. He hated himself, so I think he wanted everybody else to have the same opinion he had of himself. It's not an uncommon thing. In fact, it happens much more frequently than people's talent giving out. People who have a talent have it there always, it's just a question of what they do with it. When Bill Inge killed himself, I remember talking to Truman about the fact that Bill felt he was out of fashion and that he couldn't write another hit play. I said, "That's just not true; Bill has allowed this depression to overwhelm him." He couldn't see anybody, he couldn't talk to anybody, and there are many writers who need that kind of contact in order to be able to write. I don't think gifts go away, they get abused. I certainly don't think Truman's ever went away. Writing's a profession that attracts so many self-destructive people. They all have this great fear that as they get older, they'll get out of touch. And then they all have the fear that they didn't deserve the success to begin with. That was a huge part of Truman's thing.

ELEANOR FRIEDE We always kept the vodka in the freezer. Truman would go into the kitchen, and he'd say, "I'm just getting a Sprite. Do you have any orange juice?" and I'd say, "Yes, darling, it's there." Then I would find that the vodka was gone that afternoon. He said he was not drinking. How can you help anybody that bad? I don't know. We all have our right to walk into the fire, even if we know it burns, don't we? I mean, that's free will.

JOAN AXELROD With people who abuse themselves that badly one was always afraid; you never know at what moment they're going to turn and pull the knife. I remember I came home one day and he was sitting in the living room. I was rather frightened by that. There was help in the house, but I was frightened by the fact that I didn't know he was coming and that he had such easy access. I was aware of the fact that there was a great element of danger involved. Mostly to himself. It was very unsettling. His speech was very slurred; he was huge. He was grotesque in his appearance. He always looked swollen to me. He wanted to talk about Gore. Part of my problem was that Gore was also a very good friend and worked with my husband from time to time. I think that's one of the reasons why Truman was so insistent on staying in touch with me. He always wanted to hear about Gore, just as Gore always wanted to hear about Truman. They thrived on this little *histoire* they had made . . .

NORMAN MAILER The sort of company he kept was part of his destruction. But I don't judge it, because he could have died of some inner-crawling disease ten years earlier if he hadn't had that. Maybe he just didn't have long to live. Maybe his life's a triumph, not a failure. Anyone else with that beginning, that size, those handicaps—*true* handicaps—would have gone under. Most people in Truman's spot don't amount to much. They have sad, old stories. And he pushed right through that. He was a ballsy little guy. But what happened was that those balls got swollen at a certain point and he lost it . . . in the early years he had a wonderful sense of irony about himself. He really knew he was little Truman and he loved it. He loved what he'd gotten away with and what he could do.

PETER BEARD We were on tour with the Rolling Stones. The Stones got a little fed up when he didn't write. Truman's minimum requirement was 2,000 words. We stayed in the same room. Truman lying there in his underwear. This was in 1972, when he started consuming too many pills with the alcohol. He'd line them up on his belly at night, washing down Jack Daniel's and taking these damn pills. He'd lie there and talk. He was always interesting. We had many other journalists on the tour, and they were just cranking out all these incredible articles; every week they would appear in the paper. Truman would say, "They'll be nothing when mine appears. No one'll even remember them." The months ticked by and he never wrote a damn thing. He used to occasionally write a couple of hundred words and he'd read them—just to pretend he was doing something—and they were pretty damn good too. He basically didn't think the Stones were as good as everyone else did; he kept saying, "Sinatra was an artist; the Stones are just entertainers." In essence, he was going over the curve. He was not his old creative self. He was an "in" person with whom to talk. He'd had a lot of very successful Johnny Carson shows, and he realized that the audience responded to him because it was the Johnny Carson show, not because of his writing. I think all of that put together helped him go around the bend. He realized that writing is so much work—it's lonely, isolated work, and that it wasn't worth it. When he could go on the Johnny Carson show and have millions of people respond to him, that ratio of input to result was more satisfying to him.

JAN CUSHING He was drinking more and more. By the time we got back here for coffee he passed out in my guestroom. I did not have a baby at that time. I was not married. Truman ended up staying four days. The building was up in arms. Mr. Capote is in the building! My French cook threatened to quit because he kept pouring cognac on all the food . . . smile . . . and pass out again. So for four days and four nights I had Capote in the guestroom. He wouldn't go home. "I want to stay here. I'm comfortable here. It's so cozy, you know." Finally, the French cook said, "Mr. Capote, there is no more liquor in the house." She had taken all the bottles away.

BRIGID BERLIN One day he called me. "Hello, dear, I don't know, I'm sick, nothing. I need you to come up here right now and bring me something to eat, some milk and eggs." So I went and got him some food at the grocery store near his house, croissants, eggs, juice, and all that stuff. I rang the bell for at least twenty minutes and he didn't answer. Finally he came to the door, slobber all over him, in a blue nightshirt, "I'm so sick." I cooked him some breakfast, and I opened the kitchen cabinet to get a plate and I never saw anything like it in my life. There was one shelf in the kitchen totally filled with pill bottles, with orange warning labels, controlled substances. Every kind of pill you can imagine. I shut the cabinet and shuddered. I went into the bedroom with a tray and I had to feed him. He couldn't lift the fork he was so out of it. He claimed to have the flu. After that I said, "Truman, I'm going to go out to the living room and have a nap there, but I'll stay with you." He said, "My dear, I'm fine, you just go right along now and do what you have to do." He wanted me out of there. I didn't know why. Finally he got up and said, "Oh, the hell with it." He walked to the kitchen, took a bottle of bourbon, poured half of it in the Waring blender with a banana, blended it up, and started drinking. That was the first time I realized how bad it really was.

JANE HOWARD He said, "Now, you must always let me know when you come out to Bridgehampton." So in the fullness of time, of course, I did. I would go out to visit friends and I'd call him up. He'd say, "Oh, darling, I'm taking the dog to have his stomach pumped. This is just a terrible time, but I'm just delighted to hear from you, but . . ."

I tried three or four times and then I thought, "Hey, I get the idea! He doesn't really want to talk to me." I wasn't on his list anymore but not to take it too personally.

GEORGE CHRISTY He told me that he was bored with New York but he didn't know where to go. He complained, "You meet the same hundred and fifty people everywhere, whether you're in Los Angeles or New York or Paris. I guess the reasons I stay in New York are because you can buy a bowl of onion soup at four o'clock in the morning, have a suit made to order in Times Square, if you really need it, at four o'clock in the morning, and you can also buy the sexual favors of a policeman at four o'clock in the morning." I quoted him in my column. Obviously it didn't bother him.

DOMINICK DUNNE I was in California in the movie business. "La Côte Basque" had been published in *Esquire*, and I don't care what anyone says, Truman never truly recovered from the snubs that happened to him after that. At the same time I had a problem in my own life—alcohol and drugs—and I was on a downward spiral in the movie business. During this time we were at a party in Hollywood given by this guy who was up-and-coming, trying to make a name for himself, and it was given in the Los Angeles County Jail. It was attended by what they used to call out there in those days a kind of "B" group party list, wannabes and has-beens. It wasn't the kind of party that Truman was used to at all . . . lots of coke being taken, and he was at his table in one cell, my table was in another, and we kind of looked across and saw each other; he understood that I understood that this wasn't how it used to be; his eyes were very, very sad.

THOMAS QUINN CURTISS I'd read in the paper that Truman had fallen off the stage in Baltimore. I asked Jack Dunphy once, "What is he doing?" He said, "Think of anything a crazy drunk does and he's done it."

JACK DUNPHY *Truman was bad when I got to the apartment. He did not seem to realize that I had just come home from Switzerland. "Do you know me, Truman?" I said to him just now. He looked at me for a long time. "Of course I do. You're Jack," he said then. He appeared here in the library trying to button on a shirt. He said Cocteau had done the pillow on the sofa. I told him that it was the embroidery work of George Platt Lyons. I think he'd picked up a biography of Cocteau in the other room. He cried softly as if over the past, past glory, telling me how he admired me and always had. He was thinking of photographs of himself. Everything he saw made him sad. When I went into the bedroom, I saw he had wet the bed. It may be that's what made him cry. He knows he's mad. He knows I know it. "Something one's thought and thought about," he said. Then he looked at me, rolling his eyes,*

holding back tears. "You know what I mean?" he asked. I said that I
did, my heart breaking. The both of us cried, but as I did not want him
to see me doing it I left him and went into the library where he
followed me.

"You weren't here last night."

"Yes I was, Truman."

MARIA THERESA CAEN The last time he was here in San Francisco
he came to lecture—the Authors and Artists lecture at the Herbst
Auditorium. It was packed. I had been with him in the afternoon
and I hadn't seen him drinking much. I certainly didn't see him
taking pills or anything. We got there and I left him backstage. He
came out to speak and he lost his way very quickly. He was clearly
disoriented. He lost his place, and then he couldn't find it. Then he
turned back another page and started to read an earlier passage, and
lost his place again. I couldn't tell whether he had gotten drunk or
what. It was very sad, and hopeless. An usher came to get me about
ten minutes later because Sydney Goldstein, who started the lecture
series, needed to pull the plug on Truman and wanted me to take
him home. She went out onstage and lied. She said that there had
been a bomb threat and we were going to have to evacuate the
building. She was so classy. She said, "I will be happy to refund your
money." Only three or four people asked for their money back.
Everyone else knew she was lying. She was saying that to save
Truman's face. It was such an amazing experience because people
were in tears. They went out very slowly, very quietly. And I took
Truman back to the hotel. In the car Truman was vague, like he
didn't understand what had happened. Then, within an hour of
being back at the hotel, he was fine. It must have been a reaction to
some medicine. It could have been one drink and a combination of
pills. At that point, he'd had too much booze, too many pills—too
much of too many things—and it was all toxic. Anything could have
set it off.

JOHN RICHARDSON When he was still making sense, he was the
most marvelous companion you could have. He was a joy. Whether
he was being mean or funny or sweet, he put on a marvelous variety

show. Once I saw him when I was walking up Lexington past Mortimer's. There are a lot of bag ladies around there because of the church; they sleep on the church portico. I thought, "What a strange little bag lady." Then I saw it was Truman. He was laden with bags—I suppose, for the bottles. I can't think what else. He was terribly exhausted, small and frail. His voice was very slow. I said, "Come back to my apartment, it's just around the corner, and have a"—I was going to say drink—and then I said, "cup of tea." So at home I sat him down and went to make a cup of tea. By the time I came back, Truman was stealthily coming away from the drink tray. He'd emptied whatever was left of a bottle of scotch. I couldn't get any more sense out of him. Not long after, I was having a late lunch in the Westbury. I saw Truman alone in a dark corner, drinking. Truman came over. He went on and on that he was still obsessed with Babe Paley. He claimed to be in love with Babe. He couldn't get over the fact that she had rejected him and how cruel she was to do it. He was writing a story about her which was to be called *Heliotrope*. As he got drunker, he kept saying, *"Heliotrope, Heliotrope."* I kept trying to get out of him what this was about, but it was all very unclear.

ALAN PRYCE-JONES He was truly in the autumn of his days the very last time I saw him; he suddenly walked right out in the middle of the traffic without looking at all. He was absolutely out. Spaced out. Two or three people rushed forward and saved him from walking in front of a bus. He was walking at random through traffic. He made no sense at all. He didn't know who one was. It was not more than, I should say, two months before the end.

ALAN SCHWARTZ Joe Fox and I, at one point, pulled back into this situation to see if we could turn things around. We got Jack Dunphy. I said, "We've got to get him into Silver Hill. I've made arrangements, Jack. Take him to Silver Hill." Jack said, "I won't take him. I can't take him."

Jack couldn't face it . . . like an old lady, he couldn't face the reality of it anymore. He really wasn't helpful. It wasn't that he didn't want to be. He just couldn't be. Truman finally did it on his own and wrecked his car on the way.

On one occasion when Truman had been in the Southampton hospital, the doctor called me. "Look, Truman gave us your name as someone we can talk to. I don't know if it's ethical, but I think it's my duty to tell you we've just done a CAT scan on Truman, and his brain has shrunk. The physical size of his brain has shrunk."

"What?"

He said, "Often when people are on the kind of drugs and alcohol that he's been on . . . the combination . . . for a long period of time, it actually shrinks their brain."

I asked what could be done. He said, "I don't know that there's anything to be done. If he stopped drinking and taking this stuff today, there is a chance we could have some kind of reversal over a period of time. If he doesn't, he will be dead in six months."

I put down the phone. I telephoned Truman at the UN Plaza, and I said, "Truman, I've got to see you right away."

"What's the matter?" He was very paranoid and suspicious.

"I'm not going to tell you over the phone."

So we made a date to have lunch across the street at the Petit Marmite. They all knew him in there. I went in. He was sitting at his table with a big glass of "orange juice," yakking away . . .

I put my hand on his arm, and I actually started to cry. I mean, tears started coming down. I said, "Truman, you've got to stop. You've got to stop now." I told him what the doctor had told me.

For the first time after all this quackery—how he doesn't drink, he doesn't do this, he's writing his book—he looked at me. "Alan," he said, "let me go. Let me go. I want to go." There's nothing I could say. What was I going to say?

1984

CHAPTER FORTY-THREE   *In Which*

TC Buys a One-Way Ticket to LA

(Jill Krementz)

GEORGE PLIMPTON Joanne Carson's house is set back on a steep
slope, with a very treacherous driveway, just off Sunset Boulevard—
a garden of roses out front, along with a small swimming pool under
the overhanging branches of eucalyptus trees. Joanne said the
temperature of the pool was kept bathtub warm; Truman enjoyed
sitting on the top step, slightly submerged, holding forth by the hour
on summer days. Joanne took me through the house—one-story,
rambling, and with so much foliage backed up against the windows
that it had a wondrous twilight feeling about it . . . like walking along
the floor of a rain forest. Quite romantic and cozy. To help with the
lighting every room had an array of votive candles on tables, on the
flagging, usually in clusters, varied sizes like organ pipes; Joanne told
me that when she and Truman had a party it took a half hour
moving through the rooms to get them all going. Joanne said she
used the candles for parties and when people came over, but
Truman felt that *they* were their best guests. So they always had the
candles lit when they were alone.

As for furnishings . . . an extraordinary blend of wicker, throw
rugs, wall hangings . . . a decor Truman affectionately referred to as
"Tibetan Eclectic." Truman's touch was everywhere. Quite a lot of it
was added after his death because Joanne purchased many of his
personal effects at auction. But then some of it was his own . . . a
string of white Christmas lights he had strung around the headboard
of Joanne's bed to "protect her," as he put it. Indeed, there was so
much Capote memorabilia around that a stranger would surely
assume the two shared the house.

"He sort of moved in on me," Joanne told me.

Always, as Joanne showed me through the rooms, Truman's
memory was evoked. Pointing at a huge wicker chair, she remarked
it was large enough for "one Truman and two Dobermans"; or that a
sepia-brown painting of a Madonna and child was "Truman's
favorite."

At the far end of the house was Truman's bedroom—really a
shrine to his memory, kept pretty much as it was when he came to
stay. Two large piñatas hung from the ceiling just off the canopied
four-poster bed. On the bedside table was a collection of candies
Truman liked—a package of Snickers, a packet of oatmeal and

raisins, Twix caramels, a round tin box of licorice comfits. (I kept notes.) A dish of rose petals. Another of seashells. A silver ice bucket. Paperweights. An overstuffed teddy bear wearing a red sweater with the words "I love you" across the front. Joanne said it was a gift from Marilyn Monroe. Two throw pillows—one a gift from Truman to Joanne with the embroidered message: "It was chance that made us meet but heart that made us friends" and the other from Joanne to Truman with the words "If life is a stage I'd like better lighting!"

We walked back through the house to a little room at the opposite end. Joanne referred to it as Truman's "writing room." She said he liked it because it was quiet, next to the kitchen and food. It was here that he died.

ELEANOR FRIEDE Jack Dunphy told me, "When I saw that room where he died, I could have killed her, because"—and he was almost weeping, looking the other way—he said, "you know how much Truman loved beauty; there wasn't one beautiful thing in that room, it was just a nasty little room where she hid him away, a nasty little room behind the kitchen, which is where you put the maid."

GEORGE PLIMPTON By the time of my visit that room was decorated with quite a lot of stuff from the auction—among other things a large papier-mâché parrot perched in a ring that once hung in the United Nations apartment. Framed photos of family members, one of his mother, and next to it a gent Joanne said was Truman's great-grandfather. A framed Milt Green poster print of Judy Garland. A lamp shaped like a goose with a lightbulb inside. A half-deflated party balloon . . . and I wondered vaguely if it contained Truman's breath.

The bathroom closet still had Truman's stuff on its shelves . . . twenty pill containers (I counted them), a shaving brush, five toothbrushes, three packages of Bic shavers. I picked up a pill container and rattled it. His name was on the prescription slip attached to the bottle. Sort of spooky. I half expected him to turn up at the bathroom door behind me and in his high querulous voice ask what the hell I was doing rattling his pills . . .

JOANNE CARSON This is a very quiet house, it's very secluded, it's very private, it's not a house that people drop into. So when he was here it was almost like two children in the house with the parents away. Most of the time we'd spend in the house together. We had dinner parties, pool parties, but it was only when Truman invited them. I didn't invite people when Truman was here. When Truman was here, I put my answer phone on and I was not available to anybody, because my time was so precious. I would rather be with him than anybody else in the world.

He would come here to get healthy. He'd drink lots of carrot juice, because I'm a nutritionist—one of my Ph.D.s is in nutrition and physiology. So he'd work out in the pool, which was always heated for him. He exercised, he'd drink carrot juice, he would not drink, though I had alcohol all over the house.

This was, as he called it, his "safe place." This was the one place he could come to no matter what. Jack would always go away to Switzerland for Christmas; then Truman would come here. He didn't want to be alone for Christmas.

The last ten years I kind of shut the house down and kind of kept it very private for him. If he didn't want to see anybody, he didn't have to. He really came here to work, to write, to get healthy. A lot of times we would fall asleep at night on my huge king-sized bed in front of the television set. In the morning he would go out and get the newspaper, climb back in bed to read it and rattle it to wake me up and say it's time for breakfast. I would fix him breakfast and then we would go for a swim. He would write until lunch. Then he would take a nap from about two to three and then a swim or sit in the pool till about four or five. Then he would work until dinner and then watch television or read or sit in front of the fireplace and talk and we'd just spend the evening together. He would read me what he had written during the day. He trusted me. These were wonderful things he would do. He'd go to a kite store and buy assembly kits, and he'd sit in the living room and put these kites together. I took a bit of exception when he tore up one of my good sheets for kite tails. I've always believed you shouldn't get attached to material things, but I said, "Truman, those are my *French* sheets, those are the ones I got from Paris." He said, "I know, I picked them out for you." He felt he was entitled to cut them up because he knew he could get me more. Truman had no fear in this house of doing whatever he wanted because he knew it was all right with me. Other people complained that he cut up their good art books for his collage-box project. I had hundred-dollar art books that Truman went through and cut pictures out of that he wanted, but to me, there was nothing more important than Truman. If he wanted to cut up an art book for a collage box, fine.

Sometimes we'd get in the car and we would just start driving somewhere, having no place in mind, to go to lunch. It would depend on how we felt. Once we went to Santa Barbara for lunch. There's also a place up there that's very famous for making split-pea soup. It's a day's drive.

We used to go to Malibu and fly our kites. Then one day he decided it was too long a drive and we could fly them right off of here in my front yard, because we had enough room to run to get them going. One day we were flying kites about five-thirty in the afternoon, heavy traffic down on Sunset Boulevard, down the hill from the house, and his kite took a nosedive and hit a Mercedes on the far side of the street. Truman dropped his string and ran into the house to hide in the bedroom. He shouted, "We've got to get out of here!" So I dropped my string and ran too. We didn't do that again. But he loved to fly kites.

We would go on these marvelous imaginary adventures. He'd call me from New York and say, "Tomorrow we're going to Paris." I would pick him up at the airport; we would come home, I would put my answer phone on, and cancel anything I had for the next day, and when I would wake up in the morning he would bring in a tray with croissants and sugar cubes from the Ritz Hotel and little jars of marmalade from the Hotel Crillon, which of course he'd lifted. Then we'd take out books from the Rodin Museum, books from the Louvre, and we'd take a trip there. "Now we're going to have lunch," he'd say; he'd pick a restaurant and we'd have a French-style cuisine here to match, and so we would spend a whole day in Paris without moving. We did the same thing with China. We went to Spain; we went to Mexico, Italy, and England. For the China trip he brought these little painted, earthenware medicine jars. We'd have Chinese food. We'd sit by the fireplace on the floor to have dinner, and then we'd look at the maps of China. He'd say, "Today, we're going to Shanghai. And here's what we're going to see." We would look through the books he'd brought. I don't know how he did it. He spent months putting these things together before we'd go on a "trip." China was very important to him. It was the only country he hadn't actually been to.

Anyway, that last week Truman called me—very upset—and said, "I don't know what's happening to me, my body is giving up on me." He said, "I didn't take any drugs, I didn't have anything to drink, but I woke up this morning and I was so sick that Jack took me to the hospital at Southampton." He said, "I want to fly out there now." It was an emergency kind of feeling. He said, "Call and make reservations." I asked, "American Airlines?" "No, I'm going to fly MGM Grand." That surprised me, because he'd always flown on American Airlines. MGM was very expensive at that time. Three times as much as American would have cost. I said, "Open return?" He said, "No, just one way." Again a surprise. In the twelve years he'd been to my house, he'd always bought an open-ended ticket. His reasoning was that he might stay longer than he thought, he didn't know when he was going back . . . I said if you don't want to go back, you can always cash it in and get the money back. No, he said, he just wanted a one-way ticket.

Joe Petrocik and Myron Clement drove him to the airport. They told me when they drove him in they knew he was going to die. Joe told me, "I knew that was the last time I'd ever see Truman."

I always called Jack Dunphy when Truman got settled in, because Jack invariably wanted to know that he got here safely. Truman arrived at noon on Thursday. On Saturday morning Truman died. I called Jack at twelve, which is the time I usually call him. And I said, "Jack, it's Jo," and he said, "Truman's dead, isn't he?" So he knew too. All these people knew . . . it was a very powerful thing that everybody felt.

On Thursday when he arrived, Truman was very pale. He said the driver from the airport had got lost for two hours, and he had become absolutely hysterical about that. It was very important that he get here. That night he wanted scrambled eggs, cottage cheese, and tomatoes, and bread pudding for dessert. So I made that for him, and we sat in the kitchen and talked, and he seemed to feel better. But he looked tired. So that night he went to bed early, and I put his glass of milk next to his bed . . .

Friday morning he was up before I was. He was his normal cheerful self. I made him breakfast. We were sitting here—he always had breakfast on a tray—and he was dressed in his bathing suit, ready to go outside and swim. We were talking about his birthday and my birthday: who we were inviting, what plans I'd made. He said, "Well, what would you like for your birthday?" I said, "Truman, I just want you to write. If you're writing, I'm happy." He said, "I'll write you something for your birthday present." He chose a pen and went outside. Normally he swam after breakfast, but this time he went outside and started writing. I took lunch out to him: his favorite lunch, cracked crab and mayonnaise. The story he was writing was called "Remembering Willa Cather." It's about three-quarters finished, I would imagine. I still have it. It's extremely good. It shows what Truman does in a first draft. There are about seventeen handwritten pages. He had borrowed one of the notebooks from my desk, a blank one, and taken it outside and started writing.

He wrote for four hours. Then we had an incredibly lengthy conversation. I remember because it was one of those warm afternoons when it feels so good to sit in the pool, and it was peaceful and quiet and reflective, and he looked at me with such intensity. We came into the house and we had an early dinner: scrambled eggs, cottage cheese, and tomatoes again.

Every Christmas I gave a gift to my friends of one of his books, which he would autograph. He said, "Tonight I'm going to autograph your books for Christmas." I said, "Truman, it's August." He said, "I'm going to get books sent out here, but meanwhile I'll autograph the ones you have." He said, "Mark the ones that are very special for people who look out for you when I'm not here." I thought that was a little odd. When he ran out of books he took his little notepad and he wrote notes. When I asked, "Why do that?" He said, "You can put them in the books." I said, "But, Truman, I'll call Monday and we'll get more books from the publisher." He replied, "No, this way I don't have to think about it."

At some point I fell asleep, but before I did, Truman said he wanted to swim early in the morning, at seven or eight. When I woke up I was on top of the covers and Truman had put a blanket over me. I remember looking on my nightstand. He had taken the blue notebook he was writing in and it was face-down next to me. It was still dark, the beginning of morning. I thought, "I really should go back to sleep because it's so early." Yet something was bothering me and I couldn't fall back asleep; I tried. "Well," I thought, "maybe if Truman is up we'll go swimming." I got up and went into Truman's bedroom. He was up, and it looked like he was trying to pull on his bathing suit, trying to get the shorts over his hips. I pulled them up, and he sat down very quickly; he looked the color of paper: just white. I said, "Truman, what's wrong?" He said, "I don't know, I feel very fragile." Which was a strange word for him to use. I said, "You're going to get chilled." I put on his blue T-shirt, and I said, "Why don't you stay here and let me bring breakfast for you?" He reached up and took my hand with the strongest grip I've ever felt in my life, and he said, "No, sit here and talk with me." I said, "Don't you want breakfast? We can't swim without breakfast." He said, "No, just stay here and talk." I took his pulse, and it was very fluttery and very weak. I thought it strange that he wouldn't let me go to the kitchen to get a cup of tea, a glass of milk, nothing. I said, "Truman, your pulse doesn't feel very good. Have you taken any drugs?" "No." "Have you had anything to drink?" "No." "Well then, what has happened?" He said, "I think I'm dying." I said, "Truman, don't you dare. You die, and I'll never speak to you again." We both laughed. It was one of those conversational kind of things; we were kidding about it, because if someone's really dying, they're not going to say to you, "I think I'm dying." So the minute he said that I said to myself, "Well, he's probably fine." We talked for hours, about his mother, about his childhood, about Jack.

Then his pulse got worse again, and I said, "Truman, I really don't like this, let me call the paramedics." He grabbed hold of me again and said, "No. No paramedics, no doctors. If you truly love me you will let me go." I said, "What do you mean, let you go?" He said,

"Just let whatever is going to happen, happen. I'm tired. I don't want any more hospitals, any more doctors, any more IVs . . . I'm very, very tired, I just want to go in peace." I said, "Truman, you can't do that. I'm a doctor. If I let that happen, I'll get into a lot of trouble." And he sat up and looked at me. He said, "Well, dummy, don't tell them!" So then I thought, "Well, he's having fun with me again."

We continued talking and laughing and going over old times. He started to get pale again, and his pulse—which I had my hand on all through this—started fluttering again. For some reason I started to cry, because there was the real possibility that he *was* dying. I said, "Truman, I just can't let you do this. I can't deal with this." And that's when he said, "If you can't deal with it, just think of me as going to China. There's no phone or mail service there."

He said, "I'm cold, hold me." He had a blanket over him, but I put my arms around him, and he was half sitting, and I was sobbing so hard, and he was talking, but very softly, and I was crying, and telling him how much I loved him, how much he meant to me, and how he would always be in my heart, and he said, "Mama." He said it three times, and I was holding him, and kind of rocking him. I said, "It's okay, it's going to be fine, it's going to be fine . . ." And because I was rocking him, and telling him it was going to be okay for the longest time, I actually don't know when he went. My cheek was against his cheek, and I didn't realize it until the temperature started to change on my cheek. I realized that there wasn't any warmth radiating from him. I knew he was not there.

I remembered something that I'd read somewhere, or that someone told me, about the spirit leaving the body: that it doesn't leave instantly but needs time to get away before somebody tampers with the body. I was conscious of holding him for as long as I could. It had to be quite some time. Then I called a friend of mine, my very closest friend, Peter Eliadees, who is a stock-market analyst . . . Truman loved him. He would come up when Truman was here to play the piano and sing and do all Truman's requests: it was our private cocktail lounge. We would sit here around the piano on stools, and we'd put a dollar in the fishbowl. I called Peter, and I said, "Peter, Truman's passed away." He asked, "Who'd you call?" I said, "Nobody." He said, "I think you'd better call the paramedics." I said, "But he's already dead." He said, "Don't take a chance." So I called the paramedics and said, "I think someone has just died, I'm not sure," and decided at that point—based on what Truman said about not telling anybody—to say that when I came into the room at twelve o'clock he wasn't there anymore.

There were police cars up here, paramedics, police all over the place. There was one very funny thing that happened. I had forgotten that I had a hairdressing appointment with Julius. Julius had always wanted to meet Truman. Julius is Nancy Reagan's hairdresser; we call him the First Hairdresser. But they kept missing each other. So this one day he was going to come up to do my hair and then meet Truman. At the White House he was used to police cars everywhere, so he drove up right through the police barricade. He came in the door; he says, "I'm here, where's Truman?" I said, "Julius, Truman's gone." He said, "That's okay, I'll be here for two hours doing your hair; what time will he be back?" Peter Eliadees said, "He's gone, gone," very seriously. Then Julius saw the policemen, and the tears streaming down my face, and he said, "Oh my God."

I forgot about Cinnamon, the Doberman. When Truman was in the house she stayed with him always. Never left his sight. Cinnamon would follow him through the house to his bedroom; if he was writing, Cinnamon would sit under his feet. They had a great love affair. He always called her "the madam of the house." He'd arrive and say, "Where's the madam of the house?" I'd say, "She's outside chasing squirrels." The morning he died she was curled up at the foot of the couch; when I left the room she stayed. Now here is a Doberman attack-trained not to let anybody in this house and yet, when they moved the glass table and put Truman on the floor to try artificial respiration, Cinnamon was just curled up at the bottom of the bed watching. She never barked, which is very unusual. It's like she must have sensed that he needed help. When they brought the gurney in and put Truman on it, she then got off the couch and followed the gurney all the way out of the house. Cinnamon sat in the driveway until they backed out and left and kept sitting there until, finally, we had to go out and put a leash on her to bring her back.

LESTER PERSKY She called me at about one o'clock her time. Her first words were: "Lester"—her voice was terrible—"we lost Truman." I said, "What do you mean we lost Truman?" She said, "We lost Truman." I said, "Where'd he go?" I mean, this is someone whom I'd had two dinners with just that week. I said, "What happened?" She said, "Oh, I woke him up and tried to get him up to breakfast, he was too tired. Then he said he wanted to go to sleep and when I went to wake him at noon, I couldn't wake him." I said, "Did you call a doctor?"

JOANNE CARSON Legally, I don't know what problems it causes if you don't deliberately try to seek help for somebody when they're in a situation like that. But because I loved Truman, I had to respect his wishes. If Truman wanted to die, I could not take the responsibility of forcing him to go to a hospital and have his life saved if he didn't want it saved; it's his life, it's not mine. So when the policeman said, "When did you find out?" I said, "I got up in the morning and went in—we were supposed to go for a swim—and he wasn't feeling well. So we didn't go for a swim. Then I came back at noon and he was gone."

It wasn't until a few days later, when all the publicity hit that he had died in my home, the police questioning me, that I thought, "My God, am I in trouble?" I didn't know what my legal ramifications were, so I called Alan Schwartz and told him the story. He said, "I would have done exactly the same thing." Truman had been very specific, saying, "If you love me, if you *really, really* love me, you will let me go. I don't want any more IVs, I don't want any more hospitals, no more paramedics, no more doctors. I don't want to do that anymore. I'm tired."

1984

CHAPTER FORTY-FOUR *In Which*

Mourners, Some of Dubious Note, Attend

Services for TC at the Westwood Mortuary

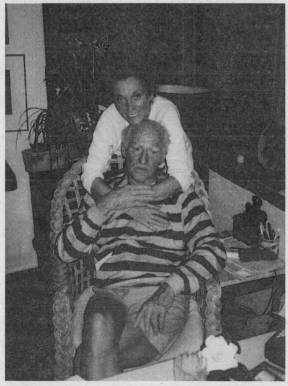

Joanne Carson and Jack Dunphy at Joanne's house after the service.
(Joe Petrocik, private collection)

GORE VIDAL Jason Epstein at Random House told me the news about Truman's death over the phone. I was here in Ravello. I said, "Good career move." I said nothing to the press. But Jason chattered. I was much quoted. I did send a message to Johnny Carson: "You know, John, I know how upset you must be by Joanne's publicity coup in having Capote die in her house. Out of friendship to you, I promise I'll die in yours." Joan Rivers told me she and Carson spent hours trying to get that on the air . . . how they could do it without being in bad taste. Happily for me, they never were able to.

JOHN GREGORY DUNNE (*writer*) Joan and I knew him only very slightly, which is why our going to the funeral was in a way so piquant. We would see him at a party and he'd say hello. Or in a restaurant. Again, very, very slightly. The night before the funeral we got a call from Carol Marcus Matthau, who asked, "Are you going to go to Truman's funeral?" We said no, we hadn't planned to. She said, "Could you as a favor to Truman go to the funeral? It's going to be at the Westwood Mortuary." It's the most expensive cemetery in Los Angeles, because it is prime Westwood real estate, completely surrounded by high-rises. It's the place where Marilyn Monroe is buried. Natalie Wood. Nora Kaye. Big-time Hollywood does not go to Forest Lawn.

BRIGID BERLIN Andy didn't go to Truman's funeral. Andy didn't go to funerals. Andy's thought about dying was "They went uptown to Bloomingdale's and they never came back. They went shopping."

JOANNE CARSON Truman and I used to go to the Westwood Mortuary and put flowers at Marilyn Monroe's crypt and also at Natalie Wood's burial plot. We would talk to Marilyn and Natalie. I mean, you know, we would take flowers to them and he'd say a little prayer. He'd say, "You are still in my heart; I miss you; I hope you're happy." That kind of thing. I thought that would be a good place for Truman because he would be with his friends.

JOHN GREGORY DUNNE The funeral was at noon. Joan and I got there at eleven-thirty. It was hotter than the hinges of hell even though it was late November or December—that kind of Santa Ana hot with that bright sun that bores right through you. We were the first two people to actually enter the chapel. There were television cameras outside. You had to go past the TV people and the paparazzi. We sat in the very back row. People began coming in. It was then that we realized why Carol had asked us to come. It was because Abe Lastfogel had died. Abe Lastfogel was chairman of the board of the William Morris Agency. Chairman emeritus, he was eighty-five. His service was the same day at approximately the same time as Truman's. Truman got the wives of the movie stars. The movie stars went to Abe Lastfogel's funeral. Truman got Carol Marcus Matthau. Walter Matthau went to Abe Lastfogel's. Felicia Lemmon was at Truman's, Jack at Abe's. That evening on TV you saw Jack, Walter, and so on wearing yarmulkes. But the wives came to Truman's. The first speaker was Robert Blake, who had been in the movie of *In Cold Blood*. The second speaker was Artie Deutsch. I couldn't figure out what the hell he was doing there, except that he lives in Palm Springs. The third was Alan Schwartz, Truman's lawyer, which was reasonable. Then, from out of left field, Artie Shaw. The fifth speaker was Joanne Carson. Christopher Isherwood was last, I think. So the speakers got up and it was as it always is at funerals: "What Truman Meant to Me," the "me" being more important than Truman.

JOAN DIDION *(writer)* There was always that thing about my first scene with Truman.

JOHN GREGORY DUNNE Yes. My first scene with Truman. Bobby Blake just went on interminably . . . about Truman calling him "Bobby B." And through every career crisis. It was endless. I thought he'd never get off. Artie Deutsch got up and said, "I suppose Truman's life hit its apex with his party, and from then on it was downhill." I nudged Joan, and I said, "Scratch Artie Deutsch from speaking at my funeral." Alan Schwartz was very nice and very brief. Then, Artie Shaw. He got up and he said, "I'm not quite sure why

I'm here. My relationship with Truman was painless at best, and anyway I haven't seen him in almost ten years." Then he went on to talk about Duke Ellington's funeral. It went on and on and on. Duke Ellington's funeral.

JOAN DIDION We were watching and suddenly a glaze came over Artie's face and he realized he was far afield. So he got a grip on himself, and he said, "And many of the same lessons apply. These were some of the same thoughts that were in my mind today!"

JOE FOX The eulogies were very peculiar. Robert Blake, who played Perry, gave one, which was egomaniacal. Wasn't about Truman at all. Artie Shaw, for some reason, gave a eulogy. He rambled on. I think he'd had a little too much to drink. His only good line was: "Truman died of everything. He died of life, from living a full one."

JOHN GREGORY DUNNE This thing was a fucking nightmare. Absolute nightmare. Then Joanne Carson got up with great rivulets of mascara coming down, like a couple of rivers, and she read from one of the stories, gulping away like people who can't control their tears. Joanne seemed to regard him as her passport into another life. It seemed as if it never would end. Boiling hot. There's a lot of glass in the Westwood Mortuary, so you could look out at the paparazzi shooting in with their cameras. There was a casket there in the center aisle. The last person who spoke was Christopher Isherwood. Christopher had snoozed through most of the service and had thought that it had gone on so long that he wasn't going to be called. Don Bachardy said, "You have to get up." And Chris did the most graceful thing of all. He said, "There was one wonderful thing about Truman. He could always make me laugh." He started to laugh, turned around, and sat down. Perfectly graceful and gracious.

CAROL MARCUS MATTHAU I'll never get over it. I'll never get over Armand Deutsch saying that it was very, very sad that a man like Truman, and Truman was a man, that whatever his sexual "things," he was essentially a very brave man. A brilliant writer. He said that the high point of his life was that *party*. Then Christopher

Isherwood—he used to tinkle on the rug at parties—he just got up there and giggled. He said, "Every time I think of Truman, I laugh." And he laughed and laughed. I think he was tinkling in his pants. It was a debacle.

JOHN GREGORY DUNNE And then it was over. People paraded past the casket. I am told that Jack Dunphy threw himself on the casket. We were in the very back of this nondenominational chapel and couldn't tell.

Joe Fox said, "Are you going to go to Joanne Carson's?" I said I'd rather go to the dentist, have a root canal. It was paralyzing hot. In December when it has the bright sun out, it feels like it's drilling a hole in your head. So we just went home.

JOE FOX Most of us went to Joanne Carson's afterward. You had to walk up a hill. A guard and a locked gate at the entrance with a big sign saying: "Beware: Doberman Pinschers." People sitting in the backyard by the swimming pool were having drinks. Joanne led me into the room where Truman had died and said she was never going to touch *anything*. Six months or a year later I was out there and found out that things *hadn't* been touched. The bed had been made, Truman's dressing gown was hanging on the back of the door. She's made that room into a shrine. Anyway, we all sat around. There was a terrible crisis because Jack wanted to have Truman cremated and take his ashes back to New York. The aunts did not. The aunts wanted to take his body back to Alabama. So there was this crisis going on behind this visibly serene wake. Everyone was trying to be on their best manners, while here and there were these hurried little whispering scenes: people on the phone, and Alan Schwartz, who was the literary executor and Truman's lawyer, trying to coax the aunts . . . this undercurrent going on. Finally it was settled in favor of Jack. Truman was cremated and Jack took the ashes to Sagaponack in a bronze book, I think it is still in Jack's bookcase with Truman inside it.

GERALD CLARKE Joanne wanted to bury Truman's ashes out there. I argued strenuously against that because Truman hated California and had no real connections—he really hated it. She wanted his ashes in the Westwood Mortuary, where Marilyn Monroe's ashes are buried.

Jack and I flew back to New York together with them. They were in a brass-bound book, very heavy. I persuaded Jack to watch a movie on the airplane because I thought it would take his mind off things. They were showing *Greystoke,* the new Tarzan with Christopher Lambert. Jack loved it! Ralph Richardson played Tarzan's grandfather. It was one of his last movies, and there was one scene in which he slid down the staircase on a tray like a kid. Wonderful! Jack had never seen a movie on an airplane.

JOANNE CARSON Truman always said that if anything happened to him, he wanted to be cremated. He wanted half of his ashes kept in Los Angeles and half in New York, so he could continue to be bicoastal. So when Truman died, since I had these instructions in a letter from Truman, I took it to the funeral home and they made up two urns. One was in the shape of a brass book with the initials "TC" on it, and the other was in a very little plain brass urn, a "little baby's box" is what they call it. I thought that would be just the thing for Truman. They made these up within a couple of days or so. Jack Dunphy left with Truman's ashes in the brass book. Jack thought he had all of Truman's ashes. I never told him, because, you know, Jack was very upset when Truman died and I didn't want to upset him further. But I also wanted to fulfill Truman's request. Dunphy didn't find out about it until a picture of Truman's bedroom with the urn on the bedside table appeared in *People* magazine. He said there was no way I could have half of Truman's ashes. But if you look at that picture, which shows the urn very clearly, on the urn it indicates that this was partial cremation of Truman Capote. So as a result Jack's not speaking to me.

JOE FOX Jack normally can't say a sentence without interrupting himself or changing the subject, so he goes from point A to point Y to point B to point Z. When he truly focused on something—which was rare—he'd say something and then there'd be a long silence. He was interviewed once on TV about Truman. He said something and then remained silent, just staring at the camera for ten or twenty seconds, which is a very long time on television, his face absolutely immobile, and then a tear would creep out of one eye. And a tear out of the other.

JOAN AXELROD I just really wanted to remember Truman the way he was—a writer—and that's the way I have him. I have him right there on the bookshelf.

1985

CHAPTER FORTY-FIVE *In Which the Mystery of* Answered Prayers *Is Examined*

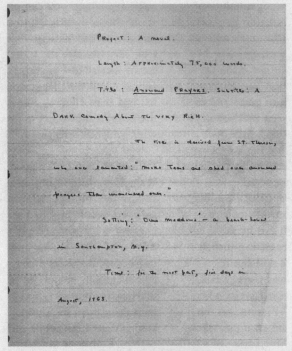

Outline of *Answered Prayers*. What was found of Truman's long-promised Proustian novel (only four chapters) was published by Random House in 1987. *(Truman Capote Papers, The New York Public Library)*

JUDY GREEN His memory was wonderful. He never forgot what a necklace looked like or the kind of wine they served or somebody's cigarette falling off the ashtray and burning the doily. I never spoke with him when he didn't say to me, "I have to go home now and rewrite what I wrote this morning. Or, I can't come over to lunch because I'll be writing all morning." Whether he was actually writing or not, nobody knows. I have a feeling he was. I don't think he just sat there doing nothing, because he couldn't do that and his self-esteem would not allow him to think that he was through as a writer. I can't believe he would say that every day he was writing and correcting and saying that this chapter was done and was fabulous if in fact he wasn't writing. It was too much of a charade and he didn't have to do that with me. He believed his last writings to be his vindication, his chef d'oeuvre: "You wait and they'll see."

He was a firm believer in good writing being rewriting. He told me that all the time. He told me, "Don't be afraid." I said, "What? To hand-carve a coffin?" He said, "Absolutely."

JOE PETROCIK I carry things of Truman's with me, his Kansas driver's license, for example. Don't ask me why. I have little notes from Truman. Epigrams. They were to go into *Answered Prayers* . . . the first at the beginning of the book and the second halfway through. The first was from Camus. "One never says a quarter of what one knows; otherwise, all will collapse. How little one says and they are already screaming." The second was a quote from Marianne Moore. "To be captured / the price of being beautiful / tropical fish go on long journeys / only to end up in a tank." These were the two. He showed these to us in Sag Harbor a year and a half before he died. He said the book was finished. He was so happy it was done. It was a Friday night; we had driven out from New York to Sag Harbor. It was late—about eleven o'clock. He said, "I'm dedicating this book to you guys." I was absolutely amazed. There were so many other people who had really been helpful to him. He never mentioned it again. Never. He read us sections of the book. Actually I was never sure whether or not he was just telling me a story. He had pages in front of him which he was apparently reading. He would look up. He was quite the actor. It was a chapter of the book called "A

Severe Insult to the Brain." I never actually did see the words on paper. When Truman would finish something, let's say "Dazzle," which was one of the stories in *Music for Chameleons,* he would give us the manuscript to read on the Long Island Expressway as we drove out of Sag Harbor. But that was not the case with "A Severe Insult to the Brain."

MYRON CLEMENT (*friend*) Incidentally, "a severe insult to the brain" was on Dylan Thomas's death certificate. Truman referred to Los Angeles as "a severe insult to the brain." He did tell us where it was going to end . . . in Sag Harbor, in a black residential community called Azurest.

ANDREAS BROWN Capote was very ambitious. He didn't want to simply be a successful writer, he wanted to be a great writer—the greatest writer of his time. He was determined. First of all, he believed that he was. He felt that, in terms of craftsmanship, his writing was superior to others', though perhaps he had some doubts about his storehouse of creative imagination.

Maybe he didn't have what Faulkner had, or Tennessee Williams, or Ernest Hemingway. But as a craftsman, a man able to construct a phrase, a sentence, a paragraph, I don't think he had any personal doubt that he was as good as or better than any of them. He was very sensitive and very alert to what the critics were saying. A considerable school of thought in contemporary American criticism at the time concluded that American creative writing had become stagnated—stuck in a kind of groove before, during, and right after World War II—and that there hadn't been any breakthroughs in style or concept. There was a lot being written about that—Trilling, Aldridge, Wilson—and Capote seemed to latch on to that. He was very sensitive to the idea of making a significant stylistic breakthrough. Certainly he talked about it . . . perhaps too much— the idea that he discovered it—this combination of journalism and fiction, bringing it together.

Critics also kept talking about the "socially significant" novel. They weren't harking back to the proletarian novel, but seemed to point to conflict in the various classes of society. They wanted something meaty and substantive.

Well, why not write about those rarefied "social standards" of café society, so far removed from the realities of the middle class and the lower middle class and the driving ambitions of America's capitalist society? At the same time, being very preoccupied with his mother's lifestyle and suicide and asking himself why this happened, what caused it, what relevance does this have to the world I live in today? The two, in my opinion, melded together perfectly. There's the motivation for his prolonged exploration leading to *Answered Prayers*. It was meant to be a scathing indictment of this lifestyle.

So then Capote, like any good researcher (and he certainly was a fine researcher, as we know from *In Cold Blood*), planned his research strategy carefully and set his mind to the challenge of becoming a part of so-called jet-set society, which was a very closed group. You simply don't get invited to the homes and the yachts and the parties of these people unless you have power, money, or glamour, or a combination of those things. So Truman, being a shrewd, clever person, felt "I can handle this." I think it proved much more difficult than he thought. First of all, that lifestyle was so rich and so glamorous, so comfortable and so much fun to be a part of, that Capote got caught up in it. In his new world, Capote found some truly wonderful people. Mrs. William Paley turned out to be an extraordinary woman. Great charm and sophistication, a delight to know, and she soon became a very important person in Capote's life. He found he genuinely liked some of her circle. This created a problem. How was he going to do a massive indictment of the lifestyle of the people he really liked? Immediately it became more complicated than he had anticipated. He continued to pursue it until he started publishing some of it, the little excerpts in *Esquire*.

About the time the first excerpts came out, Mrs. Paley came down with terminal cancer. This threw Capote into a terrible funk. He desperately wanted to go to her, console her, and renew the friendship knowing that she was dying. She refused to see him under any circumstances. This was very hard on Capote. He never recovered from the rejection. That was the greatest loss in this whole creative project, his relationship with Mrs. Paley. Clearly, he was trying to write a Proustian novel. He really wanted to write the inside story on what these people were like and how they lived. Had he been able to keep his private life more stable and control the problem of drugs and alcohol, he might have written an important novel, one of the significant American novels of the twentieth century. He was capable of doing it, the timing was perfect, and he had access to the people.

There are only three possibilities that I can think of regarding the alleged missing manuscript of *Answered Prayers*: (1) Capote never wrote them, (2) Capote wrote them but destroyed them himself because he wasn't satisfied with them, (3) Capote wrote them and somebody took them. I'm inclined to think that he did write at least some of them based on the fact that he read significant excerpts to close friends. Some are even able to basically construct the plot lines of some of those excerpts. So something existed, at least at one time. I lean toward the suspicion that Capote destroyed them himself. He admitted writing much of the later drafts of *Answered Prayers* during some of his most serious drug and alcohol problems and the quality was probably rather uneven. During more sober moments when Capote would sit down with a clear head, say, after he came out of one of his detox programs, and read these manuscripts, he probably found them unsatisfactory. Because he was an absolute perfectionist, he may well have destroyed the manuscripts. He was known to have destroyed major manuscripts early in his career that he wasn't satisfied with. He talked about that: "I tore it up into a million little pieces."

ALAN SCHWARTZ We went to the UN Plaza apartment after Truman died. I was sure we were going to find the manuscript of *Answered Prayers*. We turned the place inside and out. I was absolutely astounded. I thought we were going to find at least half the book because Truman had kept after me. "Tell Joe Fox I've got half the book done. I want half the advance now." I kept renegotiating his contract. Joe kept asking, "Hey, come on. Where's the manuscript? Where's half of it?"

During this time, he kept telling us about *Answered Prayers*. We believed him. He was very articulate about the book. "There's a chapter called 'A Severe Insult to the Brain,' " he'd tell us. "There's a chapter called . . . this is the story so far. I'm halfway through the book. You must think of the book as a series of tails on a kite."

At one point Truman said that John O'Shea had it . . . and had stolen it. He actually instructed me to file suit against O'Shea for the return of these chapters, which I did. He had persuaded me and everybody else that they were in the trunk of O'Shea's car and gone with him to Florida. The upshot of it was that we were more or less persuaded that O'Shea didn't have them. So we didn't pursue the suit. In the midst of this, Truman arranged to blow up John O'Shea's car. Apparently, he wanted to scare him for two reasons: one, so that he'd never bother him again, and two, so that somehow this would force him to redeliver the manuscripts. Truman's version of this was: "Well, one day little Johnny went downstairs, and his car wasn't there. Instead there was a big puddle where a car used to be."

CLAY FELKER He wanted to sell me the last chapter of *Answered Prayers* when I became the editor of *Esquire*. I was willing to pay $35,000. Approximately thirty thousand words. He described it in such detail that whether it existed or not, it was certainly interesting to hear what he was planning. He made a major effort to sell me this thing . . . spending a morning describing it in detail at my house.

I *did* want the story because the other two excerpts from *Answered Prayers* under previous editors had been such a success. So I talked to him about it, and we agreed on the $35,000. But I said, "I want to read the story first." He said I could read it over the weekend. My house was about two miles away from his in Wainscott. That weekend, I rode my bike over and knocked on the door. Finally he answered it. He was very shaky. "Listen, I've got this terrible pain, terrible headache. I've just taken a lot of Percodan and I can't make sense right now, so I'll see you tomorrow."

The next morning he came over while we were having breakfast—just an ordinary breakfast with grapefruit juice. He'd like some of that, he said, and could we put some vodka in it. So I gave him a drink and he proceeded to describe the chapter. It was essentially about Kate McCloud. She is on her bed at 550 Park Avenue one morning talking on the telephone to Jerry Zipkin in Beverly Hills. While she is talking, her lover is going down on her. Zipkin is telling her all the Hollywood, Beverly Hills, Bel Air gossip.

The situation was kind of a dramatic clothesline on which to hang all of these gossip stories Truman had been collecting. He told me that from time to time Kate McCloud and her lover would switch places. Truman wasn't going to tell me the lover's name, but he was a real person . . . a figure he'd used in other stories. Finally, as Truman described it, Zipkin says, "The reason I'm calling you is that I've been calling Maggie all weekend long and I'm worried about her."

He was referring to Margaret Case, who was a well-known society editor. She lived at 550 Park. So over the phone Zipkin says, "Can you go upstairs and knock on the door and find out if she's all right?"

At that point, Kate looks up and sees this body hurtling past the window. She goes to the window and there's Margaret Case, a suicide, down on the pavement below. She goes back to the phone and tells Zipkin, "Well, yes, I *can* tell you."

That was the end of the story, more or less. Capote said, "Everybody will wonder who she is. They won't understand that I took her from another period and placed her in the contemporary scene."

I remember he was wearing a nubby pink sweater and he seemed to be in good shape—jolly and witty and decisive. My stepdaughter was amazed at the amount of grapefruit and vodka he was consuming, though it didn't seem to affect him. I finally asked when I could expect it, said I'd run the whole thing in the magazine.

"I just have to tighten a few screws."

He set the price. I said okay. Nothing could have gotten my editorship off to a better start than running this story. The first *Answered Prayers* stories had been the biggest success *Esquire* had had in recent years. I would have paid anything. He could have asked for $100,000 and I would have considered it.

JOHN RICHARDSON In the evening he would try out stories on us. He didn't actually read us anything out of *Answered Prayers,* but he obviously had a lot of it by heart. And very fascinating it was. Truman was more like a professional storyteller in Marrakesh than a raconteur. In those days he was still so magical and quick-witted.

JAN CUSHING Truman said, "I've got the most *perrr*fect chapter in *Answered Prayers* on Jerry Zipkin. Do you know how the coroner's report often refers to 'a severe injury to the brain'? Well, the title for my chapter on Zipkin is 'A Severe Insult to the Brain.' It begins with my description of him: 'His face was the shape of a bidet.' "

MARELLA AGNELLI He wanted to make a great gesture, all the people to know about it. At that time, he was on a great ego trip. He was preparing this Proustian project. We talked a lot about this book. He said, "You must realize that I am going to do to America what Proust did to France." In a way, I think, with that black-and-white ball he was gathering the characters who were going to be in the novel.

KURT VONNEGUT I don't think he had a high enough opinion of himself to do the Proust thing. There's very little evidence he valued himself very highly. To do a Proustian thing, a Joycean thing, whatever, you have to be very well balanced . . . ballasted . . . have some sense of your own wit.

GORE VIDAL Truman thought Proust accumulated gossip about the aristocracy and made literature out of it. Truman clung to that fantasy. But he had never read Proust. I quizzed him once, rather sharply, on the subject. He was incapable of reading Proust: he didn't have that kind of concentration, and, of course, he had no French or interest in history. He didn't realize that although Proust wrote about a real world, it was not a café society world at all. It was a world, a great world—at least in Proust's eyes and in its own eyes—and he made something extraordinary of it. Truman thought that if you just gossiped about famous people and how Mona Williams, say, started out from a Lexington horse trainer family and how she gets one rich man and then another, you've got a story to tell. But then he didn't even know that world well enough to write about. If you are going to be a writer along the Proustian or, indeed, Jamesian or Louis Auchincloss line, you've got to know your cast. He never really learned anything, which startled me. He could never sort things out. He didn't know the difference between society and café society, a division back in those days and one which a Proust would have spun a glittering web about. He thought everyone was just like him: made up, on the make, malicious.

NORMAN MAILER He had to feel that his social life was swallowing him. Because the warmth, the entertainment, the humor, the creativity he brought to his relations with all these people had to have its reverse side, which is that he'd slowly get to hate them more and more because they swallowed his talent. He was very divided. One half felt, I think, that he had to burn all his bridges. The other half felt, "I am so powerful that I can do whatever I want. I will not injure myself socially with this book because they are all so terrified of me. In fact, I will increase my power." There was always that little Napoleon in Truman. But it turned out to be a double miscalculation. For he didn't understand the true social force of New York—that even he could be eighty-sixed. He didn't understand that he'd really crossed the line—that certain things he wrote could not be forgiven. The way he treated Babe and Bill Paley, for instance, was not going to be forgiven. But then he also misjudged his own resources. He did not have the stuff left to say "A plague on your house" and write the book he could write. That book had probably died in him ten years earlier. One of the things we do in our lives as writers is to keep saving certain books, but when we get to the point where we think we're ready to write them, we no longer can. The material has crumbled into powder. You could write a collective biographical work about all the writers of our generation and how in our separate way each of us got eaten out a little more than we expected, until we couldn't bring off all the things we thought we could.

MARGUERITE YOUNG The *Answered Prayers* stuff was so horrible, so embarrassing. He had such a talent, a very beautiful one . . . a Ronald Firbank delicacy. But he went through a kind of alteration of personality after *In Cold Blood,* and when he decided to give the black-and-white ball to the beautiful people, I think it was a physiological alteration. That's what a friend of mine who is a psychiatrist told me. I asked, "Won't he come back to his original lyric style?"

"*No,* never. He can't. He's no longer the beautiful fairy boy."

He maintained that ethereal talent as long as he could. He wanted to develop beyond his original ground, but he could not. He didn't have that kind of talent. If I had been with him as I was with his early writing, I'd have said, "Stick to your original talent. It is good enough. You don't have to be an epic writer."

I don't think he could have been an epic writer because that requires a formidable strength. It requires an education. Philosophy, theology, psychology, sociology, morality, and an infinite sense of human comedy and tragedy. Like many American writers, he existed in tidy vignettes of limited dimensions. No one could be better at that. But just stringing them together doesn't make an epic. An epic has to have a vast undertow of music and momentum and theology. Joyce knew St. Augustine and Plato and the Church Fathers. Sterne is an amalgam of Hume, Locke, Berkeley . . . Herman Melville had his great conflict between Catholicism and Protestantism.

I don't think Truman ever developed those resources . . . partly because he was a native singer from the South (where folklore, thank God, was on his side) and because he didn't read enough books. He didn't know anything. He was ignorant. He knew his Maupassant. He read his Proust quite late. When I went to Europe with Carson McCullers, she was reading Proust for the first time and reading it through *blue* sunglasses. That's how educated those people were. Newton Arvin felt Truman was a literary talent which should not be spoiled by reading too much. Truman was a ballad singer. But what he did was suddenly to become an admirer of all the people he hated. He parted company with most of the people he loved. Those of us who understood and appreciated his lyric talent rarely saw him—for instance, Leo Lerman or others who had encouraged his talent. It's just tragic, but it's not unusual, is it? He went around with people he really used to hate. At the very last he realized something was gone. If he could just find his way back! I don't think he could have, because at that time he was writing little waves, little wavy lines. Someone saw the manuscript and it was just wavy lines.

LOEL GUINNESS He never told *me* about his Proustian novel. I don't think I'd have understood it, would I? Well, I've never read anything of Proust's and I very much doubt if I ever will. Not the sort of thing that's quite my cup of tea. I think I'd have gone to bed if they started talking about Proust, or tried to.

JOHN KNOWLES Once he came to my house in Nyack, which he adored. Truman named it originally. Tree House. There were trees all around, and after lunch one day Truman came to see it when it was about three-quarters finished. We had to take a stepladder up to the master bedroom, and out onto the deck off it. By this time you're really in the treetops, three stories high. He said, "It's a *tree house!*" I said, "Well, all right, that's the name." I had a bronze sign made. He adored that house. He came there hundreds of times . . . to lie on a couch much longer than he was. He would lie there and after a while he'd get up and go over to the sideboard and make himself his "orange drink"—which had to be pure freshly squeezed orange juice and vodka. His "orange drink"! it sounded so innocuous. One day he had with him what he said was the manuscript for *Answered Prayers*. He started to show it to me. There was a lot of it, much more than has been published. Much more than has ever been found. I said, "Oh, later," which was madness on my part because he was making a great concession by showing me something of a work in progress. He never offered to show it to me again. I'm absolutely certain that he wrote a great deal more of that book and burned it.

Truman was a terrible liar, we all know that. But I can tell his truth from fantasy, and I'm sure he wrote a great deal more of that book than was published. It was hundreds of pages. He had been talking about it for years in a way which I'm sure was authentic. He said, "It's absorbing everything, it's taking in everything."

Then one day at McCarthy's restaurant in Southampton, Truman said to me, "I've been working, working, working, working, and you know, sometimes you look back at your work and you see that it just isn't any good." I think he had come to that point. Whether he was right or wrong about his own work, I don't know. I think he burned hundreds and hundreds of pages because he thought they weren't any good.

DAVID DIAMOND (*composer*) I know he told me that he wanted a section in *Answered Prayers* about a certain house which we all went to on Saturdays back in the sixties—Constance and Kurt Askew's. Everyone, but everyone went in the world of art: writers, painters, musicians. He would remember that we were all there. Even the young Leonard Bernstein. Truman was knocked out by him because Lenny would go to the piano and play the Ravel piano concerto and sing the orchestral parts. Truman was flabbergasted. We all were. Virgil Thomson—that alone could have been a marvelous part, equal to the great receptions at the Verdurins' or Guermantes'. He could have made a marvelous character out of Pavel Tchelitchew. He told me these were things he was planning. I assumed he was writing them and I was one of those stupid people who would always say, "Truman, how's the book getting on? Have you gotten to anything about the Askews? Remember that night when . . . Remember when . . ." "Oh, I'll get around to it. Right now I've got to . . ." So there was always something in the way. But I always thought he was working on it. Because he told me so many things that he planned for the book.

FRANK PERRY There was already talk that maybe *Answered Prayers* was blocked and wasn't happening and he was having trouble writing. I asked him how everything was going and he said, "It's wonderful." We were in his bedroom. He pointed to his worktable and said, "Look at that, finished pages, two and a half inches. It's wonderful."

Later on, being a cynic, I drifted over to riffle through the manuscript. It turned out to be a Missouri bankroll, which is to say, the top three pages had typewriting on them and the rest were blank. It was for show. It wasn't a clean ream of paper, they were work pages. It looked like a manuscript and yet it was blank. What do you say to someone who is a friend . . . ?

BOB COLACELLO I do not believe there is some secret copy of *Answered Prayers* somewhere. I think there are lots of notebooks. I'm sure Truman must have kept extensive notebook-type diaries. What happened to those? Those, I think, are the basis for *Answered Prayers*. Lady Coolbirth's speech must have been a composite of a lot of lunches with Slim Keith and maybe a couple of other people thrown in. Those things had to come out of some notebooks, because there's really no way you can retain such large sections of dialogue. With Brigid Berlin, he dragged out notebooks and read from them to her. Brigid came back to the Factory and told Andy that Truman was reading something to her he said was *Answered Prayers*. Andy said, "Did you tape him?" She said, "No, I didn't tape him. Why should I tape him?" Andy said, "You could have given me the tape and we could have made it into a play." "But, Andy," Brigid said, "I can't do that to Truman. This is his book." He said, "Brigid, who do you work for? You don't work for Truman. I'm paying you." "Andy! You want me to steal Truman's work and then bring it to you and then you're going to call it your goddamn work." He said, "Brigid, you don't understand."

LESTER PERSKY No one was supposed to know he'd finished it. At Truman's request I made a copy and I remember putting it in a black, stiff cardboard binder with a snap. I had it in my apartment. It's disappeared. But there are still two cabinets I haven't opened. I lost the keys. I'm going to go back and break them. It may just be in there.

ALAN SCHWARTZ You should see the correspondence I have with Lester Persky, who said he had Truman's manuscript in a cabinet next to his bed. He finally said, "We pried it open. There's nothing in it. I don't know what happened to it."

I can't think what advantage there'd be to Lester at this stage *not* to deliver it if it was there. So very reluctantly, Joe and I have concluded that either there wasn't any manuscript or if he had written any part of it he destroyed it because he didn't like it. That Truman was forever mendacious was part of what made him such a good fiction writer. His take between reality and fiction sort of got mixed up. He loved secrets. He loved to make you think there were major secrets involved that he would never be able to disclose or only under certain circumstances at the right time, and to you only.

JOANNE CARSON Truman had a sense of timing; he did not want those missing chapters to be found for some time. I know they exist. They're in a safe-deposit box; I had a key to the safe-deposit box, which I gave to Alan Schwartz. But the problem is, there's no number on the key. Truman gave it to me the morning he died.

Always when I would say to him, "I would be very unhappy if anything happened to you, I would be lost without you," he'd say, "Don't worry, nothing's going to happen to me. I have to finish *Answered Prayers* first. When that's finished, then you can worry."

So when it seemed that morning that there was a possibility he was dying, I said to him, "Truman, what happens to *Answered Prayers;* it's not finished yet." He said, "Oh, yes it is." I said, "How will anybody know where or how to find them if something happens to you?" He said, "Don't worry, they will be found when they are ready to be found." I said, "But you know there are a lot of people who say you never finished *Answered Prayers.* If something happens to you and these aren't found, people are not going to be convinced."

I questioned him about it enough to know they are in a safe-deposit box. I asked, "Where? What bank? What city?" He said, "Well, they could be on Long Island, in Manhattan, or they could be in Palm Springs, or maybe they're in San Francisco. Or maybe right here in Los Angeles. Texas, even New Orleans."

I read those three chapters. Very long. One of them was called "The Nigger Queen Kosher Cafe," a place on Long Island. That was the final chapter. Another one was called "Yachts and Things"— about the beautiful people in New York who eat baby vegetables, how people use money like an artist uses oils, using money to create a picture. The other one was called "And Audrey Wilder Sang." It's about Hollywood, the beautiful people of Hollywood and New York, and how they're not so beautiful. There was one vivid scene where a woman is talking on the phone in a business office and somebody jumps off the roof above and goes past and she just continues talking.

JOAN DIDION He was always at work on a story about Hollywood. He was going to call it "And Audrey Wilder Sang."

JOHN GREGORY DUNNE You'd go to parties and there Truman was. This was a period when the morning report on parties would end: ". . . and Audrey Wilder sang." That meant what a wonderful party it had been. "And Audrey Wilder sang!" Actually, at all those parties I went to I only heard Audrey Wilder sing once. We had always heard when we were kids that there were these parties where Judy Garland got up and sang and sang and sang. Well, I never went to one where she sang. But once I heard Audrey Wilder sing. Warren Beatty played the piano, "Blue Moon," that sort of stuff. "Audrey Wilder sang" meant it was really a terrific party. That was Truman's title: "Dot, dot, dot and Audrey Wilder sang."

JOAN DIDION I really wanted him to finish that book. The stuff that came in and that I read at least was unfinished and quite . . . well, not good, but it could have been improved. The book might have worked if it had been more polished.

GEORGE PLIMPTON I saw Alan Schwartz the day after Joanne told me about the key to the safe-deposit box. It wasn't the most important thing on my mind by any means. What was fresh about my talk with Joanne that afternoon was the enchantment of listening to someone who truly couldn't find anything *wrong* to say about Truman, and what's more, was talking about him amidst all the paraphernalia of his life—a kind of Miss Havisham scene, except everything was in place, neat, as if Truman had just gone out shopping and would be back in twenty minutes.

Anyway, I went to see Alan and we talked for a couple of hours about Truman. I mentioned the key at some point, but Alan shook his head and said he couldn't remember anything about a key. I thought, "Well, that's that." But then just as I was leaving for the airport, standing out in the driveway, Alan suddenly said, "You asked me about a key."

ALAN SCHWARTZ Yes, I think there was a key. There was no clue as to what it did unlock, or if it did, what was inside. We could never find the safe-deposit box. There was a key, and we tried to track it everywhere. We couldn't. So we're left with that.

1985

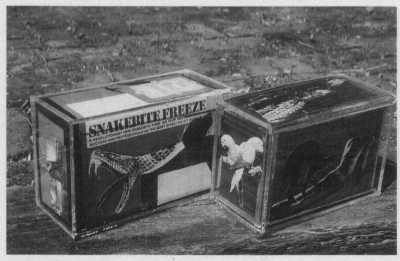

Two of Truman's collage boxes—snakebite kits covered with new and/or vintage photographs, erotic messages, magazine clippings, etc., enclosed in lucite and signed. Seen here (right): "Tombstone Box: With Loving Memory," the gravestones of dead "yag" writers (he hated the word "gay," so he always inverted it); and (at left): "Snake with Blue Tongue." The first is from the collection of Joe Petrocik; the second from the collection of Myron Clement. *(Joe Petrocik, private collection)*

ANDREAS BROWN The Gotham Book Mart is historically a writer's bookstore, and a significant number of writers have come here sooner or later. This goes back to the 1920s, and '30s, when Ezra Pound, T. S. Eliot, Gertrude Stein, James Joyce, D. H. Lawrence, and all the major writers of that era . . . this was their store. Today, it's Norman Mailer, John Updike, Arthur Miller, Tennessee Williams, Samuel Beckett, Saul Bellow, and the new generation. Capote was an infrequent customer, but would occasionally buy a book from us, only rarely stop in and browse. A year or so before his death, he called the bookshop one day and said, "Could I make an appointment to see you?" Because we do a great deal of work with writers in the handling of their literary archives, their manuscripts and things, we assumed that's what Truman wanted to talk about. So we made an appointment and we went to his apartment at the UN Plaza. When we got there, he said, "I want to discuss with you a personal project." We were a little nonplused by that. He said, "This is something that nobody knows about and for the moment I don't want anyone to know about it, so when I tell you about it, it must be confidential." This seemed to us to be a rather surprising request from Capote, who had a very well-known reputation for not keeping confidences. But we gave him our assurance.

He said, "Okay, I will explain. I not only have this apartment in the UN Plaza, but I have a small studio apartment here which is rather secret—people don't know about it: it's where I go when I'm doing my writing. I've had that room for quite some time but now I'm giving it up. I'm moving out of there and I'm bringing my things—typewriter, desk and chair, books and things—back here into the apartment."

Then he said, "There's something else I've been doing in my secret little hideaway. I've been making some art objects, some boxes, in the tradition of Joseph Cornell. This has been a very secret project of mine. Even Jack Dunphy doesn't know about it. Jack's in the country and will be coming back soon and I don't want him to see these. I would like you to store them for me at the Gotham Book Mart Gallery."

I said, "Well, I guess so."

"It's important to me if you do that. Could you take them right away? Today?"

"Well," I said, "I guess I can get some fellows over from the shop with some boxes and we'll come over and get them."

Then he took us into the room off of the living room, which had been converted into a kind of library. In there were these stacks of Plexiglas boxes which contained boxes covered with collage designs. They were rather astonishing. They were snakebite kits covered with different kinds of colored paper, metallic paper, and then applied to that paper collage designs made up from images he had cut from magazines, newspapers, art books to fit the theme of whatever that particular box might be. Occasionally, he would use photographs. On some of the boxes were written comments or aphorisms, little phrases, sometimes very cryptic, sometimes in French. These boxes were a little larger than a Kleenex box. As protective containers, he had designed custom-made clear Plexiglas boxes which were hinged on one side. On one panel of the Plexiglas box, he had his signature in facsimile printed in red, white, or blue enamel. He had made the collage boxes with specific themes, or about particular people or events. A few did not have an obvious theme. He didn't discuss them with us. He was really anxious to pack them up and get them out of there. So we did so, not really knowing why. As often happens, writers ask us to do favors and we do them. My best recollection is Marianne Moore calling the Gotham Book Mart one day to tell us her plumbing wasn't working. She couldn't get a plumber. Was there anyone on staff that could come and fix her plumbing? We sent one of our staff members down with plumbing tools to her apartment in the Village and repaired her sink.

So we brought Capote's material back and I stored it and thought no more about it.

Capote wandered into the shop a few weeks later and said, "Let's go up to the gallery."

Capote looked around the gallery, which is up on the second floor, and said, "This is just going to be perfect for my exhibit." Or something to that effect.

I said, "What exhibit, Mr. Capote?"

"The boxes. We're going to exhibit the boxes here."

"Are we really? What exactly do you have in mind?"

He proceeded to describe the most elaborate kind of exhibit you could possibly imagine. The boxes were to be contained within some kind of a viewing box lined with mirrors so that you could see the different sides. The boxes would stand on pedestals. He had this very elaborate plan.

I stopped him mid-sentence and said, "Mr. Capote, I can't afford to do that kind of installation. That's a very expensive proposition, what you're talking about."

He said, "Don't you worry about all that. It'll all be done and it'll be splendid and all you have to do is provide the space and help promote it."

I asked, "When is this supposed to take place, Mr. Capote?"

"Next year when everything else is going to happen. It's going to be a sensation. Some of the boxes will create scandals and everybody will want one. We'll make a lot of money."

I asked, "What kind of money are you thinking about?"

"Well, I don't know about that. Maybe they'll sell for $5,000 apiece, maybe they'll sell for $500 apiece."

I don't think he'd decided if he wanted them inexpensive so his friends could have first shot at the boxes designed for them, or if he wanted to ask $5,000 a box and see if he could really play Joseph Cornell. Anyway, he was convinced that it would be a big sensation. In retrospect, my suspicion was that he was hoping to have *Answered Prayers* published, Gerald Clarke's much-anticipated biography, and now the exhibit of his collage boxes, and any number of other carefully orchestrated events—all to happen in one year. It would be sort of a Truman Capote festival year. I think he was planning all of these things to come together. I wasn't at all happy with Capote's obvious attempt to manipulate us into exhibiting his boxes. I didn't think it was something we could accomplish as he envisioned it. I turned him down. He wasn't pleased, but he didn't make a scene. He asked if we could continue to store the boxes and we agreed. We never heard from him again. Unfortunately, he died within a year of that time. When he died, I had to contact the estate and tell them I had these boxes.

So I contacted Alan Schwartz, his attorney, and I said, "Alan, this is probably going to be the most peculiar asset you're going to hear about regarding the Capote estate, but I have some thirty snakebite kits covered with collage work . . ." You can realize how strange that sounded to anyone who didn't know what they were. Mr. Schwartz eventually came by, looked at them, and thought they were quite astonishing and peculiar and strange and really didn't know what to think.

Eventually, Mr. Schwartz asked us if we would exhibit and sell the boxes for the estate.

So, with my staff, I started to do a lot of homework. I studied each collage box very carefully, trying to determine what they were all about. They're quite mysterious, for the most part—a lot of very carefully thought-out imagery in each. They're probably going to be the basis for a doctoral dissertation or master's thesis someday, and an interesting one. I went back and reread everything Capote wrote. I discovered, through his writings and his many interviews, that the snake as an image, as a metaphor, was extraordinarily important. He had been bitten by a snake when he was a small child and was very, very ill. Whether he almost died, as he claims, I don't know. Snakes fascinated him as a child. He was terrified of them and at the same time he was attracted to them, as people often are with things that are dangerous or exciting. Capote had that mixed feeling, almost ambivalence, about snakes. His apartment had a number of snake images. He had a stuffed, coiled rattlesnake; a strange beaded snake; he had a very antique coiled copper snake; he had a carved, wooden-jointed snake—all these things in a room. He evidently enjoyed sitting in this room among these images. He had one that was particularly dramatic—a branch of a tree with a snake coiled in it, so it hovered out over him if he sat in the chair underneath. There were photographs of Capote posing with some of these snakes. After all, these are snakebite kits. I had asked Capote, "Where in the world did you get the idea of using them?" He said, "I walked into a little rural store in northern Alabama, way off in the sticks where they need snakebite kits to go off into the swamps. Great stacks of these kits were on the counter of the store and I was quite taken with them."

The kits actually have several snake images on them—a rattlesnake with its mouth open and its fangs showing—part of the pitch to sell the kit. Capote bought two or three cases of these things. He used about thirty for his collage boxes and he must have had another twenty-five of them still in the original packing boxes in the closet of his apartment.

We finally concluded that he saw the snakebite kit as some kind of talisman, a kind of protective charm. By having a Capote box in your home, it would be a kind of protection from the dangers of life, the adversities, symbolized in the poisonous snake. That's perhaps a simplistic explanation, but I think I'm right about that.

Some of them are very negative personal attacks on individuals; some are attacks on attitudes, perhaps reflecting his attitude, for instance, about jet-set society.

JOE PETROCIK The show took place upstairs at the Gotham Book Mart, the boxes laid out on two or three tables with price tags on them. Two or three dozen people were there. Of course, the estate gave some of the boxes to friends—Joe Fox got one. C. Z. Guest, Kate Harrington. Gerald Clarke, Lester Persky. Myron and I each got one—Myron's, in a decorative red satin, has this cat looking around and about to leap up at the backside of a man. Mine has got a title, "Gay Dead Authors" . . . photos of various tombstones—Proust, Wilde, Noel Coward—surrounded by cats, snakes, and owls. Just above the instructions on the snakebite kit (DO NOT PANIC) it reads, "With deepest sympathy." Truman's signature is on the bottom of the box. Actually, I recognized part of the box. One of the photographs I had snapped myself—at Firefly, Noel Coward's place in Jamaica where he is buried. We were shown around by a Jamaican who told us, "The master died in my arms." It's a small house—two grand pianos squeezed into the living room. I remember a large painting. The Jamaican said, "That is the master with some gentlemen in bathing suits at the bottom of a hill." There was a clothing closet with fifty or sixty silk robes hanging in it. I photographed the tombstone. I showed it to Truman. "Mmmmm . . . wouldn't that be an interesting addition to my collection," and he put it in his pocket. He had a sort of reputation for doing that sort of thing . . .

DOTSON RADER Truman had this Joseph Cornell fixation. When he couldn't finish *Answered Prayers* he got like Tennessee Williams. The last few years of his life, Tennessee painted feverishly. He thought his whole new career was going to be as a painter. Tennessee would pop off two or three paintings a day and I'd carry them to the art gallery on Duval Street in Key West where this poor woman would try to sell them. Actually, he got good money—about $1,500 a shot. He signed his paintings "T. Williams." When the writing totally collapsed he could always be the next Gauguin. Truman's were like Cornell boxes. They'd have a little doll on them and a thimble. A lot of snakes. He'd cut pictures out of magazines and paste them on the back and do little scenes. I take Truman's box stuff like I take Norman Mailer's . . . Norman had done a portrait of me. And Kurt Vonnegut draws. Everybody I know draws. I think it's a back-pocket career move possibility. Sort of insurance money.

ANDREAS BROWN I think we had about twenty-five boxes in the exhibit, some marked "The property of . . ." and which were not for sale. There were some partially completed ones, which have an element of mystery about them . . . what they might have been.

After Capote's death we purchased his New York library from the estate. In the apartment we found manila envelopes of things he'd obviously torn from magazines and art books and that he was planning to cut up . . . a collage collection he was using to make the boxes. Apparently, visiting people as a houseguest, or at a party, he'd be in the library going through art books, and was known to tear a page out of a book if it had something that he wanted. Joseph Cornell bought his materials; Capote took them.

The most interesting thing that turned up were uncashed royalty checks. This was speculation on our part, but if he was reading and the phone rang, he would pick up something off his desk to mark his place, and maybe not go back to the book. It was a fair amount of money by the time we got done emptying all that kind of thing out of books. Hundreds and hundreds of dollars. We turned it over to the estate.

Capote's snakes from the apartment were used in the exhibit because they tied in so effectively with the theme of the boxes. He had a dead tree branch with little twigs on it painted white, a snake intertwined in it; it hovered out over a chair. I asked Joe Fox and Alan if we could borrow that from the apartment and put it in the gallery, so that if you walked in, you saw this thing hovering over the first glass cases. It was very dramatic.

October 1, 1994

CHAPTER FORTY-SEVEN   *In Which*

TC and Jack Dunphy Are Reunited in

Crooked Pond

The memorial stone in Bridgehampton, Long Island.
(Joe Petrocik, private collection)

MYRON CLEMENT We had gone out to the funeral with Jack Dunphy. He didn't bring any shoes with him; he was going to the services in his sandals. He didn't have a tie.

JOE PETROCIK That was not surprising. Jack either dressed in the most elegant clothes or he'd wear tank tops, cutoff jeans, and his clumpy sandals and sit in the very first row at the New York City Ballet—the very first row! For Truman's funeral, I selected a tie, a yellow tie, and gave it to him. We came to the services in a limo Joanne Carson had rented. We walked into the chapel expecting a few dozen people to be there. I was amazed to see television cameras outside. And more than anything—because I knew Truman had been cremated the day before—I was not expecting to see a casket. I thought, "My God, what is a casket doing at the altar of this Westwood funeral chapel with nothing in it." After all, Joanne herself had told us she wanted to put the ashes in a vault next to Marilyn Monroe and Natalie Wood—in a wall. In any case, Jack brought Truman's ashes back with him the day after the funeral— only half of them, according to a cockamamie story of Joanne's. A few years later she said that her half had been stolen off a bedside table at a Halloween party. It's all really bizarre.

When he got back to Sagaponack, Jack took all Truman's clothes and put them in a big plastic bag, which he dumped in a bin for the St. Vincent De Paul Society in front of the Bridgehampton shopping center. Just dropped them in there.

The last time we saw him alive was when we drove over to see him at his house in Sagaponack. Nobody was in the house, but we saw his car, so we knew he had to be somewhere. Truman's and his house were very close together. I said to Myron, "How nicely Jack keeps the hedge trimmed and the lawn mowed." We looked around very quietly. I said to Myron, "I wonder if Jack isn't possibly snoozing in Truman's house." We walked up to the kitchen door. I saw Jack sitting at a table with an enormous bowl of berries—strawberries, blueberries, blackberries, all fresh fruit—and he was reading Latin and Greek poets. It was about eleven-thirty on a Sunday morning, He said, "Oh, come in," and said, "I'm not going to offer you anything because it's so good and there's just enough for me."

GERALD CLARKE From the time that Jack Dunphy died in 1992, I had Truman's ashes. They were in a brass container that looked like a book, with the initials "TC" on the front. They had sat on a bookshelf in Jack Dunphy's apartment for several years. When Jack died I thought it was time that Truman's remains be put to rest, and Jack's as well. They loved this part of Long Island, and, at my suggestion, Jack left their houses in Sagaponack to the Nature Conservancy. I wanted a memorial for both of them, and the Nature Conservancy let me choose from three of their preserves. One was an acre or so on the beach, but it was surrounded by houses. Another was Sagg Swamp, but I could already hear jokes about the "Capote and Dunphy Swamp." Then there was this one on Crooked Pond. It's quite beautiful, so still and serene, you wouldn't know you were in the Hamptons. It's really very private. "This is the one," I said. And the Nature Conservancy agreed.

Then I wanted to have a memorial service—there had been no funeral for Jack—and I picked the first Saturday in October. October out here is usually so glorious. The day following the memorial was gorgeous, the day before also had been gorgeous. But that Saturday it poured.

KAREN LERNER (*journalist*) There was no wind but it was very foggy and rainy. We met at a parking lot in Sag Harbor because it was felt we couldn't find our way to Crooked Pond on our own. So there was a bus that took us there. Twenty, twenty-five people, no more. In a kind of yellow school bus. It was sort of a sad turnout.

MYRON CLEMENT Crooked Pond is halfway between Bridgehampton and Sag Harbor on the Sagg Main Road. There, just by a house that is shaped like a pumpkin, is Widow Gavits Road. You go for about a mile—a very rough road, the pavement gone in a lot of places—and about fifty yards beyond a house and kennels is a little path that goes down to the pond. You can drive halfway down that path and then there's a barrier. You have to get out and walk the rest of the way.

JOE PETROCIK Jack's brother was there along with a few relatives. Jack's sister, Fay, who'd suffered a stroke, was in a wheelchair, which had to be guided down this steep, quite muddy path to the pond. She brought a bouquet of roses with her.

KAREN LERNER I walked down to the pond with Joe Fox. We all had umbrellas. Gerald Clarke was walking along with this Saks shopping bag. I wondered, "God, I wonder why he's bringing a *shopping bag*. I wonder what's in there." And Joe said, "Truman."

GERALD CLARKE I read a quote from *Other Voices, Other Rooms* for Truman. It's inscribed on a memorial plaque which is set on a large rock by the pond's edge. Bob Dunphy and I found an appropriate one from Jack's memoir *Dear Genius*. So they're side by side.

KAREN LERNER Gerald dropped Truman's ashes in from a box he must have been carrying in that shopping bag. Jack's nephew Bob shook out his ashes. They walked out to the end of this little six-foot-long dock to do it. When the ashes were dumped in, Truman's were white and Jack's were gray. Joe and I looked at each other. I thought it was kind of sweet, though I don't know what the symbolism might be. In reality, Jack's were less old. Anyway, the two clumps kind of sat there on the pond's surface; it was foggy with just the slightest breeze and they sort of went around.

JOE FOX It was quite striking . . . how much darker Jack's were. There were ducks or geese at the other end of the pond and I remember thinking that something ought to be done to dissipate the ashes—perhaps striking at them with sticks—or the ducks or geese would get them, which wasn't what anybody had in mind.

GERALD CLARKE The quote I found from *Other Voices, Other Rooms* reads: "The brain may take advice, but not the heart, and love having no geography knows no boundaries." Jack's is from *Dear Genius*. "I was grieving the way earth seems to grieve for spring in the dead of winter, but I wasn't afraid, because nothing, I told myself, can take our halcyon days away."

It's a beautiful spot, an ideal resting place after the storms and turbulence.

CHAPTER FORTY-EIGHT *Coda*

GEORGE PLIMPTON Every year during what are called the "proceedings" at the annual meeting of the American Academy and Institute of Arts and Letters, commemorative tributes to members who have died during the year are read. The year after Truman died, James Dickey offered the tribute at a dinner meeting in the Academy Meeting Room.

Dickey was somewhat surprised to be asked (he was invited by letter) since he barely knew Capote. Indeed, his only firm recollection was a chance meeting in New York's Gotham Book Mart at which—as Southerners tend to do—the two talked about relatives: Capote had an aunt "up 'round Buford way."

"Still," Dickey recalls, "I felt, when asked, I ought to pick up the gauntlet, get up there, and try. I worked on it right hard, because I wanted to say some things about Capote that people would *not* have thought about him . . . to go in there along with what everyone *did* think about him."

JAMES DICKEY *(poet)* With certain deaths a double vision sets in among the living; there is no escaping it. When a noted person has just died, there is that gap, that disparity, that possible sameness with regard to what the press, in all its clamorous efforts to summarize, finds fit to say, and a kind of private estimate in the mind of each of us. If the person is someone we knew or admired, or disliked, we are inexorably drawn—or driven—to the press to see how the public summation compares with ours. Speaking for myself, I was deeply shocked and terrified at the death of Truman Capote and, like others, went to the newspapers to see what the world felt about him. I was afraid of what I would find, and I was not mistaken. The journals I read, some of them quoting friends and acquaintances of the deceased, were about a writer of real ability who had produced a best-seller from which a movie was made, and he had ruined himself—his talent along with his health—for money and publicity.

It would be foolish to deny the international-café-society, jet-set, beautiful-people, name-dropping Capote, or to downplay this aspect of his life. If we don't include it, we are not really talking about the person who existed. I was never bothered, myself, by this side of Truman Capote's career—that is, the careerism—but always rather enjoyed from afar the intimations of the fabulous that it contained. If there is any magic in American life, it is to be found where great sums of money are spent in groomed and luxurious settings which exist for exposure and pleasure: a corrupt and debilitating magic, but the only one in which our culture truly believes. Scott Fitzgerald was right, far more perceptive than Hemingway in the famous exchange, when he said that "the very rich are different from you and me." They are, and *how* they are different fills the magazines, the newspapers, the films, and television every day we go into the world that surrounds us.

In regard to this last medium, incidentally, I think of the opportunities that the life and career of Truman Capote could give to the literature of soap opera! Could a man—a young man many took, for years of his adulthood, to be a child—born in the South, product of a broken home, shunted around among relatives in obscure villages, cultivate in secret a literary talent which would bring him into international society, a close acquaintanceship with movie stars, high politicians and their wives, millionaires and millionaire hostesses on four continents? *Could* such a thing happen to a writer, particularly if he were a *good* writer, introspective and poetic in the true rather than the conventional sense? It seems unlikely, and yet something like this happened, and is the only case of its kind. Strange indeed, and unignorable.

As I said, my response to all this was more favorable than not; at least *one* of us had made it! I remember enjoying public photos of Capote, who had written "Miriam" and "The Headless Hawk," disporting with selected friends on the rocks of Taormina, and dancing cheek to cheek with Marilyn Monroe, rich and famous as few writers are—again, a few *good* ones. I lived this part of Capote's existence with considerable vicarious relish, when I was not deviled with envy, a dark shape usually somewhere in the background. To wear a white sequined mask at one's own ball at the Plaza *and* to have written "The Headless Hawk" too, the real and private accomplishment underlying the publicity, the money, and the pleasure! Where else would you find it?

Yet a reaction against the talk-show Capote, the masked-ball Capote, was inevitable, and Capote suffered from it more than he should have had to. The notoriety, the campy put-on quality of some of the episodes, the cattiness, the public fights, the lawsuits—all of those things were regarded by many as evidence of a falling-off, a sellout, a deterioration, a waste, a betrayal, an outrage, a tragedy. But were they? Were they *entirely* so?

Unfulfillment continues in the mind. I cannot help being reminded, for example, of certain parallels between the situations of Truman Capote and Marcel Proust. I am not talking about performance—that would be ridiculous—but of the similar opportunities that both writers had for observing at first hand and at length the crumbling-away, the loss of morale and sense of consequence, the desperate and defiant secret lives, the hyperactive despair and ruinous lack of self-discipline of the monied class of our time: of being highly observant and intelligent witnesses to the Decline of the West itself, spies in the house of Trimalchio. This is, I realize, a lot to charge Truman Capote with having the ability to carry off in any such manner as did Proust; the four published excerpts of his unfinished novel, *Answered Prayers,* are not strong evidence that he had either the capacity or the desire. Yet I continue to be haunted by the undone, the opportunity. Proust's world, various and multilayered, is, even so, limited to a very small segment of the population, and geographically confined to Paris and a few small French villages. In contrast, Capote had the chance to observe the glittering process of decay at work in many places and kinds of situations, many climates, many languages. And he had talent as well, of a different order and scope than Proust's, it is true, but plenty of it just the same. He had the will, when he wanted to use it, and he had the vantage point, an overview of a doomed society that very few have, or have ever had: the Death of the Soul in America, Italy, France, Africa, Russia, all over the place! *What* a death, and what a work of literature might have resulted!

All speculation, indeed, but death brings on and encourages speculation as nothing else can. Could Capote have done something like this? If one surmises that he might have come to attempt it, what would be the factor that caused him to try? The belief in his own talent. Did this exist? It did; indeed it did.

The talent of Truman Capote: that is where we can engage him, all speculation aside. This small childlike individual, this self-styled, self-made, self-taught country boy—what did he teach himself? To concentrate: to close out, and close in: to close with. His writing came, first, from a great and very real interest in many things and people, and then from a peculiar frozen detachment that he practiced as one might practice the piano, or a foot position in ballet. Cultivated in this manner, his powers of absorption in a subject became very nearly absolute, and his memory was already remarkable, particularly in its re-creation of small details. He possessed to an unusual degree this ability to encapsulate himself with his subject, whatever or whoever it might be, so that nothing else existed except him and the other; and then he himself would begin to fade away and words would appear in his place: words concerning the subject, as though it were dictating itself. In the best of his work, this self-canceling solipsism, if this be not too self-contradictory an estimate, amounted to Truman's vision of things, and he could call it into service under any circumstances, and with any person, from Marlon Brando or Isak Dinesen to Bobby Beausoleil in San Quentin or Perry Smith on death row in Kansas. All Truman's work was a result of this power of isolation-with, of concentration and super attention. His journalism, including his so-called nonfiction novels, was made possible by means of it, but I prefer to speak of a deeper, more lasting thing than the pursuit of fact allows, and look, if only momentarily, at what came to Truman in the form of words when he closed not with Marilyn Monroe or Perry Smith, but with himself and his own life: what words then took the place of *him?*

Words standing for one of the purest and most generally felt conditions of our human time, or of any human time: isolation, loneliness, forsakenness, lostness: the lostness that tends to hallucination, dementia, paranoia: "The notion of some infinitely gentle / Infinitely suffering thing," but which also, taking as refuge and resource the imagination, calls another order of being into play, into existence:

"You ever see the snow?"
Rather breathlessly Joel lied and claimed that he most certainly had; it was a pardonable deception, for he had a great yearning to see bona-fide snow; next to owning the Koh-i-noor diamond, that was his ultimate secret wish. Sometimes, on flat boring afternoons, he's squatted on St. Deval Street and daydreamed silent pearly snowclouds into sifting coldly through the boughs of the dry, dirty trees. Snow falling in August and silvering the glassy pavement, the ghostly flakes icing his hair, coating rooftops, changing the grimy old neighborhood into a hushed frozen white wasteland uninhabited except for himself and a menagerie of wonderbeasts: albino antelopes, and ivory-breasted snowbirds; and occasionally there were humans, such fantastic folk as Mr. Mystery, the vaudeville hypnotist, and Lucky Rogers, the movie star, and Madame Veronica, who read fortunes in a Vieux Carré tearoom. "It was one stormy night in Canada that I saw the snow," he said, though the farthest north he'd ever set foot was Richmond, Virginia.

   I find myself returning often to *Other Voices, Other Rooms,* but
more often to the shorter pieces of *The Tree of Night,* and I believe I
do this because I think of Capote's gift as essentially lyrical, poetic:
the stamp-minted event, the scene stunning with rightness and
strangeness, the compressed phrase, the exact yet imaginative word,
the devastating metaphorical aptness, a feeling of concentrated
excess which at the same time gives the effect of being crystalline.
One can say of these stories, like "Miriam" and "Shut a Final Door,"
which in other hands would bear too many resemblances to gothic
movies, with lots of melodrama, props, grotesque stage businesses,
that they are saved by the only quality that can save any writer's
anything: his personal vision, which in Capote's case runs to
unforgettable images of fear, hopelessness, and dream-death: in
addition to cold, also its opposite: airlessness, heat, ripe rot, the
submerged corpse green in the moveless pool.

   It is maybe paradoxical, but not finally so, that such images—
many of his best—of the stultified, the still, the overhot and
overripe come like the others from Truman Capote's lenslike
detachment, and suggest, rather than lushness and softness, things
wrought by the engraver's delicate hammer, the artist working with
otherworldly intensity upon materials from the world, as the
universe makes a snowflake, the most fastidiously created of
artifacts, resulting in a true work of literature, which, unlike the
snowflake, keeps on existing. The sure-handed crystal-making
detachment, the integrity of concentration, the craft of the artist by
means of which the intently human thing is caught, Truman Capote
had, and not just at certain times but at all times. This we
remember, and will keep, for it gave us what of him will stay. Keep
him we will, and from such a belief come these few lines,
something.

Chronology

1924 Truman Streckfus Persons, son of Lillie Mae Faulk Persons and Arch Persons, is born on September 30 in New Orleans, Louisiana.

1930 Sent to live in Monroeville, Alabama, with Lillie Mae's guardian and first cousin, Jennie Faulk, and her sisters Sook and Callie and brother Bud.

1931 Lillie Mae moves to New York, meets Joseph Capote, and divorces Arch Persons.

1932 Lillie Mae marries Joseph Capote. She changes her name unofficially to "Nina."

1933 Truman moves to New York with his mother and enters the fourth grade at Trinity School, at that time an all-boys high episcopal school on the Upper West Side of Manhattan.

1935 Full custody of Truman is granted to his mother. Joseph Capote adopts him, renaming him "Truman Garcia Capote."

1936 Enters St. John's Military Academy, an all-boys military boarding school.

1937 Returns to Trinity School.

1939 The Capotes move to Greenwich, Connecticut. Truman enters Greenwich High School, and falls under the guidance of English teacher Catherine Wood.

1942 The Capotes return to New York City. Truman repeats his senior year and graduates from the Franklin School, a now defunct private school on the Upper West Side.

While still at school he secures part-time employment as a copy boy at *The New Yorker*.

1944 Fired from *The New Yorker* by Harold Ross over an incident involving Robert Frost at the Breadloaf Writers Conference in Vermont. Moves south to stay with various relatives while attempting a novel, *Summer Crossing,* which he never completes.

1945 Rents a room in New Orleans and begins *Other Voices, Other Rooms*. Later that year he moves back to New York.

1945 "Miriam" is published in the June issue of *Mademoiselle* and given an O. Henry Memorial Award in 1946.

1946 Attends Yaddo, the writers and artists' colony in Saratoga Springs, New York, and meets Newton Arvin.

1948 *Other Voices, Other Rooms* is published by Random House in January.

In the fall, Truman meets Jack Dunphy.

1949 *Tree of Night and Other Stories* is published. In February, Truman and Jack depart for Europe, staying until December.

1950 *Local Color* is published. Truman and Jack return to Europe, settling in Taormina, Sicily.

1951 Truman and Jack return from Sicily in August. Truman's second novel, *The Grass Harp*, is published in September.

1952 The stage version of *The Grass Harp*, produced by Saint Subber, opens on Broadway at the Martin Beck Theater.

In April, Truman and Jack return to Europe, where Truman begins work on John Huston's film *Beat the Devil*.

1953 Truman's mother swallows a lethal dose of Seconal and dies on January 4, 1954. Truman returns to New York.

1954 *Beat the Devil* is released.

Musical version of the story "House of Flowers" opens on Broadway at the Alvin Theater.

1955 Truman is introduced to the William S. Paleys at their home in Round Hill, Jamaica.

Joe Capote pleads guilty to charges of forgery and grand larceny, enters Sing Sing Prison (released May 14 1956).

1956 *The Muses Are Heard,* an account of Truman's travels in the Soviet Union with the cast of *Porgy and Bess,* is published, first in two installments in *The New Yorker,* and then in hardcover by Random House.

1957 "The Duke in His Domain," a portrait of Marlon Brando, is published in *The New Yorker.*

1958 *Breakfast at Tiffany's* is published.

1959 Richard Avedon's book of portraits, *Observations,* with text by Truman, is published.

Truman reads in the *New York Times* (November 16) about the murder of the Clutter family in Holcomb, Kansas, and begins research for *In Cold Blood.*

1960 Truman writes a film adaptation of Henry James's *Turn of the Screw.* The film, entitled *The Innocents,* is directed by Jack Clayton and stars Deborah Kerr and Michael Redgrave.

1961 Truman buys a condominium in Verbier, Switzerland.

1963 *The Selected Writings of Truman Capote* is published.

1964 Truman buys a house on Long Island, in Sagaponack, New York. Soon after, he buys the one next door for Jack.

1965 Perry Smith and Dick Hickock, the convicted murderers of the Clutter family, are hanged on April 14. Truman attends the hanging.

In Cold Blood is serialized in *The New Yorker* on September 25, October 2, 9, and 16.

1966 *In Cold Blood* is published in hardcover by Random House.

Truman hosts the black-and-white ball at the Plaza Hotel in New York City in November.

Truman buys a two-bedroom apartment at the UN Plaza on First Avenue and Forty-ninth Street in New York.

1967 Film version of *In Cold Blood* opens, directed by Richard Brooks.

Truman launches Lee Radziwill's acting career, first in *The Philadelphia Story* at the Ivanhoe Theater in Chicago in June, then in the ABC television remake of *Laura*.

1968 *The Thanksgiving Visitor* is published.

Truman buys a house in Palm Springs, California, and makes his first appearance on "The Tonight Show" with Johnny Carson.

1970 Truman meets "the air-conditioning repair man."

1971 Truman writes a film adaptation of *The Great Gatsby,* which is eventually rejected by Paramount.

1972 Truman covers the North American tour of the Rolling Stones with Peter Beard and Jann Wenner for *Rolling Stone* magazine.

1973 Truman meets John O'Shea.

1975 "Mojave," the first excerpt from the unfinished novel *Answered Prayers,* is published in *Esquire* magazine, followed by "La Côte Basque, 1965."

1976 Truman plays the role of Lionel Twain in Neil Simon's film *Murder by Death.*

Two more chapters of *Answered Prayers,* "Unspoiled Monsters" and "Kate McCloud," are published in *Esquire.*

1980 *Music for Chameleons* is published.

1984 Truman dies in the home of Joanne Carson on August 25.

Biographies of Contributors

DANIEL AARON, professor emeritus of English at Harvard University, was a colleague and friend of Newton Arvin's at Smith College.

SLIM AARONS is a photographer known especially for his portraits of high society.

ADOLFO is a designer whose clients have often graced the best-dressed list: the Duchess of Windsor, Claudette Colbert, Betsy Bloomingdale, Nancy Reagan, and Gloria Vanderbilt.

MARELLA AGNELLI worked as a photographer and editor for Condé Nast in Italy. In 1953 she married Gianni Agnelli, the chairman of the board at Fiat S.P.A. Her books include *Gardens of the Italian Villas* and *Il Giardino di Ninfa*.

SHANA ALEXANDER has written for *Life* and *Newsweek*. She was an editor at *McCall's* and a commentator for the TV show *60 Minutes*. Her book *Haunted by Elephants* was published in 1998.

BARBARA ALLEN was a contributing editor and photographer for *Interview* magazine.

STEVEN M. L. ARONSON, a former publisher, is the author of *Hype* and the coauthor of *Savage Grace*. He is writing the biography of Leland Hayward.

LOUIS AUCHINCLOSS is a lawyer and novelist. He has written over forty books, including *The Rector of Justin*.

WILLIAM AVERY is a publicist in New York City.

JOAN AXELROD is married to screenwriter and film producer George Axelrod, who produced *Breakfast at Tiffany's*, as well as such movies as *The Seven-Year Itch* and *The Manchurian Candidate*.

LAUREN BACALL is famous for her roles in *To Have and Have Not, The Big Sleep, Key Largo, How to Marry a Millionaire,* and *Murder on the Orient Express*. She received the Tony Award for Best Actress in a Musical in both 1970 and 1981.

DON BACHARDY, an illustrator and artist, was Christopher Isherwood's companion for many years.

JACK BARR was a Kansas state senator from 1960 to 1968. He is also a banker, rancher, and sculptor.

DR. CLAIRE BAYLES was a professor of chemistry at Alabama Southern Community College in Monroeville, Alabama, who knew Truman as a child.

PETER BEARD is a photographer and adventurer who lives outside of Nairobi, Kenya, at Hog Ranch and in Montauk, New York. He has photographed Africa since 1955.

CHRIS BEARDE is a television producer living in Hollywood. He produced *The Sonny and Cher Comedy Hour.*

PEARL KAZIN BELL is a critic and editor who lives in Cambridge, Massachusetts.

MARISA BERENSON, an actress and a model, is the granddaughter of fashion designer Elsa Schiaparelli. Her films include *Death in Venice, Cabaret,* and *White Hunter, Black Heart.*

CANDICE BERGEN stars in the television show *Murphy Brown,* for which she has won the Emmy Award for Leading Actress in a Comedy Series five times. She was married to the late Louis Malle.

BRIGID BERLIN is a writer living in New York. She was an editor of *Interview* magazine and a chronicler of life at the Warhol Factory.

ELIZABETH BISHOP's first book of poems, *North and South,* was published in 1946. In 1956 she was awarded the Pulitzer Prize for poetry, and in 1970 she won the National Book Award for her *Complete Poems.*

KARL BISSINGER, a photographer, now works for the War Resisters' League as an organizer and fundraiser.

DENISE BOUCHÉ is the widow of the portrait painter and illustrator René Bouché.

PAUL BOWLES, an expatriate author and composer who lives in Tangier, has written a number of books, including *A Distant Episode, Up Above the World, Without Stopping,* and *The Sheltering Sky.*

BEN BRADLEE is the former executive editor of the *Washington Post* and the author most recently of *A Good Life: Newspapering and Other Adventures.*

JOHN MALCOLM BRINNIN is a poet, critic, biographer, and social historian. His books include *Dylan Thomas in America, Sextet: T. S. Eliot, Truman Capote and Others,* and *Truman Capote: Dear Heart, Old Buddy.*

RICHARD BROOKS directed the film version of Truman's *In Cold Blood*. His film credits as a director include *Blackboard Jungle*, *The Professionals*, and *The Happy Ending*.

ANDREAS BROWN is the owner of the Gotham Book Mart in New York City, specializing in literary archives.

CLARENCE BRUNER-SMITH has been associated with New York's Trinity School for seventy years. He has served as head of the English Department, principal of the Upper School, college admissions advisor, and advisor to the school publications.

DORIS BRYNNER is the widow of actor Yul Brynner.

WILLIAM F. BUCKLEY, JR., is editor-at-large of the *National Review*, host of the weekly television show *Firing Line*, and author of many books. His most recent book is *Nearer, My God*.

SUSAN PAYSON BURKE crashed Truman's black-and-white ball in 1966.

HERB CAEN wrote a daily column for the *San Francisco Chronicle* for over fifty years, beginning in 1936, and for the *San Francisco Examiner* from 1950 until 1958. In 1949 he was awarded France's Médaille de la Liberation. His widow, MARIA THERESA, is a literary agent based in San Francisco.

JOE CALDWELL is a playwright and novelist who won the Prix de Rome, awarded by the American Academy of Arts and Letters, in 1980. His most recent novel is *The Uncle from Rome*.

HORTENSE CALISHER is the author of seventeen works of fiction, most recently *Age*, which was published in 1987. She is a former president of the American Academy of Arts and Letters and a former president of PEN.

VIRGINIA CARR is a professor of English at Georgia State University. She is the author of *The Lonely Hunter: A Biography of Carson McCullers*.

JOANNE CARSON was a television hostess for twenty-six years, received a master's degree in psychology, and holds a Ph.D. in nutritional biochemistry and physiology. She is now in private practice in Los Angeles. She was married to Johnny Carson.

JENNINGS FAULK CARTER is Truman's first cousin. He lives in Monroeville, Alabama.

CHRISTOPHER CERF is a Grammy and Emmy Award–winning songwriter and producer and an author of several bestselling books, including *The Official Politically Correct Dictionary and Handbook* (with Henry Beard).

GEORGE CHRISTY writes a thrice-weekly column in the *Hollywood Reporter* and is the author of two books, *All I Could See from Where I Stood*, and *The Los Angeles Underground Gourmet*.

GERALD CLARKE wrote Truman's official biography, *Truman*, and is now working on a biography of Judy Garland.

JACK CLAYTON is a British movie director. He won a short-subject Oscar for *The Bespoke Overcoat* in 1955 and worked on many of Truman's film projects, including *Beat the Devil* and *The Innocents*.

MYRON CLEMENT is a public relations consultant on tourism for France and the French West Indies. He lives in New York City and Sag Harbor.

BOB COLACELLO is a special correspondent for *Vanity Fair*, covering art, fashion, and society. From 1970 to 1983, he was an editor of *Interview* magazine; his memoir of those years, *Holy Terror: Andy Warhol Close Up*, was published in 1990.

THOMAS QUINN CURTISS is a columnist for *The International Herald Tribune* in Paris.

JAN CUSHING lives in New York City and Newport, Rhode Island.

ALVIN DEWEY, the KBI agent in charge of the investigation of the Clutter murder case, died in 1987. His wife, MARIE, continues to live in Garden City, Kansas.

DAVID DIAMOND is a composer of classical music. He received several Guggenheim Fellowships and was on the faculty at the Juilliard School of Music from 1973 to 1997.

JAMES DICKEY, poet, novelist, filmmaker, and critic, is known most widely for his bestselling novel *Deliverance* and for *Buckdancer's Choice*, which won the National Book Award for poetry in 1966. He died in 1996.

JOAN DIDION, an essayist, novelist, and screenwriter, is the author of several books, including *Slouching Toward Bethlehem*, *The White Album*, and *The Last Thing He Wanted*. She is married to the writer John Gregory Dunne.

PETER DUCHIN, for many years America's preeminent dance band leader, led his orchestra at Truman's black-and-white ball.

DOMINICK DUNNE's bestselling novels include *A Season in Purgatory, An Inconvenient Woman, People Like Us,* and *The Two Mrs. Grenvilles.* He is a special contributor to *Vanity Fair.*

JOHN GREGORY DUNNE's books include *The Red White and Blue, True Confessions, Vegas, Playland,* and *The Studio.* With his wife, Joan Didion, he has worked on a number of screenplays, most recently *Up Close and Personal.*

JACK DUNPHY, Truman's lifelong companion, was the author of five novels and a memoir called *"Dear Genius . . .": A Memoir of My Life with Truman Capote.* He died in 1992.

LEE EISENBERG is the former editor in chief of *Esquire* magazine and the founding editor in chief of *Esquire UK.* He is now editor for special projects at *Time* magazine.

JASON EPSTEIN has been an editor at Random House for over thirty years. He cofounded the *New York Review of Books.* In 1988 he received the first National Book Awards medal for "distinguished contribution to American letters."

MIA FARROW is famous for her roles in *Rosemary's Baby, The Great Gatsby,* and numerous Woody Allen films, including *Hannah and Her Sisters, Crimes and Misdemeanors,* and *Husbands and Wives.*

CLAY FELKER was founding editor of *New York* magazine, later editor of *Esquire.* He now teaches at the Graduate School of Journalism at the University of California at Berkeley.

MICHAEL FEZNICK is an actor and a nightclub operator in New York City.

ROBERT FIZDALE is a duet pianist who performed with his partner, ARTHUR GOLD. Together they also wrote several books, including *The Divine Sarah: The Life of Sarah Bernhardt, Misia: The Life of Misia Sert,* and *The Gold and Fizdale Cookbook.*

JILL FOX, who lives in Vermont, was at the time of the black-and-white ball married to Truman's editor at Random House, Joe Fox.

JOE FOX was Truman Capote's editor at Random House for many years. He died in 1996.

GRAY FOY is working together with Stephen Pascal on a biography of Leo Lerman.

ELEANOR FRIEDE was a book publisher for many years, at Macmillan, World Publishing, and then had her own imprint at Delacorte Press.

GWEN GAILLARD is a restaurateur and year-round resident of Nantucket Island, Massachusetts.

JOHN KENNETH GALBRAITH is the Paul M. Warburg Professor of Economics Emeritus at Harvard University and a member for literature and past president of the American Academy of Arts and Letters.

BRENDAN GILL has worked at *The New Yorker* for nearly sixty years, which he writes about in *Here at "The New Yorker."* He is most recently the author of *Late Bloomers.*

ARTHUR GOLD (see Robert Fizdale).

KATHARINE GRAHAM is publisher of the *Washington Post* and the author of an autobiography, *A Personal History.*

JUDY GREEN is the author of several novels, including *Winners, The Young Marrieds, Sometimes Paradise,* and *Unsuitable Company.*

SAM GREEN ran an art gallery in Philadelphia.

WINSTON GROOM is the author of eight books, most notably *Forrest Gump,* which was made into an Academy Award–winning film.

LOUISE GRUNWALD is married to Henry Grunwald, the former CEO of Time-Life and subsequently the American ambassador to Austria.

LOEL GUINNESS, the British financier, was married to Gloria Guinness, one of Truman's "swans."

JANE GUNTHER was married to John Gunther, the author of the well-known "Inside" books.

ANTHONY HADEN-GUEST is a contributor to *Vanity Fair* and *New York* magazine and most recently the author of *The Last Party,* a chronicle of New York's underground nightlife.

ANTHONY HAIL is an interior decorator living in San Francisco. His work often appears in *Architectural Digest.*

JOE HARDY was a theater director who worked with Truman on *House of Flowers.* Most recently, he directed the television show *Ryan's Hope.*

KATE HARRINGTON, the daughter of John O'Shea, was an editor at *Vanity Fair.*

CRAWFORD HART attended Greenwich High School with Truman.

ASHTON HAWKINS is executive vice president and counsel to the trustees at the Metropolitan Museum of Art in New York City.

R. COURI HAY is a writer, columnist, and TV reporter who lives in New York City and Maine.

LENORE HERSHEY was an editor at *McCall's* and *Ladies' Home Journal*.

GEOFFREY HOLDER was born in Trinidad. He is a dancer, actor, choreographer, and director, and in 1950 he founded his own dance company.

CLIFFORD HOPE was Herb Clutter's attorney in Kansas. He is now a writer of historical biography. He is a former Kansas state senator and Finney County Commissioner.

LEONORA HORNBLOW is the author of two novels, *Memory and Desire* and *The Love-Seekers,* and is completing a third, *Listen to the Sad Songs.* With her late husband, Arthur Hornblow, Jr., she wrote six books for children.

HORST P. HORST was a photographer who collaborated on many books with his partner, VALENTINE LAWFORD, including *A Salute to the Thirties* and *Vogue's Book of Homes, Gardens and People* (with an introduction by Diana Vreeland).

JANE HOWARD, a former journalist at *Life,* wrote several books, including *A Different Woman, Families, Please Touch,* and *Margaret Meade: A Life.*

JOHN HUSTON was a director, actor, and screenwriter. Among his many films are *The Maltese Falcon, The Man Who Would Be King,* and *The African Queen.*

DAVID JACKSON's stories have appeared in O. Henry Prize volumes. He was James Merrill's companion for many years and now lives in Florida.

TONY JEWELL is the retired president and general manager of KIUL Radio in Garden City, Kansas.

ALFRED KAZIN is most recently the author of *God and the American Writer, Writing Was Everything,* and *A Lifetime Burning in Every Moment,* and the first recipient of an award in memory of Newton Arvin, established by the Truman Capote Literary Trust.

SLIM KEITH, one of Truman's "swans," was married to Howard Hawks, Leland Hayward, and Sir Kenneth Keith.

NAN KEMPNER is an international representative for Christie's and is married to the financier Thomas Kempner.

JAMES KIRKWOOD was the coauthor of *A Chorus Line* and the author of several novels, including *There Must Be a Pony, P.S. Your Cat Is Dead,* and a memoir, *Diary of a Mad Playwright.*

JOHN KNOWLES lived for twenty years in the Hamptons on eastern Long Island, where he was a friend and neighbor of Truman Capote's. One of his nine novels, *A Separate Peace,* is an American classic, taught throughout the country.

POLLY KRAFT, a painter who lives in Washington D.C., is married to the *Newsweek* columnist Joseph Kraft.

KENNETH JAY LANE is a famous costume jewelry designer.

LEWIS LAPHAM, the editor of *Harper's* magazine, is also an essayist and the author of several books, among them *Money and Class in America, Waiting for the Barbarians,* and *The Wish for Kings.*

VALENTINE LAWFORD (see Horst P. Horst).

BARBARA LAWRENCE has worked as a magazine editor, first at *The New Yorker* and then at *Harper's Bazaar, Redbook,* and *McCall's.*

IRVING LAZAR was a literary agent for over fifty years. As well as Truman Capote, his clients included Richard Nixon, Jesse Jackson, Larry McMurtry, Cole Porter, Orson Welles, Lauren Bacall, and Humphrey Bogart, who nicknamed him "Swifty." He and his wife, MARY, both died in 1993.

LEO LERMAN, a friend of Truman Capote's from 1946, wrote widely about writers and artists for over fifty years, becoming best known as an editor at *Mademoiselle, Vogue,* and *Vanity Fair.* He died in 1994.

KAREN LERNER, formerly an editor and writer for *Time* magazine, has produced a number of documentary films.

DORIS LILLY was a syndicated gossip columnist and the author of *How to Marry a Millionaire, How to Make Love in Five Languages,* and *Those Fabulous Greeks: Onassis, Niarchos, and Livanos.*

PIEDY LUMET, associate editor of Rolling Stone Press and advisory editor to *The Paris Review,* compiled a book of children's stories entitled *Wonders.* She is married to film director Sidney Lumet.

CHARLES MCATEE was the Kansas Director of Penal Institutions during the Clutter murder case. Now a lawyer in Topeka, Kansas, he has also served as a special agent for the FBI and as Assistant United States District Attorney.

NORMAN MAILER was born in 1923, has written thirty books, and now lives in Provincetown with his sixth wife, Norris.

JERRE MANGIONE is professor emeritus of English at the University of Pennsylvania. His books include *The Dream and the Deal, An Ethnic at Large,* and *Mount Allegro: A Memoir of Italian American Life.*

PETER MATHIESSEN has been nominated in both fiction and nonfiction for the National Book Award, which was won by *The Snow Leopard* in 1978. His most recent work is the novel *Lost Man's River.*

CAROL MARCUS MATTHAU is married to Walter Matthau, whom she met while acting in George Axelrod's play *Will Success Spoil Rock Hunter?* She is the author of two books, *The Secret in the Daisy* and *Among the Porcupines.*

DR. RUSSELL MAXFIELD was the physician for the Clutter family in Garden City, Kansas.

KAY MEEHAN, one of Truman's "swans," was married to Joseph Meehan, the former head of the New York Stock Exchange.

AILEEN MEHLE is the society columnist also known as "Suzy." Her column appears in *Women's Wear Daily* and *W.* She has written for many magazines, including *Vogue, Harper's Bazaar, Town & Country,* and *Architectural Digest.*

JAMES MERRILL, a poet, novelist, and playwright, won the National Book Award for his *Nights and Days,* which was published in 1966. In 1976 he was awarded a Pulitzer Prize for his *Divine Comedies.*

MILAN is a designer who lives in Los Angeles.

MARIANNE MOATES is a freelance writer, Capote lecturer, and writing consultant. A native Alabamian, she is the author of *Truman Capote's Southern Years: Stories from a Monroeville Cousin.*

ALICE MORRIS was the literary editor at *Mademoiselle* before replacing Mary Louise Aswell, Truman's mentor, as fiction editor at *Harper's Bazaar.*

WILLIE MORRIS, former editor in chief of *Harper's,* is the author of, among other works, *North Toward Home;* its sequel, *New York Days,* and the recent bestselling *My Dog Skip.*

NATALIA MURRAY, a representative for two of Italy's major publishers, Mondadori and Rizzoli, edited a volume of Janet Flanner's letters to her entitled *Darlinghissima*.

BODIE NEILSON, a Danish-born writer, is a regular contributor to *Avenue* magazine and publications specializing in architecture.

JOHNNY NICHOLSON has been the proprietor of Café Nicholson, a restaurant in New York City, for the past fifty years.

HAROLD NYE was a law enforcement officer for thirty years. He retired in 1975 after twenty years with the Kansas Bureau of Investigation.

GEORGE PAGE, the host and narrator of the PBS-TV series *Nature,* was a correspondent for NBC News and covered the Vietnam War. He is currently writing a book about animal intelligence.

GORDON PARKS is a photographer, film director, writer, composer, poet. He is the author of twelve books of poetry, fiction, and nonfiction, including the autobiographical *Voices in the Mirror*.

ELEANOR PERÉNYI, the author of *Liszt* (a biography of the composer) and *Green Thoughts,* was formerly an editor at *Harper's Bazaar* and *Mademoiselle*.

FRANK PERRY, a motion picture executive, director, producer, and writer, coauthored *Trilogy: An Experiment in Multimedia* with Truman.

LESTER PERSKY is a Hollywood film producer who owns the rights to Truman's *Music for Chameleons*.

ARCH PERSONS, Truman's father, died in 1981.

JOE PETROCIK is a partner with Myron Clement in a public relations firm in New York City. He lives there and in Sag Harbor.

TOMMY PHIPPS is a screenwriter who lives in Southampton, New York.

NORMAN PODHORETZ, editor, critic, and essayist, was editor in chief of *The Commentary Reader*.

JAMES POST, now retired, was the chaplain of the Kansas State Penitentiary at the time of the Clutter murders.

HAROLD PRINCE has directed and/or produced over fifty musicals, plays, and operas. He serves as a trustee for the New York Public Library and served on the National Council of the Arts of the NEA for six years. He has received twenty Tony Awards.

ALAN PRYCE-JONES was a drama critic for *The Observer* in London, the book critic for *The International Herald Tribune,* and the editor of the *Times Literary Supplement* for twelve years. His autobiography is entitled *The Bonus of Laughter.*

DOTSON RADER is the author of a number of books, including *Blood Money* and *Tennessee: Cry of the Heart.*

LEE RADZIWILL, one of Truman's "swans," lives in East Hampton and New York with her husband, Herbert Ross. She is the sister of the late Jacqueline Onassis.

PAUL RANDOLPH is an automobile executive living in Grosse Point, Michigan.

MATTHEW RHODES, a native of Lynchburg, Virginia, now resides with his wife in Mobile, Alabama. He is currently involved in local politics and serves as a consultant to the Monroe County Heritage Museum.

JOHN RICHARDSON was born in England and has lived in the United States since 1960. For the last ten years he has devoted his life to writing Picasso's biography. Two out of four projected volumes have been published.

NANCIE B. ROBINSON is a longtime resident of Monroeville, Alabama.

NED ROREM is a Pulitzer Prize–winning composer and also the author of fourteen books, including *The Paris Diary* and *Knowing When to Stop.*

MARIE RUDISILL, also known as "Tiny," is Truman's aunt—the youngest sister of Lillie Mae Faulk, Truman's mother. She is an antiques dealer and the author of a book about Truman's childhood.

JOHN BARRY RYAN is managing director of Oppenheimer & Co., Inc., director of national sales administration and corporate communications. He worked on *Beat the Devil* with Truman as John Huston's assistant.

NANCY RYAN, a former writer for *Life* magazine, traveled to Russia with Truman for the *Porgy and Bess* tour.

JOHN T. SARGENT's career at Doubleday spanned over fifty years. He retired in 1987 as chairman of the board. He is a trustee of the New York Public Library, the American Academy in Rome, and the Academy of American Poets.

SYLVAN SCHENDLER was a professor of English at Smith College when Newton Arvin taught there. With Daniel Aaron, he edited a collection of Arvin's essays entitled *American Pantheon*.

ARTHUR SCHLESINGER, JR., writer and historian, is a two-time Pulitzer Prize winner and served as special assistant to President Kennedy.

JOEL SCHUMACHER, director of such films as *St. Elmo's Fire, Lost Boys, Cousins, Flatliners, Dying Young, Falling Down, The Client, Batman Forever, A Time to Kill,* and *Batman and Robin,* currently lives in Los Angeles, California.

JAMES SCHUYLER, poet, novelist, and playwright, was awarded the Pulitzer Prize in 1981 for *The Morning of the Poem.* He died in 1991.

ALAN SCHWARTZ is a partner in Manatt Phelps Phillips, the Los Angeles law firm, and was Truman's attorney and friend for many years.

BOBBY SHORT, the pianist and singer, has performed at the Café Carlyle in New York City for the last thirty years.

NEIL SIMON is an award-winning playwright whose plays include *The Odd Couple, Brighton Beach Memoirs, Biloxi Blues, Broadway Bound,* and *Lost in Yonkers,* which won the Pulitzer Prize for drama and the Tony Award for best play in 1991.

BABS SIMPSON is a former editor of *Harper's Bazaar* and *Vogue* magazine.

HARRISON SMITH was the court-appointed defense attorney for Richard Hickock and Perry Smith in the Clutter murder trial.

LIZ SMITH is the veteran syndicated gossip columnist whose column appears in sixty major newspapers. She has worked for *Newsday,* the *New York Post,* and the *New York Daily News.*

STEPHEN SONDHEIM has written the music and lyrics for *Company, A Little Night Music, Sweeney Todd,* and *Sunday in the Park with George,* which won a Pulitzer Prize in 1984.

WILLIAM STYRON, a native of Virginia, is a novelist, essayist, and short story writer. A biography of the writer, *William Styron: A Life,* by James L. W. West, was published by Random House in 1998.

VIRGINIA TAYLOR grew up in Monroeville, Alabama.

VIRGIL THOMSON was a composer and music critic. His opera *The Mother of Us All*, for which Gertrude Stein wrote the libretto, is based on Susan B. Anthony's fight for women's rights.

DIANA TRILLING, the wife of critic Lionel Trilling, was a fiction critic for *The Nation*. Her books include *Reviewing the Forties, Mrs. Harris: The Death of the Scarsdale Diet Doctor*, and a posthumous edition of her husband's complete works.

KATHLEEN TYNAN, novelist, journalist, and screenwriter, wrote *The Summer Aeroplane, Agatha*, and a biography of her husband, Kenneth Tynan.

GORE VIDAL, novelist, essayist, playwright, has written over thirty books, most recently a memoir entitled *Palimpsest*. He won the National Book Award for nonfiction for his book *United States: Essays, 1951–1991* in 1993. He lives in Ravello, Italy.

PETER VIERTEL, a novelist and screenwriter, has lived in Spain for almost thirty-five years. He has written a novel about the bullfighter Luis Miguel Dominguín.

KURT VONNEGUT, the author of thirteen novels, including *Slaughterhouse Five*, lives in New York City with his wife, Jill Krementz.

DIANA VREELAND was a fashion editor at *Harper's Bazaar* before becoming editor in chief of *Vogue*. A consultant to the Metropolitan Museum of Art's Costume Institute, she was awarded France's Legion of Honor.

PHOEBE PIERCE VREELAND is a writer and former magazine editor living in New York City. She is working on a book on Manhattan in the 1940s and '50s.

PHYLLIS CERF WAGNER was married to Bennett Cerf, a cofounder of Random House and the publisher of Truman's books.

EUGENE WALTER, a writer born and raised in Mobile, Alabama, has received a Eugene Saxton Fellowship, an O. Henry Citation for fiction, and a Prix Guilloux for translation.

JANN WENNER is the editor and publisher of *Rolling Stone* and the chairman of Wenner Media, Inc., which also publishes *Us* and *Men's Journal*. He also founded *Outside* and *Family Life*.

DUANE WEST, now semiretired, was the prosecuting attorney in the Clutter murder trial.

MONROE WHEELER was involved with the Museum of Modern Art for over five decades. The Monroe Wheeler Reading Room was established at the museum in 1988, the year of his death.

DONALD WINDHAM, poet, novelist, and playwright, is the author of *Footnote to a Friendship: A Memoir of Truman Capote and Others*. He lives in New York City.

MARGUERITE YOUNG is the author of two books of poetry, *Prismatic Ground* and *Moderate Fable*; one novel, *Miss MacIntosh, My Darling*; and a work of nonfiction, *Angel in the Forest*. She died in 1996.

Sources

Printed Material by Truman Capote and Jack Dunphy

page 8: *As a child I lived for long periods of time* from "Guests" by Truman Capote, *McCall's*, February 1977.

page 10: *Once more, the creek,* from *The Dogs Bark: Public People and Private Places* by Truman Capote (Random House, 1974).

page 13: *. . . I started writing when I was about eight,* from "'Go Right Ahead and Ask Me Anything' (And So She Did)," an interview with Truman Capote by Gloria Steinem, *McCall's*, November 1967.

page 14: *Harper Lee . . . wanted to be a lawyer,* from "'Go Right Ahead and Ask Me Anything' (And So She Did)."

page 38: *The last thing in the world I would do,* from *Conversations with Capote* by Lawrence Grobel (Plume, 1985).

page 52: *dear bob,* from a letter from Truman Capote to Robert Linscott, May 1946, in the Random House Collection, Columbia University.

page 57: *marylou, my angel,* from an undated letter from Truman Capote to Mary Louise Aswell, in the collection of Pearl Kazin Bell.

page 71: *Marylou, my beloved,* from an undated letter from Truman Capote to Mary Louise Aswell, in the collection of Pearl Kazin Bell.

page 80: *Do you remember the young boy,* from an interview with Truman Capote by Eric Norden, *Playboy*, March 1968.

page 100: *It was very much being talked about,* from *The Dogs Bark*.

page 102: *Best about Ischia were its cliffs,* from *"Dear Genius . . ." A Memoir of My Life with Truman Capote* by Jack Dunphy (McGraw-Hill, 1987).

page 107: *At Fontana we used to go down to the water,* from *"Dear Genius . . ."*

page 109: *. . . a little town near Taormina,* from *"Dear Genius . . ."*

page 113: *I came back to the hotel Choiseul,* from *"Dear Genius . . ."*

page 125: *The last few weeks have been filled with peculiar adventures,* from an undated letter from Truman Capote to Andrew Lyndon, in the Truman Capote Papers, The New York Public Library.

page 137: *I am a completely horizontal author,* from an interview with Truman Capote in *The Paris Review,* 1957.

page 196: "In Which TC Discusses . . . *In Cold Blood* and the Form He Claims to Have Invented—the Nonfiction Novel," from an interview in the *New York Times Book Review* by George Plimpton, January 16, 1966.

page 414: *Truman bad when I got to the apartment,* from *"Dear Genius . . ."*

page 468: "You ever see the snow?" from *Other Voices, Other Rooms* by Truman Capote (Random House, 1948).